ANNALS OF COMMUNISM

Each volume in the series Annals of Communism will publish selected and previously inaccessible documents from former Soviet state and party archives in the framework of a narrative text that focuses on a particular topic in the history of Soviet and international communism. Separate English and Russian editions will be prepared. Russian and American scholars select and annotate the documents for each volume; together they explain the selection criteria and discuss the state of relevant research and scholarly interpretation. Documents are chosen not for their support of any single interpretation but for their particular historical importance or their general value in deepening understanding and facilitating discussion. The volumes are designed to be useful to students, scholars, and interested general readers.

# The Secret World of
# American
# Communism

Harvey Klehr, John Earl Haynes,
and Fridrikh Igorevich Firsov

*Russian Documents Translated by Timothy D. Sergay*

Yale University Press

New Haven and London

TO OUR WIVES

*Elizabeth Klehr*

*Janette Haynes*

*Lidia Mikhailovna Firsova*

Designed by James J. Johnson and set in Sabon and Melior Roman by The Composing Room of Michigan, Inc. Printed in the United States of America by Vail-Ballou Press, Binghamton, New York.

*Library of Congress Cataloging-in-Publication Data*

Klehr, Harvey.
    The secret world of American communism / Harvey Klehr, John Earl Haynes, and Fridrikh Igorevich Firsov.
        p.    cm. —(Annals of communism)
    Includes bibliographical references and index.
    ISBN 0-300-06183-8

    1. Communism—United States—History—Sources.    I. Haynes, John Earl.    II. Firsov, Fridrikh Igorevich.    III. Title.    IV. Series.
HX83.K557    1995
320.5′32′0973—dc20                                                    94-3596
                                                                              CIP

A catalogue record for this book is available from the British Library.

The paper in this book meets the guidelines for permanence and durability of the Committee on Production Guidelines for Book Longevity of the Council on Library Resources.

10  9  8  7  6  5  4  3  2  1

Publication of this volume was made possible in part by a generous gift to Yale University Press from the Daniel and Joanna S. Rose Fund, Inc. We are grateful for their vision and support.

Yale University Press gratefully acknowledges the financial support given for this publication by the Foundation for Cultural Initiative (Moscow), the John M. Olin Foundation, the Open Society Fund (New York), and the Smith-Richardson Foundation.

# Contents

# Documents Reproduced in Facsimile

# Preface

Until 1992, Soviet archives dealing with Communist activity in America were closed to everyone except a few Soviet Communist party researchers. The collapse of communism in the Soviet Union led to a welcome opening of archives documenting relations between Soviet and American Communists— archives that shed a great deal of light on Soviet espionage in America and on the American Communist party's covert activity. One of the most important archives for studying the American Communist party (CPUSA) is the Russian Center for the Preservation and Study of Documents of Recent History (RTsKhIDNI).

Documents in RTsKhIDNI are organized into a series of collections and stored in folders. Each folder has a short description of its contents printed in well-organized and detailed finding aids prepared by RTsKhIDNI archivists. In this volume, a three-part numerical citation is given to each document. The first part is the number of the collection (*fond* in Russian), the second part provides the number of the subseries or description (*opis*) of that collection, and the third part gives the number of the file or folder (*delo*) in which the document is found. Thus, a document cited "RTsKhIDNI 495–37–65" refers to *fond* 495 (the Communist International, or Comintern), *opis* 37 (the American Commission of the Executive Committee of the Communist International), *delo* 65.

Using the finding aids prepared by RTsKhIDNI archivists to choose the most promising candidates, we examined more than a thousand Comintern and CPUSA files containing scores of thousands of pages of documents. The RTsKhIDNI attaches to each file a record of prior use. In the case of Comintern files, these records show occasional use over the years by Soviet researchers and use by Western researchers only since 1991. In many cases we were the first non-Soviet researchers to examine the files. In the case of the CPUSA files (*fond* 515), virtually all prior-use records for the hundreds of files we examined were blank, indicating that the files had not been used since they were organized by Russian archivists. Being the first to examine these files was a thrill few scholars are fortunate enough to experience.

Ninety-two documents dealing with various aspects of clandestine activity are reproduced in this volume. We selected the most significant and illustrative documents we were able to find. In order to convey the richness of these documents and provide ample context, the full text of a document is usually included, although only portions may be relevant to the questions under discussion in this book. In some instances, however, only an excerpt is included because the entire document would have presented readers with a text of unnecessary and tedious length.

We explain the significance of the documents, provide their historical context, and describe particular historical controversies that these documents help illuminate. When documents leave historical puzzles unsolved, we discuss various possible interpretations. A glossary of names will aid the reader in identifying people and organizations that appear frequently. A chronology of the history of American communism is included to assist in relating the activities detailed in the documents to the broader history of the CPUSA.

Two of the authors have devoted many years to the study of American communism based on primary sources available in the United States, and the third has spent many years in Russia studying the history of the Comintern. All three of us are intimately familiar with the problem of documentary authenticity. We have no doubts about the authenticity of the documents held by RTsKhIDNI; none of the documents that we examined were forgeries. There is no evidence that false documents were planted in the collection to mislead the unwary. As with all archival documents, however, it is possible that some authentic documents contain erroneous information. The creator of a particular document may have been misinformed, may have been incompetent, may have been repeating gossip, or may have been lying to mislead contemporaries. An example of an authentic but easily misunderstood and even misleading document (number 69) is discussed in chapter 6.

In selecting documents for this volume and those that will follow, we had open access to the vast collection of Communist International and CPUSA records at the RTsKhIDNI. Our books are not intended to provide a comprehensive documentary history of American communism. Instead, they will reproduce documents from the RTsKhIDNI that are not known to exist in the

United States and that provide new information, settle old controversies, or provide unexpected illumination of historical events.

Most of the documents in the CPUSA collection and the American-related files of the Comintern deal with the promotion of communism as a political and ideological movement in the United States. In subsequent volumes, we will present documents delineating aspects of the CPUSA's dealings with the Comintern, its role in labor strife in the 1930s, its attempts to organize black Americans, its involvement in mainstream politics, and its relationship with intellectual supporters, as well as Comintern directives to the CPUSA regarding the presentation of the Nazi-Soviet Pact and the activities of American Communists in the International Brigades in the Spanish Civil War. In this volume, we concentrate on the clandestine activity of the American Communist party and Soviet espionage in the United States.

# Acknowledgments

We incurred numerous debts in the preparation of this book. It was the most complicated and challenging research project any of us has ever undertaken, and it would not have been possible without the cooperation, assistance, expertise, and goodwill of many people and institutions.

The two American authors each made two trips to Moscow to work in the Russian Center for the Preservation and Study of Documents of Recent History (RTsKhIDNI). We greatly appreciate the help and assistance of the directors and staff of the archive. Russian archivists face daunting problems, not the least of which is dealing with American scholars used to different rules and a different pace of research. We are grateful for all the assistance we were rendered and for the many ways the RTsKhIDNI staff made our task easier. We particularly want to acknowledge the aid of Kiril Mikhailovich Anderson, archive director, Oleg Vladimirovich Naumov, associate director, and, most important, Svetlana Markovna Rosenthal, who had the unenviable task of reproducing the thousands of documents collected for this project.

Two Russian scholars spent many months reading files to make our visits more productive. We owe a great debt of gratitude to Mark Isaakovich Lapitsky and Inna Mkrtychevna Tatarovskaya, not only for their research, but also for their friendship and hospitality. Nikolai Petrovich Yakovlev, Yale University Press's representative in Moscow, was helpful in many ways. Todd Weinberg arranged housing for us in Moscow.

Our Russian translators were indispensable. Nikolai N. Silin arranged Harvey Klehr's first visit to the RTsKhIDNI and worked tirelessly and selflessly to ensure that the visit was a success. On subsequent visits, Datia Lotareva translated for John Haynes and assisted in identifying much obscure material.

Svetlana Savranskaya worked as a translator in both Moscow and Atlanta. She is a treasure. Moshe Haspel assisted both with translation and with making sure we were able to function in Moscow. Laura Kennedy did many of the initial translations from Russian. Both Laura Van Assendelft and Jody Cornish provided helpful assistance during the project. Timothy Sergay prepared the final translations for this volume; his skill and ingenuity are much appreciated.

Lowell Dyson and Ronald Radosh were kind enough to read parts of the manuscript and make detailed comments and suggestions; they saved us from numerous errors. Herb Romerstein read the entire manuscript and was extraordinarily generous in making available his own collection of material from the RTsKhIDNI, as well as his encyclopedic knowledge of American communism. Jim Ryan loaned us Margaret Browder's FBI file, made available under the Freedom of Information Act. Sam Tannenhaus generously shared his own research on Whittaker Chambers, and Alan Cullison, his research assistant, was equally helpful. David Hornstein shared his knowledge of the Pan-Pacific Trade Union Secretariat. Edward Epstein discussed his own research on Armand Hammer and alerted us to the significance of some of our material on him. Andrea Graziosi offered useful advice on the background to Raisa Browder's role in the Bolshevik Revolution in Ukraine. Vernon Pedersen, having just finished his own dissertation on communism in Maryland, volunteered to accompany us to Moscow in the summer of 1994; he was a great help, and we could not have covered as much ground without his research assistance. Thomas Remington of Emory University frequently made available his talents and Russian expertise. For much of the background material, we drew upon the rich resources of the Library of Congress.

The administrative staff of the Political Science Department at Emory University—Karen Salsbury, Esther Nerenbaum, Denise Brubaker, and Sherry Friedman—were, as usual, efficient, helpful, and considerate to those of us who are organizationally challenged.

Our debt to the people at Yale University Press is substantial. John Ryden, the director, has believed in this book from the beginning; his encouragement has meant a great deal. We are also grateful to Jane Hedges, James Johnson, and Elaine Maisner for their help. Our deepest debt goes to our editor, Jonathan Brent. He has pushed, prodded, and pleaded with us to make this a better book. His enthusiasm, support, and faith in what we were doing went beyond the call of duty. In addition to learning what a superb editor he is, we are delighted to have become good friends. To him belong most of the virtues of this project.

Several foundations provided critical financial assistance. Without the generous support of the Lynde and Harry Bradley Foundation, the John M. Olin Foundation, and the Smith-Richardson Foundation, none of our research would have been feasible. We are very grateful for their confidence. We also acknowledge the use of material we first published in the *American Spectator* in December 1992.

Last, but certainly not least, our families deserve decorations. Our wives, Elizabeth Klehr and Janette Haynes, put up with our long stints in Moscow; our children, Benjamin, Gabriel, and Joshua Klehr and Amanda and Bill Haynes, endured huge piles of papers and hours spent in front of word processors. We promise not to return to Moscow for at least a year.

HARVEY KLEHR
JOHN EARL HAYNES

# A Note on the Documents

The reproduction of the documents included in this volume is intended to preserve their original character. Grammatical, spelling, and stylistic errors in the original documents have been retained. Orthographic and typographical errors that were corrected by the author of the document (words or letters crossed out—for example, "comm~~u~~unicates") and clerical notations that are irrelevant to the content of the documents and that were added when the documents were placed in the archive have not been reproduced. Handwritten comments added to the documents are included and appear in *italic* type. Our interpolations, as well as illegible or indecipherable words, are enclosed in brackets. <u>Single underlining</u> indicates that a word or phrase was underlined using a typewriter; <u>double underlining</u> indicates that the underlining was done by hand. The headnote accompanying each document provides information about the language of the original document, the archival citation, and any exceptions to the guidelines presented here.

# Glossary of Individuals and Organizations

Individuals, organizations, and acronyms are identified when they first appear in the text. Listed here are individuals and organizations mentioned in more than one chapter.

**Abraham Lincoln battalion:** Spanish Civil War infantry unit (battalion 58) of the XV International Brigade made up largely of American volunteers. Best known of the American units fighting for the Spanish Republic against the nationalist forces under General Franco. Often mislabeled the Abraham Lincoln Brigade. The veterans' organization of all Americans who served with the International Brigades, including those in other battalions, is called Veterans of the Abraham Lincoln Brigade.

**Abraham Lincoln Brigade:** See Veterans of the Abraham Lincoln Brigade.

**Anarcho-syndicalism:** A left-wing political ideology that envisioned the abolition of private property and the replacement of the political state by a voluntary association of labor unions and worker cooperatives. Anarcho-syndicalism was strong in Europe in the late nineteenth and early twentieth centuries. In America, the Industrial Workers of the World held views resembling anarcho-syndicalism. After the Bolshevik Revolution, the anarcho-syndicalist movement split, with part joining the new Communist movement. Those who remained anarcho-syndicalists tended to be hostile toward communism because of Communist support for the creation of an all-powerful political state dominated by the Communist party. Anarcho-syndicalism remained a significant force in France and Spain until the end of the 1930s.

**Anglo-American Secretariat:** Section of the Comintern that supervised Communist parties in America, Canada, Britain, and certain other English-speaking territories.

**Baker, Rudy** (1898–? ): Little-known CPUSA official who replaced J. Peters as head of the CPUSA's underground organization. He returned to his native Yugoslavia after World War II.

**Bentley, Elizabeth** (1908–1963): Former Communist who named more than forty government employees as sources for a Soviet espionage ring she ran in the 1940s.

**Bolsheviks:** Members of a revolutionary Russian political party led by Lenin; they advocated Marxism-Leninism and took power in Russia in 1917; founders of Soviet communism.

**Brother-Son network:** A World War II CPUSA espionage network directed by Rudy Baker, head of the CPUSA's secret apparatus. The Brother-Son network included Morris Cohen and others who took part in Soviet atomic espionage.

**Browder, Earl** (1891–1973): Early Communist party organizer and first head of the Comintern's Pan-Pacific Trade Union Secretariat. Led the CPUSA in the 1930s, its period of greatest growth, but was driven from the leadership in 1945 and expelled from the party in 1946 when his policies lost favor in Moscow. His attempts to win reinstatement in the late 1940s were rebuffed.

**Budenz, Louis** (1891–1972): A member of the CPUSA Central Committee and editor of the *Daily Worker* who split with the party in 1945 and converted to Roman Catholicism. He became a conservative anti-Communist, writing extensively about the dangers of communism and testifying against the CPUSA at various trials and congressional hearings.

**Bukharin, Nikolai** (1888–1938): Prominent Bolshevik leader defeated by Stalin in the struggle to succeed Lenin. He was accused of right-wing deviation from Marxism-Leninism and was later executed by Stalin.

**Bukharinite:** Follower of Nikolai Bukharin. Jay Lovestone and his followers in the CPUSA were accused of holding Bukharinite views.

**Central Committee (CC):** Consisted of the CPUSA's national leaders along with leaders and representatives of its regional bodies and its auxiliary organizations.

**Central Control Commission (CCC):** CPUSA body charged with supervising internal discipline and security.

**Chambers, Whittaker** (1901–1961): Former Communist and Soviet spy who accused Alger Hiss of espionage and asserted the existence of a large Washington Communist underground in the 1930s.

**CNT:** Confederación national del trabajo (National confederation of workers). Radical Spanish anarcho-syndicalist labor federation hostile to Communist control of the Spanish Republican government.

**Cohen, Morris** (1910– ): CPUSA member, soldier in the International Brigades, and Soviet spy. In 1994, still living in retirement in Moscow.

**Coles, Ann Cadwallader** (1882–1969): Artist and member of the CPUSA underground.

**Comintern:** Abbreviation for Communist International. Founded by Lenin in 1919 as the international headquarters of and directing body for all Communist parties. Disbanded in 1943.

**Comparty:** Comintern abbreviation for Communist party.

**CPSU:** Communist Party of the Soviet Union.

**CPUSA:** Communist Party of the United States of America. The name of the American Communist party from 1929 until the present. Its predecessor organizations, formed in 1919, were the Communist Party of America and the Communist Labor Party. During the 1920s, the CPUSA used the titles United Communist Party, Workers (Communist) Party, and Workers Party. For a period in 1944 and 1945, it used the title Communist Political Association.

*Daily Worker:* Flagship newspaper of the CPUSA.

**Dennis, Eugene** (1905–1961): CPUSA organizer and Comintern agent who became general secretary of the CPUSA after Browder's ouster in 1945. He led the party until 1959.

**Dies committee:** Special Committee on Un-American Activities, a committee of the U.S. House of Representatives headed in the 1930s and early 1940s by Representative Martin Dies (Democrat, Texas).

**Dimitrov, Georgi** (1882–1949): A Bulgarian Communist who gained international fame as a defendant in the Reichstag fire trial in Nazi Germany in 1933. After his acquittal, he became head of the Communist International and enunciated the policy of a Popular Front against fascism at the Comintern's Seventh World Congress in 1935. He remained head of the Comintern until its dissolution in 1943. In 1945 he became head of the Communist regime installed in Bulgaria by the Soviet Red Army.

**ECCI:** Executive Committee of the Communist International, based in Moscow.

**FBI:** Federal Bureau of Investigation, chief American internal security agency.

**Fitin, Pavel Mikhailovich:** Head of the foreign intelligence directorate of the NKVD from 1940 to 1946.

**FOIA:** Freedom of Information Act. Documents obtained from a U.S. government agency under the Freedom of Information Act are cited as FOIA documents.

**Foster, William Z.** (1881–1961): Trade union organizer and syndicalist who joined the Communist movement in 1921. Foster headed CPUSA trade union operations in the 1920s and early 1930s and was the party's presidential candidate in several elections. He was a contender for party leadership throughout his life, but he never achieved the most powerful post, that of general secretary.

**George, Harrison** (1888–? ): Longtime Comintern and CPUSA organizer and head of the San Francisco bureau of the Pan-Pacific Trade Union Secretariat. He was expelled from the party in 1946 as an ultra-leftist.

**George Washington battalion:** Spanish Civil War infantry unit of the XV International Brigade made up largely of American volunteers, later merged into the Abraham Lincoln battalion.

**Gitlow, Benjamin** (1891–1965): One of the chief founders of the Communist Labor Party in 1919. He became general secretary of the CPUSA in 1929 but was expelled the same year on Stalin's orders for being a member of the Lovestone faction. He later became a conservative anti-Communist, writing and speaking against the party.

**Golos, Jacob** (1890–1943): CPUSA official who headed some of its underground and espionage operations. Elizabeth Bentley was his courier, lover, and successor.

**GPU:** Gosudarstvennoe politicheskoe upravlenie (State political directorate). Predecessor to the KGB.

**GRU:** Glavnoe razvedyvatelnoe upravlenie (Chief intelligence directorate of the Soviet general staff). The Soviet military intelligence agency. The foreign intelligence operations of the GRU were extensive, although smaller than those of the KGB.

**Gulag:** Russian acronym referring to the system of forced labor camps to which millions were sent during the Communist era. During the height of the Stalin regime, the death rate among those sent to the camps was very high.

**Hammer, Armand** (1898–1990): Businessman who, together with his father, Julius, established early commercial links between the United States and Soviet Russia. He later became the head of Occidental Petroleum.

**Hammer, Julius** (1874–1948): Founding member of the Communist Labor Party who, together with his son Armand, established early commercial links between the United States and Soviet Russia.

**Hiss, Alger** (1904– ): A high-level government official imprisoned for perjury (he was convicted of lying about having provided government documents to a Communist espionage ring). Whittaker Chambers was the chief witness against Hiss. Hiss continues to deny his guilt.

**ILS:** International Lenin School. Comintern school for mid- and upper-level foreign Communists and for Soviet Communists who worked with foreign Communists.

**International Brigades:** Comintern volunteer army of about 30,000 soldiers that fought with the Spanish Republic against rebellious nationalist forces led by General Francisco Franco in the Spanish Civil War of 1936–1939.

**KGB:** Komitet gosudarstvennoi bezopasnosti (Committee for state security). Chief security service (secret political police) of the USSR. The foreign intelligence arm of the KGB was the largest and principal Soviet intelligence agency. The KGB and its foreign intelligence directorate have a complex organizational history. The predecessor organzations to the KGB include, using their Russian acronyms, the Cheka, the GPU, the OGPU, the NKVD, the NKGB, the GUGB, the MGB, and the MVD. In some periods the foreign intelligence apparatus was organizationally separated from the much larger internal security apparatus.

**Koide, Joe** (1903–1976): Pseudonym of Nobumichi Ukai, Japanese immigrant and CPUSA member. Attended the International Lenin School from 1930 to 1933 and then worked with the Pan-Pacific Trade Union Secretariat. Became a government witness against the CPUSA.

**Lautner, John** (1902–1977): CPUSA organizer who specialized in work among Hungarian immigrants and who later became an official in its security apparatus. After false accusations that he was a U.S. government agent, he was expelled from the CPUSA. He subsequently testified against the party.

**Lenin, Vladimir Ilich** (1870–1924): Leader of the Bolshevik Revolution in Russia, founder and first leader of the Soviet state, and creator of Marxism-Leninism and the modern Communist movement.

**Lincoln battalion:** See Abraham Lincoln battalion.

**Lovestone, Jay** (1898–1990): Early Communist leader who became general secretary of the CPUSA in 1927 after the death of Charles Ruthenberg. He was expelled in 1929 on Moscow's orders for adhering to the views of Nikolai Bukharin. Lovestone later became a highly effective anti-Communist labor organizer and chief foreign policy adviser to George Meany of the AFL-CIO.

**Lovestoneists (Lovestoneites):** Followers of CPUSA leader Jay Lovestone, expelled from the CPUSA in 1929 for Bukharinite ideological deviation. Although comprising only about two hundred activists, the Lovestoneists included a number of talented individuals, among them Will Herberg, later a prominent theologian, Bertram Wolfe, writer and historian, and Lovestone himself, an influential foreign policy adviser to the AFL-CIO.

**McCarthy, Joseph** (1908–1957): Republican Senator from Wisconsin who espoused harsh anti-Communist views and accused prominent liberals and Democrats of links to the Communist party.

**Mackenzie-Papineau battalion:** Spanish Civil War infantry unit (battalion 60) of the XV International Brigade. It was nominally a Canadian battalion, but many of its soldiers were American volunteers.

**Nazi-Soviet Pact:** Also known as the Hitler-Stalin Pact and the Molotov-Ribbentrop Pact. The August 1939 treaty between Nazi Germany and the USSR provided for Soviet neutrality when Nazi Germany attacked Poland and for the division of Eastern Europe between the two nations.

**Nelson, Steve** (1903–1993): High-ranking political commissar in the International Brigades and a prominent CPUSA official in the late 1930s and 1940s. He was accused of involvement in atomic espionage but was never indicted. In the 1950s, Nelson was convicted under the federal Smith Act as well as a Pennsylvania "little Smith act" statute. In a landmark case, the Supreme Court reversed Nelson's conviction, holding that the federal government had preempted and invalidated state sedition laws with federal statutes. Nelson dropped out of the CPUSA in the late 1950s.

**NKVD:** Narodnyi komissariat vnutrennikh del (People's commissariat of internal affairs). Predecessor to the KGB.

**OGPU:** Obedinennoe gosudarstvennoe politicheskoe upravlenie (United political directorate of the state). Predecessor to the KGB.

**OMS:** Otdel mezhdunarodnykh svyazei (Department of international relations). Department of the Comintern dealing with international communications and clandestine operations.

**OSS:** Office of Strategic Services, chief agency for American intelligence and covert action in World War II. Officially disbanded in 1945. The remnants of its officers and functions were transferred to the State Department and in 1947 transferred to the newly organized Central Intelligence Agency.

**OWI:** Office of War Information, chief American propaganda agency in World War II, directing information at both foreign and domestic audiences.

*Pan-Pacific Worker:* Publication of the Pan-Pacific Trade Union Secretariat, edited and printed in California.

**Peters, J.** (1894–1991): Also known as J. Peter. A CPUSA official accused by Whittaker Chambers of heading the party's underground organization in the mid-1930s. He was deported to Hungary in 1949 and remained there until his death.

**Piatnitsky, Osip** (1882–1939): Comintern official who headed the Comintern's International Relations Department (OMS) in the 1920s and remained one of its ranking officials in the 1930s. In the late 1930s, he fell victim to Stalin's Great Terror and died in prison, probably executed, in late 1939.

**Political Bureau:** The highest executive agency in the CPUSA, consisting of the general secretary and the party's chief officials. Also known as the Polburo, PB, and Politburo.

**Profintern:** Russian acronym for the Krasnyi internatsional professionalnykh soyuzov (Red International of Labor Unions). Sometimes known by the English acronym of RILU. The Profintern was the Comintern's trade union arm.

**Randolph:** Pseudonym used by a series of American CPUSA representatives to the Comintern in the 1930s.

**RCP(b):** Russian Communist Party (Bolshevik). The official title of the Soviet Communist party from 1918 until 1925, when it became the All-Union Communist Party (Bolshevik), or AUCP(b). In 1952 it became the Communist Party of the Soviet Union (CPSU).

**Red:** Term for Communists, taken from the Communist use of red flags and banners.

**Reed, John** (1887–1920): Well-known American journalist and one of the chief founders of the Communist Labor Party. He died of typhus in Soviet Russia in 1920 and was buried beneath the Kremlin wall with a Red Army honor guard.

**Rosenberg, Julius** (1918–1953) and **Ethel** (1915–1953): Obscure American Communists executed for their role in Soviet atomic espionage. They denied their guilt and denied that they were Communists.

**RTsKhIDNI:** Rossiiskii tsentr khraneniia i izucheniia dokumentov noveishei istorii (Russian center for the preservation and study of documents of recent history). Archive holding records of the Comintern, the CPUSA up to 1944, and the CPSU up to 1953.

**Russian Center for the Preservation and Study of Documents of Recent History.** See RTsKhIDNI.

**Ruthenberg, Charles** (1882–1927): One of the chief founders of the Communist Party of America in 1919 and first general secretary of the party after it merged with the rival Communist Labor Party. He remained head of the American Communist party until his death in 1927. He was buried beneath the Kremlin wall in Moscow with a regiment of the Red Army in attendance.

**Smedley, Agnes** (1892–1950): Well-known journalist who championed the cause of the Chinese Communists in the 1930s and 1940s. She denied having any official links to the Comintern.

**Sorge ring:** Soviet espionage network operating in China and Japan in the 1930s and early 1940s headed by the German Communist Richard Sorge. Sorge, who operated under the cover of a pro-Nazi German journalist, became an unofficial adviser to the German ambassador to Japan. Sorge's access to the German embassy and that of his subagents to the Japanese government allowed him to provide the Soviet government with highly valuable intelligence on both Japan and Germany.

**Stalin, Joseph [Joseph Vissarionovich Djugashvili]** (1879–1953): Soviet dictator who ruled the USSR from Lenin's death in 1924 until his own death in 1953.

**Subversive Activities Control Board (SACB):** U.S. agency charged with registering Communist-controlled organizations in the 1950s.

**Syndicalism:** See Anarcho-syndicalism.

**Toohey, Pat** (1904–1978): CPUSA trade union organizer and representative to the Comintern in the late 1930s.

**Trade Union Educational League (TUEL):** Trade union arm of the American Communist party in the early 1920s, headed by William Z. Foster.

**Trade Union Unity League (TUUL):** Trade union arm of the CPUSA in the late 1920s and early 1930s, successor to the TUEL.

**Trotsky, Leon [Lev Davidovitch Bronstein]** (1879–1940): Second only to Lenin in the Bolshevik Revolution, Trotsky was defeated by Stalin in the struggle to succeed Lenin. He was accused of ultra-revolutionary left deviation from Marxism-Leninism and was later assassinated by a Soviet agent while living in exile in Mexico.

**Trotskyists (Trotskyites):** Followers of Leon Trotsky, a Bolshevik leader defeated by Stalin in the struggle to succeed Lenin; accused of left-wing ultra-revolutionary ideological deviation.

**Veterans of the Abraham Lincoln Brigade (VALB):** Veterans' organization for Americans who served with the International Brigades in the Spanish Civil War. The best-known American unit in the Spanish Civil War was the Abraham Lincoln *battalion*. Consequently, the veterans' organization adopted the title Veterans of the Abraham Lincoln Brigade.

**Wallach, Albert** (1912–1938): American volunteer with the International Brigades who died in Spain—executed by the International Brigades security police, according to some accounts.

**Washington battalion:** See George Washington battalion.

**White:** A term used during the Bolshevik Revolution and in the 1920s and 1930s to describe anti-Communist forces; the opposite of "Red."

**Wolff, Milton** (1914– ): Last commander of the Abraham Lincoln battalion in the Spanish Civil War, leader of the Veterans of the Abraham Lincoln Brigade, and OSS officer in World War II.

**YCL:** Young Communist League, youth arm of the CPUSA.

# Chronology of American Communism

1917    Lenin and the Bolsheviks seize power in Russia.

1919    Communist Party of America and Communist Labor Party founded in the United States. Both parties go underground in emulation of the conspiratorial Bolsheviks and in response to government harassment.

1921    Under pressure from the Communist International (Comintern), the two American parties merge and form the Workers Party, later renamed the CPUSA, controlled by the underground.

1924    After considering Robert La Follette, the Communist Party of America nominated William Z. Foster for president instead.

1925    Comintern prevents Foster from becoming party leader and gives control to Charles Ruthenberg.

1927    Ruthenberg dies; Jay Lovestone succeeds him as party leader.

1928    Followers of Leon Trotsky expelled from the CPUSA. Comintern proclaims new era of revolutionary upsurge.

1929    CPUSA leaders Jay Lovestone and Benjamin Gitlow expelled from CPUSA on Stalin's orders.

1930    Communists take lead in demonstrating against unemployment in America.

1931    Communists lead fight for the Scottsboro boys and focus attention on plight of Southern blacks.

1932    Calling for a Soviet America, Communists on a ticket led by Foster get 102,991 votes in the national election. Secret apparatus established under direction of J. Peters.

1934    Earl Browder becomes general secretary of the CPUSA.

1935    Georgi Dimitrov proclaims Popular Front against fascism at the Seventh Congress of the Communist International.

1936    Communists help form the Congress of Industrial Organizations (CIO) and begin to support President Roosevelt and his New Deal.

1937    Communists organize Abraham Lincoln battalion to fight in the Spanish

Civil War. Communists active in many civic and political organizations whose membership is chiefly noncommunist.

1938    House of Representatives Special Committee on Un-American Activities charges widespread Communist infiltration of American life.

1939    CPUSA membership approaches 100,000 before Nazi-Soviet Pact destroys Popular Front. Liberals abandon Communist-dominated organizations.

1941    Popular Front resuscitated after German attack on the USSR.

1943    Stalin dissolves Comintern as gesture to Western allies.

1944    Browder leadership dissolves the CPUSA and replaces it with the Communist Political Association.

1945    Moscow's displeasure with Browder's policies leads to his removal as leader and to the reconstitution of the CPUSA.

1946    Eugene Dennis becomes general secretary of the CPUSA.

1947    Truman administration creates loyalty program for government employees. CPUSA leaders, including Eugene Dennis, indicted for violating the Smith Act.

1948    Elizabeth Bentley names numerous government employees as Soviet agents. Whittaker Chambers accuses Alger Hiss of Communist ties and espionage. Communist effort to enter mainstream politics through the Progressive Party and the presidential candidacy of Henry Wallace fails.

1949    J. Peters deported to Hungary. Hiss tried for perjury.

1950    Senator Joseph McCarthy charges that Communists have infiltrated the State Department. Julius and Ethel Rosenberg are charged with atomic espionage. Morris Cohen vanishes from New York. Congress establishes the Subversive Activities Control Board. The CIO expels Communist-led unions.

1951    Supreme Court upholds constitutionality of the Smith Act. Several Communist leaders jump bail and go underground. Anticipating the coming of American fascism, the CPUSA creates an elaborate underground apparatus to hide its cadre.

1953    Rosenbergs executed.

1956    Khrushchev denounces Stalin's crimes. The CPUSA is torn apart by Khrushchev's speech and by Soviet suppression of Hungarian Revolution.

1957    Supreme Court makes prosecution of Communists under the Smith Act virtually impossible.

1958    CPUSA membership falls to 3,000; hard-liners win control of the party.

1959    Gus Hall replaces Eugene Dennis as party leader.

1989    USSR cuts secret subsidies to the CPUSA. Party membership, which had been rising slowly, declines after collapse of communism in Eastern Europe.

1991    Nearly half of CPUSA's 3,000 members quit after Gus Hall supports attempted hard-line Communist coup against Soviet leader, Mikhail Gorbachev.

1994    CPUSA has about 1,000 registered members.

The Secret World of American Communism

# CHAPTER ONE

# Background

IN 1943 WOLFGANG LEONHARD, a young German attending a Communist International (Comintern) school for foreign Communists near Ufa, a city 750 miles east of Moscow, received an unusual assignment. The Comintern's archives had been transferred to Ufa when the Nazi army was threatening Moscow, and Leonhard was among a group of students given the task of putting the chaotic archives into order. His assignment was to organize the records of the American Communist party. In his memoir written in 1958, a decade after his break with communism, Leonhard noted:

> The Communist Party of the U.S.A. was readily conceded first place for chaos and confusion. The sacks belonging to my American comrades contained not only whole bundles of Party documents which had simply been stuffed in without even a file-cover being put round them, but also the remains of cinema advertisements, old numbers of the *New York Times*, broken pencils and every kind of rubbish that had not the slightest connection with the archives. . . .
>
> There were so many things that I would have liked to have read— protocols of sessions of the Central Committee, struggles with the factions, justifications for the expulsions of leading Party officials—but unfortunately there was not the slightest possibility. I had to open the sacks, put the material in folders, and write on the outside "Trade

Unions" or "Miscellaneous" or "Party 1921–1923" at the pace of a
Stakhanov. With every day that passed, we were urged more and more
often to pay less attention to accuracy than to speed.[1]

The Soviet Union never acknowledged possession of this archive,
much less allowed scholars access to it, and until very recently it was
not known whether this valuable resource for the study of American communism had survived. Fortunately, these records do exist;
they form part of the vast Comintern collection, which is held by the
Russian Center for the Preservation and Study of Documents of
Recent History (RTsKhIDNI). Fifty years after Wolfgang Leonhard
sorted through these documents, the authors of this volume had the
opportunity to study them. This book is the first of several volumes
that will present and explain how this material can enlarge our
understanding of American communism and twentieth-century
American history.

## A Brief History of the American Communist Party

Few political organizations have excited as much controversy as the
Communist Party of the United States of America (CPUSA). From
its founding in 1919 until it subsided into obscurity during the
1960s, the CPUSA was constantly in the news or on the minds of
government officials. Frequently involved in spectacular or violent
demonstrations, strikes, or other public events, it was also a contin-
ual target of local or federal agencies. Some of the most important
Supreme Court cases of this century dealing with fundamental issues of civil liberties arose from cases involving American Communists. From 1947 until the mid-1950s, no other problem was as
contentious or aroused as much political disharmony as the issue of
communism and Communists. The newly declared Cold War was
then in its most dangerous phase. Joseph Stalin ruled the USSR, and
communism's influence was expanding on every continent. Most
Americans regarded the fight against the CPUSA as simply the
domestic front of a Cold War whose ultimate winner was undecided. Democrats and Republicans, Congress and the executive

1. Wolfgang Leonhard, *Child of the Revolution* (Chicago: Henry Regnery, 1958),
231. As a youth, Leonhard was taken to the USSR by his mother, a German Communist fleeing Hitler. Stakhanov was a model Stalinist worker who set records for
working at a furious pace.

branch, liberals and conservatives all struggled to convince the nation that they were tougher on communism than their counterparts.

The movement that aroused this ire was inspired by the sudden, violent seizure of the Russian government by the Bolshevik party, led by Vladimir Ilich Lenin, in November 1917. The triumph of Marxist socialism in Russia electrified radicals around the world; encouraged by the Bolshevik success, Marxist revolutionaries seized power in several European nations and made bold attempts to do so in others. In the political and social turmoil that followed the end of World War I, it seemed as though the Marxist millennium was near. Even in the United States, enthusiasm for the new regime swept through the ranks of the Socialist party, then a small but lively presence in American politics. William Z. Foster, an avowed radical who later became a prominent American Communist, led hundreds of thousands of steelworkers out on strike, and in Seattle a general strike led by a Bolshevik admirer shut down the city. Political terrorists detonated bombs, killing dozens and injuring hundreds.

In this heady atmosphere, American radicals founded two Communist parties in 1919. The Communist Party of America, led by Charles Ruthenberg, had about twenty-four thousand members. The rival Communist Labor Party, led by John Reed and Benjamin Gitlow, had about ten thousand. Fewer than four thousand members of both groups spoke English; most of these new American Communists were immigrants from the former tsarist empire. Not until the 1930s were a majority of American Communists English-speaking and native-born.

Both Communist parties proclaimed themselves dedicated to the violent overthrow of the American state and issued terrifying threats. In 1919 one early Communist, Carl Päiviö, wrote in the newspaper he edited that "a rioting mob is the one and only possible means for organizing a fight . . . in these last open and decisive blood-battles between the capitalists and the working classes. . . . To hell with the teachings of peaceful revolution. The bloody seizure of power by the working classes is the only possible way."[2] Public

---

2. *Luokkataistelu* (Class struggle), May 1919, quoted in Joint Legislative Committee Investigating Seditious Activities, *Revolutionary Radicalism, Its History, Purpose and Tactics, with an Exposition and Discussion of the Steps Being Taken and Required to Curb It* (Albany: J. B. Lyon, 1920), 1191.

authorities took no chances. New York prosecutors, for example, briefly imprisoned Päiviö for his violent editorial under New York's criminal anarchy law. Between 1919 and 1922, local, state, and federal agents detained hundreds of Communists for advocating violent revolution. In California alone, more than five hundred Communists were arrested, and more than half were imprisoned for short terms. Although neither Communist party was outlawed and party membership by an American citizen was not a crime, non-citizens could be deported, and federal immigration officials did deport nearly a thousand alien radicals during this era.

Both of the newly formed Communist parties went underground. Their leaders adopted pseudonyms and changed residences, their party papers were printed secretly, and their members divided into small cells that met at secret locations. These actions were under-taken in part to protect members who were not American citizens but also because Communists were convinced that a revolutionary upheaval was imminent and that the conspiratorial Bolshevik model was the path to victory.

This early romantic revolutionary era did not last long. Although Lenin consolidated power in Russia, the Bolshevik-inspired revolutions in Germany, Hungary, Latvia, and Finland failed. When Poland repulsed a Soviet invasion in 1921, the threat of a Red revolution sweeping Europe diminished. America's Red Scare of 1919–1922 subsided and with it the fear that American society could be overthrown by a small group of underground Communists.

Meanwhile, Lenin set about bringing under control the various revolutionary movements inspired by the Bolshevik Revolution. His instrument was a new body, the Communist International. In 1919 the Bolsheviks invited radical parties from around the world to join together to promote world revolution. Although the first Com-intern congress was largely composed of individuals representing tiny groups or no one but themselves, within a few years Commu-nist parties around the globe had been either formed or detached from previously existing socialist groups. The Comintern set up headquarters in Moscow and received offices, equipment, and staff from Lenin's government. Most important, the USSR also supplied the Comintern with generous funding, much of it in the form of jewels, gold, and silver confiscated from tsarist holdings, to subsidize the nascent Communist parties.

In theory the Comintern was a worldwide brotherhood of like-minded revolutionaries, and all Communist parties, including the USSR's, were its branches. In practice, the Soviet party dominated the organization. Stalin's rise to power in the late 1920s further consolidated Soviet government control of Communist parties around the world, and his government directed Comintern policies to serve Soviet foreign policy interests.[3]

Under Comintern guidance and pressure the two American Communist parties merged in 1921, and Charles Ruthenberg soon emerged as leader. Comintern representatives also ordered the American party to organize itself as an aboveground organization, while still retaining a covert arm. But the Comintern was unable to end the bitter factionalism that characterized the early American Communist movement. Deeply divided, spending much of their energy struggling against each other, the factions had little time and less ability to make much of a mark on American society for the rest of the 1920s. In all cases, the Comintern was the final arbiter of party feuds. The winner of each fight was always decided when disputing leaders went to Moscow for a Comintern ruling or when a Comintern representative residing in America picked the winner on the spot.[4]

In 1929, party leaders Jay Lovestone and Benjamin Gitlow (Ruthenberg had died in 1927) were expelled on Stalin's orders after they defied Comintern instructions to relinquish power to their factional rivals. Stalin accused Lovestone of ideological kinship with Nikolai Bukharin, a Soviet leader whom Stalin had bested in the struggle to succeed Lenin after the latter's death in 1924.

3. As one of the authors noted in a study of the Comintern, as early as 1920 "all principal questions of the Comintern's activities were discussed and tentatively resolved in the RKP(b) Central Committee" prior to their consideration by the Comintern itself (Fridrikh Igorevich Firsov, "Mechanism of Power Realization in the Comintern," in *Centenaire Jules Humbert-Droz: Colloque sur l'Internationale communiste* [La Chaux-de-Fonds: Fondation Jules Humbert-Droz, 1992]). The RKP(b) was the Russian Communist Party (Bolshevik), the title in 1920 of what became the Communist Party of the Soviet Union (CPSU).

4. A subsequent volume will reproduce documents demonstrating the Comintern's control over the internal affairs of the American movement.

Stalin had accused Bukharin of demonstrating "right-wing" tendencies because he opposed Stalin's plans to use coercion to collectivize the Soviet peasantry. The removal of the "Lovestoneites" ended organized factionalism in the Communist Party of the United States of America (the party's name from that year onward). Within a year, Earl Browder, an American born in Kansas but fresh from Comintern work in China, emerged as party leader; he held the reins until he was deposed for defying Soviet policy in 1945.

The onset of the Great Depression of the 1930s briefly restored Communist dreams of revolution, and the party gained widespread publicity by leading a series of dramatic strikes and demonstrations. The CPUSA was the first group to organize nationwide demonstrations against the rapid increase in unemployment during the early years of the Depression. Notable also was CPUSA leadership of violent strikes by textile workers in Gastonia, North Carolina, and by coal miners in Harlan County, Kentucky, and its championing of the cause of nine black youngsters in Alabama convicted of raping two white women. The age of the defendants, the lynch mob atmosphere of the trial, and the considerable evidence that no rape had occurred turned the Scottsboro case into one of the major symbols of Southern racism. Little wonder that some idealistic Americans (several of whom will appear later in the pages of this book) searching for greater social justice turned to communism and the Communist party.

Still, throughout the first half of the 1930s, the CPUSA remained a small organization on the fringes of society. Even though the Depression radicalized some Americans, many more were attracted to Franklin Delano Roosevelt's New Deal and his program of energetic reform within the confines of America's democratic traditions. Undaunted and with Moscow's approval, Communists denounced Roosevelt as a reactionary seeking to save capitalism and termed his New Deal an American version of fascism.

The growing threat of Nazi aggression altered Soviet foreign policy, the Comintern's orientation, and, inevitably, American Communist behavior. At the Seventh Congress of the Communist International held in Moscow in 1935, the new Comintern leader, Georgi Dimitrov, a Bulgarian Communist who had gained international fame as a defendant in the Reichstag fire trial in Nazi Germany in 1933, called for a Popular Front against fascism. Communist parties, which had been denouncing liberals and socialists, now called for an alliance with them to fight the spread of fascism.

In the United States, the CPUSA embraced Roosevelt's New Deal. In the 1920s the CPUSA had created the Trade Union Unity League (TUUL) and a series of explicitly revolutionary trade unions as rivals to the American Federation of Labor and its moderate trade unions. As part of its Popular Front strategy, the CPUSA dissolved the TUUL and sent its militants into the mainstream labor movement. The Congress of Industrial Organizations (CIO), newly formed and dominated by John L. Lewis, was eager to organize such mass production industries as automobiles, steel, and electrical machinery, needed capable organizers, and quietly made use of Communist aid. The CIO grew rapidly, and with it Communist influence. By the late 1930s, a quarter of the CIO's members were in unions led by Communists.[5]

Aided by the Popular Front stance, Communists could soon be found in dozens of organizations, dealing with every aspect of American life. Prominent writers, artists, and intellectuals flocked to Communist-dominated groups such as the League of American Writers and the American League against War and Fascism. The American Youth Congress, a federation of the largest youth groups in the United States, was Communist led. The CPUSA raised large sums of money in Hollywood, capitalizing on its role in sending several thousand young men to Spain to fight on behalf of the Spanish Republican government in a civil war (1936–1939) against fascist-supported insurgents.

Many liberals remained suspicious of Communists, but others were impressed by the CPUSA's support for Roosevelt and by its fervent antifascism and were willing to cooperate with it. In a few states and cities, the Popular Front alliance of liberals and Communists became a political force. In New York, one such coalition took control of the American Labor Party, a state-level grouping that held the balance of power between Republicans and Democrats. In Minnesota, a Popular Front faction took control of the Farmer-Labor Party, which dominated Minnesota politics in the 1930s.

5. Documents dealing with the role of the CPUSA in the labor movement in the 1930s will be presented in a subsequent volume.

When it merged with the Democratic party in 1944, Communists and their allies became a major force in the resulting Democratic-Farmer-Labor Party. Communists and their Popular Front allies also won control of the Washington Commonwealth Federation, the leading New Deal body in Washington state. Operating through similar alliances, Communists also became important, albeit not dominant, actors in the Democratic parties of California, Wisconsin, and Michigan. By 1939 nearly a hundred thousand Americans were members of the CPUSA.

The CPUSA's growth and the spread of its influence in American society came during the same years that the Soviet Union experienced the worst torments of Stalin's rule. Millions of Soviets died during the collectivization of agriculture in the early 1930s and millions more died later in the decade when Stalin purged Soviet society and the CPSU itself of all he regarded as politically unreliable. The totalitarian nature of the Soviet state prevented much of the news of Stalin's oppression from reaching America. And the information about the purges that did reach the West was often not believed or was rationalized by American Communists and their sympathizers.

The CPUSA's successes, however, were always hostage to Soviet foreign policy. The triumphs of the Popular Front had been predicated on an antifascist policy. In 1939 Stalin shifted his foreign strategy from opposing Hitler to seeking mutual accommodation with him. The two dictators divided Eastern Europe: Hitler acquired western Poland and a sphere of influence in Central Europe, while the USSR annexed eastern Poland, Latvia, Lithuania, Estonia, and part of Romania. Once the Nazi-Soviet Pact was signed in August 1939, Hitler, assured of Soviet neutrality, was free to attack Poland and begin World War II. The Nazi-Soviet Pact required the CPUSA to abandon its support for an anti-Nazi foreign policy and attack Roosevelt as a warmonger for his continued support for the beleaguered democracies of Europe. The Popular Front bodies so painstakingly built up in the 1930s collapsed under the weight of the new Communist policies. The League of American Writers lost so many of its prominent members that its letterhead had to be discarded. So many liberal members abandoned the

American League for Peace and Democracy (formerly the American League against War and Fascism) that it simply dissolved. Disillusioned, thousands quietly dropped out of the CPUSA itself. In addition to these internal difficulties, in late 1939 the federal government launched a legal attack on the CPUSA, expanding Federal Bureau of Investigation (FBI) surveillance of party activities, and, in 1941, imprisoning Earl Browder for using a false passport. The FBI also exposed the company World Tourists as a front for Soviet clandestine work. World Tourists was ostensibly a travel agency run by a CPUSA official, Jacob Golos, whose name will appear later in this book in connection with Elizabeth Bentley.

The German invasion of the USSR in 1941 saved the Communists from their own folly. The party dropped its peace program and demanded American aid for the Soviet Union and American intervention in the war. After Pearl Harbor, the CPUSA endorsed Roosevelt's war policies, called for a quick American invasion of Europe to relieve Nazi pressure on the Soviets, and vehemently denounced any interference with the war effort as treasonous. These policies allowed the rebuilding of many of the Popular Front relationships destroyed during the period of the Nazi-Soviet Pact. The heroic Soviet resistance to the Nazi army also lessened the pervasive anti-Communist sentiment of the American public.

Released from prison in 1942 as a symbol of goodwill toward America's Soviet allies, Earl Browder became convinced that the Soviet Union's wartime alliance with the United States and Great Britain was permanent. Emboldened by the dissolution of the Comintern in 1943, Stalin's gesture to his Western allies, Browder dissolved the CPUSA in 1944 and reformed it as the Communist Political Association, intending to make Communists the left wing of the Democratic party. He announced that socialism would not be on the American agenda in the foreseeable future, a step that disconcerted some members of his own party.

At this point, the Soviet Union intervened once more. In the spring of 1945, Jacques Duclos, a French Communist only recently returned to Paris from Moscow, wrote an article denouncing Browder's policies as examples of class collaboration. Taken by the CPUSA as a signal of Soviet disapproval, the Duclos article led to an upheaval. Browder's colleagues expelled him and resurrected the CPUSA. Eugene Dennis, a veteran of Comintern work in China, South Africa, and the Philippines, became the new party leader.

As the Cold War developed, the reborn CPUSA demanded that its liberal allies accommodate Soviet foreign policy goals and oppose President Harry Truman's policy of containing Soviet expansion. In 1948 Communists threw all of their strength into Henry Wallace's presidential campaign and supported the Progressive Party as a Popular Front alternative to the Democrats. The failure of the Wallace campaign (it garnered only 2.3 percent of the national vote), however, left anti-Communists in firm control of the Democratic party and American liberalism. CIO leaders such as Philip Murray and Walter Reuther, deeply angered by the Communist role in the Wallace effort, drove Communists and Communist-dominated unions out of the labor federation, destroying what had been one of the CPUSA's chief sources of strength.

By the late 1940s, as the Cold War intensified, more Americans began to view the CPUSA as the domestic ally of America's most dangerous enemy, and the party began its irreversible decline. A series of spectacular spy cases, beginning at the end of World War II and continuing through the early 1950s, buttressed many Americans' belief that Communists were disloyal. The most visible symbols of alleged Communist perfidy were Alger Hiss and Julius and Ethel Rosenberg. The former was a respectable high-level government official whose conviction for perjury (for lying about having provided government documents to a Communist espionage ring) stoked fears that the United States government had been infiltrated by spies.[6] The Rosenbergs were obscure Communists (they, in fact, denied being Communists) whose conviction for involvement in a spy ring responsible for atomic espionage suggested that ordinary Communists would not hesitate to betray the nation's most vital military secrets. The Rosenbergs' conviction reinforced the distrust that had been generated by congressional hearings in the late 1940s over alleged widespread Communist subversion in the preceding decades. After the Korean War broke out in 1950 and American soldiers died fighting Communist troops, the CPUSA lost virtually

6. The statute of limitations prevented Hiss's trial on an espionage charge; his trial for perjury was tantamount to a conviction for espionage.

all of its allies. Beginning in 1948, the U.S. Justice Department used the Smith Act to imprison more than a hundred Communist leaders, including Eugene Dennis, for conspiring to teach and organize the overthrow of the government by force and violence.

Expecting the emergence of full-fledged fascism in the United States, the CPUSA sent hundreds of its cadre into hiding in its underground organization in 1951. The CPUSA was never outlawed, however, and continued to function openly, albeit with difficulty. After Stalin died in 1953, the Cold War stabilized. With its sense of crisis easing, the CPUSA ordered its hidden cadre to resurface in 1955 and 1956. The Communists, however, were immediately dealt an even more serious blow. In 1956 Soviet leader Nikita Khrushchev admitted Stalin's crimes, including the purges in the 1930s that had killed not just millions of ordinary Russians but hundreds of thousands of Communists as well and had created an atmosphere of terror. The admission confirmed the long-standing views of many anti-Communists and devastated American Communists. The damage was reinforced by the USSR's brutal suppression of the 1956 Hungarian Revolution and exposés of Soviet anti-Semitism. Their morale broken by these revelations about the internal life of the Communist system, Communists left the party by the thousands.

By the late 1950s, the American government had ended most of its legal attacks on the party, which was, by this point, a shattered organization. Immediately after World War II, membership in the CPUSA was seventy thousand; by 1956, it had dropped to twelve thousand, and in 1958, following Khrushchev's speech and the Hungarian Revolution, membership plummeted to three thousand. In 1959 Gus Hall, a Soviet loyalist trained at the International Lenin School in Moscow, replaced the ailing Eugene Dennis as CPUSA general secretary. Under Hall the party continued to limp along, sustained by its hard-core loyalists and by secret Soviet subsidies, earning a reputation as the most slavishly pro-Soviet Communist party in the industrialized world.

In the aftermath of the Vietnam War, which ended the anti-Communist consensus in American politics, and the waning of the New Left movement of the 1960s and 1970s, the CPUSA gained some respectability and some members, although its numbers probably did not exceed ten thousand. It entered its death throes in 1989, when Soviet leader Mikhail Gorbachev cut off Soviet subsidies in response to Hall's criticism of Gorbachev's reform program. The CPUSA split in 1991 over Hall's continued backing of Communist hard-liners, with about half of its members and most of its younger leaders quitting. In 1994, the eighty-four-year-old Hall remains in charge of an elderly remnant of about a thousand members.

## The Clandestine Activities of the CPUSA

Many questions remain about the CPUSA's role in American political and social life. One of the most contentious and important issues concerns the party's clandestine activities. Did the Communist party conceal key aspects of its organization in a secret apparatus? Did secret members of the party infiltrate government agencies in the 1930s and 1940s? Did the Communist party and its members commit espionage on behalf of the Soviet Union? Strictly speaking, only the last was a crime. The maintenance of a concealed underground organization, however, marked the CPUSA as an abnormal participant in democratic politics. And the manipulation of government agencies to promote Communist policies was a form of political subversion.

By any measure, dislike of communism has always been strong in the United States, with only the degree of aversion varying over time. The CPUSA's overt and covert ties to the Soviet Union accounted for a large measure of the fear and loathing with which most Americans regarded the party. Particularly during the era of intense popular anticommunism in the late 1940s and 1950s, American Communists were perceived as spies, either actual or potential, or as "ideological termites" burrowing away within American institutions and seeking to weaken them fatally.

In addition to the cases of Alger Hiss and the Rosenbergs, other charges and accusations about Communist subversion abounded. Whittaker Chambers, who named Alger Hiss as a spy, described an extensive Communist underground that existed in Washington in the 1930s. Elizabeth Bentley, a former Communist, named more than forty government employees as sources for a Soviet espionage ring she ran in the 1940s. Right-wing groups charged that Franklin

Roosevelt and his administration assisted in Communist infiltration of the government.[7] Relatively few of the charges, however, had sufficient evidence to back them in a court of law. A few spies were convicted and imprisoned, but even they were seldom caught red-handed. And even when persuasive evidence existed, it was rare that anyone confessed. Both the Hiss and the Rosenberg cases remain the subjects of controversy, with those who maintain their innocence or reaffirm their guilt continuing to add to the small libraries of books and articles on these episodes.

## The Question of Joseph McCarthy

The documents in this volume also require us to examine the legacy of Senator Joseph McCarthy. In the early 1950s, anticommunism was in its harshest phase. The Soviet Union had consolidated its control of Eastern Europe and emerged as a nuclear-armed super-power, Communist forces had conquered China, and fifty-four thousand American troops died fighting invading Communist troops in Korea. Emotions aroused by the Hiss and Rosenberg spy trials combined with the fear and anger kindled by Communist advances overseas to produce an atmosphere in which demagogues, frauds, and charlatans could use anti-Communist sentiment for their own, often unsavory purposes. In McCarthy's hands, anti-communism was a partisan weapon used to implicate the New Deal, liberals, and the Democratic party in treason. Using evidence that was exaggerated, distorted, and in some cases utterly false, he accused hundreds of individuals of Communist activity, recklessly mixing the innocent with the assuredly guilty when it served his political purposes. With passions against communism as strong as they were, McCarthy's demagoguery and that of others like him found a ready audience for several years. Some innocent people

7. The classic extremist statement of this position was a 14 June 1951 Senate speech by Senator Joseph McCarthy (Republican, Wisconsin), who accused Dean Acheson, secretary of state under President Truman, and George C. Marshall, army chief of staff under President Roosevelt and secretary of state and secretary of defense under Truman, of having been part of "a conspiracy on a scale so immense as to dwarf any previous such venture in the history of man. A conspiracy of infamy so black that, when it is finally exposed, its principals shall be forever deserving of the maledictions of all honest men."

were ruined by the irresponsible use of unverified charges and even faked evidence concocted for political gain. In addition, much of the legal attack on the CPUSA in the 1950s was excessive, inspired by political pandering to strong public anti-Communist emotions, and of doubtful constitutional propriety. The government needed a security program, but its implementation was sometimes needlessly intrusive and crude.

The excesses of this era brought several reactions. McCarthy was censured by his colleagues in the U.S. Senate in 1954 for his repeated assaults on political civility and was effectively neutralized. The courts invalidated many of the most abusive anti-Communist laws. And a consensus developed that "McCarthyism," meaning the reckless use of unverified charges and guilt by association, was a moral wrong, and the term conveyed political opprobrium.

Reaction to the excesses of the McCarthy era has also confused the debate over historical issues surrounding American communism, particularly in regard to its clandestine activities. Because McCarthy and those like him used the issue of American Communist involvement in Soviet espionage to assail liberals and Democrats, some people concluded that anyone who suggested that the CPUSA was involved in covert activities and espionage was a McCarthyite—McCarthy's guilt-by-association technique in reverse. To recognize the excesses, mistakes, and injustices of McCarthy's anti-Communist crusade is not to accept the distorted view that anticommunism was an irrational and indefensible persecution of a group of American reformers or that it was impossible for the CPUSA to have been engaged in nefarious activities. Indeed, the documents in this volume demonstrate that the widespread popular belief that many American Communists collaborated with Soviet intelligence and placed loyalty to the Soviet Union ahead of loyalty to the United States was well founded. Concern about the subversive threat of the CPUSA and worries that Communists employed in sensitive government jobs constituted a security risk were equally well founded. None of this, however, offers any vindication for Senator McCarthy or McCarthyism.

## The Historiographic Debate

In addition to specific information, the archival documents offer a new perspective on the more general historiographic issues. Two views of the history of the CPUSA are in contention. The older view, first developed in the 1950s, holds that the CPUSA was never an independent American political party but a creature given life and meaning by its umbilical ties to the Soviet Union. Seeing the Soviet connections as the defining aspect of American communism, these scholars, while acknowledging the importance of studying the myriad local activities of the CPUSA, focus on the party's willingness to alter its policies to suit Soviet needs and on the key roles played by the party leadership in defining the Stalinist nature of American communism.[8]

The revisionist view, the dominant perspective among academic historians for the past twenty years, holds that the American Communist movement was a normal, albeit radical, political participant in American democracy.[9] This assessment sees American commu-

---

8. The chief works advancing this view are Irving Howe and Lewis Coser, *The American Communist Party: A Critical History, 1919–1957* (Boston: Beacon Press, 1957); Theodore Draper, *The Roots of American Communism* (New York: Viking Press, 1957); Theodore Draper, *American Communism and Soviet Russia: The Formative Period* (New York: Viking Press, 1960); Max Kampelman, *The Communist Party vs. the C.I.O.: A Study in Power Politics* (New York: Praeger, 1957); Harvey Klehr, *The Heyday of American Communism: The Depression Decade* (New York: Basic Books, 1984); and Harvey Klehr and John Earl Haynes, *The American Communist Movement: Storming Heaven Itself* (New York: Twayne Publishers, 1992). Draper summarizes his views and replies to critics of this interpretation in Theodore Draper, "American Communism Revisited," *New York Review of Books* 32, no. 8 (9 May 1985); Draper, "The Popular Front Revisited," *New York Review of Books* 32, no. 9 (30 May 1985); and Draper, "The Life of the Party," *New York Review of Books* 41, nos. 1 and 2 (13 January 1994).

9. Chief among these works are Maurice Isserman, *Which Side Were You On? The American Communist Party during the Second World War* (Middletown, Conn: Wesleyan University Press, 1982); Mark Naison, *Communists in Harlem during the Depression* (Urbana: University of Illinois Press, 1983); Ellen W. Schrecker, *No Ivory Tower: McCarthyism and the Universities* (New York: Oxford University Press, 1986); Fraser M. Ottanelli, *The Communist Party of the United States from the Depression to World War II* (New Brunswick: Rutgers University Press, 1991); and the essays by various writers in Robert W. Griffith and Athan Theoharis, eds., *The Specter: Original Essays on the Cold War and the Origins of McCarthyism* (New York: New Viewpoints, 1974); and in Michael Brown, Frank Rosengarten, Randy Martin, and George Snedeker, eds., *New Studies in the Culture and History*

nism as a domestic American movement with its roots in America's democratic, populist, and revolutionary past. While sometimes admitting that American Communists took their ideological inspiration from Soviet communism, this school insists that the linkages to Moscow were either superficial or ritualistic and that at the grass roots, American Communists paid little attention to ideological abstractions and concentrated on fighting racism, organizing unions, and promoting American democracy.

The revisionists have either denied or downplayed arguments about what others have described as the dark side of American communism—a side often emphasized by disaffected members from its early days. Former Communists described Soviet funding of the CPUSA, orders and directives from Moscow, and recruitment of American Communists for espionage. The revisionists dismissed these stories as inherently unreliable or exaggerated, as tales tainted by the tellers' disillusionment with communism and inspired by their desire to reap monetary rewards and benefit from America's obsessive anticommunism. And, certainly, some former Communists inflated or exaggerated what they knew. Others lied or strained credulity with charges that kept them employed or in the limelight. And some made honest mistakes in trying to reconstruct past events.

The documents presented here, and the more massive documentary record now available, provide a powerful challenge to the revisionist perspective. It is no longer possible to maintain that the Soviet Union did not fund the American party, that the CPUSA did not maintain a covert apparatus, and that key leaders and cadres were innocent of connection with Soviet espionage operations. Nowhere in the massive Comintern archives or in the American party's own records did the authors find documents indicating that Soviet or CPUSA officials objected to American Communists cooperating with Soviet intelligence or even having second thoughts about the

*of U.S. Communism* (New York: Monthly Review Press, 1993). Isserman presents the case for the revisionist argument in Maurice Isserman, "Three Generations: Historians View American Communism," *Labor History* 26, no. 4 (Fall 1985).

relationship. Both the Soviet Union and the American Communist leadership regarded these activities as normal and proper. Their only concern was that they not become public.

CHAPTER TWO

# Clandestine Habits: The 1920s and the Early 1930s

## The Comintern and Covert Operations

IN THE EARLY 1920s, the Comintern conducted covert operations and acted as the Soviet Union's foreign intelligence agency. As the USSR matured, the predecessors of the KGB, the state security organization (the GPU, the OGPU, and the NKVD), and the Soviet military intelligence service (GRU) established their primacy in the country's intelligence hierarchy. The romantic revolutionaries of the early years of communism gradually gave way to professional agents. In the 1930s, the operations of the Comintern overlapped with those of the KGB and GRU, but the Comintern continued to conduct covert operations until its dissolution in 1943. The Comintern was a useful apparatus through which to recruit agents and sources. Foreign Communists who might balk at working directly for the Soviet Union's espionage services could be persuaded that they were serving the international headquarters of world revolution.

In the 1920s there was close cooperation between the OGPU and the Comintern's International Relations Department, known as the OMS (Otdel mezhdunarodnykh svyazey), which oversaw the financing of foreign parties and the activities of Comintern emissaries. In 1935 Osip Piatnitsky, head of the OMS, was replaced by Mikhail Trilisser, who used the name Moskvin. Trilisser had directed the OGPU's foreign espionage operations from 1921 to 1929. Trilisser's dual role as OGPU officer and Comintern official illustrates the close relationship between the two agencies.

Soviet intelligence was able to make use of the Comintern and its operatives because, from its foundation, the Communist International had encouraged Communist parties to maintain both a legal political organization and an illegal or underground apparatus. Among the twenty-one conditions required for admission to its ranks, the Comintern in 1920 stipulated that all Communist parties create an illegal "organizational apparatus which, at the decisive moment, can assist the Party to do its duty to the revolution."[1] These underground apparatuses were intended both to defend the Communist movement from police repression and to promote secret political subversion.

Comintern representatives often traveled on false passports, entered countries illegally, and carried large amounts of cash and valuables to distribute secretly to local party leaders and organizations. The Comintern maintained clandestine courier services, secret mail drops, and systems of coded telegraphic and radio communications with foreign Communist parties. Year after year the Comintern issued instructions and pleas to its member parties to form secret units, train cadres to operate illegally, and prepare systems of safe houses and fake identification documents to protect its key officials in case of repression by hostile governments. Communists, in short, were not novices at the kind of work required for espionage. Soviet intelligence agencies quickly recognized that they could piggyback on these activities for espionage operations.

## John Reed and Clandestine Funding of American Communism

The United States did not officially recognize the USSR until 1933. Before that date, Soviet money for the American Communist movement had to be sent by way of secret couriers. The earliest known subsidies were sent in 1919. **Document 1** is a Comintern accounting sheet listing sums given during 1919 and 1920 to various individ-

1. "Thesis on the Conditions of Admission to the Communist International," in *Theses, Resolutions and Manifestos of the First Four Congresses of the Third International* (London: Inks Press, 1980), 93. The Comintern's 1922 order that the American Communist party end its underground existence reflected its judgment that the American movement, in an excess of conspiratorial zeal, had placed too many of its assets in the underground. The Comintern view was that, given the freedom of American society, the bulk of the Communist movement could operate openly with only necessarily covert activities assigned to the underground.

uals to finance newly formed Communist parties around the world. Four payments are listed for America: 209,000 rubles to Kotliarov on 16 July 1919, 500,000 rubles to Khavkin on 30 September 1919, 1,008,000 rubles to John Reed on 22 January 1920, and 1,011,000 rubles to Anderson on 31 January 1920. Three of these names are unknown, but John Reed was a famous American journalist, one of the founders of American communism, and author of *Ten Days That Shook the World,* a book that painted a romantic, idealistic picture of the Bolshevik Revolution. The date of the payment coincided with Reed's arrival in Soviet Russia as the international delegate of America's newly organized Communist Labor Party.

---

## Document 1

"Corresponding with Krumina's Receipts . . . ," RTsKhIDNI 495–82–1. Original in Russian. This undated document illustrates the enormous extent of Soviet subsidies of foreign Communists; the four payments for American activities, set here in boldface, were not unusual. The account lists the denomination of payments for American operations as in "value," indicating jewels, gold, or other valuables rather than currency. The cash-equivalent is listed in Russian rubles. The original document is entirely handwritten, worn, and some words and numbers are illegible.

Corresponding with Krumina's receipts, held in the archives, which were released by her

| [Year] | Month | Date | Released to | Doc. # | Denomination | Amount |
|--------|-------|------|-------------|--------|--------------|--------|
| 1919 | Sept. | 1 | Hungarian Comm. Govt. Rudnianok for Dige | 1/7 | value | 250,000 |
| | Dec. | 6 | " D. Zerlei | 2 | " | 207,000 |
| | " | 15 | " Brasler Kalush | 3 | " | 194,000 |
| 1920 | unknown | 24 | Bohemia Iv. Sinekom for Genglerzh and Mush | 4 | " | 288,000 |
| 1919 | Nov. | 19 | " [illeg.] | 5 | " | 215,000 |
| | May | 30 | Germany Reich for Thomas | 1/2 | " | 300,500 |
| | | | to him | " | DM | 100,000 |
| | | | " | " | Sw. Kron. | 3,000 |
| | | | " | " | Finn. M | 4,500 |
| | | | " | " | Russ. Rub. | 6,500 |

| | | | | | | |
|---|---|---|---|---|---|---|
| | Sept. | 9 | " Proletariat | 1/8a | value it seems | 250,000 |
| | Oct. | 28 | " Rudolf Rothegel | 6 | value | 639,000 |
| 1920 | Feb. | 20 | " Rozovski for Reich [all 3] for Thomas | 7 | " | 275,000 |
| 1919 | May | 20 | Italy Liubarskii —Carlo | 1/2 | DM | 15,200 |
| | | | " | " | Finn. M | 331,800 |
| | | | " | " | Sw. Kron. | 13,000 |
| | | | " | " | Russ. Rub. | 300,000 |
| " | Sept. | 21 | " via Berzin [illeg.] | 8 | value | 487,000 |
| " | **July** | **16** | **America Kotliarov** | **1/4** | " | **209,000** |
| " | **Sept.** | **30** | **" Khavkin** | **1/9** | " | **500,000** |
| **1920** | **Jan.** | **31** | **" Anderson** | **9** | " | **1,011,000** |
| " | " | **22** | **" John Reed** | **10** | " | **1,008,000** |
| 1919 | July | 5 | England Levin | 1/3 | " | 500,000 |
| 1919 | July | 15 | England Levin via Kantorovich [undecipherable to whom] | 11 | " | 1,039,000 |
| " | Sept. | 29 | See what is for Engl. Krasin | 12 | " | 7,040,000 |
| " | July | 30 | Balkan countries | 1/5 | " | 1,000,000 |
| 1919 | Dec. | 29 | Yugoslav. Beloshevich | 13 | value | 300,000 |
| " | Dec. | 26 | [?] Comm. Part. [Shchao?] Mikhail | 14 | " | 503,000 |
| " | Aug. | 13 | unknown to which country Sgurski | 1/6 | " | 297,000 |
| " | Sept. | 1 | " Inoderev gr. Balabanov | 1/8 | [Kron.?] | 83,300 |
| " | Oct. | 28 | " Leo [illeg.] [undecipherable] | 15 | value | 2,020,000 |
| 1920 | May | 5 | " unknown to whom | 16 | " | 5,239,000 |
| PAGE 2 | | | | | | |
| 1919 | Oct. | 19 | Roiters | 17 | Sw. Kr. | 10,000 |
| | | | also | | DM | 5,000 |
| | | | " | | value | 4,050,000 |
| | | | " | | Pounds | 50 |

| | | | | | | |
|---|---|---|---|---|---|---|
| | Dec. | | Swedish Office | 18 | Pounds | 4,000 |
| | | | A. Ioffe | | | |
| | | | also | | Dollars | 4,000 |
| | | | " | | Sw. Kr. | 52,000 |
| | | | " | | Marks | 25,000 |
| | | | Poland looks as if values | | | |
| | | | no receipts | 19 | | 10,000,000 |
| " | Dec. | 27 | Group Loriot Kost | 20 | value | 280,000 |
| | | | [both] to A. Groshov | | | |
| 1920 | June | 18 | Thomas | 21 | value | 1,000,000 |
| | | | to him also | | roman. | 150,000 |
| | | | " | | DM | 1,600,000 |
| | | | " | | " | 35,600 |

These four subsidies alone add up to 2,728,000 rubles. The value of the ruble on foreign exchange markets fluctuated wildly from 1919 to 1922 before the Soviets stabilized the "hard" ruble used for international trade at between $1 and $2. The Comintern document records that the subvention for American operations was in "value," a term in Comintern bookkeeping meaning that the sums were transmitted in the form of gold, silver, or jewels rather than currency. Thus, this account reveals that in this period the Comintern supplied the tiny American Communist movement with the equivalent of several million dollars in valuables, an enormous sum in the 1920s.[2]

Not all of this subsidy found its way to America. Reed left Russia secretly in February 1920. He was arrested by Finnish police while trying to stow away on a ship. The Finns confiscated $1,500 in various currencies and 102 diamonds estimated to be worth $14,000, a small fortune in 1920.[3] Although these diamonds never made it to America, others did. Benjamin Gitlow, one of the early

2. Rudolf Pikhoia, chairman of the Committee on Archival Affairs of the Russian Federation, estimates the value of the jewels given to Reed to be $1.5 million. See Michael Dobbs, "Yeltsin Aides Seek to Link Gorbachev to Terrorism," *Washington Post,* 6 June 1992. Soviet funding of the CPUSA from 1919 to 1989 is described in John Earl Haynes and Harvey Klehr, " 'Moscow Gold,' Confirmed at Last?" *Labor History* 33, no. 2 (Spring 1992): 279–93, and 33, no. 4 (Fall 1992): 576–78. Part of document 1 was reproduced in *Revelations from the Russian Archives: A Report from the Library of Congress* (Washington, D.C.: Library of Congress, 1993), 29.

3. Reed was tried and imprisoned by a Finnish court for illegal border crossing, but Finnish authorities later exchanged him for a Finn held by the Soviet govern-

leaders of the Communist movement, was expelled from the CPUSA in 1929. A decade later he testified before a congressional committee that in its early years the party often received its Soviet subsidies in the form of diamonds and jewelry, which it then converted to cash with the aid of sympathetic businessmen.[4] But, like so many defectors from communism, Gitlow has frequently been regarded as an unreliable witness and his testimony discounted.

The Comintern continued to provide regular subsidies to the American party. By the early 1920s, jewelry had largely given way to direct cash payments. The amounts of these secret subsidies were substantial and were often earmarked for specific projects. **Document 2** is a 1923 letter notifying the American Communist party that the Comintern's "B.C." (budget committee) had set its 1923 subsidy at $75,000, "of which two thirds is to be spent on the legal work of the C.P." It follows that the other $25,000 was to support illegal operations of various sorts. Carr and Marshall, mentioned in the letter, were pseudonyms for two leading American Communists, Ludwig Katterfield and Max Bedacht. Joseph Brodsky was the party's lawyer, and Philip Rosenblit (Rosenbliett), a New York dentist, was in the Communist underground organization. Rosenbliett is an illustration of how elements of the party's underground were later used by Soviet intelligence services for espionage work. As this document demonstrates, he was providing one of several way stations for Soviet funds destined for the American party, an illegal act but one of political subversion rather than espionage. By the 1930s, however, Rosenbliett was a participant in Soviet espionage in the United States, working closely with Whittaker Chambers.[5] Similarly, Max Bedacht was the Communist official who first recruited Chambers for underground work.

---

ment. See Robert Rosenstone, *Romantic Revolutionary: A Biography of John Reed* (Cambridge: Harvard University Press, 1990), 367; Eric Homberger, *John Reed* (Manchester: Manchester University Press, 1990), 204.

4. Gitlow testimony, 11 September 1939, House Special Committee on Un-American Activities, *Investigations of Un-American Propaganda Activities in the United States*, 76th Cong., 1st sess., 1939, 7:4687–88.

5. On Rosenbliett, see Whittaker Chambers, "Statements to the Federal Bureau of Investigation," January–April 1949, 58–59, Freedom of Information Act (FOIA) document; Adolf Berle's memo of his 1939 interview with Whittaker Chambers, reproduced in Senate Subcommittee to Investigate the Administration of the Internal Security Act, *Interlocking Subversion in Government Departments*, 83d Cong., 1st

# Document 2

"To the Communist Party of America," 22 February 1923, RTsKhIDNI 495–19–608. Original in English. "M" may be Marshal[l].

To the Communist Party of America.

During the Congress and in the presence of Carr and Marshal, the B.C. decided that out of the sum allocated for 1922, 10,000 dols. should be sent immediately and that 8,000 dols. be retained until the organisation by the C.P. of a book store and the publication of a definite quantity of printed matter. Of the 10,000 dols. Carr took 1,000 with him and two sums of 3,750 dols. were sent to the addresses of Brodsky and Rosenblit respectively and 500 dol. was remitted to the account of the C.P. immediately after the close of the Congress. The balance of the sum due for 1922 will be remitted when the condition indicated above will have been fulfilled.

For 1923 the sum of 75,000 dols has been allocated to you, of which two thirds is to be spent on the legal work of the C.P. We can send you a fourth of this sum, but we have not yet had confirmation of the receipt of the 7,500 dols, nor do we know whether Carr has arrived and handed over the money he had to the C.P. Furthermore we have no address to which to send. In addition to all this M. informs us that the representative present at the Workers' Famine Relief Conference in Berlin did not pay him 10,000 dols. As the Orgbureau is decidedly opposed to any money collected for the work of the organisation of which M. is the head being detained. no money will be sent until this question has been cleared up. We await a reply to this and an account for 1922.

22.2.23

N51                                                                       [illegible]

## Julius and Armand Hammer

One route for Soviet subsidies to American communism was through the future successful American businessman Armand Hammer. Controversy about his ties to the USSR dogged Hammer for most of his long and fascinating life. He always maintained that

---

sess., 6 May 1953, pt. 6:328–30; Allen Weinstein, *Perjury: The Hiss-Chambers Case* (New York: Knopf, 1978), 122–23. A case similar to Rosenbliett's is that of Julius Heiman. According to Benjamin Gitlow, Heiman arranged to convert the jewels sent by the Comintern in 1920 and 1921 into cash for the American party. During World War II, Heiman reappears as an associate of Arthur Adams, a Soviet spy engaged in nuclear espionage. Adams escaped U.S. government surveillance in 1945 and disappeared (House Committee on Un-American Activities, *Report on Soviet Espionage Activities in Connection with the Atom Bomb*, 80th Cong., 2d sess., 28 September 1948, 167–77).

he was simply a businessman whose example demonstrated that it was possible to make profits by dealing with a Communist regime. He first established relations with the Soviets shortly after the Bolshevik Revolution, bringing medical supplies to Moscow on behalf of his father's business. Received by Lenin himself, he was soon granted one of the first Soviet concessions for foreign entrepreneurs and manufactured pencils in the USSR for several years. During a later career, he sold Russian artwork in the West. Reestablishing his ties to the Soviet Union in the 1970s, Hammer, then president of Occidental Petroleum, signed contracts with the Soviet state worth tens of millions of dollars.

Comintern records establish for the first time that in the early years of the Soviet regime, Armand and his father were actually an official part of the Comintern's covert financial network. Hammer's father, Julius, was a founding member of the Communist Labor Party. In 1917 he set up the Allied Drug and Chemical Company. Ludwig Martens, who served as Soviet Russia's unofficial representative in the United States until he was deported in 1921, held half of the stock in the company. Allied Drug and Chemical Company functioned as a conduit around the economic boycott the Western powers applied to the Soviet regime in its early years, purchasing vitally needed chemicals and medicines for shipment to Soviet Russia.

In 1919, Julius Hammer, a doctor, was convicted of manslaughter after a patient died following an illegal abortion. After his release from prison in 1923, Julius moved to the Soviet Union, where he and Armand occupied an elaborate prerevolutionary mansion. In 1924 the Hammers purchased an Estonian bank, ostensibly to finance the export of butter from Russia. The U.S. State Department worried, however, that Soviet authorities might have provided the funds used by the Hammers to purchase the bank in order "to obtain a means of transferring funds abroad surreptitiously if desired."[6]

The concern was justified. In 1927 British police raided the London offices of Arcos—the All-Russian Co-Operative Society—an agency ostensibly engaged in promoting Soviet-British trade. Docu-

6. Steve Weinberg, *Armand Hammer: The Untold Story* (Boston: Little, Brown, 1989), 62.

ments seized in the raid listed Joseph Moness and his Moness Chemical Company as a way station for money for the American Communist movement "upon special instructions from the Profintern," the Comintern's trade union arm.[7] Acting on information supplied by the British, New York police raided the Moness Chemical Company on Broome Street in Manhattan. Moness had disappeared, but papers seized in his office showed that he had received large sums of money from Harry Hammer, Armand's brother. The Moness documents seized by the police, however, did not show that the Hammers' payments to Moness were made on behalf of the Comintern, and the American government's suspicions about the Hammers remained unproven.[8]

The evidence is now at hand. **Documents 3 and 4** disclose for the first time that both Julius and Armand Hammer were laundering Soviet money. The first is a December 1925 telegram to Armand, then in Berlin, from his father. Julius tells him a "friend" of "Mr. Moness" will deliver $6,400 to him in Berlin and Armand should have the Hammers' New York office give $6,400, less expenses, to Moness in New York. Document 4 is a deciphered copy of a June 1925 telegram sent from Charles Ruthenberg, then head of the American Communist party, to Osip Piatnitsky, head of the Comintern's International Relations Department (OMS). Complaining that the financial condition of the *Daily Worker,* the party's flagship newspaper, was "critical," Ruthenberg charged that Hammer—it is not clear whether he is referring to Armand or Julius—had not yet delivered $7,000 given to him by the Profintern. Moreover, Hammer was also late in delivering a sum given to him for the TUEL, or Trade Union Educational League, the American party's trade union arm. Ruthenberg complained again in a July telegram: "Hammer of allied trading corporation now holding sixteen thousand of party and TUEL money received from Comintern and Profintern which he fails to deliver in spite of all our efforts. Seven thousand hold for a year and nine thousand for three months. Urge

7. "List of Addresses Found in the Possession of Anton Miller," *Documents Illustrating the Hostile Activities of the Soviet Government and Third International against Great Britain,* Russia No. 2, 1927 (London: His Majesty's Stationery Office, 1927), 25.

8. John Costello and Oleg Tsarev, *Deadly Illusions* (New York: Crown, 1993), 103–9.

he be summoned before Comintern secretariat and sharply insisted acted to make immediately settlement. . . ."9

---

## Document 3

"Translation of Com. [Comrade] Hammer's Letter to His Son Armand . . . ," 4 December 1925, RTsKhIDNI 495–19–612. The original document is a Russian translation of Julius Hammer's cable in English. The notation "Accurate" on the document signifies that the translation was confirmed.

---

Translation of Com. Hammer's letter to his son Armand in Berlin, 4 Dec. 1925.

I hope that by the time this letter gets to Berlin you will be there to get it.

A relative of Mr. Moness, the pharmacist in New York, came to see me and told me that $6,400 should be coming from their friend in Berlin; he wants us to accept that money and telegraph our New York office with instructions to pay that sum to Mr. Moness.

Please arrange this. You can deduct the telegraph costs from the total sum being transferred.

Your loving father, J. Hammer.

ACCURATE.

---

## Document 4

Ruthenberg to Piatnitsky, 8 June 1925, RTsKhIDNI 495 19 612. Original in English. A Russian translation of the cable was written on the bottom of the original document.

---

Comrade Piatnjitsky Hammer owes us seven (7) nought (0) nought (0) nought (0) (7.000) dollars received from Profintern last year june about which I cabled early may stop Daily Worker in critical condition and we ask you to compel Hammer pay this [sum] immediatel also sum for fuel he received as April stop cable answer stop N letters from you since leaving in april stop Ruthenberg 8.VI.25

Dechiphriert am 9,VI.25.

---

9. Ruthenberg telegram, 11 July 1925, noted as deciphered on 14 July, RTsKhIDNI 515–1–422(I). The last sentence is garbled, probably owing to errors made in coding or decoding the message.

The Hammers must have finally delivered the money, for the Comintern continued to use them as a conduit. In 1926 the Comintern informed the American party: "According to your request . . . we send you today through Berlin—Julius Hammer—the following sums: $7,500 for the edition of Lenin's works (according to indication of comrade Bedacht); $5,777—your debt to TUEL (according to the requests of comrade Foster). . . . We send you also $1,500 for the Com. Party of Canada. This sum is composed of the balance of its last year's money and of part for the first quarter of 1926. Please send it to our Canadian Party." In the same period, an OGPU report on Armand Hammer that described his signing a concession agreement to develop a Soviet asbestos mine also noted that "on the return trip, Dr. Hammer, at the request of the Comintern, carried over and delivered to the Communist Party of America $34,000 in cash."[10] (Armand Hammer, like his father, was a medical doctor.)

As late as 1930 the Hammers continued to work with the Comintern. In December of that year William Weinstone, the CPUSA's representative to the Comintern, sent the following report to the party's leaders: "*Hammer,* I took up the telegram with the old man Piat[nitsky] after discussing it with Hammer. The latter is willing to return but has difficulty settling his affairs. I cannot interfere with such matters. The old man thinks that he compromised himself in the matter in which he handled the business. I shall write for official word about the situation. But as I wired you, do not count upon his return at an early date."[11]

10. Comintern to Ruthenberg telegram, 13 April 1926, RTsKhIDNI 495–19–613. Ruthenberg also cabled the Comintern to request that the Hammers deliver a late 1926 payment to the party's lawyer, Joseph Brodsky, because the scheduled recipient had died. Ruthenberg to Comintern, 16 November 1926, RTsKhIDNI 495–19–613. The OGPU document quoted is undated, but it is located in a file labeled 1923–1926. This document is quoted and its provenance is discussed in Jerrold L. Schecter and Yuri A. Buranov, "Documents Tie Hammer to Communists," *We* 1, no. 7 (15–28 June 1992): 1, 3.

11. Weinstone to Secretariat, CPUSA, 6 December 1930, RTsKhIDNI 515–1–1870. Emphasis in the original. The Secretariat was the executive leadership of the CPUSA.

*Other Secret Communications*

Both the Comintern and the CPUSA mixed covert funding for CPUSA political activities with more mysterious clandestine operations. **Documents 5 and 6** are 1929 telegrams sent in code from Moscow to the United States. In document 5, Piatnitsky warns someone named Thomson that only one person should learn "Bob's" real name, asks why "Bent" needs $3,000 in addition to the $5,000 he already received, and suggests the United States as the base for an unspecified operation. The only identifiable name in the message is that of William Z. Foster, who directed Communist trade union work. Foster, part of the CPUSA's top leadership from the early 1920s until his death in 1961, was the party's presidential candidate in three elections. In document 6, Piatnitsky rejects Thomson's suggestion of London as a base for the unnamed operation, saying, "If there is slightest chance of receiving and sending coded telegrams *from America* to Bents destination country, then we must choose America as our base. . . . Did you receive telegram with radio sending symbols"? Bent's identity and the country to which he was being sent remain unknown. His mission, whatever it was, was clearly a Comintern operation for which the CPUSA was providing technical aid and transmitting Comintern funds.

---

# Document 5

"To Thomson from Piatnitsky" telegram, 28 November 1929, RTsKhIDNI 495–19–133. Original in Russian.

---

1/FK

BY CIPHER.
TELEGRAM

NEW YORK

To Thomson from Piatnitsky stop Indicate why Bent needs three thousand dollars he received five thousand in full stop Bob telegraphed about the youth money through Foster stop Check to see who knows of Bobs stay stop Imperative that only one person deal with Bob and that his real name never be mentioned anywhere stop If at all possible I suggest choosing America as base stop NR

1/1518.
28 Nov. 1929

# Document 6

"To Bent from Piatnitsky" telegram, 22 December 1929, RTsKhIDNI 495–19–133. Original in Russian.

---

2/LA

BY CIPHER

AMERICA

To bent from Piatnitsky stop In reply to yours No. 4 stop I strongly object to meeting with Clemens stop I do not understand your monetary calculations stop To Thomson and Bent from Piatnitsky stop In reply to yours of 21 december stop I am firmly against base in London due to criminal investigation stop If there is slightest chance of receiving and sending coded telegrams *from America* to Bents destination country comma then we must choose America as our base stop I await reply stop Did you receive telegram with radio sending symbols stop When does Laud leave to visit us stop *I await reply stop* NR #7,8/1660.
22 December 1929

---

The Comintern's channels of communication with the United States required subterfuge. Not only was it necessary to transmit information and money secretly, but an elaborate system of mail drops was required. **Document 7** is the first page of a November 1925 letter from the Workers Party of America, as the CPUSA was then known, to the Comintern's Organization Department. It provides five new mailing addresses that the Comintern could use to send messages to the American party. The system is clearly still amateurish, and the Americans complain that sloppy procedures in sending letters to previous addresses risked exposing them as Communist mail drops. One of the addressees, Lydia Beidel, was found on the list seized by British police in the Arcos raid; that list also specified that the inside envelope should be marked "for Rogers."[12]

---

12. "List of Addresses Found in the Possession of Anton Miller," 20. When asked about the Arcos documents, Joseph Brodsky, the CPUSA's attorney, suggested that the British government had forged them (Brodsky testimony, 6 September 1939, House Special Committee on Un-American Activities, *Investigations of Un-American Propaganda Activities in the United States*, 7:4494–95). This and other Comintern documents demonstrate the authenticity of the Arcos documents.

# Document 7

Excerpt from Workers Party of America to Organization Department of the Comintern, 25 November 1925, RTsKhIDNI 515–1–426. Original in English on Workers Party of America letterhead.

## WORKERS PARTY OF AMERICA
### NATIONAL OFFICE
### 1113 W. WASHINGTON BLVD., ROOM 301
### CHICAGO, ILL.
### PHONE MONROE 4714

Organization Department          November 25 1925
Comintern                             #151-25
Moscow

Dear Comrades

Your cable requesting a change in mail addresses of our country has been received and we are giving you below five new addresses to be used FOR LETTERS ONLY.

Mrs. D. Wilson
1416 North Kolin Ave
Chicago, Ill.

Miss Fannie Golden
2848 Augusta St
Chicago Ill.

Miss Lillian Burt
3004 Blaine Place
Chicago Ill.

Miss Anna Lawrence
1625 North Dayton
3rd Floor
Chicago, Ill

Miss Lydia Beidel
1654 West Marquette Rd
Chicago Ill

Inside envelope for all should be marked "For Rogers".

In this connection we again call your attention to the fact that all the addresses which you have been using previously have been exposed by the careless method of sending mail to us. In place of the individual letters being sent, we have received ten to fifteen letters in one envelope which made the package so bulky that it was sent to the customs authorities for examination befor delivery and the letters opened exposing the fact that there were ten to fifteen individual letters in a large envelope addressed to various Party organizations. This practice must be stopped. No address is safe if all such packages go to the customs department and are opened before being delivered to us.

Communist secrecy was not confined to international communications. **Document 8** is a 1934 directive from the party's national
organizational commission to regional leaders reminding them of
the importance of secrecy, of using mail drops, and of using "special
channels," presumably couriers, for factual information about the
party's secret work in trade unions and other mass organizations.
Clandestine habits affected even the lowest levels of the American
Communist movement. **Document 9** is a 1933 directive from the
California Communist party to party functionaries and local unit
leaders. The directive states that "units must meet in homes, not
offices or halls and must change meeting places every week. No
notices of unit meetings are to go thru the mails. . . . No regular
minutes are to be kept by units containing names of comrades. . . .
Keep all membership lists in a safe place, and in cipher. . . . No
records of any kind [are] to be kept in headquarters, offices, etc."
The directive also contains instructions on the design of two simple
but effective codes.[13] While such security precautions were designed to protect the secrecy of the Communist movement from
outsiders, they also provided Communists with training in clandestine procedures that were readily adaptable to the needs of Soviet
intelligence agencies.

---

# Document 8

Org. [Organizational] Commission to Dear Friends, 2 November 1934, RTsKhIDNI, 515–
1–3459. Original in English.

---

November 2, 1934.

Dear Friends:

In the last few months, there has been a decided loosening up by the districts
in the matter of sending important letters to the Center. We have been and are
receiving letters and other material from the districts, which if they fell into
the hands of the authorities, would not only endanger many individuals, but
certain organizations as well, and would certainly expose certain plans of the

13. A far more complex cipher for CPUSA use in 1940 was also found. CPUSA
cipher instructions, RTsKhIDNI 515–1–4204.

organization. We have warned the comrades many times not to use the open mailing address for _any_ inside communications. Every district already has an established special apparatus through which to send such communications.

You are very well aware that our open address (Box 87, Sta.D), is well known by the authorities, not only in New York, but all over the country. Mail sent to this box is not only in danger of being opened in New York, but also in your district, because it is known that P.O. Box 87 is the address of the Center. At the same time, all letters sent by us with the return address, is also apt to be opened, not only here, but also at the city to which it is addressed.

A small commission here going through the mail for the last week or so, found that a large percentage of these letters could be cut down very easily if there would be more initiative on the part of the districts. We must keep in mind that the enemy is alert, and diligently collects material which it can use against our organization. It would be criminal to help them collect this material by supplying it through the mail.

We have therefore made the following decisions:

1. The Center will stop using its present postoffice box for return address.
2. The Center will rent two other boxes, well covered, about which you will receive instructions very shortly. Letters which are sent today to the present box number, shall be sent in the future to the _new_ box number.
3. The present box number (P.O. Box 87) will remain for the purpose of receiving material which is distributed openly (leaflets, shop paper, etc.). This is the only kind of material which shall be sent to the present box number.
4. All factual material, Org. reports, problems about our work in various mass organizations, trade unions, etc., must be sent through special channels,— and not to the new box number.
5. The districts must cut down the number of letters to the Center, limiting themselves to the most important problems; at the same time avoid taking up within the same letter various problems which require the attention of more than one department.

As it stands now, there are cases where letters addressed to the Center, refer not only to political and organizational problems of the Party, but to matters of a technical nature regarding the I.L.D., F.S.U., trade unions or of other mass organizations, etc., using the Center as a clearing house. These letters simply obstruct the work of the Center, inasmuch as in order to make the necessary reply to these, it is necessary to call in the comrades of the various organizations.

Train the fractions of the various mass organizations to send their letters to the leading fractions of the specific organizations, i.e., I.L.D. problems to the leading fraction of the I.L.D., trade union problems (A.F.L.) to the leading fraction of the A.F.L. opposition; T.U.U.L. to the leading fraction of the T.U.U.L., etc. For such letters, the fractions of the various organizations must have their own confidential mailing apparatus. Until this is built up, this material shall be sent in double envelope to the new box number, and we will forward it to the respective fractions.

Page 2.

There have been numerous cases where districts have been sending Bureau Minutes through open mail. We are checking up very carefully every such letter, and the most severe action will be taken against those who violate the elementary principles of conspirative work.

In order to safeguard the material sent from the Center to the districts, special arrangements must also be made in the Districts. It would be advisable for each District center to rent a postoffice box under the name of a private person or business firm. The Center will stop using the open addresses of the districts entirely.

Many letters which are sent today to the Districts will be shifted to the special channels. This will increase the number of letters to the addresses given to us and will endanger the safety of these addresses. It is necessary, therefore, to get more addresses in each district. We therefore expect every District to send us, in the shortest possible time, 3 more addresses, which can be continuously used by us.

You received an outline on special mailing sometime ago. In this we emphasized the necessity of using only onion skin paper for communications. Only a few districts adhere to these directives.

We gave to the Districts, 2 or 3 addresses, but many of the districts use only 1 of them. It must be understood that we could kill an address if we overburden it. Therefore, it is imperative to use all the addresses—not only one. If you send 3 or 4 letters a week to the Center, change the addresses continuously,—that is, alternating them.

We propose that the District Organizers in each district, shall immediately call a meeting of the functionaries in the apparatus, discuss this question very thoroughly, instruct everyone involved as to the future procedure concerning

## Document 8 *continued*

communications, and take the necessary control steps to see that these instructions are being carried out.

Comradely yours,

ORG. COMMISSION CC

P:K

## Document 9

"Special Instructions for: Efficient Party Apparatus . . . ," District 13, 24 April 1933, RTsKhIDNI 515–1–3296. Original in English. In a 1933 file with a handwritten annotation, "letter sent IV/24," April 24.

No. 125                          *District #13*

Special Instructions

For: Efficient Party apparatus
Protection of Comrades
Preparations for illegality
Conduct of Comrades

Our unit meetings can be made alive and interesting if 90% of the time is used for Marxist-Leninist education and discussion of Party campaigns and no time of the meeting is spent on doling out to each comrade endless amounts of tickets, Western Workers, leaflets and other assignments. These practical steps are vitally important and they can be handled easily as follows:

I.    a) Before the next unit buro meeting, the unit organizer is to prepare a list of the unit comrades, grouped into squads of 3, 4 or 5 comrade depending on the size of the unit; one comrade of each squad is to be squad captain. (Group the comrades according to nearness of their places of work or homes so the captain can reach them on short notice; also according to kind of Party work they are best fitted for; and whatever other local points must be considered)

The list is then to be acted on by the buro and after the captains are notified of the members in his or her squad, the list should be destroyed. The organizer must remember who is in each squad and who the squad captains are. Squad captains must remember names and addresses of his squad members.

b) Comrades are to be notified of all assignments made by the buro thru the squad captains; Western Workers are given to each squad captain for his squad members; tickets and leaflets also. Thus, instead of handing out bundles of material to each of 12 or 20 comrades, 3 or 5 captains receive their squad's material and after the meeting they distribute the material to each squad member.

c) Units must meet in homes, not offices or halls and must change meeting places every week. No notices of unit meetings are to go thru the mails.

d) Organizers are responsible for attendance and activities of squad captains; squad captains are responsible for attendance and activities of his squad.

e) New members are to be immediately assigned to a squad by the organizer or buro. His squad members are to make friends with him, help him learn about the Party and go together for leaflet distribution, factory gate and house-to-house Western Worker sales, etc.

f) Meetings are to start on time and last not longer than 2 hours at the most. Agenda must be well prepared by buro before the meeting starts.

g) No regular minutes are to be kept by units containing names of comrades, etc. The organizer is to keep notes for check-up to see that decisions are carried out.

II. Every unit member is to be instructed by his squad captain who is to constantly check up on the following:

a) Not to carry around membership books nor lists of names and addresses, party documents, etc., in pockets or briefcases, except when on a specific assignment which makes this necessary.

b) All non-citizens must use Party names. (Citizens may also).

c) No talk of any kind about inner Party decisions anywhere outside of the actual meetings where they are made or checked up such as unit or committee meetings and avoid gathering in restaurants or public places and discussing such Party questions or decisions.

d) Do not gossip about or discuss Party activities nor give name of comrades, meeting places nor time over the telephones.

e) Do not give information of any kind about Party comrades or the organizational apparatus to strangers who come around asking all kinds of questions.

f) Comrades (especially functionaries) should not dress or behave in any unusual or flashy manner so as not to attract undue attention.

g) Do not openly carry or read Party press or literature in street cars, restaurants, etc.

h) Do not loiter around the front of halls and homes after meetings.

III. Functionaries are instructed:

   a) To keep all membership lists in a safe place, and in cipher (code). (See attached for simple methods of cipher).

   b) No records of any kind to be kept in headquarters, offices, etc. Whatever is needed for work there during the day should be taken away at nite.

   c) Especially before demonstrations, headquarters should be absolutely clear of all documents; also machinery (typewriters, mimeographs) should be put in safe places and brought back to the office after the demonstration. In some localities it is better even now to have such machinery in a special place where mimeographing, etc., can be done instead of at the offices or headquarters.

   d) All leading functionaries to move to new places which are known to no one and where no meetings are to be held. (It is advisable to take such apartments or rooms under assumed names).

IV. Sections and Units are instructed to:

   a) Create Defense squads which are to function during demonstrations, mass meetings, etc., to protect speakers and be on alert against provocation.

   b) Special instructions regarding use of mail for Party material will be given to each Section. Mails to be used only when it is impossible to convey matters in person.

V. Action regarding stool pigeons:

   a) A close check-up on all applicants thru "new members" committees.

   b) If there is any suspicion of a member his squad captain or other reliable comrade is to follow him up and become friendly and try to find proof of stooling.

   c) Members under suspicion should be carefully eliminated from responsible committees or functions and used only for routine work (leaflet distribution, literature sales, house-to-house work with another comrade, etc.). Such cases should be immediately reported to the Section or District Committee.

> All the above instructions must be carried out explicitly. A strict check will be made on all units and functionaries and the sharpest discipline faces comrades responsible for violations of these instructions.

* * * * * *

# Document 9 *continued*

The above is based on experience thus far. The comrades should think about this, and any further suggestions should be given to the unit organizers for transmission to the Section Organizers. Section Organizers will give these suggestions to the District Committee.

## Simple Ciphers

I.

Method:   1) Choose a page in a book or an article from a newspaper or magazine.

2) Designate the letters to be ciphered by numbers according to the position they are found on the page of the book or article.

Example:   Key: Western Worker, April 10, 1933, Page 4 - Editorial Column.
First line of text (exclude titles) to be counted as line 1.
To be ciphered: A. Comrade, 30 Grove Street.
(Note: "a" is found in the 1st line, 8th character. It would be designated as 1/8. "C" is found in the 2nd line, sixth character, and would read 2/6, etc.) The cipher would read as follows:
1/8. 2/6 1/3 3/1 2/5 2/1 1/4 1/5, 15/28 15/29 3/23
5/12 3/2 5/10 4/3, 5/5 1/1.

———

II.

Method:   Write the name on one side of paper and the street on the other side, house number in the middle and the street on the other side, but add (or deduct) a certain number from the house number. Then cut the sheet in three and keep pieces in separate places.

Example:   Address to be noted - A. Comrade, 30 Grove Street,
John Jones, 148 Fell Street.

| A. Comrade | 52 | Grove Street |
|---|---|---|
| 360 | John Jones | Fell Street |

Note: 2 was added to each figure of the address.

Simple Ciphers

I.
Method:  1) Choose a page in a book or an article from a newspaper or
            magazine.
         2) Designate the letters to be ciphered by numbers according
            to the position they are found on the page of the book or
            article.

Example:  Key: Western Worker, April 10, 1933, Page 4 - Editorial
               Column.
               First line of text (exclude titles) to be counted as
               line 1.

          To be ciphered: A. Comrade, 30 Grove Street.

          (Note: "a" is found in the 1st line, 8th character. It
          would be designated as 1/8. "C" is found in the 2nd line,
          sixth character, and would read 2/6, etc.) The cipher
          would read as follows:

          1/8.  2/6 1/3 3/1 2/5 2/1 1/4 1/5, 15/28 15/29 3/23

          5/12 3/2 5/10 4/3, 5/5 1/1.

-------------

II.
Method:  Write the name on one side of paper and the street on the
         other side, house number in the middle and the street on the
         other side, but add (or deduct) a certain number from the
         house number. Then cut the sheet in three and keep pieces
         in separate places.

Example:  Address to be noted - A. Comrade, 30 Grove Street,
                                John Jones, 148 Fell Street.

| A. Comrade | 52         | Grove Street |
|------------|------------|--------------|
| 360        | John Jones | Fell Street  |

Note: 2 was added to each figure of the address.

DOCUMENT 9. Last page of "Special Instructions for: Efficient Party
Apparatus . . . ," District 13, 24 April 1933.

## The Pan-Pacific Trade Union Secretariat

One of the most fertile breeding grounds for American Communists who would later turn up in Soviet espionage operations was the Pan-Pacific Trade Union Secretariat (PPTUS). This secretive organization intermingled overt and covert political organizing with a heavy dose of clandestine practices, as was also habitual with the Comintern. Created in 1927 by the Profintern, the Comintern's trade union arm, the PPTUS was charged with promoting Communist trade unions in China, Japan, Korea, the Philippines, and other nations in the western Pacific. Earl Browder, an obscure leader of the American Communist party's Trade Union Educational League in the early 1920s, was a key figure in the early years of the Pan-Pacific Trade Union Secretariat and its first general secretary. Browder spent most of 1926 in Moscow assisting in Profintern planning for the PPTUS. The first meeting of the trade union secretariat took place in Hankow, China, in 1927. When Browder and the Profintern's delegation to the Hankow meeting entered the city, they passed beneath a banner welcoming the "Earl of Browder"— local Chinese Communists thought the unknown American was a British nobleman!

### Earl Browder and Undercover Operations in Asia

Browder spent most of the next two years in Asia. He returned to the United States in 1929, and was soon tapped to lead the CPUSA. Although one of Browder's chief aides was a Canadian woman, Katherine or Kitty Harris, the Pan-Pacific Trade Union Secretariat recruited a large number of Americans. Jim Dolson and Philip Aronberg, both veteran American Communists, worked in China. Eugene Dennis, later Browder's successor as CPUSA leader, was in the Philippines in 1931 as a Comintern representative and in Shanghai in 1933 and 1934. In 1933, Steve Nelson, fresh from a stint at the International Lenin School in Moscow, undertook Comintern missions to India and China, delivering Soviet subsidies to the Chinese Communist party. Margaret Undjus and her husband, Charles Krumbein, both veteran CPUSA leaders, also served in China.

Krumbein was deeply involved in the Comintern's clandestine service and paid a price for it. British authorities arrested him in

1930, and he served six months in prison for using a false passport. After his release, the Soviet consulate issued travel documents to him, and he left for Moscow and from there traveled to China. In 1934, after his return to the United States, American authorities arrested him for using a fake American passport. He spent fifteen months in prison. **Document 10** is an excerpt from a 1936 Comintern document reviewing candidates for the Political Bureau of the CPUSA, its most powerful agency. This document, written by André Marty, a French Communist and a member of the Executive Committee of the Comintern, illustrates Moscow's control of CPUSA officials and will be reproduced in its entirety in a subsequent volume. There were two types of members of the Political Bureau, full "members" and a junior rank of "candidate" members. The CPUSA had recommended Krumbein for candidate membership. Marty recommended that the Comintern reject the CPUSA suggestion that Alexander Bittleman be promoted to the Political Bureau and instead upgrade Krumbein from candidate to full member. The Krumbein entry includes the comment that he is "at present temporarily in prison in connection with passport issues raised by his work along our lines outside the country." "Line" was Soviet jargon for a network or activity, generally clandestine. Thus, the reference to "our lines" indicates that Krumbein's passport mishap involved work for a Comintern operation. Krumbein became the CPUSA's national treasurer in 1938 and retained this office until his death in 1947.

---

## Document 10

Excerpt from "Information on Candidacies Nominated for the PB CC CPUSA," signed "M" [André Marty], 7 February 1936, RTsKhIDNI 515–1–3966. Original in Russian. "PB CC CPUSA" stands for Political Bureau of the Central Committee of the CPUSA.

---

1706/3/fr. orig./A.B.                                    TOP SECRET.
Feb. 7, 1936
Information on candidacies *nominated* for the PB CC CPUSA (*in connection w/dispatch fr/ Robert . . .*
*(from secretariat Com Marty)*

. . .

Instead of Bittleman it is expedient to promote the PB member Krumbein, currently nominated candidate for the PB.

8. KRUMBEIN, Charles—mem. CC, nominated candidate for the new PB. American, born in 1894, in the party since 1919, was a worker. One of the leading party comrades. Recently was secretary of the largest New York party district and acquitted himself well at that work. At present temporarily in prison in connection with passport issues raised by his work along our lines outside the country. His candidacy raises no objections.

If Bittleman's candidacy to PB membership falls away, and no other candidacy is found, then Com. Krumbein, is perhaps the best candidate for membership in the PB, and in that case it would be expedient to promote him from candiate for PB, as he is currently nominated, to membership in the new PB.

---

Communist activity was illegal in most of Asia, so much of the Pan-Pacific Trade Union Secretariat's work was clandestine. **Document 11** is a memo originating in Shanghai to someone named Alexander, who appears to be the Soviet official supervising the PPTUS, from J. Crosby and Marion. Crosby was the pseudonym used by Pascal B. Cosgrove, a shoe workers' union organizer from Massachusetts, when he attended the first Profintern congress in Moscow in 1921. In testimony to Congress, Benjamin Gitlow stated that the CPUSA had sent Cosgrove to Shanghai to assist Browder in 1929.[14] This document confirms Gitlow's statement. "Marion" was probably Marion Emerson, another veteran American Communist working for the Pan-Pacific Trade Union Secretariat.[15] Crosby and Marion make clear that Shanghai police are

14. Gitlow testimony, 7 September 1939, House Special Committee on Un-American Activities, *Investigations of Un-American Propaganda Activities in the United States*, 7:4681. Browder led the American delegation to the 1921 Profintern congress. Crosby is identified as Cosgrove's pseudonym in Theodore Draper, *The Roots of American Communism* (New York: Viking, 1957), 316.

15. In the late 1930s, State Department investigators turned up evidence tying Marion Emerson and W. A. Haskell to the Pan-Pacific Trade Union Secretariat. Nothing is known of W. A. Haskell (U.S. Department of State Passport Division brief of a conspiracy charge against World Tourists and the CPUSA, reprinted in Senate Subcommittee to Investigate the Administration of the Internal Security Act, *Scope of Soviet Activity in the United States*, 85th Cong., 1st sess., 1957, app. 1, pt. 23-A:A109, A113). The records of the Special Branch (internal security) of the Shanghai Municipal Police contain extensive surveillance and informant reports on Browder (pseudonym George Morris), Katherine Harris (called Harrison and using the pseudonym Alice Read), Dolson, Dennis (pseudonym Paul Walsh), Undjus, Emerson, and Haskell. See D. S. McKeown report, "History of the Communist

looking for Browder (Morris was his Shanghai pseudonym) in late 1928. Following guidance from Stein (whose real name is unknown), Marion and Crosby ordered Kitty Harris to vacate the residence she shared with Browder; but the two complain that Harris has ignored their directive.[16]

---

## Document 11

J. Crosby and Marion to Alexander, 30 January 1929, RTsKhIDNI 534–4–283. Original in English.

---

*To Alexander*

Jan. 30, 1929

In view of the fact that certain rumors are being circulated to the effect that the affair of Morris being wanted by the authorities is a scheme and without foundation we wish to present the following statement regarding the affair.

Some time after Morris left in December, our houseboy came and told us that a foreign and a Chinese plainclothesman was here looking for Mr. Morris and that the Chinese detective was here every day. He said they had the picture of Mr. Morris, that he saw it and the number II42 was under it and that they asked all manner of questions about him as to what he did and where he was etc.

---

Movement in Shanghai," 8 May 1933, box 1, document 5; Special Branch report, "Earl Browder Alias George Morris," 30 September 1931, box 6, document 62; D. S. Pitts report, "The Oriental Trading and Engineering Corporation—Activities in China," 9 June 1937, box 3, document 21; Special Branch report, "Communist Activities in China, Federated Malay States, etc. (The 'Noulens Case')," box 4, document 30; all in Record Group 263, Formerly Security Classified Records Relating to Espionage Activities in Shanghai, 1926–1948 (Willoughby Collection), Shanghai Municipal Police Files, National Archives, Washington, D.C. The Shanghai Municipal Police was a British-dominated organization that reported to the Shanghai International Settlement, an international body that ran the commercial center of Shanghai and was jointly controlled by British, French, American, Japanese, and other non-Chinese representatives.

16. Harris and Browder were reputed to be lovers at the time. In testimony to Congress, Gitlow discussed Harris's work with Browder in the Pan-Pacific Trade Union Secretariat at length (Gitlow testimony, 7 September 1939, House Special Committee on Un-American Activities, *Investigations of Un-American Propaganda Activities in the United States*, 7:4681). The relationship is also elucidated in a U.S. Department of State Passport Division brief of a conspiracy charge against World Tourists and the CPUSA, reprinted in Senate Subcommittee to Investigate the Administration of the Internal Security Act, *Scope of Soviet Activity in the United States*, A86; and in McKeown, "History of the Communist Movement in Shanghai."

We immediately took care of things after ascertaining that this was true and saw Kitty telling her of the danger and to keep away, and to liquidate her place at once (this on the instruction of Stein). When told she remarked "Yesterday when I went there my arms were so full of papers from the postoffice that I could not pay the ricshaw man and the house coolie paid for me. When I got on the lift I noticed a Chinese man standing by it and when I came down an hour later he was still there and as I left the lift the boy said "I not see your master long time" and I said, is that so."

For four weeks this detective has been coming to this building (both of us have seen him) asking the boy about Mr. Morris and if he has been there and one day he even went to the boy's home trying to get information, according to the boy's story. Later he said he had located where Mrs. Morris was staying in the French concession and asked the boy to go with him to identify her but the boy avoided him and did not go. He also asked the boy what labels were on our trunk when we came and if he knew where we came from, also what our business was.

Three weeks after being notified to liquidate her place Kitty called us on the phone asking Marion to meet her and at that time she was still living there thereby endangering herself and those she was in contact with. She has made statements that this is all lies and part of a scheme although refusing to see the boy and talk with him himself about the affair.

J. Crosby
Marion

---

**Documents 12, 13, and 14** deal with Philip Aronberg, a veteran American Communist and Pan-Pacific Trade Union Secretariat agent who later had ties to the NKVD. Document 12 is a 1934 letter from Jack, a pseudonym for Japanese Communist Sanzo Nosaka, regarding the purchase of "J types," referring to Japanese language printing type, and the deficit in the budget that will be "made up from the money which our Second Salesman brought here." Second Salesman is identified in document 13 as "Phil A." for Philip Aronberg. Document 13 is a financial report showing that Aronberg traveled from the United States to the Philippines, Japan, and China and back during a five-month period. He was arrested in Japan while carrying $5,505, a large sum at that time. He was held for forty-nine days, released, and had his money returned, less payment for a hotel bill and $328 retained by the police. The money lost to the police was deducted from Aronberg's wages.

# Document 12

Jack to Uncle, 12 December 1934, RTsKhIDNI 495–19–617. Original in English. Stamped "Secret" in Russian. *Inprecor* is a Comintern magazine: International Press Correspondence.

Dec. 12, 1934.

SECRET

Dear Uncle,

As I informed you already, I ordered J types to J in early Sept. and received almost all of them (except some of special types) early Dec, without difficulty.

The number of types amounts to 150,000 (size: 7.5 point with "rubi"— almost the same size with J daily paper's types.) With the present number of types we can print in a month five pamphlets of 48 pages of the size of the present J Inprecor. Meanwhile they are sufficient for us.

We are now trying to build our own plant.

In connection with the financial problems, as the separate Financial Report shows, the costs in the past amount to $367.56 and the cost for the future accommodations amount to around $50.00; therefore the total costs reach to $410.00. We received from you $300.00 for these works and should like to remind you that there is $110.00 in deficit from the original budget. This deficit can be made up from the money which our Second Salesman brought here.

Yours sincerely,

JACK/

Jack

# Document 13

"Financial Report (Second Salesman)," 12 December 1934, RTsKhIDNI 495–19–617. Original in English. The line "[illegible] in Yokohama." was crossed out but clearly legible in the original.

Secret

Financial Report (Second salesman)

Part 1:

| | |
|---|---|
| Wages July, $130.00 | $130.00 |
| Wages Aug. Sept. Oct. Nov.@$150 | 600.00 |
| Part 2: | |
| Passport and visas | 28.00 |
| Expenses on clothing, dissolving apartment, and incidental expenses on preparation; also fare to LA | 318.00 |
| (Above includes per diem expense for five days.) | |

Part 3:

| | |
|---|---:|
| Ticket, round trip, LA to Manila | 312.00 |
| 44 days on ship both ways, LA to Shanghai, expenses | 50.00 |

Part 4:

| | |
|---|---:|
| Hotel in LA, 9 days in July (per diem) | 36.00 |

Part 5:

[illegible] in Yokohama.

Expenses disbursed by police from funds, shown as follows:

(was in prision for 49 days)

| Had when arrested: | Turned back by police: | Spent by police: |
|---|---|---|
| $5,505 | $4,745 | $760.00 |

(Note: 8 days hotel before arrest was also paid by police from above $760)

Part 6:

| | |
|---|---:|
| Hotel in Shanghai (per diem @$4) 15 days | 60.00 |

Part 7:

| | |
|---|---:|
| Hotel in LA., per diem @$4, 10 days | 40.00 |
| Total | $2,328 (see note) |

Note: Of the total expense of $2,328, the sum of $328 is stricken out because this money was spent by the police; and although actually spent is not included. Therefore, the toal expense is arbitrarily reckoned as $2,000. This $328 is deducted from wages due as listed in Part #1.

| | |
|---|---:|
| Additional expense, ticket by RR to NY from LA | $132.00 |
| Four days, per diem @$4 | 16.00 |
| | $148.00 |

*Phil A.*

*Approved by* <u>Jack</u> *Dec. 12, 1934.*

Document 14, a 1942 message to the Comintern, indicates that the NKVD had heard that Earl Browder, head of the CPUSA, had prohibited party members from maintaining any connection with Aronberg. The message asked for a report on this because "the issue of connections with Phil Aronberg is of very immediate concern to us," indicating that Aronberg had a close link to Soviet intelligence. Browder's remark may have been a security measure to discourage an open CPUSA official from inadvertently compromising Aronberg's clandestine work.

# Document 14

Kislenko to Sorkin, 28 February 1942, RTsKhIDNI 495–74–486. Original in Russian. The heading of the message, "ECCI to Com. [Comrade] Sorkin," indicates that the message was sent to Sorkin at the Executive Committee of the Communist International, not that it was an ECCI message to Sorkin. In the original, Aronberg's name was typed "Arenberg" and hand-corrected.

TOP SECRET
Copy No. 1
29

### ECCI to Com. S O R K I N

According to information we have received from the NKVD, a year and a half ago Com. BROWDER advised one of the leading workers of the American Comparty to dismiss a certain Phil Aronberg from all [party] business and prohibited all party members from maintaining a connection with him as a corrupt and dangerous individual

In view of the fact that the issue of connections with Phil Aronberg is of very immediate concern to us, we urgently request that you share with us any information you have on him, and advise us whether Com. Browder actually issued such a directive regarding Aronberg.

*KISLENKO*

28 February 1942
No. 66051ss
2 copies printed
28 February 1942, to No. 16

*They have agreed to check again in the US*
*29 February 1942.*

---

## Harrison George and the Secret Work of the PPTUS

Harrison George, a veteran Communist with long experience in covert politics, undertook a variety of missions for the Pan-Pacific Trade Union Secretariat. George had been a prominent leader of the syndicalist Industrial Workers of the World (IWW), the most notorious radical organization in America in the first two decades of this century. In 1917, along with other IWW leaders, he was arrested and convicted of conspiracy to interfere with American war mobilization during World War I. He secretly joined the Communist party in 1919 but remained a public member of the IWW, attempting to convert it to communism from within. Not until 1924 did he openly announce his party membership. In 1927 he served as the American representative to the Profintern in Moscow. By 1929 he was in China and "was engaged on an international assignment of confidential nature" according to a letter he wrote to the Anglo-American Secretariat.[17] **Document 15** is a telegram indicating that Browder—his middle name was Russel—had recruited George for "special work," a party euphemism for underground activities.[18]

---

## Document 15

Cass to Gabin, 2 January 1929, RTsKhIDNI 534–6–138. Original in English.

---

Telegram

GABIN 2070 DAVIDSON BRONX NEW YORK
RUSSEL COMING WANTS HARRISON FOR SPECIAL WORK CASS

"2.I.29

---

In **document 16** Browder indicates that he wants George to publish the "monthly" out of San Francisco. The monthly was the *Pan-Pacific Worker,* the journal of the Pan-Pacific Trade Union Secretariat developed and edited by Browder. **Document 17** is a 1932 report to Moscow in which Harrison George discusses his publication operations and notes that Earl Browder had informed him that the scope of his operations would be wider than anticipated. George would have "a larger apparatus," and he would be receiving "special instructions."

---

17. Harrison George to Anglo-American Secretariat, 9 January 1929, RTsKhIDNI 495–37–53.

18. On the meaning of "special work," see Harvey Klehr, *The Heyday of American Communism: The Depression Decade* (New York: Basic Books, 1984), 440. Document 15 is addressed to Gabin. Gabin, Philip Aronberg's wife, was the addressee for many cables from Comintern agents (Joseph Zack Kornfeder testimony, 9 July 1958, Senate Subcommittee to Investigate the Administration of the Internal Security Act, *Communist Use and Abuse of Passports,* 85th Cong., 2d sess., 1958, pt. 1:18).

# Document 16

Browder to Arctic, 2 February 1929, RTsKhIDNI 534–4–283. Original in English on Western Union cablegram form.

ARCTIC

MOSCOW

RECEIVING NO MATERIALS FROM SHANGHAI URGE THEM ACTIVITY STOP PARTY CENTRAL POSTPONES RELEASE HARRISON STOP WE PROPOSE HE GOES SANFRANCISCO IN THREE DAYS STOP CAN PUBLISH MONTHLY WITHIN ONE WEEK RECEIPT MATERIALS

BROWDER

# Document 17

Harrison to Dear Comrade, 29 March 1932, RTsKhIDNI 534–4–422. Original in English. A handwritten annotation directs the message to Alexander. Harrison's signature is in Cyrillic script. The "Wallace" mentioned in this message is unknown. "Grace M." is probably Grace Maul, also known as Grace Granich, Browder's secretary, later sent to China to work with Agnes Smedley. RILU is the Red International of Labor Unions, better known as the Profintern.

March 29, 1932

Dear Comrade:

Enclosed find Minutes No. 7. You will notice that our publication is beset by technical difficulties, which to overcome will sooner or later require that we equip our own printery. We wrote about this before, and indeed about other things, but have received no reply. Indirectly, though Grace M., we learned that letters you intended for us, were sent to another comrade who happened to be using the name "Wallace". She said (March 14) that she was sending to him to get these letters back to forward to us—but over two weeks have gone and . . . nothing. I have in fact no means of knowing if these letters of mine are being received there, aside from the receipt at the bookshop here of a bundle of RILU magazines I had asked be sent. It is not good that we be left without information, advice and material in this fashion. Particularly it is annoying to expect funds and not get them, because altho we are stretching out what we had, lack of assurance of any more prevents us progressing with the work in any way that will involve expense.

From Earl, I just received a copy of the Directives for work here. These indicate a far larger work than I was given to understand; also a larger apparatus. In addition, Earl says I will soon receive "special instructions". I hope so. At least I should be enlightened on what relation our present plan of work has to these Directives he sent, since they vary so widely.

Greetings,
Harrison

(Alexander)

**Document 18** presents the minutes of a March 1932 meeting of the San Francisco bureau of the Pan-Pacific Trade Union Secretariat that have been signed in Cyrillic with the names Harrison [George] and Takeda. The minutes discuss including the "Tanaka Memorandum" in an upcoming issue of the *Pan-Pacific Worker*. The Tanaka Memorandum (often referred to as the Tanaka Memorial) was a 1929 memo from General Baron Tanaka, prime minister of Japan from 1927 to 1929, to Japan's emperor. It was a chilling blueprint for the Japanese conquest of the world. Japan denied the document's authenticity, and the consensus of historians is that internal errors in the Tanaka Memorandum reveal it as a forgery, a type of disguised propaganda known today as disinformation. Who forged the Tanaka Memorandum is not known, although the Soviet OGPU (the KGB of that era) is the most likely candidate. The document first surfaced in China and was circulated worldwide through Comintern channels, one of which was Harrison George's *Pan-Pacific Worker*.

Takeda, the other signer of document 18, was the pseudonym of Tsutomu Yano. Yano arrived in California in the early 1930s to help revive the CPUSA's Japanese section because many of the section's leaders, mostly immigrants, had been deported in 1930. Yano's duties also included recruiting espionage agents to assist Soviet intelligence. In 1931 Yano recruited Yotoku Miyagi. Born in Japan in 1903, Miyagi immigrated to the United States in 1919. An aspiring painter, Miyagi attended the California School of Fine Arts in San Francisco. However, his chronic tuberculosis prompted him to move to the drier climate of southern California; there he graduated from the San Diego Public Art School in 1925. He settled in Los Angeles to pursue art while supporting himself as a co-owner of a restaurant. In the late 1920s he joined the Proletarian Art Society, a CPUSA affiliate; in 1931 he formally joined the CPUSA. In 1933, Yano sent Miyagi back to Japan, where, using the freedom of movement and lack of regular employment given by his cover as a tubercular artist, he became part of a Soviet spy ring headed by Richard Sorge. Sorge, a German Communist, operating under the cover of a pro-Nazi German journalist stationed in Japan, became an unoffi-

# Document 18

Minutes No. 4, San Francisco Bureau of the PPTUS, 2 March 1932, RTsKhIDNI 534–4–422. Original in English. The minutes are signed in Cyrillic with the names Harrison and Takeda.

MINUTES NO. 4
(San Francisco Bureau of the Pan-Pacific Trade Union Secretariat)
March 2, 1932

Present: Takeda, Harrison.

Agenda: 1) Publication of "P-P Worker"; 2) Completion of the Bureau; 3) Connection with Seamen.

1. Report made that although articles for first issue are all translated and checked through, being ready for the printer, Comrade N, who is entrusted with getting them through printshop, was suddenly hospitaled for operation, unavoidably delaying going to press for a fortnight. Japanese type has been ordered from Japan as per previous arrangement, and the search for an inexpensive press is proceeding. The "Tanaka Memorandum" discussed.

Decision:—In view of the time required on translations, to at once begin translating the Tanaka Memorandum (from the English to Japanese) for featuring with our own introduction in the second issue.

2. Investigation of qualifications of local Chinese comrades proceeding, with better prospects of adding a Chinese comrade to Bureau.

Decision:—To interview Comrade Orden Lee with view to test his political qualification.

3. Reported that in spite of difficulties, preliminary contact has been made with three more Japanese seamen on passenger boats, and there is some prospect of improving our effective apparatus in this respect, by using a certain connection. But these contacts all have yet to be developed by political examination before it can be determined if they will be useful to the work or not. As a general rule, the seamen of freight steamers are more class conscious and daring than those of passenger ships, but our comrades, although trying very hard, are simply barred from going aboard freight ships. Our conference with the local head of the (American) Marine Workers Industrial Union delayed by his absence out of town.

Decision:—To intensify our contact work on passenger-ships, with the additional comrade (making two) if he can be successful in the subterfuge planned, and to await the results of consultation with the Marine Workers Industrial Union to determine how to get around the difficulties in making connections with Japanese freight seamen.

Adjourned

For the Bureau
Harrison
Takeda

cial adviser to Germany's ambassador. Sorge's access to the German embassy and that of his subagents to the Japanese government allowed him to provide the Soviet government with highly valuable intelligence on both Japan and Germany. When Sorge first arrived in Asia, he operated from Shanghai, and in 1932 the Shanghai Municipal Police identified him as part of the Pan-Pacific Trade Union Secretariat, a relationship that helps to explain why the San Francisco bureau of the PPTUS would recruit Miyagi for Sorge.[19]

Miyagi was one of Sorge's chief Japanese assistants, but his American Communist past was the undoing of the Sorge ring. In 1940 Japanese security police began an investigation of Communists among Japanese expatriates who had returned to Japan. The investigation turned up a returnee who had joined the CPUSA in Los Angeles at the same time as Miyagi, who knew him as a fellow Communist, and who also had contact with him after returning to Japan. The returnee told all, and the police put Miyagi under surveillance, arresting him in October 1941. He attempted suicide by leaping headfirst from the second-floor window of the police station, but the shrubbery beneath the window saved his life. Under intense, perhaps torturous interrogation he confessed, and the security police rolled up the rest of the Sorge network. Miyagi, in poor health even before his arrest, died in prison in 1943. Sorge was executed in 1944.

Another Comintern agent who also died in prison may have been one of Harrison George's recruits for the secret world: his own son. George had a number of short-lived marriages and was even mar-

---

19. The record is unclear concerning whether Miyagi was an American citizen. Takeda's identification as Tsutomu Yano can be found in F. W. Deakin and G. R. Storry, *The Case of Richard Sorge* (New York: Harper and Row, 1966), 127–35. A transcript of Miyagi's statement to Japanese security police about his recruitment by Yano is reprinted in House Committee on Un-American Activities, *Hearings on American Aspects of the Richard Sorge Spy Case*, 82d Cong., 1st sess., 1951, 1190–93, 1206. Also see discussions of Miyagi's role in the Sorge network in Gordon W. Prange with Donald M. Goldstein and Katherine V. Dillon, *Target Tokyo: The Story of the Sorge Spy Ring* (New York: McGraw-Hill, 1984); "The Case of Richard Sorge," in *Covert Warfare*, ed. John Mendelsohn, vol. 7 (New York: Garland, 1989); and Chalmers Johnson, *An Instance of Treason: Ozaki Hotsumi and the Sorge Spy Ring* (Stanford, Calif.: Stanford University Press, 1990). D.S.I. Everest report, "Dr. Sorge, Suspected Communist," 10 January 1932, box 2, document 18; and Special Branch report, 18 May 1933, box 1, document 10, Willoughby Collection.

ried for a time to Earl Browder's sister, Margaret.[20] From one of his
earlier liaisons came a son, Victor Allen George, born in 1909.
Harrison left Victor's mother while Victor was still an infant; she
later married a man named Barron, and Victor assumed that name.
Harrison George had little contact with his son until the early
1930s, when young Victor Barron approached him. Shortly thereafter Barron was on his way to the Soviet Union. Years later the U.S.
government raided the offices of World Tourists, the travel agency
run by Jacob Golos, a senior CPUSA official. Records seized in the
raid showed that Barron obtained a passport in 1932 and that
World Tourists arranged his passage with costs billed to an account
funded by the CPUSA.[21]

Victor Barron reappears in 1935 in Brazil using the cover of an
American machinery salesman. Actually, he was running short-
wave radio operations for Arthur Ewert, a German Communist and
a veteran of the Pan-Pacific Trade Union Secretariat, who was assisting with preparations for a left-wing coup in Brazil. Ewert used the
cover of an American businessman; both he and his wife had false
American passports furnished to them by the CPUSA. The coup,
however, began prematurely and was crushed by Brazil's Vargas
dictatorship. Both Ewert and Victor Barron were arrested.[22] In
March 1936 Barron, who had probably been tortured, jumped
(according to Brazilian police) or was thrown (according to skep-
tics) from a high prison window and died.[23]

20. Browder testimony, 5 September 1939, House Special Committee on Un-
American Activities, *Investigations of Un-American Propaganda Activities in the
United States*, 7:4440.

21. U.S. Department of State Passport Division brief of a conspiracy charge
against World Tourists and the CPUSA, reprinted in Senate Subcommittee to Investigate the Administration of the Internal Security Act, *Scope of Soviet Activity in the
United States*, A22.

22. Ibid., A90, A109–10, A116, A122. Ewert was severely tortured and driven
insane. He was released from prison in 1947 and sent to East Germany.

23. On Victor Barron and the Brazilian coup, see David P. Hornstein, *Arthur
Ewert: A Life for the Comintern* (Lanham, Md.: University Press of America, 1993),
200–203, 207, 267–77; and Fernando Morais, *Olga* (New York: Grove Weiden-
feld, 1990), 56, 61–62, 65, 82, 94, 108–11, 123–24, 129–33. The short interval
between the time Victor contacted his father and the time of his CPUSA-funded travel
to the Soviet Union has led several writers to conclude that Harrison recruited Victor
for secret work. Hornstein writes: "In 1933, when Harrison George heard of the
opening of Mirov-Abramov's Podlipki school in Moscow for Comintern clandestine
radio operators and the search for suitable young communists of various nation-

George's Pan-Pacific Trade Union Secretariat apparatus also provided an apprenticeship into the secret world for Eugene Dennis, then a young Communist just beginning his lifetime career as a professional revolutionary. Dennis moved to San Francisco in 1929 to assist George in editing the *Pan-Pacific Worker*.[24] After a few months, Dennis was sent to southern California to organize agricultural laborers, many of them immigrant Filipinos. Early in 1930 Dennis was arrested and charged with criminal syndicalism.[25] He jumped bail, fled to Moscow, and turned up in the Philippines a year later as the Comintern representative to the Filipino Communist party. In 1934 he moved to Shanghai, and the local security police identified him as a Comintern agent who was using the name Paul Walsh.

George also served at least one covert tour in the Philippines. In October 1932 he wrote to "Charlie" about Pan-Pacific Trade Union Secretariat work there. (Charlie may be Charles Krumbein or possibly Charlie Johnson, an official of the Profintern's eastern department, which had jurisdiction over Asian activities.) This letter, **document 19**, discusses Browder's suggestion for a business cover for the Pan-Pacific Trade Union Secretariat's operations: serving as an agent for secondhand films. George writes that he has a different idea, one "which does not require so much travelling—nor so much capital." The letter describes his plans to go to the Philippines for some time; he appends a note that "to every Filipino I will be known as 'Pedro' and you must refer to me as such." Pedro was one

---

alities to be trained there for eventual assignment to covert duties abroad, he used his considerable influence to assure that his son, for whom he continued to feel a sense of responsibility, was one of the first candidates selected" (202–3). Morais's book tells a similar tale. Although both the Hornstein and Morais volumes are serious books, they are intended for the educated public rather than for scholars and lack documentary citation. In the absence of direct documentation, the authors regard it as possible, but not proven, that George recruited his son.

24. Peggy Dennis, *The Autobiography of an American Communist: A Personal View of a Political Life, 1925–1975* (Westport, Conn.: Greenwood, 1977), 39. Peggy Dennis was Eugene's wife.

25. During or after World War I, a number of states made promoting the violent overthrow of the government a crime. These laws were generally called laws against criminal syndicalism because at the time the chief radical organization advocating violent revolution was the syndicalist Industrial Workers of the World.

of George's many aliases; this letter, for example, was signed "Fisher."[26]

---

## Document 19

Excerpts from a three-page letter, Fisher to Charlie, 1 October 1932, RTsKhIDNI 534–4–423. Original in English. The identity of "Al" is unknown.

Oct. 1, 1932.

Dear friend Charlie:

. . .

There is a devil of a lot of delay here in getting "fixed up". You know what that is, I think. I have now only just gotten the first thing that I need to get something else, savvy? Now I have to get out and <u>fix</u> finish up. Time goes by— but what can one do? To leap out into space without proper preparation is folly. If I get lined up as I intend, I think that, barring a piece of bad luck, I can stay where I'm going a lot longer than you imagine.

My trip here gave one excellent result. I have a comrade lined up to devote time and attention to sending a steady stream of literature to my objective— postage, literature and all to be at the cost of the American Party. This comrade has 200 addresses and will mail everything covered, as all literature is being nabbed by the customs [unreadable]. I do not know whother or not you have a better way; but if not, everything you think is useful to our people, may be sent here to Earl, and oar marked for the PI.

. . .

When I came here, Earl had a business in mind for me to use, but as when Al arrived I found that some of the expenses that I must make were not reckoned upon by you, I had to choose another business that is cheaper—though I believe just as good for my special purpose. The one Earl found, I wish to explain to you, as both Al and Earl think that you have need of that kind of business which will allow someone to travel frequently and keep up connections between all points in the Far East. One cannot be a capitalist without some <u>capital</u> and get away with it long.

The business Earl found is that of an agent for second-hand films, mostly "silents", for which there is a real demand in all the Far East that owing to language difficulty with "talkies". There is a dealer here in such films who has

---

26. There are several pieces of evidence establishing that Harrison George is Fisher. During the 1934 maritime strike on the West Coast, Fisher wrote a series of angry letters to party leaders denouncing the strike strategy of the local Communist leadership. Responding to this criticism, California party leader Sam Darcy referred to Fisher as "Comrade H.G." See Sam D. [Darcy] to Browder, 22 June 1934, RTsKhIDNI 515–1–3613.

many orders from India, Java, Singapore, China, etc. But he does not get their orders because, firstly, he wants to be sure to get paid for them, but secondly, [unreadable] sends them and the buyers have no chance to inspect them before paying—and these buyers simply will not pay before inspection as they have been stung so much in the past and paid for films only to receive films that fell to pieces. This dealer is, therefore, very anxious to find someone who can take films to all these points and show them to the buyers, so all his orders can be filled and he can make money—it is every bourgeois' aim. The job is to sell to local film exchanges, not to theaters direct. The exchanges then rent them around. Please understand that these are <u>not</u> the big expensive films that a lot of fuss is raised over. And the average "silent" costs this dealer $10 to $15 and sells for $25 to $30. Nevertheless, since films are a mystery to most people, a fellow selling films <u>may be</u> estimated "A-1" by the average person. If one of our people took this up, he would have time for work outside of business, he would be free to travel as desired, and money put into films can be liquidated—not a whole lot need be put in, since [unreadable] can be made upon re-ordering.

Get this clearly, I am not taking this film business, but telling you about it at Earl's suggestion, in case you have someone who can connect up for it as a cover for visiting all these Far Eastern points. Earl and a friend who can put us on with this dealer (who is entirely innocent) figured that from $300 to $350 would give a person a <u>genuine</u> cover—and this would not be lost, either.

Take that for what you can make out of it. I am getting another line, on which does not require so much travelling—nor so much capital. I think I can get fixed up for less than $100, and still make a showing of real business. That is about the minimum you could expect to give for a genuine legitimate front. And I promise that it will not be allowed to interfere with work more than is needed to keep appearances. Nor should anything be lost. Anyhow, I'll do my best on that.

. . .

> Best of good wishes to you and your wife.
> *Fisher*

note: To every Filipino I will be known as <u>"Pedro"</u> and you must refer to me as such

The business cover George developed was unusual. Al Richmond, a Communist journalist who worked closely with George in California, noted in his memoir that one of George's eccentricities was a zeal for colonic irrigation (therapeutic enemas), a medicinal practice that had some popularity in that era. In his memoir, Richmond wrote that "as a cover for a Pan-Pacific Trade Union Secretariat operation in Manila," George "set up a colonic irrigation dispensary."[27]

After his tour in the Philippines, George returned to San Francisco to head the Pan-Pacific Trade Union Secretariat's American-based operations. Part of this work involved recruiting Asian seamen on ships traveling between California and Japan, China, or other Asian ports. Among other purposes, these contacts were sought in order to smuggle Communist literature into Asian ports, particularly into Japan, where the ruthless security police had suppressed most Communist activity. George's apparatus printed much of this literature, translating and adapting it to the requirements of the different nations for which it was intended.

George was directing these Pan-Pacific Trade Union Secretariat operations when the 1934 West Coast maritime strike broke out. He vehemently disagreed with the strategy followed by local Communists. The strategy, however, was a success, and Harrison George was removed from the Pan-Pacific Trade Union Secretariat. In a 1935 letter (see document 20) Browder informed Georgi Dimitrov (head of the Comintern) that "Comrade Bradford" was the unanimous choice of the Profintern, the Eastern Secretariat of the Comintern, Comrade Okano of the Japanese Communist party, and Browder himself to direct the Pan-Pacific Trade Union Secretariat.[28]

In this period the Fisher (Harrison George) letters in the Profintern files discussing the secretariat's work are replaced by letters from "Betford." Bradford and Betford are probably pseudonyms for the same man. Most likely, Betford was the veteran American Communist Rudy Baker, who, like others involved in the Pan-

27. Al Richmond, *A Long View from the Left: Memoirs of an American Revolutionary* (New York: Delta, 1972), 277. Richmond also noted that Harrison George was an avid fisherman; the hobby may have given rise to the Fisher pseudonym. In 1947, after his expulsion from the CPUSA for ideological deviation, George published a pamphlet defending his views and calling for internal party reform. One chapter was called "Principles of Party Cleansing from Below," a title that greatly amused those familiar with George's particular health enthusiasm. See Harrison George, *The Crisis in the C.P.U.S.A.* (Privately printed, December 1947).

28. Document 20 also deals with "Comrade Gerhart." This is Gerhart Eisler, a German Communist who carried out Comintern missions in many countries, including America. Browder says that after discussing the issue with four leading Comintern officials (Wilhelm Pieck [a German who later became president of the German Democratic Republic], Dmitry Manuilsky [a Russian], Otto Kuusinen [a Finn], and Ercoli [the pseudonym of the Italian Communist Palmiro Togliatti]), he wanted Eisler to return to the United States. Eisler did, in fact, return.

Pacific Trade Union Secretariat, will appear later in this volume in connection with Soviet espionage operations during the 1940s. Substantiating evidence can be found in the 1953 testimony of Joe Koide, a Japanese Communist who immigrated to the United States, concerning his work editing the Japanese-language section of the PPTUS's *Pan-Pacific Worker.* Koide testified that Harrison George had supervised his work in 1933 and 1934 but that George was replaced in 1935 by Rudy Baker.[29] Baker, said Koide, headed the San Francisco operations of the Pan-Pacific Trade Union Secretariat into 1937. Document 27, discussed more fully in chapter 3, includes Baker's own comment that he had spent 1936, 1937, and the first half of 1938 doing "secret work" in California. Baker also taught about China at a 1941 CPUSA training school, an expertise he probably picked up from his work in the Pan-Pacific Trade Union Secretariat.[30]

### Agnes Smedley, Comintern Agent

Under Betford/Baker the Pan-Pacific Trade Union Secretariat had a number of connections with the well-known American journalist Agnes Smedley. Smedley, born in 1892, first achieved notoriety in 1918 after being indicted with a group of Indian revolutionaries in New York who were seeking to overthrow the British Raj. She was also a close associate of birth-control advocate Margaret Sanger. Her 1929 autobiographical novel, *Daughter of the Earth,* solidified her reputation as a militant feminist and radical. Smedley spent time in the Soviet Union in the 1920s and traveled to China in 1928 with journalistic credentials, but she really hoped to build links between the Indian and Chinese nationalist movements. She quickly became enamored of the Chinese Communists and was convinced they would be the saviors of China.

Apart from a brief trip to the United States and Russia in 1933–1934, Smedley remained in Asia until 1941. She then returned to the United States and championed the cause of the Chinese Communists. With their victory, the polemics in the United States about

29. House Committee on Un-American Activities, *Investigation of Communist Activities in the San Francisco Area—Part 5* (5 December 1953), 83d Cong., 1st Sess., 1954, 3422–28.
30. Herbert L. Packer, *Ex-Communist Witnesses: Four Studies in Fact Finding* (Stanford, Calif.: Stanford University Press, 1962), 188.

"who lost China" grew increasingly shrill, and Smedley came under attack. The U.S. Army released a report in 1949 about the Sorge espionage network. The report, by Major General Charles Willoughby, General Douglas MacArthur's intelligence chief in World War II, accused Smedley of being a spy and a key link in the Sorge network. Willoughby's evidence, although strong, was largely circumstantial. After Smedley threatened to sue for libel, the army withdrew the charges and apologized.[31] Nevertheless, Smedley decided to leave the United States. The Chinese Communist government provided her with money, but she fell ill and died while returning to China in 1950.

There is no doubt that Smedley was close to many figures in the Sorge ring: she had a love affair with Sorge himself while he was in Shanghai. A recent biography, nonetheless, has insisted that she "was a freelance revolutionary operating on a global scale" who did not work for the Comintern or any Soviet agency.[32] Documents from the Comintern archives demonstrate, however, that Smedley was an integral, although ill-disciplined, part of the Comintern apparatus in China. In **document 20** Browder urges the Comintern to approve and fund "the proposal to assist Agnes Smedley, now in Shanghai, to publish an English language anti-imperialist newspaper there." Browder said the CPUSA would "provide her with helpers, politically and technically qualified." Browder also noted that the Chinese Communist party approved of Smedley's plan "with the provision that these comrades in Shanghai shall not have connections with the Chinese Party which would endanger its work." Dimitrov evidently agreed, because shortly thereafter Smedley established her journal, *Voice of China*, and Browder carried out his pledge of CPUSA aid by dispatching his secretary, Grace Granich, and her husband, Manny, to help edit the paper.[33]

31. Although the army officially withdrew the charges against Smedley, Willoughby did not (Charles Andrew Willoughby, *Shanghai Conspiracy: The Sorge Spy Ring, Moscow, Shanghai, Tokyo, San Francisco, New York* [New York: Dutton, 1952]).

32. Janice R. MacKinnon and Stephen R. MacKinnon, *Agnes Smedley: The Life and Times of an American Radical* (Berkeley: University of California Press, 1988), 142.

33. Manny, sometimes known as Max, was the brother of Communist literary critic Mike Gold. In Shanghai, he was known as Max (D. S. Henchman to HBM Consulate-General, "Eastern Publishing Company and Max Granich," 24 June 1937, box 1, document 4, Willoughby Collection).

# Document 20

Browder to Dimitrov, 2 September 1935, RTsKhIDNI 495–74–463. Original in English. Okano was the pseudonym for Sanzo Nosaka, a leading Japanese Communist. Gerhart was Gerhart Eisler, who served as a Comintern representative in the United States.

Dear Comrade Dimitrov;

I am sorry that my quick departure makes it impossible for me to talk with you before I go. Of course, the main line of our work is clear since the Congress, and the C.P.U.S.A. will exert all its energies to realize it in life. There are still a few questions which will require decisions, and with which you should be acquainted. I will mention them briefly, and Comrade Gerhart can give you any details you wish:

1) After discussions with Pieck, Manuilsky, Kuusinen, and Ercoli, it is my opinion that the wish of the CC CPUSA that Comrade Gerhart return to America, at least until our Party Congress early in 1936, can be confirmed, while at the same time Comrade Gerhart can be serving the German Party in America and be prepared for its work when called upon. Comrade Gerhart will be of very great value to the CPUSA precisely in this period of preparing our next Congress.

2) We have worked out plans for the Pan Pacific Trade Union Secretariat, jointly with plans for help to the CP Japan, with Comrade Okano, the Eastern Secretariat, and the Profintern. All are agreed with the plan, including the important point of sending Comrade Bradford (now in Europe for Profintern) to America to direct the work. If you agree with the plans, nothing remains except formal decision, and provision of funds.

3) The proposal to assist Agnes Smedley, now in Shanghai, to publish an English language anti-imperialist newspaper there, should be finally decided. She writes that conditions grow more favorable; such a paper would be of great influence. The CPUSA can provide her with helpers, politically and technically qualified. The Chinese comrades agree, with the provision that these comrades in Shanghai shall not have connections with the Chinese Party which would endanger its work. The poltical value of the project is clear. It will require formal approval and provision of necessary funds.

These three questions are our chief <u>undecided</u> problems. Quick decisions will help us work effectively.

Finally I want to express my own deep satisfaction with the Congress and its results, and my opinion that this Congress will bring the CPUSA and the whole world party out into a new high field of experience. I will be delighted to receive any calls from you for whatever the American Party can contribute to this end.

With warmest fraternal greetings
*Earl Browder*
Earl Browder

Moscow, Sept. 2, 1935

Dear Comrade Dimitrov:

I am sorry that my quick departure makes it impossible for me to talk with you before I go. Of course, the main line of our work is clear since the Congress, and the C.P.U.S.A. will exert all its energies to realize it in life. There are still a few questions which will require decisions, and with which you should be acquainted. I will mention them briefly, and Comrade Gerhart can give you any details you wish:

1) After discussions with Pieck, Manuilsky, Kuusinen, and Krooll, it is my opinion that the wish of the CC CPUSA that Comrade Gerhart return to America, at least until our Party Congress early in 1936, can be confirmed, while at the same time Comrade Gerhart can be serving the German Party/And be prepared for its work when called upon. Comrade Gerhart will be of very great value to the CPUSA precisely in this period of preparing our next Congress.

2) We have worked out plans for the Pan Pacific Trade Union Secretariat, jointly with plans for help to the CP of Japan, with Comrade Okano, the Eastern Secretariat, and the Profintern. All are agreed with the plan, including the important point of sending Comrade Bradford (now in Europe for Profintern) to America to direct the work. If you agree with the plans, nothing remains except formal decision, and provision of funds.

3) The proposal to assist Agnes Smedley, now in Shanghai, to publish an English-language anti-imperialist newspaper there, should be finally decided. She writes that possibilities conditions grow more favorable; such a paper would be of great influence. The CPUSA can provide her with helpers, politically and technically qualified. The Chinese comrades agree, with the provision

-2-

that these comrades in Shanghai shall not have connections with the Chinese Party which would endanger its work, the political value of the project is clear. It will require formal approval and provision of necessary funds.

These three questions are our chief undecided problems. Quick decisions will help us work effectively.

Finally I want to express my own deep satisfaction with the Congress and its results, and my opinion that this Congress will bring the CPUSA and the whole world party out into a new high field of experience. I will be delighted to receive any calls from you for whatever the American Party can contribute to this end.

With warmest fraternal greetings

Earl Browder

Moscow, Sept. 2, 1935

DOCUMENT 20. Browder to Dimitrov, 2 September 1935.

Although Smedley's political loyalty was never questioned, she came to be viewed by the Comintern as unfit for covert work. In **document 21**, Betford/Baker indicated that Smedley has been a vital part of the apparatus, delivering money and instructions to an agent named Young, probably a Chinese involved in labor organizing. Betford forwarded to the Comintern "her frantic requests for funds" but stated that he was proceeding with his instructions "to break all connections with her." Betford complained that Smedley "has acted on her own authority" but added, "I did not condemn her for these acts because the documents sent to me at least partly proved that she was making the work of Young and trade union apparatus possible in absence of other connections."

---

# Document 21

Excerpts from a five-page letter, Betford to Alexander, 8 May 1936, RTsKhIDNI 534–4–518. Original in English. Alexander was probably a PPTUS functionary. In this document Betford mentions instructions to break the "little sister communication system." "Little sister" is unknown, as is "Liangpu." Alec, a link between Betford and Smedley, is also unknown.

---

### ON CHINESE CONNECTIONS

According to my original instructions I made no effort to make connections with trade union apparatus in China. I wrote to Smedley and Alec for Shanghai publications, clippings and translations on trade union and strike problems in general, for the english press release which I am preparing to issue and quantities of Chinese postage stamps for our work.

In answer to my letters I received her frantic requests for funds which I immediately forwarded to you. I continued communications with her on this and other matters until $1,000 was forwarded to Young, connections with "little sister" broken and I established other connections for my trade union and strike information.

I believe you understand that mail communications with Smedley were carried on through Alec and her letters to me through a business institution. Different names being used in all cases.

Your instruction to break all connections with her will be realized in few weeks when I answer an expected letter from her giving me the final information relative to Youngs departure.

As I allready cabled you Young is due to leave Shanghai via Vladivostok at end of April. He will no doubt explain many matters including reasons for maintaining connections with little sister and Agnes. It appears that home instructions to break little sister communication system arranged by Liangpu and myself never reached Shanghai untill I wrote to them from here. It further appears that connections were made with Agnes due to break in connections with original sources of funds.

I am now enclosing several more letters recently received from Agnes. Since my correspondence with Agnes I have received following documents from Young.
1) "Reports On Trade Union Work on Railroads in North China."
2) "Report on Strikes in Hopei Jan-June 1935"
3) "Iron Hammer June 1935, #7 "
4) "Iron Hammer October 1935, #8 "
5) "Iron Hammer March 1936,#9 "
6) "Three trade union pamphlets"

The strike report was sent to C.C. in N.Y. for translation and original forwarded to you. The others I am striving to get translated with local reliable forces and forward original to you. These documents are of value because they indicate activity of our trade union forces and show that Young maintained most of his contacts up to present time.

In my earlier letters to Smedley I informed her to stop advancing further funds to Young untill authorized to do so. I also warned of need of extreme carefullness to guarantee safety of Young and others.

To me it is clear that Agnes has acted on her own authority in contacting Young and advancing funds for his work. Nevertheless I did not condemn her for these acts because the documents sent to me at least partly proved that she was making the work of Young and trade union apparatus possible in absence of other connections.

With the departure of Young this situation becomes automatically liquidated. Now other and satisfactory arrangements can be made by you and contact with Agnes eliminated.

The departure of Young has also altered your proposal to make connections with trade union forces in China from here. The little sister connections is now liquidated. Alec alone remains. But Alec had only connections (very rare) with Young. Now Young is temporarily gone but he no doubt left some other

## Document 21 *continued*

connections behind. I shall make no effort to secure new connections untill I hear from you. . . .

Betford

---

Document 22, an excerpt from another Betford report, indicates that Smedley, despite being told to stop her activities, "continues to act as a self-appointed unofficial representative in China." Betford notes that her past role in delivering financing for trade union and party work had "strengthened" her position, and "she does nothing else but holds meetings with party, trade union and student groups. She is taking no part in the editing of Voice of China. There are numerous complaints against her. It is necessary to liquidate this situation once and for all or else grave consequences will follow."

---

# Document 22

Excerpts from an eight-page letter, Betford to Alexander, 20 July 1936, RTsKhIDNI 534–4–518. Original in English.

---

TRIP TO CHINA

As I allready informed you by wire I am leaving for Shanghai at end of August and will return at end of October. The work here will not be handicapped very much due to recent strenghtening of our forces. . . .

In view of this situation and discussion with Lampson I agreed that it is vey important that I spend a week with Young in order to explain our new unity policy and to establish direct and permanent connections for future work. This becomes especially important due to the dangerous situation in which Smedley continues meeting with Young and also certain party leaders. While I have stopped corresponding with Smedley she nevertheless continues to act as a self-appointed unofficial representative in China. Her position is strenghtened due to fact that she has helped financing both trade union and party work for many months. My information in that she does nothing else but holds meetings with party, trade union and student groups. She is taking no part in the editing of Voice of China. There are numerous complaints against her. It is necessary to liquidate this situation once and for all or else grave consequences will follow.

I might mention that I have received information to the effect that Young has made connections with the party in China and now receives some financial aid from them. I have no further details on this. Lately I was informed that the Party has decided to send him to Moscow. I have immediately replied that he should not leave under any circumstances.

I expect to organize reliable means of communication with Young and send him a number of documents and instructions written by Lampson.

At present my sole means of reaching him is through Alec who is a loyal and reliable sympathiser by who maintains contact with Smedley. It is necessary that this contact with Smedley be broken. This cannot be done by mail. Alec is a personal friend of Smedley and she introduced him to me. Hi [He] did not and does not know who I am except that I too am a close friend of Smedley. Hence a letter to him to break contact with Smedley would only create distrust and confusion. Personal explanation alone can get results. In addition to this I have certain other neutral connections in Shanghai established while I was in New York. This creates possibility of creating several different and safe connections for further communication and connections with Young. This too requires a personal visit. . . .

. . .

Fraternally Yours,
Betford

In **document 23**, Betford reports that Young, the labor organizer, may have "fallen into the hands of the enemy" and suggests that Smedley's continued contacts with him may have put him in danger. Betford complains about "the reckless nature of her activity" and notes that in addition to maintaining contact with Young against orders, Smedley "proceeded to establish many new connections. With these connections she deeply involved our neutral friends into activities of [the] party. She told our neutral friend who is not a party member, that leading comrades authorized her to do this work. In general she assumed the authority of a special representative." Her activities became so disruptive that Browder "sent her instructions to return to U.S." Smedley, though, did not obey; she left Shanghai for Shensi. Nonetheless, Betford notes that "the special dept which previously had connections with her has broken all connections."

# Document 23

Excerpts from a three-page letter, Betford to Alexander, 20 October 1936, RTsKhIDNI 534–4–518. Original in English.

Oct 20, 1936.

Alexander:

My journey to Shanghai has been postponed for three or four months. The first delay arose over the unclarity whether Young has left for your city or not and what connections he had left behind him. It took several months to clarify this point. Now it is clear that a trade union commission has been set up to replace him. This commission however has connections with the special organ of the party that has not been verified as to its trustworthiness. On it are people who are under suspicion which extends to the period of severe losses of two yours ago. Under these conditions Lampson and I agreed that it is unwise to make the journey. Instead we have taken measures to isolate the trade union commission from the party organ and have sent a message to seek out two of reliable friends of Lampson. When this message reaches the right individuals they will go to an address known to them alone and there receive final instructions how to make connections with us. When this is completed I shall make the journey.

In meantime I have sent $1,000 by courier to be at disposal of trade union commission after they have broken off all party connections. This measure was necessary in order that work may continue after stopping party connections. Simultaneously a series of documents embracing the modified trade union policy has been sent to the trade union commission through special channels.

I might mention that all these arrangements have been made without assistence or use of Smedley in any way. Connections with her have been severed last spring and new channels established with which she has no connection and no knowledge.

In the developement of this new system of connection a courier system of reliable seamen has been set up and will be strenghtened as time goes on.

CASE OF YOUNG

Young has left Shanghai via the short route late in May or early in June. I have received cable and letters to this effect and I have tried to verify this fact. The repeated messages from your friends to the effect that he has never arrived alarmed me considerably. It is quite possible that he has fallen into the hands of the enemy. He maintained weekly connections with Smedley up to his departure. It was through her that all his technical arrangements for the journey were made. How he came to make connections with her I have already explained in one of my earlier letters.

### CASE OF SMEDLEY

Upon your request last April I have stopped corresponding with Smedley. In my last letter to her I urgently advised her to break all her personal connections with Young. She has not done so despite the fact that Young could have easily received funds and mail through a neutral friend and address. Both this friend and address are known to Lampson. It is the person we know as "Alec"

She not only did not stop this connection but proceeded to establish many new connections. With these connections she deeply involved our neutral friends into activities of party. She told our neutral friend who is not a party member, that leading comrades authorized her to do this work. In general she assumed the authority of a special representative.

When this information reached me I notified Lampson and together we sent messages to trade union commission informing them that Smedley had absolutely no authority and that connections with her were very dangerous. In view of the fact that she involved our neutral friends into this kind of work and spoiled their address for our future use I also notified them of the position and harmfull role of Smedley.

It appears that these messages finally reached their destination. At the same time the reckless nature of her activity has resulted in voluntary breaking of connections with her. She has finally left Shanghai for Shensi. What she is doing there is not known. The general reputation which she possesses based on her books will cause some inexperienced comrades to approach and confide in her. Comrade E. has also sent her instructions to return to U.S. From several sources informations has arrived that her mental health is breaking down. On one occassion she pulled a revolver and threatened to commit suicide unless our friend Alec agreed to do certain work for her. This incident supported by others indicates that she is on verge of a mental breakdown which only aggravates the dangers that she is creating with her activity. She had shamelessly accused two reliable comrades of being Trotskyists and careerists. Number of letters that she wrote to these comrades clearly portray mental disintegration. I have forwarded some of these letters.

It is in view of her irresponsible acts that I am worried of the fate of Young. In conclusion I want to state that she did not and does not have have any connections with the T.U. commission. Further that the special dept which previously had connections with her has broken all connections. What her remaining connections are I do not know.

Taken as a whole, the documents in this chapter demonstrate some of the many ways in which clandestine habits of mind and behavior pervaded all levels of the Communist party—from well-known party figures like John Reed and Earl Browder, to prominent businessmen like Armand Hammer and journalists like Agnes Smedley, to obscure and ordinary party functionaries. For some Communists, like Miyagi and Aronberg, the clandestine activities of the Comintern led directly to association with Soviet intelligence agencies. And, as we shall see, they were not the only American Communists to transfer their allegiance from the Comintern to the NKVD—the predecessor of the KGB.

# CHAPTER THREE

# The Secret Apparatus of the CPUSA: The Early Years

## The CPUSA Establishes Its Secret Apparatus

IN 1930 THE EXECUTIVE COMMITTEE of the Comintern reminded its member parties that "legal forms of activity must be combined with systematic illegal work."[1] This illegal work was designed to escape the surveillance of hostile police and protect special party assets from exposure, with members carrying out surveillance and infiltration of enemy groups and undertaking other clandestine tasks. That same year, B. Vassiliev, a Comintern official based in Moscow, sent a memo to the CPUSA pointedly noting that "all legal Parties are now under the greater responsibility in respect to the creation and strengthening of an illegal apparatus. All of them must immediately undertake measures to have within the legally existing Party committees an illegal directing core."[2]

American Communists had no disagreement with Moscow about the need to prepare for the day when Communists would forcibly seize control of the government. The manifesto adopted at the movement's founding convention in 1919 declared that "Com-

1. "Resolutions of the Political Secretariat of the ECCI on the Situation and Tasks of the CPUSA," Theodore Draper Papers, box 1, folder 1, Emory University Library, Atlanta, Georgia.
2. B. Vassiliev, "How the Communist International Formulates at Present the Problem of Organization," Draper Papers, box 1, folder 21, pp. 12–28.

munism does not propose to 'capture' the bourgeois parliamentary state, but to conquer and destroy it. . . . It is necessary that the proletariat organize its own state *for the coercion and suppression of the bourgeoisie.*"[3] In the mid-1930s and later, the CPUSA would downplay and even deny its commitment to revolution, but it was an open goal as late as the early 1930s. In 1932 William Z. Foster, the CPUSA's presidential candidate, wrote:

> One day, despite the disbelief of the capitalists . . . the American workers will demonstrate that they, like the Russians, have the intelligence, courage and organization to carry through the revolution. . . .
>
> By the term "abolition" of capitalism we mean its overthrow in open struggle by the toiling masses, led by the proletariat. . . . To put an end to the capitalist system will require a consciously revolutionary act by the great toiling masses, led by the Communist party; that is, the conquest of the State power, the destruction of the State machine created by the ruling class, and the organization of the proletarian dictatorship. . . .
>
> Under the dictatorship all the capitalist parties—Republican, Democratic, Progressive, Socialist, etc.—will be liquidated, the Communist party functioning alone as the Party of the toiling masses. Likewise, will be dissolved all other organizations that are political props of the bourgeois rule, including chambers of commerce, employers' associations, rotary clubs, American Legion, Y.M.C.A., and such fraternal orders as the Masons, Odd Fellows, Elks, Knights of Columbus, etc. . . .
>
> The press, the motion picture, the radio, the theatre, will be taken over by the government.[4]

In the 1920s the CPUSA was more involved in fighting factional wars within its own ranks than it was in trying to overthrow the American government. Once this factional warfare ended in 1929, the CPUSA was better able to fulfill the goals laid down for it by the Comintern. It doggedly worked to transform itself into a mass organization, a process marked by very slow progress until the mid-1930s. The party also took to heart the Comintern's frequent in-

3. "Communist Party Manifesto," reprinted in Joint Legislative Committee Investigating Seditious Activities, *Revolutionary Radicalism, Its History, Purpose and Tactics, with an Exposition and Discussion of the Steps Being Taken and Required to Curb It* (Albany: J. B. Lyon, 1920), 782. Emphasis in the original.

4. William Z. Foster, *Toward Soviet America* (New York: International Publishers, 1932), 67, 121–213, 271–75, 317.

junctions to establish a secret, conspiratorial wing. During the 1920s the party had an underground, but, upset by the vicious internal battles, it did not systematically maintain its covert apparatus. However, in 1929 the CPUSA pledged to "make all necessary preparations for illegal functioning of the leading organs of the Party."[5]

## J. Peters and the Secret Apparatus, 1932–1938

The person chosen to revitalize the CPUSA's secret apparatus was J. Peters. He had a remarkable career in the Communist movement. His Comintern autobiography, **document 24,** written in 1932 while he was on assignment in Moscow, details his journey from a working-class Jewish family to the party. Although known in historical literature as J. Peters, in Communist documents he used "Peter" as frequently as "Peters." This autobiography, for example, uses "Peter" and bears his "Peter" signature; when he retired to Hungary he used "Peter" rather than "Peters." At various times he used other names, including Isidor Boorstein, Goldfarb, and Alexander Stevens. Born in Cop, then part of the Austro-Hungarian Empire, later incorporated into Czechoslovakia, Peters finished high school and briefly attended a university but dropped out without earning a degree. He joined the army in 1914, enlisted in the Communist movement in October 1918, and was part of the movement when it briefly seized power in Hungary. Many Hungarian Communists fled to Moscow after the successful counterrevolution, but Peters continued to work for the party in the Hungarian-speaking section of Czechoslovakia where he had grown up. In 1924 he immigrated to the United States and was transferred to the American Communist party. After working in a factory for less than a year, Peters became a functionary in the Hungarian bureau of the party; by 1927 he was its secretary.

---

5. *Daily Worker,* 17 October 1929. Symptomatic of the indifference of the American authorities toward the CPUSA in 1929 and the sense of security of CPUSA officials, the *Daily Worker* openly published a resolution about its intent to form a secret organization.

# Document 24

"Autobiography of J. Peter of C.P. U.S.A." with "J. Peter" handwritten signature, 25 January 1932, RTsKhIDNI 495–261–5584. Original in English. C.I. is the abbreviation for the Communist International.

---

### AUTOBIOGRAPHY OF J. PETER OF C.P. U.S.A.

I was born in August 1894 in Cop (Hungary, now Czehoslovakia). My father, son of a needletrade worker, was employed on the railroads as brakeman. After a short service, he was released, I don't know the reason why, and got a job together with my mother in a restaurant in Cop. A few years later they opened a small restaurant of their own in the same town, which had about 2000 inhabitants. They alwais struggled to keep up the family.

My mother, daughter of a locomotiv fireman, was cooking in the restaurant. My father died in 1913. Mother lives now in America with my brother, working in restaurants as cook. In the last months, she is unemployed. During the Hungarian revolution she was active among the women. Today she is reader of the Party paper and good sympathizer of the Party.

I was brought up by my grandfather, in this time already locomotiv engineur on the railroads in Debrecen. Was there from the age of five years, going home to see my parents only on school vacations. Finished my schools in Debrecen. After graduating from the highscool (gymnasium), registered in the university in Kolozsvar. Never attended the lectures in the university because had no ways and means to keep up myself. Was working in an office in Debrecen, and went for examination only. Because of lack of funds was compelled to teach students from lower grades in the high school.

In 1914 at the beginning of the world war was enlisted in the army. Was serving in the infantery. After a few months drilling was sent to the front, where after a few months became an officier authomatically. (According the laws the high school graduates will be promoted to reserve officiers) Was at the front, with a few ferloughs, till Sept 1918, when got a longer ferlough. From this ferlough never went back to the army, the revolution broke out.

Have two brothers. Both of them actively participating in the Hungarian revolution. One of them skilled machinist, the other unskilled factory worker. Today both good sympathizers, read Party press, support Party, vote Communist. Have two uncles in Hungary. One a machinist, actively participating in the Hungarian revolution, jailed by the whites after the revolution, today not active, but good sympatizer. My other uncle petiburgois businessman, never sympatized with the movement. Have nobody in the family *who belongs* to any other political parties.

Have divorced my wife. She was and is a member of the Party and Y.C.L. since 1924. Today she is an active Party worker.

INTELLECTUAL DEVELOPMENT AND EDUCATION

I have mentioned before that had four years elementary school, eight years in high school (gymnasium) and 3 semesters (year and half) in the university.

## Document 24 *continued*

During this period, especially when attended high school, got in contact with the labor movement through my grandfather and uncle, who were members of the railroad and machinist unions. Attended many union meetengs. Later I lost my interest in this problem and only during the war started to think about these questions.

Did not finish my study because the war broke out and had to enlist in the army. In 1918 had a chance to continue my study, but gave it up, because of the change of my conceptions about everything. Was already classconscious fighter.

In the Party did not have any schooling. All my knowledge is from study circles and selfeducation. I read Marxist literature since 1918. Mostly independently. Read and fairly intensively studied Political Economy. (From Marx; Capital, Value-Price-Profit. Wage Labor and Capital, Contribution to the Critic of Political Economy. From Hilferding; Das Financkapital, From Luxemburg; Die Akkumulation des Kapitals, From Lenin; Imperialismus the Last Stage of Capitalism, and other books on this subject, like Bogdanov, Lapidus etc. The same time I read some of the books of burgeois authors on Pol. Economy.) Read Marx's-Engels writings on the French, German and Hungarian revolutions. Read superficially Marxian literature on philosophy. Read and studied Lenin's following books: State and Revolution, Infantile Sickness, The Proletarian Revolution and the Renegade Kautsky, Very deeply studied Lenin's works on organizational questions (What is to be done, One Step Forward.) Have all collected works of Lenin published in German and read it superficially. Studied more intensively Lenin on the national and peasant questions. Reand and studied Stalins works published in German, especially the organizational part of Leninism. Carefully followed the thesises and resolutions of the C.I. congresses and plenums. In the last two years especially studied the organizational problems of the C.I. and the Communist Parties.

Have no much experience in literary work. Was writing articles about actual organizational problems in the Party publications.

Speak, read and write perfectly Hungarian, read perfectly, speak not fluently German, (lack of experience) speak, write, and read english (not perfect).

POLITICAL LIFE

Did not belong to any other Party before joined the Communist Party. Joined the Party 1918 (october) and since than I am a member without interruption. I was among those who organized the first Party group in Cop among the railroad workers in 1918. During the Karolyi regime the Party group did good work among the railroad workers in this very important railroad center. Before the revolution the locomotiv repair shop was organized almost entirely. The Party had influence in every department of the railroad center, with the exception os the locomotiv engeners and station officials. But in both places had good connections.

During the revolution was elected in the Directorium of Ung county. In this period most of my time was spent among the railroad workers. Participated in the fight against the Czeh and Roumanian white army around Cop. Organized workers in the Red Army. After the revolution was working in the Uzhorod [Uzhgorod] district of the Party. Was appointed as sub district organizer in a peasant territory with the Headquarters in Cop.

Was working there for two years. Agitating in small towns among the peasant, organizing the agricultural workers in a big farm (Tisra-Salamon) and organizing a strike for higher wages better conditions, for recognition of the union, collective agreement. This militant strike was won by the workers. Organized a strike among the ditchdigger on a government job. Strike was hundert percent, but was broken by terror. We were arrested, with all the leading workers.

We had a militant union in the locomotiv repair shop and among the locomotiv firemen.

During the mobilization against Horthy at the time of the royalist puch [putsch], was organizing Party groups in the regiment in Cop. With fairly good succes. The Internacional became the official song of the soldiers. The regiment became unreliable.

In 1921 was called in to Uzhorod and was assigned to work with Gaty, who was the head of legal office of the Party (Party attorney). During the period when Gaty was in jail, I lead the office and [illegible].

In 1922 was elected on the District Convention in the Controll Committee, 1923 as chairman of this Committee. As such became a member of the District Executive Committee.

The following were my activities during this period. Organized and lead the first big study circle in Uzhorod and Cop. Was the instructor in these circles.

Reorganized the Party on the Vertrauensmanner (delegate) system. Was the had of this body in Uzhorod.

During the municipal election was responsible for the Uzhorod elections. In the same time the District Committee assigned me to help the Cop Section Committee in the election campaign. Organized the campaign in this territory and agitated in Cop and the surrounding peasant towns. In this election we succeded to get the majority of the votes in 3 towns in this Section. In Cop even up to day the Party has the majority of all votes and majority of the town council.

The Party appointed me as representativ of the Party in one of the subcommittee of the Uzhorod City Council.

1922– and 1923 was the organizer and head of the Proletkult movement in Uzhorod Districts. Organized the red scouts group in Uzhorod.

In 1924 was transferred to the C.P.U.S.A. On the end of this year the Buro of the Hungarian Federation appointed me as organizer in Chicago Districts. Was working there about 9 months. Spending all mine time organizing and agitating among the mineworkers in Southern Illinois, steelworkers in Gary, Ind. Harbor, Hammond, automobil workers So. Bend.

In 1925 was called back to New York to work on the editorial staff of the Uj Elore. Was elected by the national Convention of the Hungarian Federation to the National Buro. In 1927 was appointed by the Central Committee as secretary of the Hungarian Buro. In 1928 was participating on the 6-th world Congress of the C.I. as fraternal delegate.

As Secretary of the Hungarian Buro has responsible with a small Committee for taking back the printing shop of the Hungarian movement, which was rented out to private persons. After this transaction the Central Committee assigned me to reorganize the printing shop so that the Daily Worker and the other Party papers could be centralized in one printing plant. We succeded to centralize the Hungarian and Freiheit press in the hand of the Central Committee (1929).

End of 1929 was drawn in the District work of the Party. Was elected as head of the Language Department of the District. In 1930 March was elected as organizational secretary of the New York District and functioned as such up to the date when was sent by the Central Committee to the C.I. as org. practicant.

As org secretary of the District was appointed as instructor to the full time schools of the District and the Central Committee assigned me to the National Training School in the same function. Was instructor in the class of Organizational Principles of the Party.

In 1927 was elected by the 5-th Convention of the Party as alternate to the Central Committee.

1930 was elected by the New York District Convention to the District Committee. Was a member of the District Secretariat till came to Moskva. (1931 Oct.)

Was appointed by the Central Committee to the Central Org. Department in 1930, was a member till came to Moskva.

Participated in all Party Conventions and Plenums from 1926, in U.S.A. Previously in all Party Conferences in the Uzhorod District (Czehoslovakia) and in the 6-th World Congress of C.I.

Have some experiences in illegal work. After the Hungarian revolution organized the literature transportation from Czehoslovakia to Hungary in one section (Cop). Was responsible for the Czehoslovakian end of the work. In New York District I was responsible with an other Comrade to build the apapratus. I must state the New York apparatus was not built properly. We entirely underestimated this face of our task.

The character of my work during the whole period more organizational than propagandist. In the first period of my party activity (Cop-Uzhorod-Chicago) was among the workers in all my activity (meetings, house to house canvassing, leaflet distribution, strike activity) later especially in the last period 1930–1931 as org. secretary of New York District was entirely working

# Document 24 *continued*

inside of the Party. The connection with the masses only through the Party members in the nuclei and fractions. (small part through the fractions) Was working in a very burocrati way during this period, because of the whole burocratic system of the Party. From the C.C. down to lowest unit of the Party. I take the responsibility for my burocratic tendencies and don't want to blame the higher Committees for it. But it would be wrong to blame one individual *only* also.

This does not mean, that I didn't participate in struggles, demonstrations. I was there, but I wanted to emphasize that I did not have in this period daily direct contact with the non party workers.

In the fractional struggle in the U.S.A belonged to the Lovestone group. Came out to U.S.A after the lessons of the Hungarian revolution was already known by us and after learning from experience in Cehoslovakia how important it is to work among the peasants. Didn't understand the american problems, but the controversy on the Farmer Labor Party issue was very simple in my mind. Supported the group, which was for the winning of the farmers. Later on supported the Ruthenberg group, because was convinced that they represent the correct bolshevik line. Was factional in my actions in the Hungarian movement with the whole Hungarian Buro on the side of Ruthenberg and later Lovestone. On the 6-th Convention of the Party had some doutht [doubt] about the correctness of the group, but the factional tigh [tie] was more stronger than anything else. Did not hesitate for a moment to carry out the decision os the C.I. and carried out with conviction.

Was never reprimanded or any way disciplined by the Party.

## PARTICIPATION IN SOCIAL LIFE

In the U.S.A belonged to the Hungarian Sick and Death Benevolent Society. Was participating in the work of a branch and of the Central Committee of the organization. The organization has about 5000 members all over the country. Was not a member of any union.

In Czehoslovakia was working among the peasants as stated above in the election campaigns, strikes. For a longer period 2–3 months was assigned to the peasant organizer (Safranko) to help in the land ditribution campaign. Was working in this campaign, going from town to town in the Hungarian section of the District, organizing the small peasants and the share croppers. Was in daily contact with the workers in the above mentioned locomotiv repair shop in Cop, even in the time when I was working in Uzhorod, because every night went to Cop and came back next morning.

Was working only about eight months in the factory in New York (from febr. 1924 till Nov. 1924) Left the factory on Party instruction.

Participated in the Hungarian revolution (facts above) in every demonstration in Uzhorod and in Cop and vicinity. In U.S.A participated in the demonstration in New York, since 1930 as org. secretary with the org. department of the district organized and in many cases lead the demonstrations. In certain demonstrations did not participate openly on the instruction of the Central and District Committee. Was participating in the strike preparation in Paterson in 1931, in the first days of the strike was out among the strikers and on the first day of the strike was helping to bring down shops. Later the District Org was assigned to this strike.

Was arrested in a strike of ditch diggers (Czehoslovakia) sentenced to two weeks. Was among those who were sentenced in their absence for their activity in the Hungarian revolution against the Czehoslovakian army to 5 years, but never was caught and later everyone got amnesty (Massaryk)

Was paid subdistrict organizer in Czehoslovakia after the Hungarian revolution till 1921. Was assigned in 1921 to the Party attorney's office, but not on the Party payroll. Worked in a shop from 1924 febr. 1924 Nov. (small metall, later small doll factory) Paid District organizer in Chicago (1924–1925). Paid member of the Uj Elore editorial staff (1925–1927) Paid secretary Hungarian Buro (1927–1929) Paid organizer-manager printing shop (Active Press) (1929–1930) Paid Org Secretary New York District (1930–1931) Org Practicant C.I. (1931–1932)

The chief points would be confirmed by the following leading Comrades.

1918–1921 Balazs-Ungvary-Cop, H. Feher (secretary Mukacevo District) all three in Czehoslovakia, E. Seidler in Moskva [Moscow].

1921–1924 E. Seidler (Moskva) Ivan Mondok (Charkov) E. Safrenko (Moskva) H. Feher (Mukacevo-Czehoslovakia)

1924–1932 Jack Stachel, W.W. Weinstone, R. Minor, I. Amter, E. Browder, C.H. Hathaway all in U.S.A.

J. Peter

January 25, 1932.

---

After the expulsion of Jay Lovestone and many of the party's leaders in 1929, a severe shortage of experienced party cadre developed. A number of leaders of the party's language bureaus were pressed into general service, Peters among them. In March 1930 he was selected to head the organizational department of the large New York district. In that capacity, he had responsibility for developing the party's illegal apparatus in New York. In document 24 he wrote:

> Have some experiences in illegal work. After the Hungarian revolution organized the literature transportation from Czehoslovakia to Hungary in one section (Cop). Was responsible for the Czehoslovakian end of the work. In New York District I was responsible with an other Comrade to build the apaparatus. I must state the New York apparatus was not built properly. We entirely underestimated this face of our task.

Whatever his own reservations about his accomplishments, Peters was selected to travel to Moscow in 1931 as "Org Practicant." **Document 25**, a CPSU report on Peters written in 1947, notes that in 1931 and 1932 he served as a "trainee in organizational issues in the Anglo-American Lander-Secretariat of the ECCI."[6]

---

# Document 25

Dzerzhinsky, "Report Peters, Joseph . . . ," 15 October 1947, RTsKhIDNI 495–261–5584. Original in Russian. Dzerzhinsky, not to be confused with the founder of the Cheka, was probably a functionary of the CPSU International Department.

---

Secret

REPORT

PETERS, Joseph (Peters Joseph), a.k.a. Boorstein, Isidor, born 1894 in the town of Cop, Austria-Hungary (later Czechoslovakia), to a worker's family. Nationality—Jew. Citizen of Czechoslovakia. Finished secondary school and the first year of university in the town of Kluzh. Knows Hungarian, English, and German.

A member of US Comparty since 1924. Was a member of the Comparty of Hungary since 1918 and a member of the CP of Czechoslovakia from 1919 through 1924.

1913–14—an office clerk in Debrecen, while also a correspondence student of the university in Kluzh (Kolozhvar).

1914–18—a private, then an officer of the Austro-Hungarian army, was at the front in World War I.

1918–19—assigned by the CP of Hungary to work among railroad workers in Debrecen.

In 1919 during the Hungarian revolution was elected a member of the directorate of the Ungsk (Uzhgorod) district. Took part in battles of the Hungarian Red army against Czech and Romanian troops.

1919–21—subdistrict organizer of the Comparty of Czechoslovakia in the Cop region of the Uzhgorod district. Arrested by Czech authorities for revolutionary activities, released after two weeks.

1921–22—employed by the legal bureau attached to the Uzhgorod Comparty district committee.

1923–24—chairman of district control commission and member of Comparty district committee in Uzhgorod.

In 1924 traveled to the US and worked eight months in a New York factory.

---

6. The Lander secretariats supervised regional subdivisions of the Comintern. The Anglo-American secretariat oversaw the Communist parties of Britain, America, Canada, and a number of English-speaking territories. The ECCI was the Executive Committee of the Communist International.

# Document 25 continued

1924–26—district organizer of the Hungarian Federation for the CPUSA in Chicago assigned to miners and metallurgical and auto industry workers in Illinois.

1925–27—on editorial staff of the Hungarian Communist newspaper Uj Elore in New York.

In 1927 at the 5th CPUSA Congress elected a candidate to the CPUSA CC.

1927–29—secretary of the National Bureau of the Hungarian Federation of the CPUSA, New York.

In 1928 visited Moscow as a delegate of the 6th Congress of the Comintern.

1928–29—during factional struggles in the CPUSA sided with the Lovestone group.

1929–30—head of national minorities department of the New York district of the CPUSA and director of the party printing office.

1930–31—organizational secretary of the New York district committee and simultaneously a worker of the organization department of the CPUSA CC.

1931–32—trainee in organizational issues in the Anglo-American Lander-Secretariat of the ECCI, Moscow.

At the end of 1932 left the country for party work in the US.

We have no information on Peters's activities for 1933–35.

1935–36—organizational secretary of CPUSA regional committee in New York.

1936–38—worker in the secret apparatus of the CPUSA CC.

In 1938 worked in the organization department of the CPUSA CC. In the same year elected a member of the CPUSA Central Control Commission. He was subsequently relieved of his duties in the CPUSA CC apparatus as a non American citizen and performed special assignments for the party CC.

There is no information on Peters for the period 1941–47.

According to a report in the US reactionary press of 9 October 1947, Peters was arrested by the American authorities on Ellis Island (New York). The Hearst press calls him a "Soviet agent."

*Dzerzhinsky (Dzerzhinsky)*

15 October 1947

3 copies printed

---

Late in 1932 Peters returned to the United States. Many years afterward, his new assignment became a matter of great political controversy, and it is still a matter of intense historical debate. In 1948 Whittaker Chambers testified that Alger Hiss, a respected member of the Washington establishment, was a secret Communist and Soviet spy. Peters played a key role in Chambers's story. According to Chambers, it was Peters who headed the Communist underground apparatus that Chambers joined in the early 1930s after having been an open member of the CPUSA. Chambers testified that among his covert assignments for Peters was assisting secret Communists who worked for government agencies in Washington in the 1930s. These groups provided the CPUSA with information about sensitive government activities and sought to promote Communist influence within the government. In particular, Chambers described the operation of the Ware group. This group, first supervised by the Communist farm-policy specialist Harold Ware, consisted of young Communist professionals who worked for the New Deal's Agricultural Adjustment Administration (AAA). One of those named by Chambers as a member of the Ware group was Alger Hiss.

Chambers testified that Peters turned underground Communists who had access to especially important information over to Soviet intelligence. Among those transferred were both himself and Hiss. Because of Peters's key role in Chambers's story, revisionist historians and defenders of Hiss have often denied that Peters was involved in any party underground or even that there was such a thing as a Communist underground.[7]

Document 27, entitled "Brief on the Work of the CPUSA Secret Apparatus," however, proves Peters's involvement in underground work. Written in January 1939, this report says of Peters that "upon his return from Moscow the CC [Central Committee] assigned him to work in the secret apparatus." Peters did not start from scratch; as he noted in his autobiography, he had organized the New York Communist party's underground in 1929 and 1930. Peters, how-

---

7. Victor Navasky, editor of the *Nation* and a defender of Alger Hiss, agrees that Peters was "a well-known Communist Party official in the 1930s" but notes that he "denied participation in any 'Communist underground,'" suggesting through the use of quotation marks that there was no such thing. See Victor Navasky, "The Case Not Proved against Alger Hiss," *Nation*, 8 April 1978, 395–96. Further, the *Nation* asked journalist Donald Kirk to stop by Peters's home in Budapest (in 1949 Peters had been arrested and deported) and chat with him. Kirk found Peters to be "a skeptic, an intellectual who cannot help but perceive humor in the posturing and maneuvering." Kirk quotes him as calling the charge that he did secret work for the American Communist party "nonsense." "This is so stupid—the 'secret Communist' and 'not-secret Communist,'" Peters said. Kirk felt bad for having "intruded upon the inner contentment" Peters and his wife had achieved "since the turmoil of their lives in America." In his Hungarian retirement, Peters used the name Joszef Peter. See Donald Kirk, "Checking Up on Peter's Smile," *Nation*, 6 May 1978, 525–26.

ever, revitalized, and provided central supervision to, what had been a scattered and uncoordinated underground. The organization that Peters put together was what the "Brief" called the CPUSA "secret apparatus."[8]

## Rudy Baker Replaces J. Peters

According to a cover note (**document 26**), the "Brief on the Work of the CPUSA Secret Apparatus" (**document 27**) was written by Rudy Baker. Baker noted in the "Brief" that he had succeeded Peters as head of the secret apparatus in June 1938. Prior to that, Baker said "its operations have been directed for that entire period by Com. PETERS."[9] Rudy Baker explained that the secret apparatus created by Peters was financed by "people who are entirely without party affiliation, and hence undercover." Baker mentions only a few specific tasks carried out by Peters's secret apparatus. Peters established relationships between the Central Committee and the states, indicating that branches of the illegal apparatus were built up in local districts. He also undertook a number of security assignments, including creating a "satisfactory and secure [system of] safeguarding especially important Central Committee documents. . . . Experiments have also been carried out by the Special Dept. in the setting up of radio links, of special equipment for [sound or signal] reproduction, of an electrical device for detecting enemies."[10]

8. Although the word chosen to translate the Russian is "secret" apparatus, the Russian word is *konspirativnyi*, a cognate of the English word "conspiracy," and the term could as accurately be translated "conspiratorial apparatus" or "conspiracy apparatus."

9. Perhaps because the secret apparatus was not an entirely new organization and because he did not take over until 1938, Baker is ambiguous about timing. In the "Brief," Baker refers to Peters taking on the secret apparatus assignment after his return from Moscow, which was in late 1932. He also refers to Peters's secret apparatus having been in existence for "about four years," placing its origins in mid-1934 if we work back from Baker's takeover in mid-1938. Document 25 states that Peters was a "worker in the secret apparatus of the CPUSA CC [Central Committee]" between 1936 and 1938. Document 25 was compiled in 1947; document 27, written in 1939, is more likely to be accurate about timing.

10. The last was probably a mechanism for detecting listening devices.

# Document 26

Andreev to Dimitrov, 28 January 1939, RTsKhIDNI 495–74–472. Original in Russian. Cover letter for document 27.

**22** File with No. 256/s
28 January 1939
Top Secret

2 copies printed
28 January 1939

**TO THE ECCI GENERAL SECRETARY**
Com. G. M. DIMITROV:

I am forwarding a brief written at our request by a member of the CPUSA Central Committee, Com. BAKER, "On the Work of the CPUSA Secret Apparatus."

Enclosure: Com. Baker's brief

HEAD OF ECCI CADRES DEPT      *Andreev*
(ANDREEV)

*GD Discuss immediately with Com. Baker, 31 January 1939. GD*

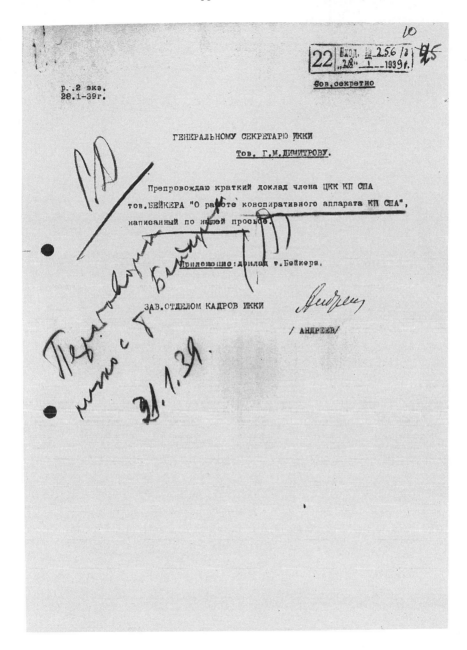

р. 2 экз.
28.1-39г.

ГЕНЕРАЛЬНОМУ СЕКРЕТАРЮ ИККИ

Тов. Г.М. ДИМИТРОВУ.

Препровождаю краткий доклад члена ЦКК КП США

тов. БЕЙКЕРА "О работе конспиративного аппарата КП США",

написанный по нашей просьбе.

Приложение: доклад т. Бейкера.

ЗАВ. ОТДЕЛОМ КАДРОВ ИККИ

/ АНДРЕЕВ/

DOCUMENT 26. Andreev to Dimitrov, 28 January 1939.

26.I.39г.
3 экв.ак.

22  Вход. № 256 /.
,,2Д" I -1939 г.

Секретно.

КРАТКИЙ ДОКЛАД О РАБОТЕ КОНСПИРАТИВНОГО

АППАРАТА   КП. США.

Конспиративный аппарат КП США существует около 4 лет. В продолжении всего этого периода работой конспиративного аппарата руководил тов.ПИТЕРС. 13 июня 1938г. он был освобожден от этой работы и назначен на другую работу, а спец-работа была поручена т.БЕЙКЕРУ.

Тов.ПИТЕРС организовал связь между Центральным Комитетом и Штатами и ввел подобную систему связи в наиболее важных округах, для этой цели недавно послав двух товарищей для развертывания этой работы в Чикаго и Кливленде.

Этот отдел создал также вполне удовлетворительное и безопасное хранение особо важных документов Центрального Комитета. Безопасное хранение секретного архива Центрального Комитета проводилось по меньшей мере в продолжении 15 лет с различной степенью безопасности документа. Секретные документы хранятся в частных домах/ на частных квартирах/. Спец. Отделом также были произведены опыты по установлению радиосвязи ,специально воспроизводящего аппарата,электрического прибора для определения противника. Для этой работы были найдены средства. Для финансирования этой работы созданы группы из людей не являющимися прикрепленными ни к какой парторганизации и т.о. являющиеся засекреченными.

Недостаток этой работы заключается в том, что всем стало известно, что эту работу проводит ПИТЕРС.

Отдел не ставил перед собой проблему разоблачения врагов внутри партии. Этот вопрос разрешался непосредственно т.БРАУДЕРОМ от центра и дисциплинарными комиссиями в боль-

DOCUMENT 27. First page of "Brief on the Work of the CPUSA Secret Apparatus," 26 January 1939.

# Document 27

"Brief on the Work of the CPUSA Secret Apparatus," 26 January 1939, RTsKhIDNI 495–74–472. Original in Russian. The text reproduced here is an English translation of a Russian original that was itself a translation of a report Baker wrote in English. This double translation has resulted in some stilted phrasing and shifting between first person and third person narration. The person designated "I. Ch." in the document is clearly John Leech from the description provided. The "I. Ch." is a translation problem stemming from the first English-to-Russian (Latin to Cyrillic alphabet) translation of what Baker probably wrote as "J. Leech."

---

**22** File with No. _256/s_
28 January 1939
Secret

26 January 1939
3 copies of doc.

### BRIEF ON THE WORK OF THE CPUSA SECRET APPARATUS

The CPUSA secret apparatus has been in existence about four years. Its operations have been directed for that entire period by Com. PETERS. On 13 June 1938 he was relieved of that position and appointed to another, and special-work was assigned to Com. BAKER.

Com. PETERS organized ties between the Central Committee and the states, and introduced a similar system of coordination in the most important districts; it was for this purpose that he recently dispatched two comrades to Chicago and Cleveland to develop this work.

This department has also created an entirely satisfactory and secure [system of] safeguarding especially important Central Committee documents. The safeguarding of the Central Committee's secret archive has been in effect for at least fifteen years, with varying degrees of document security. Secret documents are held in private homes (in private apartments). Experiments have also been carried out by the Special Dept. in the setting up of radio links, of special equipment for [sound or signal] reproduction, of an electrical device for detecting enemies. Resources were found for this work. For the financing of this work, groups were formed of people who are entirely without party affiliation, and hence undercover.

The problem with this work was that it became generally known that this work was being directed by PETERS.

The department did not address the problem of exposing enemies within the party. This issue was resolved directly from the center by Com. BROWDER and disciplinary commissions in the majority of districts. Issues of evaluation and verification of cadres were handled by the CC Organizational Dept. Issues of internal communications were handled by special persons not linked with the functioning of the Organizational Dept.

New, or Current Work Regime

Comrade Baker has been assigned to special-work. This is known only to Browder, Stachel, Weiner, Peters, and now Pat Toohey. This became possible only because Baker is actively involved in the Control Commission, in the commission on the struggle for peace, and in the Eastern affairs and education commissions. There is no reason for anyone to reflect or puzzle over what sort of work Baker is doing. Although this is an unfavorable working condition, in so far as work in the commission on the struggle for peace and in the other commissions consumes a great deal of time and effort, the aim is, however, achieved, in that Baker's special-work goes unnoticed and unknown. His position as a member of the Central Control Commission makes it possible to raise issues of document safeguarding, communications, and the exposure and weeding out of enemies before district organizations.

At the present time systematic efforts are being applied to improving communications, developing and testing [arrangements for] safeguarding important documents, and conducting experiments in radio links. Attention is mainly focused on enlarging the apparatus and training its cadres in proper methods of detecting and exposing the enemy within our own party and in the workers' movement. This work is in its very initial stages in all party organizations.

The recent rapid growth of the party, the broad scope and variety of forms of mass party work, and significant improvement in the legalization of the party have all served to distract the attention of our leading party workers in district organizations from the need to expose and weed out the enemies in our ranks. Vigilance in the party dropped off in comparison with the earlier period, when the party was smaller, semilegal, and often persecuted. It was not so long ago that party organization secretaries in California and Pittsburgh were informed of the presence of a spy in the leadership of those district committees, however, those leaders proved helpless to expose that spy and appealed for the assistance of the Central Committee. Such incidents are not isolated ones. The districts lack competent comrades assigned to study this problem and to study cadres, accumulating experience and knowledge relevant to this work. An exception to this rule is the New York District Committee, which has formed such an apparatus and appointed an outstanding comrade to head it; that comrade trains cadres and has already exposed quite a number of sophisticated spies and Trotskyists in the ranks of the party. This comrade infiltrated the Lovestoneist organization and obtained important materials of great significance for the entire party. This is unrelated to the discovery of the Lovestoneist archives—that discovery was made by a specific person. Highly successful efforts are being made to infiltrate the New York Trotskyist organization. The work of the New York apparatus is being carried out under the direct leadership of Com. BAKER. The work of that apparatus serves as a field for advanced experimentation, an instructive model of the proper development of comparable activity in the other districts. It is considered most preferable to develop this work in the following major districts:

CALIFORNIA
ILLINOIS (CHICAGO)
MICHIGAN (DETROIT)
OHIO (CLEVELAND)
PENNSYLVANIA (PITTSBURGH)

In the indicated districts, work should begin with the reinforcement of disciplinary commissions and the selection of a reliable comrade to elaborate and study the problem of exposing enemies within the party. At first this work is carried out on behalf of the Central Control Commission. Currently, Com. Baker has at his disposal a qualified and experienced comrade directing work along these lines. He ("JOHN") is now in California, where he was sent for a month to work on exposing suspect elements in the district leadership apparatus and to assist in forming the district's own apparatus to continue that work. This was done at the request of the secretary of the California Party District Committee.

After this work is completed here, JOHN will depart for the states of Washington, Illinois, Michigan, Ohio, and Pennsylvania, where he will spend two weeks in each state for the same purpose. Issues connected with this work are to be discussed with a local comrade selected for this work, and also with the secretary of the party district committee.

Each of the above-mentioned districts will be assigned the following simple tasks:

Compile a comprehensive list of Trotskyists and Lovestoneists on its territory, including their names, addresses, biographies, connections, the organizations to which they belong, who their friends and wives are, and so on. In other words, provide complete information on each of these enemies. Alongside this task, present a comprehensive list of the various espionage agencies, their addresses, information on their activities, and so on.

Despite the fact that the above-mentioned tasks are in and of themselves simple, they will draw the attention of our comrades to systematized and active methods of struggle; they will require increased activity and involvement on the part of many comrades in this work, and will serve as a means of stimulating the vigilance of party members.

Throughout its entire existence, our party has exposed and weeded out spies and traitors. The party has accumulated considerable experience in this area. However, that experience has never been studied, never been passed on to the entire party, and the center has never been guided by that experience.

On the whole, all of that was primitively handled. One of our tasks is to generalize that experience with advanced knowledge in this area, and to make that experience available to the entire party. Espionage agencies, chiefly their Trotskyist and Lovestoneist sections, have become more sophisticated and wily.

Of course, it would be impossible and impermissible to set forth all of that experience of directives and leadership in writing, in documents. Therefore, people like JOHN will be regularly sent to train party cadres in the exposure of enemies.

In principle, this problem is a political and ideological, as well as an organizational one. In the present brief report, issues of the political, ideological and mass struggle against Trotskyism and Lovestoneism and spies will not be touched on, in the first place, because that is the task and duty of the leadership party organs. However, I am aware that here there can be no demarcation between organizational and political forms of that struggle. Our experience has shown that in those districts where no serious political and ideological struggle was waged against Trotskyism and Lovestoneism, not only did enemies inflict significant damage on the workers' movement, but—as happened in Detroit—counterrevolutionary ideology penetrated the party under various disguises.

The foregoing plans and measures are all that the special apparatus of the Central Committee is currently undertaking. Comrade BAKER answers directly to Com. BROWDER. Com. Baker has at his disposal a special fund and receipts that are independent of the Central Committee's finances, being instead under Com. Weiner's control.

The CC secret apparatus is partially connected with the work of the Control Commission, however, the Control Commission is completely unaware of the work of the special apparatus, its staff and activities. From time to time, as changing conditions and increased workloads dictate, new, carefully selected persons will be drawn in to the work of the special apparatus. These new people, too, will not be secret, but perhaps openly connected with some conventional, well-known work. A certain highly qualified group of technical workers will be completely isolated from the party in view of the special nature of their work. For various reasons I had no opportunity to discuss all phases of this work in detail with Com. BROWDER.

Browder was above all concerned that this work be passed on to me in such a way that my participation in the work of the special apparatus not become generally known, as had been the case with Com. PETERS. This required my participation in other areas of work, but since I had not been directly involved in the work of the American Comparty for six years, it took me some time to get reacquainted. It was also necessary to make a thorough study of all issues relating to that work. Next, Com. Browder expressed the wish that all phases of that work be discussed here.

## Document 27 *continued*

The task of evaluating and verifying cadres is one of those tasks that the special department has not managed successfully. I think that Com. Baker would do well to work more closely with Com. Krumbein, who is currently assigned cadre work in the CC, and work jointly with him to devise means and mechanisms for checking the biographies of our cadres, determining whether the facts reported in them are accurate, and whether the comrades have omitted any of their shortcomings. For carefully checking the most dangerous weaknesses of our cadres, for instance, alcoholism, unhealthy social relations and habits, conduct of sexual life, cowardly tendencies, serious criminal records, etc.

Com. ANDREEV's suggestions to the effect that the CC should consider the problem of retaining our leadership cadres in case of war, mobilization, and a possible transition to illegal status. I will inform Com. Browder of all these matters upon my return.

The issue of informers in the CC will also be discussed with Com. Browder in light of its practical application here; it will also be necessary to discuss the issue of the fuller use of CC members in district work, as well as the encouragement of rank-and-file party members to forward their complaints directly to the CC, to the Control Commission, or to the newspaper Daily Worker.

Brief report on the staff of the
CPUSA Central Control Commission

The CPUSA Central Control Commission was elected by the Central Committee immediately after the 1938 Party Congress. It answers to the Central Committee. The following information on the CC staff is sketchy and incomplete.

Chairman of the Central [Control] Commission:

ROBERT MINOR

Member of the CC and Politburo. Artist (caricaturist). A member of the party since its early years. Before the founding of the party he belonged to the anarchists of the American school and was a friend of TOM MOONEY. After the October Revolution he traveled to Moscow, met LENIN and joined the CPUSA. He is a firm, devoted, indefatigable party worker. Popular in the party and with the masses.

Secretary of the Control Commission:

CHARLES DIRBA (LAPIN): Secretary of the Control Commission for many years. Also secretary of the Latvian bureau of the CPUSA CC. An accountant by profession. Relieved of duty as Control Commission worker.

BAKER: See his biography.

PETERS: Baker does not know the details of his situation. His [own] biography ought to be in the Comintern, since he worked for a year, 1932, in the Organizational Dept. In 1930–31 he was Com. Baker's organizational secretary in the New York District Committee. Upon his return from Moscow the CC assigned him to work in the secret apparatus. He was at this post until June of 1938. He currently works in the CC Organizational Dept. under the supervision of Brown and Stachel. He has no experience of mass work. With the exception of his work as org. secretary of the New York district committee, he has held no other post involving political responsibility. He is a Jew from Vienna.

[JACOB] MINDEL: Emigrated from Russia long before the Revolution. Was a dentist by profession. Came [to the USSR] to study at the ILS in 1933. Returned at the end of 1933 or 1934. Assigned by the CC to the organization of the three-month party school. In 1936 he was one of the members of a committee of three on the organization of the six-month party school. Currently one of the directors of the national school commission. He has organized and himself taught in many party schools. He is one of the best and [most] beloved party instructors. He has earned special recognition from Com. Browder for his outstanding teaching activities. Highly respected and loved by the thousands of students whom he has trained. A member of the party since the day it was founded.

ROSA AUERBACH: Garment worker. Currently working in a factory workshop. Possibly born in Russia. Arrived in the US long before the Revolution. A Jewess. Very active in the party and the trade union. Baker does not know her well, but she is very popular in the party.

[LEO] HOFFBAUER: Metal worker. Works in a factory shop. Baker first met him in 1921 in the IWW and in the New York party organization. Evidently a German, since he speaks English with something of a German accent.

KINGSTON: Negro. Joined the party in Philadelphia in 1924 or 1925, while Baker was secretary there. Currently working as a party worker in New York (Brooklyn). One of the senior and steadfast Negro comrades in our party.

. . . ? . . . Jewess. Possibly emigrated from Russia, many years ago, before the Revolution. Speaks English well. 45–50. Garment worker. Currently working in factory workshop. One of our most active comrades in the trade union. Very active in party and trade-union work in New York.

The latest instances of negligence in the CPUSA

Vigilance and the ability to expose spies are not one and the same in the party. In New York, for instance, a great deal of attention is given to this work. The same is true of party organization leaders in Cleveland and Chicago. In . . . . . . in view of serious leak[s] of secret material, the comrades are persistently requesting assistance. Directives, advice and concrete assistance would be appreciated in the majority of districts.

For the next two and a half years I carried on secret work and encountered the following instances. I bring up these instances not because I want to single out California, but because I observed them personally. The center was aware of these instances, or if not, I reported them orally during my frequent trips to New York.

The California party organization is considered one of the best, certain shortcomings notwithstanding.

ROSS: Editor of the party newspaper in California (a weekly) and a member of the district committee bureau. Abandoned his wife and child. Conducted himself suspiciously. The comrades felt that he was "strange" and different from the other responsible comrades. Reports came in saying he was on the police payroll. Such information is often directed against responsible comrades for the purpose of fostering an atmosphere of mistrust toward leadership. At the same time it became known that critical decisions reached at a party bureau of five meeting had become known to an association of businessmen. Ross was in that bureau of five. The usual procedures for verifying these suspicions produced nothing. The secretary of the party organization sent a request to the CC to transfer Ross to New York in connection with the dangerous situation in San Francisco and the inability of the district committee to confirm these suspicions on its own. Next, Ross was dismissed from all responsible posts in connection with a Trotskyist article that had appeared in the newspaper during his absence and with his discontinuing child support. Upon arriving in New York he worked in the trade union.

Even in New York it has been impossible to produce any evidence of his guilt. His case remains open.

I. Ch [JOHN LEECH].: Worker. Later became a small businessman. Bankrupted during the crisis. Joined the unemployed movement in a desperate attempt to obtain financial assistance, and subsequently became involved with the Comparty. Because he was an American, he was quickly promoted to the leadership, and after two years he became secretary of the party organization in Los Angeles (California). He had a wife and five children, and a good reputation as a family man. He was paid 10 dollars a week, later his salary was increased to 17 dollars. He had a large sum of secret-fund moneys at his disposal, and after engaging in sexual relations with a certain girl, he squandered more than 25 dollars with her in a single night. Many more instances of suspicious and negligent work practices aroused the attention of the state party committee. It was at least two or three months before he was permitted to resign his job voluntarily. This instance of extreme negligence, which took place during a period of intensive electoral campaigning and a looming strike, while our leadership was working day and night under great pressure, and contending with a disciplinary committee staffed with inexperienced people. Even after he was removed from his post and transferred to a different district (that district was put on notice that he would be coming). The state committee delayed his expulsion and public denunciation for several months, fearing that he knew too much about the secret organization and would reveal this information in Hollywood.

SCOTT: Served a prison term for his role in criminal case brought against miners, became a friend of TOM MOONEY. On his release from prison he joined the party and was appointed by Darcy to important secret work. For a time he headed cadre work. Had access to all secret documents in San Francisco, especially during the critical strike of 1934. Remained on important work after Schneiderman's arrival. Some time later, Schneiderman grew suspicious of Scott and removed him from all responsible posts. He set out for Los Angeles, robbed a number of homes, and to secure his freedom, gave the police a mixture of certain falsifications and significant material on the internal and secret work of the party. The party published an announcement of his expulsion.

This instance is symptomatic of the inexcusable promotion of a new, unverified and undependable person to secret work.

TOM JOHNSON: A very capable organizer and leader. At least ten years in the party. Expelled from the party after he had quit work at the most critical junctures no fewer than four times. In Los Angeles he had been assigned responsible work in the leadership of the committee of industrial organizations, despite a warning about his irresponsible tendencies. Johnson's wife was the secret secretary of the district party organization, and during the period of Johnson's arrest in connection with the Scott case, she had meetings with [his] sister, a known Trotskyist.

The foregoing instances cannot be taken as a characterization of party activities in the area of weeding out internal party enemies. However, the fact that such instances could take place in our party, and in one of its best districts, serves to illustrate the fact that work in this area is weak, and the most serious attention must be given to this work in the immediate future.

In all the above-mentioned instances the Central Control Committee severely criticized the work of the state committees and constantly called for decisive actions. However, the Control Commission lacked the high authority and prestige of the Central Committee. The Central Committee has since strengthened the Control Commission significantly, reinforcing it with newly elected comrades and charging it with more responsible tasks. In my view, the current Control Commission is carrying out its work on a broader political basis, with a more profound political understanding of that work, and is providing the party with serious leadership, and therefore, with the help of the Central Committee, which will help to lend it a breadth of authority and prestige, which are the result of a real capacity to perform its appointed tasks.

While I am not inclined to fault the old Control Commission for its lack of corresponding authority and, therefore indirectly excuse its negligence in the instances indicated by me above, I wish, however, to emphasize that no competent and able control commission can be effective if the task of exposing and weeding out enemies in the party is not successfully carried out by the lower ranks.

Translated from the English by

REFERENT [ASSESSOR] OF ECCI CADRES DEPT.

*Povolotsky* (POVOLOTSKY)

Baker's report does not explain why J. Peters was relieved as head of the secret apparatus in June 1938. Indeed, not until this document was found has it been known that Peters was replaced in 1938 or that Baker was his successor. The timing strongly suggests that the defection of Whittaker Chambers—who gained national notoriety in the Alger Hiss case—precipitated Peters's removal. Chambers had worked closely with Peters for several years. Disillusioned and fearing Stalin's then ongoing bloody purge of the Soviet intelligence apparatus, Chambers vanished in April 1938. In May his brother-in-law received a message asking that Chambers contact "Steve," one of Peters's pseudonyms. Around the same time, Peters and Boris Bykov, his Soviet controller, dispatched the literary agent Maxim Lieber to Baltimore in an unsuccessful attempt to locate Chambers.[11]

Chambers would have been able to identify Peters and link him directly with Soviet espionage. In fact, in 1939 Chambers wrote an essay entitled "The Faking of Americans" for Herbert Solow, a journalist and friend. It began with a warning that Chambers was prepared, if provoked, to identify who "is the organizer of most of the illegal activities of the Communist Party in America, . . . organizing the Party 'underground' in what Communists call 'strategic places'—to mention only the least strategic, the Post Office . . . ; the Labor Department . . . the Treasury department." In the essay Chambers described Peters under the name "Sandor" and wrote that he "sits, in the person of his underground Communists, in the councils of the American government."[12]

Drawing on Chambers's article, which was never published, Solow prepared an account of how the CPUSA underground obtained fake American passports for Soviet espionage.[13] The centerpiece of both articles was the Robinson-Rubens case. In 1937 Stalin had purged his intelligence services and among those arrested were an

11. Chambers's defection is described in Allen Weinstein, *Perjury: The Hiss-Chambers Case* (New York: Knopf, 1978), 306–28. Weinstein's book is the most thorough and complete study of the Hiss-Chambers case.

12. Karl [Whittaker Chambers], "The Faking of Americans," Herbert Solow Papers, Hoover Institution on War, Revolution and Peace, Stanford University, Stanford, California.

13. Herbert Solow, "Stalin's American Passport Mill," *American Mercury* (July 1939): 302–9.

American woman, Ruth Boergers, and her Latvian husband, Adolf Rubens. Their arrest and disappearance in Moscow in December 1937 had led to the partial uncovering of a ring that procured fraudulent American passports for Soviet agents. Adolf Rubens, a Soviet agent, had had many contacts with Peters, whose secret apparatus had supplied the false passports. By the spring of 1938, American authorities had arrested several of the Americans involved in the operation. The Robinson-Rubens fiasco and Chambers's defection, both early in 1938, likely combined to bring about Peters's removal as head of the secret apparatus in June.[14]

## The Washington Communist Underground, 1933–1943

### The Ware Group and the La Follette Committee

A number of critics have refused to credit Chambers's testimony that a Communist underground existed inside various government agencies in Washington in the 1930s. As the preceding documents have shown, a thriving Communist underground was in place in the 1930s. Other documents demonstrate that this party underground was active within the federal government itself. The benign view is that those Communists who did work within the government were present only as individuals and never acted in concert, were not supervised by the CPUSA or a Soviet agency, and did not provide the party with information and, further, that their communism did not affect the content of their work or the activities of any government agencies. In sum, their Communist loyalties were of no more relevance to their government activities than their membership in the Methodist church or the Shriners would have been.

The testimony of Whittaker Chambers about the existence of the Ware group in the Agricultural Adjustment Administration has been amply confirmed by three members of this group, Nathaniel Weyl, Lee Pressman, and John Abt, as well as by Josephine Herbst, whose husband had been a member.[15] Even so, revisionist histo-

14. The case is known as the Robinson-Rubens case because American authorities discovered that the couple had fraudulent American passports under both names.

15. After leaving the AAA, Weyl directed the CPUSA's School on Wheels; the mobile classroom toured agricultural areas, its staff tutoring farmers on Communist

rians prefer the characterization of the Ware group offered by Pressman. After years of denouncing as liars those who said he was a Communist, Pressman admitted in 1950 that he had been a Communist in the 1930s, had belonged to the Ware group, and had met with Peters. However, Pressman depicted the group as an innocuous study club of government employees who met to discuss Marxism.

John Abt cast the same benign light on the Ware group in his 1993 autobiography. Like Pressman, Abt had spent most of his life damning those who said he was a secret Communist as smear-mongering liars. In his autobiography, however, he relates that Harold Ware recruited him in 1934 and describes how his party membership was kept a closely held secret in order to protect his usefulness during his government service and, later, in the labor movement. Only Ware, Earl Browder, and a few other colleagues knew he was a CPUSA member. Abt wrote that after Ware's death in an auto accident, J. Peters became his link to the CPUSA, as well as an intimate and trusted personal friend; Abt even visited his old friend in Hungary after Peters's deportation. Like Pressman, Abt depicted the Ware group as a discussion club and Peters as an occasional guest. Abt did allow that members provided the CPUSA with analysis of government activities, noting, however, that what they provided was not classified information.[16]

In 1935, irritation with the left-wing policies emanating from within the AAA led its chief to fire most of the members of the Ware group. Although Abt was not among those fired, he soon moved on to other government agencies. His most influential position was as chief counsel for the Civil Liberties Subcommittee of the Senate Education and Labor Committee, generally known as the La Follette committee after its chairman, Senator Robert La Follette, Jr. (Progressive, Wisconsin). The La Follette committee, which re-

---

agricultural policies. He broke his silence about his Communist activities after the Korean War began. He later wrote two books: *Treason: The Story of Disloyalty and Betrayal in American History* (Washington, D.C.: Public Affairs Press, 1950) and *The Battle against Disloyalty* (New York: Crowell, 1951) on the nature of disloyalty. Josephine Herbst was a well-known novelist of the 1930s; her husband was John Herrmann. Pressman and Abt, who both became well-known labor lawyers, are discussed below.

16. John Abt with Michael Myerson, *Advocate and Activist: Memoirs of an American Communist Lawyer* (Champaign: University of Illinois Press, 1993), 39–42, 45–46, 178–79.

ceived considerable staff support from the Roosevelt administration (Abt was actually employed by an executive branch agency and loaned to La Follette's committee), exposed the efforts of employers to resist union organizing drives by means that were sometimes violent or abusive. Abt's position enabled him to ensure that a share of the subcommittee's professional staff consisted of fellow secret Communists, such as Charles Flato, Allan Rosenberg, and Charles Kramer, another Ware group veteran. Kramer, Flato, and Rosenberg will come up again in chapter 8.

La Follette later stated that in time he came to realize that a caucus of secret Communists on his subcommittee's staff manipulated his subcommittee's work.[17] When asked about this by a historian in 1963, Abt, who at that time still denied his own Communist loyalties, said, "I just don't know what he [La Follette] was talking about," and denied that there had been an organized Communist presence among the subcommittee's staff.[18]

In 1937 and 1938, two of the La Follette committee Communists, Kramer and Rosenberg, joined the staff of the National Labor Relations Board (NLRB), created by the Wagner Act of 1935 to regulate collective bargaining and protect the rights of workers to form unions. One of the major issues the NLRB had to deal with in the late 1930s was the fierce rivalry between the AFL and the CIO; both union federations often attempted to organize the same body of workers. By its decisions about the appropriate bargaining unit and the steps necessary to gain union recognition, the NLRB could influence the outcome of a battle between AFL and CIO unions or decide whether an employer would be required to recognize a particular union. By law the NLRB was neutral and allowed workers to decide the issue. However, the CPUSA had almost no influence in the AFL, preferred the CIO's policy of organizing unions on an industrial basis rather than the AFL's craft basis, and regarded the CIO as its best hope for expanding its influence in labor.[19]

17. Robert M. La Follette, Jr., "Turn the Light on Communism," *Collier's,* 8 February 1947.

18. Jerold S. Auerbach, *Labor and Liberty: The La Follette Committee and the New Deal* (Indianapolis: Bobbs-Merrill, 1966), 168.

19. Communists led or were dominant partners in the leadership of one large CIO union, the United Electrical, Radio and Machine Workers, and seventeen smaller CIO affiliates. By the end of World War II, CIO unions with Communist-aligned leaders represented about 1,370,000 unionists, one-quarter of the CIO's total mem-

Nathan Witt, a secret Communist and a former member of the Ware group, became the first secretary (staff director) of the NLRB and hired many secret Communists. One of the first three NLRB commissioners, Edwin S. Smith, also became a close ally of the CPUSA. The Communist group in the NLRB held regular caucuses to decide on policy and also communicated regularly with Lee Pressman, the former Ware group member who was also the chief attorney for the CIO. The result was a pronounced NLRB bias in favor of the CIO to the detriment of the AFL and employers who resisted CIO organizing drives. The NLRB's pro-CIO bias became so obvious and the rumors of the existence of the Communist caucus inside the NLRB so strong that by 1940 it became an embarrassment for the Roosevelt administration.[20] Witt was forced to resign from his post, and President Roosevelt refused to reappoint Smith when his term as NLRB commissioner expired in 1941. Smith went on to become a registered agent (professional lobbyist) for the Soviet Union. The officials Roosevelt appointed to replace Smith and Witt quickly dispersed the Communist group in the NLRB.[21]

**Documents 28 and 29** bear on the role of secret Communists in the La Follette committee and the NLRB. Both are 1939 Comintern documents conveying information provided by Raymond (Rudy) Baker, head of the CPUSA secret apparatus. Document 28 states:

---

bership. In addition, Communists were partners, although not dominant ones, in the ruling coalition of the million-member United Auto Workers, the CIO's largest affiliate. Communist unionists also controlled the leadership of many state and local CIO councils, particularly those in New York City, California, Minnesota, Wisconsin, and Washington. On the Communist role in the CIO, see Bert Cochran's *Labor and Communism: The Conflict That Shaped American Unions* (Princeton, N.J.: Princeton University Press, 1977); Harvey A. Levenstein's *Communism, Anticommunism, and the CIO* (Westport, Conn.: Greenwood Press, 1981); and Max Kampelman's *The Communist Party vs. the C.I.O.: A Study in Power Politics* (New York: Praeger, 1957).

20. In 1940 the CPUSA had become savagely hostile to President Roosevelt in accordance with the requirements of the Nazi-Soviet Pact. Communist unionists were uncooperative with the administration's attempts to maintain labor peace in the rapidly expanding armaments industry, and this may have contributed to the Roosevelt administration's decision to move against the Communists inside the NLRB.

21. The role of Communists in the NLRB in the 1930s is set out in Earl Latham, *The Communist Controversy in Washington: From the New Deal to McCarthy* (Cambridge: Harvard University Press, 1966), 124–50.

President Roosevelt now has a federal commission in San Francisco working on actions directed against the workers' movement. That commission has exposed thousands of spies in the workers' movement and has also assisted in exposing spies in the California CP.

LEECH, of the party District Committee for Los Angeles, has been expelled from the CPUSA as a spy.

Wicks figures among those expelled from the party there. He is possessed of great resources; it is my belief that he is a spy.

There are Communists taking part in the work of that commission (Roosevelt is unaware of this).

Communists found their way into that commission through the Communist faction of Washington officials.

## Document 28

Andreev to Dimitrov, 21 January 1939, RTsKhIDNI 495–74–472. Original in Russian.

**22** File with No.180/s
21 January 1939
Secret.

TO THE ECCI GENERAL SECRETARY
Com. G. M. DIMITROV:

On 16 January of this year a discussion of cadre issues was held in the ECCI Cadres Department with a member of the CPUSA Central Control Commission, Com. Raymond Baker, who reported the following:

The CPUSA Central Control Commission consists of 9 members:

1. MINOR, Robert—Chairman of the CCC.

2. LAPIN (DIRBA)—Secretary of the CCC, Latvian by nationality, Secretary of the Control Commission for 10–15 years.

3. MINDEL (Russian)—member of the CPUSA CCC.

4. AUERBACH (American)—"          "     ".

5. PETERS (Hungarian)—    "          "     ".

6. BAKER (Yugoslav)—      "          "     ".

7. HOFFBAUER (German)— "          "     ".

BAKER does not recall the names of the remaining members.

The Communist Party of the US is legal, and therefore certain comrades underestimate [the need] to observe the strictest party secrecy, and fail to demonstrate true vigilance. Registers of active party members, minutes of CC meetings and other vital party documents are stored outside the CC building at an especially secure site.

# Document 28 continued

The safeguarding of documents is being very poorly handled in the District Committees, where apparatus workers often leave party documents on their desks and then leave the room, thus providing an enemy the opportunity to make use of the documents.

The Control Commission is gradually ridding itself of its old staff members, replacing them with new people. Many comrades of the old staff have been working for many years, and they are well known, whereas we must have unknown people on special assignment in the CCC.

Formerly, the CCC concerned itself primarily with breaches of party discipline; at present, the Control Commission is engaged in the most relentless struggle against spies, Lovestoneists, Trotskyists and provocateurs among the working class.

This takes on special significance now that the party has grown significantly and is continuing to grow, and there are greater opportunities for the infiltration of enemy elements into the party.

Apart from the CC, a discipl[inary] commission is in place, dealing with issues of party discipline. The discipl[inary] commission did not deal with issues pertaining to the struggle against espionage and Trotskyism. The last Party Congress found this to be an error, and that commission now has a special person directing special work exposing Trotskyists and spies. He is undercover. That commission has been reinforced with authoritative comrades.

Formerly, the Control Commission devoted itself to investigating complaints. At present, the CC is studying the reasons behind violations of party discipline.

The CC is demanding that in every district lists be compiled of known Trotskyists and Lovestoneists with complete information about them (where they work, their connections).

Formerly a Trotskyist would be called forward at a meeting and expelled from the party on the spot, and that would be the end of the matter; now he is exposed and his connections discovered. The work of uncovering Trotskyists requires considerable experience as well as trained and qualified cadres.

The CCC instructs subordinate organizations on the requisite procedures.

A great deal of this work is being directed by John (Baker does not recall his last name). He is a highly qualified specialist in phone tapping and party secrecy.

The CC possesses many documents incriminating Lovestoneists.

Copies are being made of documents from the Lovestoneists' archive, and that archive will be forwarded to the ECCI in the near future.

It must be admitted that only the CC of the New York organization is doing decent work. The other CCs are working poorly. The key is to select good comrades for membership in the CCs.

# Document 28 *continued*

VERIFICATION OF CADRES

Many biographies of the leadership staff have been compiled. A special person has been assigned this task. However, these biographies are being insufficiently utilized. The accuracy of the information reported in [membership] questionnaires is not being verified.

There are provocateurs operating in San Francisco and Pittsburgh, and information is being passed on to them. Obviously there are provocateurs among the leadership of those district party organizations, but to date the district leadership has been completely powerless to expose them.

President Roosevelt now has a federal commission in San Francisco working on actions directed against the workers' movement. That commission has exposed thousands of spies in the workers' movement and has also assisted in exposing spies in the California CP.

LEECH, of the party District Committee for Los Angeles, has been expelled from the CPUSA as a spy.

Wicks figures among those expelled from the party there. He is possessed of great resources; it is my belief that he is a spy.

There are Communists taking part in the work of that commission (Roosevelt is unaware of this).

Communists found their way into that commission through the Communist faction of Washington officials.

Party work at Ford companies is badly organized. This is attributable to the prohibition of trade unions, the lack of any trade unions there. Thus, at a factory with some 80,000 workers, only 60 are in the party.

The CPUSA CC has assigned the party membership the task of regularly gathering information on the work of enemies of the party. The CPUSA CC has no informers, consequently the Central Committee often does not know how its resolutions are being implemented.

With Com. Browder's consent, an experiment was carried out in New York: informers were sent into [certain] Trotskyist and Lovestoneist organizations. Cadres for this assignment were selected very carefully and screened very thoroughly in advance.

Com. Baker has asked the Cadres Department for guidelines on organizing the struggle against provocation and espionage. In that connection, I request that you authorize Com. Baker to familiarize himself with the document you have approved on the struggle against provocation and espionage.

DIRECTOR OF ECCI CADRES DEPARTMENT     *Andreev*     (ANDREEV)
*He may familiarize* [himself with
the document] *GD*
*24 January 1939*

# Document 29

Illegible to Dimitrov, attached to Andreev to Dimitrov, 21 January 1939, RTsKhIDNI 495–74–472. Original in Russian.

Georgy Mikhailovich!

Comrade Andreev is sending you material on a discussion of cadre issues with a member of the Central Control Commission of the CPUSA, Comrade BAKER, R.

The following particulars are noted in that material:

1. The safeguarding of party documents is being very poorly handled in the District Committees.

2. The CCC possesses many documents incriminating Lovestoneists. Copies are being made of Lovestoneist archival documents, and the archive will soon be sent to the ECCI.

3. Provocateurs are operating in San Francisco and Pittsburgh; information is being passed on to them. Obviously there are provocateurs among the leadership of those district party organizations, but to date the district leadership has been completely powerless to expose them.

4. President Roosevelt now has a federal commission in San Francisco working on actions directed against the workers' movement. That commission has also assisted in exposing spies in the CP of California. There are Communists taking part in the work of that commission (Roosevelt is unaware of this).

5. Com. Baker requests that the Cadres Department provide guidelines on organizing the struggle against provocation and espionage. In that connection, Com. ANDREEV requests that you authorize Com. Baker to familiarize himself with the document you have approved on the struggle against provocation and espionage.

[Signature illegible]

21 January 1939

---

Document 29 recapitulates: "President Roosevelt now has a federal commission in San Francisco working on actions directed against the workers' movement. That commission has also assisted in exposing spies in the CP of California. There are Communists taking part in the work of that commission (Roosevelt is unaware of this)."

In neither document is the federal commission in question identified. The NLRB and the La Follette committee are the most likely candidates.[22] These documents are dated January 1939. In the summer and early fall of 1938, the NLRB undertook an investigation of informers used by West Coast business interests against various CIO unions, including an investigation of the Associated Farmers. Associated Farmers, a large California agribusiness group, felt that Communists were behind the attempt to unionize farm workers and was one of the CPUSA's most active opponents in California.

The NLRB findings encouraged a more extensive investigation by the La Follette committee in the fall of 1938 and during 1939. Committee investigators went after the Associated Farmers, not only looking into its use of labor spies and vigilante assaults on farm unionists but also investigating its support of the campaign to deport union leader Harry Bridges and its infiltration of informers into the gubernatorial campaign of Culbert Olson, a New Deal Democrat. Olson was allied with the California CIO, and a number of secret Communists were appointed to state offices during his administration.[23] John Leech, named in document 28, was a former California Communist party official who testified against Harry Bridges, the militant head of the West Coast International Longshoremen's and Warehousemen's Union. In 1938 the U.S. government unsuccessfully attempted to deport Bridges, an Australian, on the grounds he was a secret Communist.[24] Harry Wicks, also named in document 28, was a prominent CPUSA official expelled by the party as a spy in 1938.

Documents 28 and 29 show that the CPUSA's secret apparatus was linked to a clandestine group of Communists in a United States government agency (probably the La Follette committee or possibly the NLRB), that the Communists manipulated the activities of the agency to serve party interests, and that the Communists had been

22. The reference in the documents to the agency being Roosevelt's "federal commission" should not be taken to mean an executive branch agency, thereby excluding the La Follette committee. To Comintern officials, separation of powers was an unfamiliar concept.

23. The investigation in the fall of 1938 was followed in the summer and fall of 1939 by highly publicized hearings on the Associated Farmers and other anti-union groups; these hearings exposed their activities and revealed their use of coercion and violence against farm workers who attempted to organize unions (Auerbach, *Labor and Liberty*, 177–96).

24. A subsequent volume in this series will reproduce documents definitely establishing Bridges's membership in the CPUSA.

able to gain entry into the agency through "the Communist faction of Washington officials."

The Communist role was a concealed one that depended on deceiving administration leaders; both documents state that President Roosevelt was unaware of the Communist presence. As noted, in 1940, when the Roosevelt administration realized that there was an organized Communist presence in the NLRB, it eliminated it. When critics attacked La Follette's committee for employing Communists, Senator La Follette believed his staff's assurances that the charges had no basis in fact and told the press that the charges were false. John Abt was La Follette's chief counsel, and La Follette entrusted him with considerable independence and authority for the committee's investigations. Abt's own memoirs show that he repaid that trust with deceit and betrayal.[25]

Many historians have failed to come to grips with the issue of Communist infiltration of government agencies or the dubious nature of the Popular Front alliance between Communists and a segment of liberals during the 1930s and 1940s. Previously, evidence of the Communist presence could be trivialized or its reliability questioned. These documents, however, are too clear to allow such evasions. In addition to their own evidentiary weight, they lend crucial support to the large mass of direct and circumstantial evidence indicating a substantial organized Communist presence in a number of government agencies in the 1930s and early 1940s.[26]

---

25. By the fall of 1938, Abt was no longer with the La Follette committee.

26. In addition to the NLRB, the AAA, and the La Follette committee, other agencies for which there is evidence of an organized Communist presence include the National Youth Administration, the Wheeler committee (Senate committee under Senator Burton K. Wheeler that investigated the railroad industry), the National Research Project of the Works Progress Administration, the Treasury Department, and the Federal Theatre Project. Particularly with reference to the La Follette committee and the NLRB, these documents throw into question such matters as the accepted history of the rise of the CIO and such key events as the bloody Memorial Day clash in 1937 between CIO demonstrators and police outside a Republic Steel plant in South Chicago. Most historians have treated the investigations and information produced by the La Follette committee as essentially free of bias. These documents do not prove, but they do suggest, that the La Follette committee's investigations and the NLRB's neutrality during the era of sharp competition between the AFL and the CIO may have been compromised by the actions of secret Communist caucuses. Historians have long known that John L. Lewis, chief founder of the CIO, made use of Communist organizers in the CIO's formative years. However, the

Clandestine activities in a democratic polity unavoidably compromise those involved. Communists lied to and deceived the New Dealers with whom they were allied. Those liberals who believed the denials then denounced as mudslingers those anti-Communists who complained of concealed Communist activity. Furious at denials of what they knew to be true, anti-Communists then suspected that those who denied the Communist presence were themselves dishonest. The Communists' duplicity poisoned normal political relationships and contributed to the harshness of the anti-Communist reaction of the late 1940s and 1950s.

## Peters and the Washington Informant Group, 1943

Other documents also indicate that the secret Communist groups in Washington were engaged in more than a theoretical discussion of Marxism. **Document 30** is a top secret 1943 message to Dimitrov of the Comintern from General Ilichev, head of Soviet military intelligence, the GRU.[27] The foreign intelligence operations of the GRU, though smaller than those of the NKVD, were extensive and included a sizable presence in the United States.

In the message, General Ilichev stated that a "representative" of his agency (that is, a Soviet military intelligence agent) had been in contact with a group of Communists operating in Washington, D.C., and that this group had been assigned by the CPUSA to do

---

extent to which this relationship was based on negotiation and agreement between CIO leaders and the CPUSA has long been disputed. Lewis never admitted any explicit understanding with the Communists, and most historians have tended to believe that Lewis simply needed a large cadre of organizers in a hurry and made use of the ready availability of dedicated Communist organizers on an individual basis; other scholars have seen at most an unspoken understanding between Lewis and the CPUSA. Documents in the Comintern archives show that the understanding was explicit and the result of active negotiations. Documentation of the negotiations and the agreement between John L. Lewis and Sidney Hillman of the CIO and Earl Browder, William Z. Foster, and Clarence Hathaway of the CPUSA, and of the list of organizers the CPUSA authorized Lewis to hire will be reproduced in a subsequent volume of this series (Clarence Hathaway, "Report of Situation in U.S.A. and Work of Party," testimony to the Marty Secretariat, 15 September 1936, RTsKhIDNI 515–1–3967, pp. 1–18).

27. Ilichev became head of Soviet military intelligence in mid-1942 and served in that post until late 1943 (Viktor Suvorov, *Inside Soviet Military Intelligence* [New York: Macmillan 1984], 179). Some sources list Ilichev's first name as Leonid; others as Ivan.

"informational work," a euphemism for spying. Ilichev noted that the group was supervised by "Peter," a representative of the Central Committee of the American Communist party. He added that several members of this group had complained that Peter was not paying sufficient attention to the information they furnished and inquired whether this group was one of the clandestine CPUSA networks operated by the Comintern.

## Document 30

Ilichev to Dimitrov, 5 March 1943, RTsKhIDNI 495–74–486. Original in Russian.

TOP SECRET.
Copy No. 1

PERSONAL.
To Com. DIMITROV

According to a report from our representative in the US, one of the Communist groups that the leadership of the American Comparty has chosen for informational work is operating in Washington.

That group is headed by a CC worker known as "PETER."

Our representative further reports that certain workers in that group are unhappy with "PETER," since he pays almost no attention to informational work and takes no interest in the information received.

Please advise whether this is your group.

Ilichev
(ILICHEV)

5 March 1943
No. 223529ss
2 copies printed
1st—to Com. Dimitrov
2d—for file.

СОВ.СЕКРЕТНО.
Экз.№ 1

ЛИЧНО.

тов.ДИМИТРОВУ.

По сообщению нашего представителя в США, в Вашингтоне действует одна из групп коммунистов, выделенная руководством американской компартии для информационной работы.

Эта группа возглавляется работником ЦК "ПИТЕРОМ".

Наш представитель далее сообщает, что отдельные работники этой группы, недовольны "ПИТЕРОМ", т.к. он почти не уделяет внимания информационной работе и не интересуется получаемой информацией.

Прошу Вас сообщить Ваша ли это группа.

( ИЛЬИЧЕВ )

"5" Марта 1943года.
№ 223529 сс
Отпечат.в 2экз.
1й — т.Димитрову.
2й — в дело.

DOCUMENT 30. Ilichev to Dimitrov, 5 March 1943.

Document 31, a follow-up message to document 30, repeats the reference to "the CC worker known as 'PETER.'"[28] "Peter" is probably J. Peters, because in CPUSA and Comintern documents the "Peter" variation of his name is used frequently, and, although no longer head of the secret apparatus, Peters worked for the Central Committee in 1943. Although not explicit about his work in 1943, document 25 refers to his undertaking "special assignments" for the Central Committee after he was removed as head of the apparatus. Documents 30 and 31 date from the period in which the NKVD and the GRU, the two chief Soviet intelligence services, took over direct supervision of several espionage rings operated by the CPUSA under Comintern supervision; the Comintern itself was on the verge of dissolution. These messages suggest that Soviet intelligence was appraising this group as a possible takeover target.

---

## Document 31

Bolshakov to Dimitrov, 5 May 1943, RTsKhIDNI 495–71–486. Original in Russian.

---

Reply given on 7 May 1943!

GD GD                                                         Top secret

                                                                   Copy No. 1

                                                                   PERSONAL

ECCI

To Com. DIMITROV:

I request that you make arrangements to expedite a reply to our letter of 5 March of the current year, No. 223529, regarding a group of workers singled out by the American Comparty CC for informational work and headed by the CC worker "PETER."

---

28. The Comintern's response could not be located.

What interests us is whether this is your group.

*Bolshakov*
(BOLSHAKOV)

5 May 1943
No. 223570ss
2 copies printed
1st—to ECCI
2d—to file
exec. com. Dashevsky
To No. 145 ab

---

### Copying Confidential State Department Letters, 1936

**Documents 32 and 33** offer additional support for Chambers's story that the Washington Communist underground provided the party with sensitive documents. Both are direct evidence of the theft of confidential information from the U.S. State Department by the CPUSA. Both were found not in the Comintern's records but in the files of the CPUSA that were shipped to the Comintern for safekeeping (see chapter 1).

Document 32 consists of seven paragraphs. The first, written by an unnamed person, probably whoever copied (stole) the material, explains that the second paragraph is an excerpt from a confidential letter written by Ambassador William Bullitt, U.S. envoy to France, to Assistant Secretary of State R. Walton Moore. (Moore, a distinguished member of Virginia's establishment, was known in Washington by the respectful sobriquet "Judge" Moore.) In the letter, Bullitt makes some observations on the improving economic situation in Europe and offers the view that tensions are easing on the continent. The third paragraph, by the unknown thief, notes that the next three paragraphs (the fourth, fifth, and sixth) are quotations from Moore's comments on Bullitt's observations. Moore considers Bullitt's view too optimistic and describes the situation in Europe as highly volatile.

In the final paragraph, the unnamed thief offers his own judgment, stating that the Bullitt and Moore quotations are "both interesting and important because they show attitudes of men in key positions. This Judge Moore has great influence on President Roo-

sevelt. And Bullitt is not undangerous in Paris." This unnamed
writer's comment is an accurate one; both Moore and Bullitt were
personal and political friends of President Roosevelt's. The comment also allows an approximate dating of the excerpts by its reference to Bullitt's being in Paris. Bullitt did not take up his post in
Paris until 13 October 1936. Thus, Bullitt wrote his letter and
Moore made his comment between that date and the date stamped
on the document, 5 January 1937. The unnamed person's reference
to Bullitt as "not undangerous" was also accurate. Bullitt was the
first U.S. ambassador to Moscow following Roosevelt's diplomatic
recognition of the Soviet Union in 1933. He began his service in
Moscow as an enthusiastic supporter of American-Soviet friendship but ended it a determined anti-Communist highly suspicious of
Stalin's foreign policy. Among Roosevelt's close advisers, Bullitt had
one of the strongest anti-Soviet voices.[29]

## Document 32

"Excerpt of a Letter Enclosed to Judge Moore," date-stamped 5 January 1937, RTsKhIDNI
515–1–4077. Original in English. In the original, handwritten brackets are placed around
the final paragraph ("Both interesting and important . . .").

Excerpt of a letter enclosed to Judge Moore of the State Department and written by Ambassador Bullitt, written confidentially.

. . . I confess that I am not nearly so pessimistic as you are. There are periods
in world history when everything is on the down grade, due usually I think to
economic disintegration which affects not only the economic and financial
phases of life, but also the political and all others. There are also times when
there is a general economic upswing, and during these periods everything
becomes easier; people become more reasonable and it is possible to achieve
something constructive. I am convinced that we are now entering a period of
economic prosperity. England is already in that period and most of the British
Empire is entering it. A considerable portion of the sterling bloc is also pro-

29. On Bullitt, Moore, and their relationship with Roosevelt, see Will Brownell
and Richard N. Billings, *So Close to Greatness: A Biography of William C. Bullitt*
(New York: Macmillan, 1987); and Orville H. Bullitt, ed., *For the President: Personal and Secret Correspondence between Franklin D. Roosevelt and William C.
Bullitt* (Boston: Houghton Mifflin, 1972).

gressing most satisfactorily. The swing-up in the United States is absolutely phenomenal. Moreover, in my opinion, it is infinitely sounder than a similar development in 1927 and 1928. The same progress is beginning to appear in Central and South America. I believe that the repercussion on all the countries of the world of this prosperity throughout the western hemisphere and the British Empire will be so great that men will begin again, in spite of lunatic ideas which are prevalent in many quarters, to behave as reasonable human beings. Therefore I feel that there is a sure basis for long-run optimism. I think we shall have anxious moments to go through in the next eighteen months, but I believe that if we can get through that period without catastrophe, there is a great chance that civilized human beings will again be able to make their influence felt throughout the world. . . .

Comment of the receiver before he enclosed it confidentially.

I enclose a copy of a copy of a paragraph from a letter just received from our Ambassador in Paris and I have also received same or nearly same interpretation from our Minister in Berne. Their interpretation of things corresponds with optimistic Nazi view: armament of whole male population under 50 years of age is a good or not a dangerous thing. That was the situation in 1914!

But to me 20,000,000 men in Europe trained for war; 5,000,000 ready to fight on a moment's notice; 10,000,000 engaged in making armaments; 20,000,000,000 dollars of international obligations unmet; and perhaps a 10,000,000,000 dollar Government promises to pay floating from bank to bank, or business firms, does not point towards prosperity. If peoples stop war preparation 20,000,000 people will be killed. Prosperity!

Into this complex 100 American corporations are making contributions arms even without pay except promises to pay! Prosperity!

Both interesting and important because they show attitudes of men in key positions. This Judge Moore has great influence on President Roosevelt. And Bullitt is not undangerous in Paris.

Document 33 is a typed copy of a letter marked "personal" and addressed to "Mr. President." The copy in the CPUSA's records does not show the sender's name, but the letter is datelined "Berlin, October 19, 1936." A check of the William Dodd papers at the Library of Congress showed that the letter was an accurate copy of a letter that Ambassador Dodd, serving in Germany, wrote to Roosevelt.[30] The letter contains a great deal of sensitive diplomatic information. Dodd reported on conversations he had held with Hjalmar Schacht, president of the Reichsbank and Hitler's chief economic adviser; Hans Heinrich Dieckhoff, shortly to become German ambassador to the United States; and Baron Konstantin von Neurath, then German foreign minister. Ambassador Dodd also gave his pessimistic views on the European situation. According to the stamped date, this document, like document 32, reached CPUSA files on 5 January 1937.

---

# Document 33

Unsigned to Mr. President [Roosevelt], 19 October 1936, date-stamped 5 January 1937, RTsKhIDNI 515–1–4077. Original in English.

---

Berlin, October 19, 1936.
PERSONAL

Dear Mr. President:

I congratulate you on what I think will be your second great popular majority. You have therefore another four years, and I fear your problems are going to be as difficult as those of Woodrow Wilson in 1917.

I

According to your request of early August, I have had three talks with officials here who see the Fuehrer often and who seem to know his purposes. The first of these talks was with Dr. Schacht, who fears war here the most. I wrote you that he was a little hopeful, but that Hitler could not participate. On the 16th of September I saw Secretary Dieckhoff, brother-in-law of von Ribbentrop, one of the favorites of the Fuehrer, now Ambassador in London. Incidentally the Times story was mentioned. He was of the same attitude as Schacht only less committal. On the 15th of October I saw Minister von Neurath, head of the Foreign Office here, and the subject of the German-British relations was discussed. When I asked whether Germany would really participate in the oft-proposed Locarno conference he said, "In case England satisfies the Italian demands." This led to a reference to the imminent danger of war her and I asked whether Hitler would agree to participate in a peace conference of the greater powers. He said, "Only in case the main points are agreed to before-

30. Dodd's copy of this letter is in box 49, William E. Dodd Papers, Manuscript Division, Library of Congress.

hand." This I took to mean a previous promise to Italy and Germany of colonies and condemnation of Russia. I asked whether the Fuehrer intended to send the Russian Ambassador home. He said no, but added, "The Russian position here is getting to be so embarrasing that I think he will go home"—no successor to be appointed. This last he did not say but made me believe.

These interviews and the statements rather definitely made, seem to me to mean no approval of a peace conference unless Germany and Italy are granted about all they want. And events in Europe since last December all point the same way: Hitler and Mussolini intend to control all Europe. If that be agreed to beforehand, a peace conference is quite possible; but what sort of a peace? Anyone who knows the sophomoric and egotistic mentalities of these men and their chief supporters can hardly fail to forecast the coming state of European civilization. Is there any way democratic countries can save the civilization which dates back to Luther, Erasmus, the Hollanders and the English?

Our country made democracy possible for Europe between 1776 and 1815, the population 3,000,000, to 8,000,000. It was a "miracle" which made the French Revolution possible, and then all western Europe became substantially democratic before 1860. The war of 1914–18 would have subjected Europe to a single dictatorship but for the intervention of our country: our one aim to save democracy. The blunders all greater nations have made since 1920 surpass anything recorded in modern history. Now we see clearly what is before us. Can our country of 130,000,000 people and more real wealth than all western Europe do anything? Our people say no; and the Senate says the Constitution authorizes one third of their members to defeat any policy the President might persuade men to accept: their treatment of Wilson' programme.

Much as I believe in peace as our best policy, I cannot avoid the fears which Wilson emphasized more than once in conversations with me, August 15, 1915 and later: the breakdown of democracy in all Europe will be a disaster to the people. But what can you do? At the present moment more than a hundred American corporations have subsidiaries here or cooperative understandings. The Du Ponts have three allies in Germany that are aiding in the armament business. Their chief ally is the L.G. Farben company, a part of the government which gives 200,000 marks a year to one propaganda organization operating on American opinion. Standard Oil Company (New York sub-company) sent $2,000,000 here in December 1933 and has made $500,000 a year helping Germans make Ersatz gas for war purposes; but Standard Oil cannot take any of its earnings out of the country except in goods. They do little of this, report their earnings at home, but do not explain the facts. The International Harvester Company president told me their business here rose 33% a year (arms manufacture I believe) but they could take nothing out. Even our airplane people have secret arrangement with Krupps. General Motor Company and Ford do enormous businesses here through their subsidiaries and take no profits out. I mention these facts because they complicate things and add to war dangers. If you wish proof of this story, talk with our Commercial Attache here, Douglas Miller, in the United States till early December.

Whether our people can prevent another world war is certainly a grave question. Yet no real democratic President can fail to realize the consequences of a world war to us. There is, however, increasing evidence here, in Rome, Paris and London that we may not have a war soon. Germany and Italy with the greatest war equipments any people have ever had, are cooperating in such a way that their dictators may do what they wish. You saw what happened last winter when Mussolini agreed publicly to support Hitler's Rhine move. Everybody recognizes the helplessness of France when Italy and Germany sent men, airplanes and arms to the Spanish revolutionists from July to October. And the second week in September Hitler, Goebbels and Rosenberg delivered offensive attacks upon democracies. If you or the English monarch delivered such an attack on neighboring powers serious results would almost surely follow among one's constituents. The democratic peoples in Europe made no protests, not even Russia. Of course, the cruel dictatorship in Moscow could hardly look for international support. At the present moment small European democracies: Czechoslovakia, Sweden, Denmark, Holland and Switzerland, according to their representatives, are contemplating some such declarations as ungrateful Belgium made the other day. These Ministers say the League of Nations and the World Court have no more value; one sees readily why small powers resort to armed neutrality.

With so many democracies nervous, even fearful of annexations, and England and France helpless as a result of their foolish decisions since 1930, why may not Hitler annex strategic parts of the Balkan area and Mussolini seize islands in the Mediterranean without war? Spain is to be a protectorate of Italy, perhaps Egypt annexed. High officials here say Germany is to have colonies in the Far East with Italian-Japanese approval. One thing is certain: these dictators mean to dominate Europe and there is a fair chance of their doing it without war.

One serious difficulty is mentioned here by men like Dr. Schacht, and that is the enormous debt situation. According to best possible figures here, Germany owes her own people 45,000,000,000 marks, only 18,000,000,000 publicly acknowledged by the Reichsbank. Debts to outside countries certainly amount to something like 15,000,000,000 with interest unpaid to many creditors. This debt situation is known to enough people to cause much uneasiness. If crops were to fail by half for a single year, there would be starvation to millions of people unless international credit could be had. The barrier system forbids imports even of foodstuffs. This dilemna is duplicated in Italy. So loans and commercial concessions may become most vital matters. Of course Germany rarely has a drouth; but five successive years of excellent crops suggest always the possibility of a short harvest. Hitler said a few days ago that a twenty percent shortage would be a calamity of the first order. A few days later Hess (intimate counseller of Hitler) said: "Do not forget that cannon are better than butter."

The second dilemna will come when German roads from Berlin to all frontiers (roads so built that all crossings are under or above and speed is said to be 200 miles an hour) and the Germany armaments are completed. That will mean three to four millions unemployed. At present Germany has only one million unemployed. Four or five millions of unemployed would be more serious here than twenty million with us. A debt here of 60 million marks is far more serious in comparison with Germany income than 60 billion dollars with us.

A dictator of sophomoric psychology would probably go to war to avoid possible difficulties, even with his submissive people. Of course successful threats, such as we have witnessed the last year or two, might bring annexations and postponement of war; but these cannot solve serious economic situations. And here comes one more opportunity of the United States to cooperate with European democracies. The stabilization matter suggests much, and increasing cooperation with the United States suggests more. But can our people ever recognize the importance of lowering tariffs for cooperating countries? Wilson's second method of bringing about world peace was freer trade. His first one was naturally the guarantee by larger powers of the borders and rights of smaller ones. Both of these have been violated almost regularly since 1920 and consequently there has been no real League of Nations.

This long story may not be altogether right; but it represents the best information I have been able to gather. One thing is certain: all well-informed people here, even distinguished Germans, think modern civilization is in grave danger, and they repeat their opinions to me: the cooperation of the United States with European democracies is the only hope we have. How can you lead our people to a correct understanding of things when they allowed a minority of the Senate (contrary to the intentions of the writers of our Constitution) to defeat Wilson's marvellous democratic foreign agreements in 1919, even if the Treaty of Versailles was bad? Certainly it was nothing like the treaty of Brest-Litovsk the year before. If you could only get the great nations to see things as they are and apply their coercive power to any leader who wishes to go back to the fifteenth century morals! That would be what Henry IV of France tried to do, what Jefferson hoped for in 1807 and what Wilson almost accomplished in 1918–19.

Sincerely yours,

---

Dodd's letter would have gone to President Roosevelt via the State Department. Bullitt's letter, of course, went directly to Moore at the State Department. The Dodd and Bullitt letters were the sort of diplomatic correspondence that circulated for informational purposes among policy-making officials in the State Department. Often other officials would make comments on the material being circulated. Moore himself refers to enclosing a passage from Bullitt's letter, together with his comments, to others for informational purposes. Most likely, documents 32 and 33 were surreptitiously copied at the State Department by a member of the Communist underground in Washington.[31]

Documents 32 and 33 do not reveal who copied the letters. Alger Hiss went to work in the State Department in September 1936, just prior to when these letters would have reached there. His position as an assistant to Assistant Secretary of State Francis B. Sayre would have given him access to the informational correspondence that circulated through Sayre's office. Many of the documents that Chambers later produced implicating Hiss in espionage were of this sort. However, it is also possible that these documents were copied by some other Communist source at the State Department. Chambers, for example, also received material from another State Department official, Julian Wadleigh (an economist in the Trade Agreements Section), and there were at least two other Communist sources in the State Department at the time: Laurence Duggan in the Latin American Division and Noel Field in the West European

---

31. Dodd's letter ultimately reached President Roosevelt, and it is possible that, given their relationship, Moore sent Bullitt's letter and his own comments to Roosevelt as well. It is therefore possible, but much less likely, that the material was secretly copied at the White House rather than at the State Department.

Division. Documents 32 and 33 would very likely have circulated through the West European Division. Although the source who copied this information and provided it to the CPUSA cannot be identified, its presence in CPUSA files confirms Chambers's story that the Communist party had sources in the U.S. State Department supplying it with sensitive material.

Hiss's partisans and revisionist historians notwithstanding, these documents take us into the intricate internal workings of the secret apparatus whose members operated as a coordinated group within government agencies. A good deal more than the abstract discussion of Marxism, as Lee Pressman would have it, was at stake in their activities. Both the CPUSA and the Comintern expected secret Communists to influence government policy in accord with a secret agenda, and the modes of influence apparently included pilfering government documents and transmitting useful information to Communist supervisors, thereby jeopardizing the integrity of the governmental process.

# CHAPTER FOUR

# The Secret Apparatus Branches Out

DURING THE SOVIET GREAT TERROR of the mid- and late-1930s, the CPUSA and its covert arm reflected Stalin's obsessions by waging their own war on ideological deviationists and suspected spies, even taking their paranoia into the Spanish Civil War.

## The Secret Apparatus under Rudy Baker, 1938–1940

The "Brief on the Work of the CPUSA Secret Apparatus" (document 27) stated that Rudy Baker took over as head of the Communist underground in June 1938. Rudy Baker, born in Yugoslavia in 1898, immigrated to the United States at an early age and became a naturalized citizen. According to a 1939 Comintern biography, **document 34,** Baker joined the American Communist party at its founding in 1919 and by the early 1920s was a professional revolutionary (functionary or cadre in Communist jargon) working for the party in a variety of posts.[1] He trained at the International Lenin School in Moscow from 1927 to 1930 and was a member of the Communist Party of the Soviet Union during that time. Although

1. The Comintern required its cadre to prepare autobiographies; from these documents and from other records, the Comintern prepared biographies. Comintern officials used these biographies to familiarize themselves with the background of their cadre and to provide evidence of shortcomings should a Comminternist be found wanting. Baker's biography, for example, contains a notation that his autobiography failed to list his membership in the CPSU and cites the reprimand he received for his factional activities. This biography was prepared by the Comintern's personnel department to accompany Baker's "Brief" when it reached Dimitrov.

theoretically equal, in practice members of any non-Soviet Communist party were not equal in status to members of the CPSU. The Soviets extended CPSU membership to selected members of foreign parties whom they judged suitable. **Document 35** lists seventeen other Americans at the Lenin school admitted to the Soviet Communist party in 1930.[2]

---

# Document 34

F. Nikov biographical report on Baker, January 1939, RTsKhIDNI 495–74–472. Original in Russian. "AUCP(b)" stands for All-Union Communist Party (Bolshevik), the name of the CPSU in 1928–1930. The ILS is the International Lenin School. The biography lists Baker's first name as Raymond, but Baker was commonly known as Rudy.

---

Secret

### REPORT

BAKER, Raymond (BLUM, RUDOLPH, JOHN TAYLOR): Member of the Central Control Commission of the CPUSA, assigned "special work" by the CPUSA CC.

Born 1898 in Yugoslavia. Yugoslav by nationality. American citizenship. Worker (machinist). Education: four years of primary school, attended evening technical school and the ILS (two years). Knows English, Russian, and a little German.

His father is a worker, himself a member of the US Socialist Party since 1914.

A member of the CPUSA since the day it was founded in 1919. 1928–30: A member of the AUCP(b). 1930: made a member-elect of the CPUSA CC. 1931–34: a member of the CPUSA CC.

1919–24: A member of party factions in various trade unions. 1924–26: A member of the party district committee in Philadelphia.

1926–27: Performed the functions of district party organizer in Detroit.

1927–30: Studied at the ILS.

1930–31: Directed the organizational department of the CPUSA CC. Partly involved in illegal work (Korea, England, Canada).

1931–39: A party functionary.

1918–22: A member of the IWW.

1918–21: A member of the International Association of Machinists.

In his autobiography Baker writes that in 1916 he was one of the leaders of a strike involving 100,000 workers.

---

2. Several on this list later became prominent in the CPUSA. Ben Gold headed the CIO's Fur and Leather Workers Union. Esther Carroll and Rebecca Grecht were longtime organizers. George Hewitt later broke with the CPUSA and testified against it.

## Document 34 *continued*

1910–12: Worked in a glass factory.

1912–21: Worked in various enterprises.

1921–27: A union functionary. Arrested several times.

1916: During a major strike, arrested and served 18 months in a US prison.

1918: Arrested for antiwar activities, jailed for 3 months.

Baker's wife is Lillian Schombald, Hungarian by nationality, a member of the CPUSA since 1924.

Baker's brother, John Blum, was a member of the Socialist Party until 1920. Raymond Baker himself sided with the Foster faction from 1925 to 1930. Throughout this period he stubbornly defended the minority policy. The party purging commission for students at the ILS pronounced the following judgment on Baker: "Failed to realize fully and adequately how entirely unacceptable was the unprincipled struggle waged by the minority faction of the CPUSA, despite repeated demands from the Comintern to discontinue that struggle. [Baker is to be] reprimanded. Consider confirmed."

In his autobiography Baker does not indicate that he was a member of the AUCP(b) from 1928 to 1930. He concealed the fact that he had been issued a party penalty—a reprimand—by the purging commission of the AUCP(b) in 1929.

His academic and social work in the ILS was favorably evaluated.

Source: Materials from personal file.
Responsible assessor from the ECCI Personnel Dept.: Nikov

Г. NIKOV

*It should have been made clear why he did not indicate having been a member of the AUCP(b), and why he concealed the fact that he'd been issued a Party penalty. 24 January 1939. GD.*

---

## Document 35

"This Is to Certify," Secretariat of CPUSA, 5 September 1930, RTsKhIDNI 515–1–1869. Original in English.

---

No. 36-T

Sept. 5, 1930

THIS IS TO CERTIFY, That the following comrades, active members in good standing of the Communist Party of the U.S.A., are hereby granted transfers to the Communist Party of the Soviet Union, where they will be staying for an indefinite period as students at the Lenin School.

1. Walter Burke,
2. Arnold Arnio,
3. Phil Bart,
4. Herbert Irwin,

5. Edwin Wickstrom,
6. Rebecca Grecht,
7. Chas. Kapanaris.
8. D.Uchida.
9. G.Hewitt,
10. Egan Anderson,
11. Kay Heikkila,
12. Alphonso Gonzales,
13. H.R.Hutchins,
14. Gilbert Lewis,
15. Frank Mozer,
16. Esther Carroll,
17. Ben Gold.
With Communist Greetings,
FOR THE SECRETARIAT.

---

When he returned to the United States in 1930, Baker became head of the CPUSA's Organizational Department, and in 1931 he became a member of the prestigious Central Committee. Later he joined the Central Control Commission, a body charged with maintaining internal party discipline and ideological purity. The Comintern's biography on Baker states that in the early 1930s he was "partly involved in illegal work (Korea, England, Canada)." This remark confirms a hitherto unsupported assertion by Louis Budenz, once a member of the CPUSA Central Committee and editor of the *Daily Worker,* who split with the party in 1945 and converted to Roman Catholicism. Although much of what Budenz wrote in his anti-Communist days was accurate, he sometimes over-dramatized or exaggerated his claims, and many historians have dismissed his entire testimony. One of the points Budenz made in a 1948 book about the conspiratorial nature of communism was that while a member of the CPUSA he had heard that Rudy Baker had worked for Soviet intelligence in Canada.[3] Document 34's mention of Baker's 1939 assignment to " 'special work' by the CPUSA CC" is a reference to his heading the CPUSA secret apparatus. As noted

3. Louis Budenz, *Men without Faces: The Communist Conspiracy in the USA* (New York: Harper and Brothers, 1948), 18–19.

No. 36-T

Sept. 5, 1930

THIS IS TO CERTIFY,
That the following com-
rades, active members in
good standing of the
Communist Party of the
U.S.A., are hereby grant-
ed transfers to the
Communist Party of the
Soviet Union, where they
will be staying for an
indefinite period as
students at the Lenin
School.
1. Walter Burke,
2. Arnold Arnio,
3. Phil Bart,
4. Herbert Irwin,
5. Edwin Wickstrom,
6. Rebecca Grecht,
7. Chas. Kapanaris.
8. D.Uchida.
9. G.Hewitt,
10. Egan Anderson,
11. Kay Heikkila,
12. Alphonso Gonzales,
13. H.R.Hutchins,
14. Gilbert Lewis,
15. Frank Mozer,
16. Esther Carroll,
17. Ben Gold.

With Communist Greetings,


FOR THE SECRETARIAT.

DOCUMENT 35. "This Is to Certify," Secretariat of CPUSA, 5 September 1930.

in chapter 2, Baker directed the clandestine work of the San Francisco bureau of the Pan-Pacific Trade Union Secretariat under the pseudonym Betford.

In the "Brief," Baker wrote that when he was named head of the secret apparatus, this was "known only to Browder, Stachel, Weiner, Peters, and now Pat Toohey."[4] Baker emphasized that he had made improvements in Peters's arrangements. Peters did not have a full-time party post that provided cover for his secret work. Consequently, Baker explained, "the problem with this work was that it became generally known that this work was being directed by PETERS." In contrast, Baker continued in his existing party posts on the Central Control Commission and several other party commissions, so "there is no reason for anyone to reflect or puzzle over what sort of work Baker is doing. . . . Baker's special-work goes unnoticed and unknown." Baker's assignment to public party duties in addition to heading the secret apparatus was in line with a CPUSA Political Bureau decision in 1934: "that those comrades of the PolBuro who are engaged in special work shall be assigned to some work in addition to their special work. Motion carried unanimously."[5] This directive also demonstrates that the top leadership of the CPUSA knew about the existence of the party's clandestine arm.

## Fighting Ideological Deviationists and Other Enemies

In document 27, Baker also found fault with the secret apparatus under Peters for its lack of emphasis on ideological purity, complaining that "the department did not address the problem of exposing enemies within the party." Baker was militant about ideological conformity.

In a bloodless imitation of Stalin's murderous purges, the CPUSA waged war in the 1930s against real and imagined ideological ene-

4. Earl Browder, general secretary of the CPUSA, was the party's leader. Jack Stachel was the party's organizational secretary and a Browder confidant. William Weiner was the party's financial secretary. Peters, as noted earlier, was Baker's predecessor. Pat Toohey was the CPUSA's representative to the Communist International in Moscow in 1939.

5. CPUSA Political Bureau minutes of 12 April 1934, RTsKhIDNI 515–1–3448.

mies, chiefly Trotskyists and Lovestoneists. The American followers of the exiled Bolshevik leader Leon Trotsky had been expelled from the CPUSA in 1928. American Trotskyists had a
number of talented leaders but very few followers and little institutional support. They loomed large in the eyes of American Communists simply because of Stalin's maniacal insistence that Trotskyism
was a powerful worldwide conspiracy. According to the Soviets,
Trotskyists had infiltrated Communist parties everywhere and were
in league with remnants of the tsarist White Guard and the secret
services of Japan, Britain, and Germany in an effort to overthrow
the Soviet state. The Lovestoneists were followers of Jay Lovestone,
CPUSA general secretary from 1927 to 1929, who had been ousted
on Stalin's orders for suspected ideological kinship with Nikolai
Bukharin, another purged Soviet leader. Stalin accused Bukharin
and his followers of joining in the Trotskyist–White Guard–
British–German–Japanese plot. This groundless accusation justified purges and executions that cost millions their lives and sent
millions of others to labor camps. Like the American Trotskyists,
the Lovestoneists had some talented leaders but only a tiny
following.

### Weeding Out Internal Enemies

Baker, in document 27, endorsed the importance of the war on the
party's splinter groups, explaining: "Our experience has shown
that in those districts where no serious political and ideological
struggle was waged against Trotskyism and Lovestoneism, not only
did enemies inflict significant damage on the workers' movement,
but—as happened in Detroit—counterrevolutionary ideology penetrated the party under various disguises." Each regional branch of
the secret apparatus was required to "compile a comprehensive list
of Trotskyists and Lovestoneists on its territory, including their
names, addresses, biographies, connections, the organizations to
which they belong, who their friends and wives are, and so on. In
other words, provide complete information on each of these
enemies."

In the "Brief," Baker said that Comrade John of the secret apparatus was then (January 1939) in California "for a month to work

on exposing suspect elements in the district leadership apparatus and to assist in forming the district's own apparatus to continue that work." Baker's statement that comrade John had established a special investigatory department in the California Communist party parallels a later remark by Communist leader Steve Nelson. Nelson wrote in his memoir that in 1939 he had been assigned to a "special control commission whose existence was known only to a few Party leaders" to seek out informants and spies in the California Communist party.[6] Baker said that after completing his work in California, John would be sent on two-week tours to Washington state, Illinois, Michigan, Ohio, and Pennsylvania to set up similar investigatory units.

In a meeting with Comintern officials, reported in document 28, Baker further praised John's work and noted that he "is a highly qualified specialist in phone tapping and party secrecy" and "he is undercover." Baker did not recall comrade John's full name, but he may be John L. Spivak. Proof is elusive, but several items, including evidence turned up in a secret FBI examination of Communist records (discussed below), point to Spivak. A left-wing journalist who always denied Communist ties, Spivak specialized in exposing the activities of right-wing organizations. In 1930 New York City Police Commissioner Grover Whalen produced several sensational documents showing that Amtorg, the USSR's trading organization, was involved in espionage. Spivak easily demonstrated that the documents were forgeries. However, the evidence Spivak produced and the circumstances of his finding it suggest that he had prior knowledge of the forgeries and that the documents had been foisted on the police with the intent of embarrassing them by Spivak's subsequent exposure of the forgeries.[7]

Spivak later published frequently in the *Daily Worker* and other Communist publications. The U.S. Justice Department identified him as a Communist in 1942, and in 1945 Elizabeth Bentley, a former Soviet spy, told the FBI in a secret statement that Spivak did

6. Steve Nelson, James R. Barrett, and Rob Ruck, *Steve Nelson, American Radical* (Pittsburgh: University of Pittsburgh Press, 1981), 42, 242–43.

7. Spivak's role in the Whalen forgeries is described in Herbert Romerstein and Stanislav Levchenko, *The KGB against the "Main Enemy"* (Lexington, Mass.: Lexington Books, 1989), 47–53.

investigative work for her espionage ring.[8] In 1952 a former CPUSA official, John Lautner, identified Spivak as a secret member of the party's security apparatus.[9] An illustration of the party's use of Spivak's services is provided in a 1934 letter from Sam Darcy, head of the California Communist party, urging the party's Organization Commission to "call in John Spivak" to investigate the fascistic Silver Shirts.[10]

Spivak was traveling in the West at the time that Baker's memo suggests.[11] Furthermore, Steve Nelson described one unnamed member of the special control commission on which he served in California as having "a certain technical expertise that enabled him to detect wiretaps and electronic surveillance," a depiction that fits with the Comintern's description of comrade John.[12] The time that Nelson specifies in his memoir coincides with the time given in

8. Elizabeth Bentley, "Statement to the Federal Bureau of Investigation, 30 November 1945," FOIA document, 26, 29, 67.

9. Lautner testimony, transcript of proceedings held before the Subversive Activities Control Board in the matter of *McGrath vs. Communist Party of the U.S.A.*, 11 February 1952, pp. 10,009–10,010 (reprinted on microfilm in *Records of the Subversive Activities Control Board, 1950–1972*, pt. 1 [Frederick, Md.: University Press of America, 1988], reel 17). In the purge trial of Hungarian Communist leader Laszlo Rajk (later executed), Stalin's agents fabricated evidence linking Rajk to American intelligence through Lautner, a twenty-year veteran of the CPUSA and a leader of its work among Hungarian-Americans. During World War II, Lautner entered the U.S. Army, where his Hungarian background and language skills led to his assignment to military intelligence and psychological warfare (propaganda) work, during the course of which he had contact with some Hungarian Communists. This contact formed the basis for the charge that Lautner was an agent of American intelligence who had subverted various Hungarian Communists. American Communist leaders interrogated Lautner at gunpoint and expelled him from the CPUSA as an "enemy of the working class." Joe Brandt and Saul Wellman, who had served in the International Brigades as political commissars, conducted the interrogation. Lautner's wife, a loyal Communist, left him. The evidence against Lautner was entirely false. After this experience, Lautner testified freely about his Communist career. Lautner's story is related in his testimony, 10 July 1953, Senate Subcommittee to Investigate the Administration of the Internal Security Act, *Communist Underground Printing Facilities and Illegal Propaganda*, 83d Cong., 1st sess., 1953, 323–26; Herbert L. Packer, *Ex-Communist Witnesses: Four Studies in Fact Finding* (Stanford, Calif.: Stanford University Press, 1962), 178–220; and Joseph R. Starobin, *American Communism in Crisis, 1943–1957* (Cambridge: Harvard University Press, 1972), 218–19, 306n.

10. Darcy to Organizational Commission, 16 May 1934, RTsKhIDNI 515–1–3613.

11. John L. Spivak, *A Man in His Time* (New York: Horizon Press, 1967), chaps. 30–33.

12. Nelson, Barrett, and Ruck, *Steve Nelson*, 242.

Baker's report for when John was in California to help the party "weed out the enemies in our ranks." When asked about this in 1992, however, Nelson said that he had forgotten the name of his special control commission compatriot but that it was not Spivak. He insisted that Spivak was not a Communist, only an "anti-Fascist journalist."[13]

### Stealing the Files of Party Enemies

In the "Brief," Baker noted that an unnamed New York agent of the secret apparatus "has already exposed quite a number of sophisticated spies and Trotskyists in the ranks of the party. This comrade infiltrated the Lovestoneist organization and obtained important materials," and now "highly successful efforts are being made to infiltrate the New York Trotskyist organization." Baker's reference to the secret apparatus obtaining Lovestoneist material refers to stealing files. **Document 36** is a letter to Dimitrov from Pat Toohey, newly arrived CPUSA representative to the Communist International. Toohey reports that "the entire archives of the notorious Jay Lovestone has come into the possession of our Central Committee. These archives are the complete records of Lovestone's letters, documents, addresses and financial dealings for the past 10 years. These records ante-date Lovestone's expulsion from the Communist Party. . . . Some of these documents refer to certain persons in the USSR who are mentioned in letters which discuss the trials of the Trotskyist-Bukharin spies." Toohey says the CPUSA will use the material "when most advantageous" and will send to Moscow those matters of interest to the Comintern. That the Comintern accepted the offer is verified in document 29. This Comintern memo states that the CPUSA "possesses many documents incriminating Lovestoneists. Copies are being made of Lovestoneist archival documents, and the archive will soon be sent to the ECCI [Executive Committee of the Communist International]." A similar statement was made in document 28.

13. In this interview, Nelson also denied knowledge of CPUSA covert operations against Trotskyists and Lovestoneists. Nelson also stated that historians should not use documents found in any Soviet archive (John Haynes's phone interview with Steve Nelson, 31 August 1992). In his memoir, Nelson mentioned a relationship with Baker in four places and noted that he had shared an apartment with him for a time (Nelson, Barrett, and Ruck, *Steve Nelson*, 28, 42, 51, 125).

# Document 36

Toohey to Dimitrov, 19 September 1938, RTsKhIDNI 495–74–466. Original in English. Handwritten annotations in Russian. The Moskvin annotation leaves unclear whether the reference is to something Moskvin sent in 1938 as director of the OMS, which supervised Comintern covert activity, or to someone or something he sent in the 1920s as head of the OGPU's foreign espionage operations.

USA                                          *Sent by Com Moskvin*
                                                    *9/19/38*

To: Comrade Dmitroff
From: Pat Toohey, Representative C.P., USA.
Subject: Message from Comrade Browder.

Dear Comrade Dmitroff:

I intended to give you this message upon my arrival but grippe and its aftermath prevented me from doing so. Because the doctors state that an excessive weakness will keep me away from work for some days, I therefore send this message.

The entire archives of the notorious Jay Lovestone has come into the possession of our Central Committee. These archives are the complete records of Lovestone's letters, documents, addresses and financial dealings for the past 10 years. These records ante-date Lovestone's expulsion from the Communist Party

These records include documents revealing Lovestone's close connection with notorious anti working class and bourgeois forces in America and in Europe. There are considerable documents relating to Lovestone's international dealings, plus letters and addresses of his European cohorts. Some of these documents refer to certain persons in the USSR who are mentioned in letters which discuss the trials of the Trotskyist-Bukharin spies. Others of these letters deal with some shady munitions deal which Lovestone was engaged in.

Some of these documents indicate that Lovestone maintains very close connection with one Mendelsohn of Canada, whom Comrade Browder believes to be a Soviet employee of an important branch (OGPU). Lovestone seems especially close to Mrs. Mendelsohn according to these records.

These records indicate that Lovestone has an approximate income of $40,000 yearly, of which $25,000 is spent on his individual expenses and living costs. He maintained four bank accounts in four names, kept up four different homes with as many separate identies.

Upon discovery of his loss of these records, Lovestone fled to Canada in Panic, but returned only after no immediate exposure was made.

While most of this material is of interest of our Central Committee, Comrade Browder desires to transmit the materials which refer to international matters to the office here. The American materials will be used when most advantageous.

Comrade Browder will turn over to "Smith" these materials if you so desire and inform "Smith" to obtain them, but bearing in mind the Mendelsohn matter and if there are others like him, Comrade Browder will transmit these materials via his own methods if he is notified to "send special materials yourself".

In conclusion, allow me to say I await most eagerly my opportunity to commence work, and am most happy to have merited the confidence of my Central Committee to be assigned to work under your direct and inspiring leadership.

> With warm Communist greetings,
> *Pat Toohey.*

I will appreciate verification of your receiving this message.

The Toohey letter also reveals that Jay Lovestone maintained connections with Soviet intelligence even after his ouster from the CPUSA. Toohey wrote that "some of these documents indicate that Lovestone maintains very close connection with one Mendelsohn of Canada, whom Comrade Browder believes to be a Soviet employee of an important branch. Lovestone seems especially close to Mrs. Mendelsohn according to these records." "An important branch" is a not very subtle euphemism for one of the Soviet intelligence services. The underlining by hand of the word *important* and the insertion of the Cyrillic letters "OGPU" after the word *branch* emphasize these intelligence ties.

Toohey's comments and the handwritten annotations confirm the hitherto undocumented statement by Benjamin Gitlow, who was expelled with Lovestone in 1929, that Lovestone continued to work with Soviet intelligence until 1936, hoping to reenter the

Communist movement. Jay Lovestone's links to the OGPU and Mendelsohn went back at least to 1926. In the Comintern archive is a memo from Lovestone to Ella Wolfe, wife of Lovestone's chief lieutenant, Bertram Wolfe. The memo instructs Ella to send a hidden Lovestone passport to Mendelsohn in Canada, making sure that the return address was not her own but an innocuous one. She was to ask Mendelsohn to get the passport (clearly a false one) renewed and obtain a visa for Germany and hold the passport and visa for Lovestone. Lovestone wrote: "You must keep in the strictest confidence, the whole transaction and every item and detail of it. Only you and Bert know about it."[14] Lovestone's contacts with Mendelsohn support Gitlow's story. This work, however, did not earn him reentry into the CPUSA, and by the late 1930s Lovestone turned harshly anti-Communist. Indeed, over time he became one of the most influential and effective, although little known, anti-Communist activists in the United States.[15]

In 1939 Lovestone testified to a congressional committee that in July 1938 his home had been burglarized, but the thief had removed only political files rather than valuables. Shortly thereafter, the CPUSA's *Daily Worker* published several of his letters in an attempt to discredit him. Lovestone said that he later learned that the burglary had been carried out by Leon Josephson.[16] The files stolen in July were undoubtedly the ones about which Toohey bragged in his September letter, document 36. In 1944, FBI agents secretly (and apparently without a warrant) entered the home of Philip Levy in

14. Benjamin Gitlow, *The Whole of Their Lives* (New York: Scribner's, 1948), 141; Lovestone to Ella, 19 October 1926, RTsKhIDNI 515-1-763.

15. Earl Latham, *The Communist Controversy in Washington: From the New Deal to McCarthy* (Cambridge: Harvard University Press, 1966), 81–85; Romerstein and Levchenko, *The KGB against the "Main Enemy,"* 11–13. The remark about Mrs. Mendelsohn also strengthens stories linking Lovestone romantically with Mrs. Mendelsohn. Gitlow and Lovestone adopted different varieties of anti-communism. Gitlow moved into conservative anti-Communist circles, whereas Lovestone remained on the left and devoted himself to the anti-Communist wing of the labor movement. He became the chief adviser on foreign policy to George Meany, head of the AFL and, later, of the AFL-CIO. Lovestone supervised the AFL's highly successful program of helping noncommunist trade unions in Western Europe beat back a determined Communist attempt to dominate the Western European labor movement after World War II, a program he later extended worldwide.

16. Lovestone testimony, 2 December 1939, House Special Committee on Un-American Activities, *Congressional Investigation of Un-American Propaganda*, vol. 11 (Washington, D.C.: GPO, 1940), 7147.

search of information on Communist activities. They found files belonging to Leon Josephson and John Spivak, along with Jay Lovestone's purloined material. The FBI concluded that the CPUSA had placed the files with Levy for safekeeping. Thus, an FBI burglary of a Communist turned up the swag of the earlier Communist burglary of Lovestone.[17] The CPUSA's theft of Lovestone's files was not an isolated occurrence. Steve Nelson, in discussing his work for the California special control commission, described the theft, photographing, and surreptitious return of files of the Associated Farmers, the California anti-Communist organization, during the time when the La Follette committee was investigating that group. For the events described in Nelson's story and in documents 28 and 29 the coincidence of timing, geography, and subject is striking, and the events may be connected.[18]

## Enforcing Ideological Conformity

Baker's absorption with the imagined Trotskyist-Lovestoneist menace was widely shared in the party. **Document 37** is a CPUSA report that illustrates the seriousness with which the party viewed ideological deviation. The document is a 1938 report from Charles Dirba, head of the Central Control Commission, to the party's leadership (plenum). Dirba calls upon the CPUSA to emulate the Moscow Trials. These were the grotesque charades in which scores of old Bolsheviks who had fallen afoul of Stalin were condemned and executed on trumped-up charges of treason. He writes: "The time has come, in our opinion, when every single leading comrade in our Party, including every branch secretary and literature agent must be thoroughly familiar with the records of the trials of the Trotskyite and Bukharinite groups of German fascist spies in the USSR. With-

17. The FBI examined the files but did not remove them. The FBI's examination became public because Judith Coplon, a Soviet spy working at the Justice Department, stole the FBI report on the break-in. The FBI, in turn, arrested Coplon in 1949 in the act of turning over the report and other FBI counterintelligence material to a Soviet diplomat. The report became an exhibit in Coplon's ensuing trial (defense exhibit 119, *United States v. Judith Coplon* [criminal case 381-49], United States District Court for the District of Columbia, 10 June 1949). The FBI report does not explicitly state that the information on the files at Levy's residence derived from a warrentless entry, but it is worded in such a way that this is the most likely explanation. Coplon is discussed further in chapter 8.

18. Nelson, Barrett, and Ruck, *Steve Nelson*, 242–43.

out looking for any too close analogies, we must say, nevertheless, that the lessons of those trials are of everyday practical use to every branch and organization of the Communist Party of the United States today."

Dirba, like Baker, calls on the CPUSA not only to expel members felt to be guilty of Trotskyism and Lovestoneism but to track down those who associate with them and find out what organizations they belong to. He also goes over the local records of expulsions for ideological deviations and criticizes such state parties as Minnesota for failing to expel sufficient numbers of deviationists.

## Document 37

Charles Dirba, "Report of the National Control Commission to the Plenum," 3 December 1938, RTsKhIDNI 495–14–95. Original in English.

Dirba

#### REPORT OF THE NATIONAL CONTROL COMMISSION TO THE PLENUM
December 3, 1938

Comrades: The present period, which the Communist International has aptly characterized in saying that the "second imperialist war" has in fact already begun, is one in which profound changes are inevitable in every phase of our work. In no phase is the effect of the peculiarities of this time more clearly or deeply evident than in the work of the National Control Commission and of the various Disciplinary Committees in the larger States and Districts.

Many of the earmarks of a war period are rapidly becoming apparent in various ways. Perhaps the most important of these, affecting immediately our Party work, is the increased activity and the developing type of activity of the various renegade groups, Trotskyites and Lovestoneites mainly, which long ago began as sectarian groups and which have rapidly gone through the cycle which has brought them down to the fully developed character of espionage agencies, working not simply "objectively," but consciously and in every respect as subsidized agencies of fascist groups.

The time has come, in our opinion, when every single leading comrade in our Party, including every branch secretary and literature agent must be thoroughly familiar with the records of the trials of the Trotskyite and Bukharinite groups of German fascist spies in the USSR. Without looking for any too close analogies, we must say, nevertheless, that the lessons of those trials are of everyday practical use to every branch and organization of the Communist Party of the United States today. Many times we have said this, but almost as many times we have failed to draw the inevitable conclusion, which is, that the whole Party must assume a much greater alertness in this period in respect to all types of dishonest agents within the Party and the labor movement. Not only is this true about the degree of alertness, but also about the kind of procedure that should be followed in protecting the Party from provocateurs.

For example, for many years, it has been customary for committees, charged with disciplinary duties, to investigate a suspicious case up to the point of establishing whether a certain person is guilty or not guilty of betraying the Party, and then, usually, acting upon this single case, to let the matter drop there. At this time, a complete change in this respect must take place.

The work of the Disciplinary Committee does not end with the simple discovery that a man must or must not be expelled from the Party, or refused membership in the Party. We have found by experience that, if we drop the matter at this point, there often remains a nest of agents of espionage and provocation, usually of Lovestoneite or Trotskyite origin, but sometimes originating with Hearst organizations and other frankly professional espionage agencies.

When a Party member is found, in the present period, to be involved in an anti-Party conspiracy or in contact with renegades or other espionage organizations, that surely is not the end, but the begining of serious work to protect the Party.

Such a phenomenon as a Trotskyite or a Lovestoneite in the Party as an isolated individual—is a phenomenon that simply never happens. Usually, the one that is caught ahs also some others inside the Party associated with him. But even if there is only one individual working inside the Party, that one is invariably an outpost for a renegade or other espionage organization outside of the Party.

It is obviously important for the Party to learn every possible detail of information as to such an organization. To learn about the connections of a spy is often far more important than even to catch the individual spy and to eliminate him alone from the organization. The party wants to know every name and address of every person associated with persons convicted, or under investigation on charges, of infidelity to the Party. We want to know who the associates of the spy are, where and how they meet and what political maneuvers may be under way on the part of their employers against trade unions or other phases of the labor movement. We must have a means of tracing every connection of a Trotskyite, Lovestoneite or other type of spy.

Here is an example from New York City. Ralph de Sola was a Trotskyite. He brought into the Party an undercover agent who was an employee of a Hearst newspaper the 'Daily Mirror', and anxious to become a successful stool-pigeon for Hearst. This second man's name was Edwin P. Banta. De Sola was expelled for Trotskyism in March 1937. But, unfortunately, the comrades who so dutifully expelled this spy, did not happen to remember that it is necessary to look up and discover every one of De Sola's connections or protegees inside and outside of the Party. Therefore, they overlooked the second rat, Mr. Banta, who remained in the Party for a period of 18 months, continuing the work of De Sola fully as well as De Sola could have done it himself. Banta facilitated his work by making himself conspicuous in some phases of Party activities, making himself appear to be the "most active" member of his branch. Then he, in turn, brought to a Party Section membership meeting another Hearst spy, a professional "investigator", by the name of Max Hall. Hall was recognized in the membership meeting by good comrades, and the right of this third spy person in a meeting was challenged. But even then, this couple of Hearst spies were able, by one of them taking the responsibility for the other's honesty and with a few smooth words, to talk themselves out of the difficulty and avoid being expelled from the membership meeting. After this, they reported to their employers although, of course, there was nothing secret to report.

Only later was Banta's record finally and correctly checked up, and he was expelled.

That is an example, perhaps not very important in itself, to show in a si ple way how necessary it is to follow up every single case, not only of proven Trotskism or Lovestoneism, but even of suspicions of Trotskyism and Lovestoneism, by looking closely into all associations of the persons most directly involved.

But there are far more important cases than that one. We have in mind the famous "siege of Detroit" by the Lovestoneite gang, which attempted the very ambitious plan of capturing one of the most important basic working-class organization in all of American machine industry—the Auto Workers union. This was an attempt to strike at the very heart of the working class, by means of the new type of organization of espionage and provocation which attempts to work in fields where a Bergdoll or Burns agency could not successfully operate. All of the Corruption that could be traced to a "Chowderhead Cohen" detective agency was present to the same degree in the Lovestoneite agency.

This was a bold attack upon the most strategic point of the whole trade union structure in the United States, engineered by those elements which are leading most clearly in a fascist direction as the basic material supporters of the fascist trend in America. Our comrades throughout the Party know perfectly well that the aim of the Lovestoneite group is to destroy those basic organizations of the working-class. We all know that these renegades have long ago ceased to have any of the character of a political grouping within the labor movement, and that there is no one single act of depraved crime in strike-breaking in which these groups do not specialize.

But it would be very interesting to have the comrades from Detroit give this Plenum useful information as to how this group was combatted in Detroit, what was done, and what was not done; so that the experiences can enter more fully into the useful armory of the Party's knowledge. We have the impression here that a much earlier and a much more thorough and effective clarification of the role of the Lovestoneite strike-breakers to the automobile workers of Detroit could have been accomplished.

Alertness is needed also before a Trotskyite or Lovestoneite or one of their associates gets into the Party. A concrete example will best illustrate this point. Jim Jaffe, a teacher and journalist, who had been in the U.S.S.R. and who had worked on the staff of the Moscow News there (not as CP member): returned to this country,—lived with a confirmed Trotskyite for a while, spent his vacation with a Lovestoneite,—and then applied for membership in the Party. He explained that he had not known of his friends having become Trotskyites or Lovestoneites, he had argued with the first, tried to set him straight, parted ways when unsuccessful. About the other, he did not know that he was a Lovestoneite even after several weeks association during the vacation. In his statement he treated these things as of no special concern. Comrades who had worked with him on Moscow News, gave favorable references. Yet, the NCC rejected his application, and feels that the facts in the case made rejection the only action that could be taken.

Another most outstanding case is that of the Trotskyites in the Teamsters Union in Minnesota. This is a history known to the whole Party, which need not be repeated, except to say that the whole political situation not only of Minnesota but of the entire United States, is affected by this little nest of corrupt agents of fascism, strategically placed where the effect of their work is a hundred times out of proportion to their numbers. It becomes for the whole Party a matter of great interest to know how it happens that in this large union, embracing great numbers of honest and healthy workers, the Party does not manage successfully to concentrate and recruit workers to be members of the Communist Party.

It is also interesting to note that the NCC has not received any reports from Minnesota on any expulsions of Trotskyites or Lovestoneites from the Party. Perhaps there have been some shuch expulsions, but it was neglected to report them to the NCC. Yet, by this time we have the right to expect that every State and District Office has established the necessary routine for sending in reports without fail. Most likely, therefore, the absence of reports denotes actually the absence of expulsions. If none were expelled, then the question arises: Are there really no Trotskyites or Lovestoneites or their followers in the Minnesota Party? Or is it rather a case of neglecting the work of uncovering them and throwing them out?!

We know of only tow states that are taking special steps toward systematic seeking out of enemy agents and their connections: namely, New York and Ohio. The exposure of Banta, just before he "testified" before the Dies Committee was the result of these special steps.

What about the other States and Districts? What shall we think of these facts,— that Illinois has so far reported only 8 expulsions this year, Michigan only 4, and Pittsburgh no more than two? Comrades, if this indicates that the Trotskyite-Lovestoneite renegades have no[t] succeeded in getting their agents into the Party—very good. We are delighted and congratulate you. But we doubt it. Unless we are badly mistaken, these are signs of the lack of alertness of our Party there, not signs of the lack of Trotskyites or other such elements which should be thrown out.

(About Jaffe)

We must not overlook that such events as the rape of Ethiopia and the Munich betrayal of Czechoslovakia and new penetration of China produce a certain amount of pessimism and consequent demoralization among the weaker elements everywhere, and that this is meat to the Trotskyite and Lovestoneite vultures. Take, for example, the upsurge of a reactionary type of distorted nationalism which has manifested itself in New York and elsewhere. We can even say that it has had an effect of confusion and disorientation on certain portions of the Negro masses in the past elections. Very strong and consistent political work is necessary to prevent serious damage resulting to the democratic unity of the masses. Also the closest observance of efforts of corrupt agencies to demoralize individuals and whole groups within the party, is indispensable.

In Harlem, in the unemployment movement the damaging effect is manifested by the work of corrupt agents who propagate the idea of throwing off all cooperation between the workers and national liberation movements, the so-called "All-Negro" movement for a separate organization of the unemployed. All over Greater New York, you find a revival of Garveyism in a very crude and degraded form, which seems to have been timed deliberately to effect the election campaign. To trace the effects of this movement within the Party, which is more strictly with the field of the Control Commission work, we can give the example of one Negro woman Party member in Brooklyn who is now known to have had contact with Trotskyites. At the height of this reactionary movement, during the election campaign, this woman went from door to door to every Party member that she could find, in the attempt to get members to drop out of the party, with an agitation to the effect that there is "no democracy in the Party" and that the Party is "not carrying on the struggle for Negro rights."

During this time, several Party members of some length of membership, such as Louis Campbell in Harlem, were expelled. Campbell was a Trotskyite, and apparently had been for some time, and we think that a certain looseness is responsible for our not having taken hold of this situation earlier and somehow prevented the damage that these people were able to do.

In our opinion, it is not an accident that just at this time, an old Party member (Harold Williams), who long ago began to lose his sense of the Party's line, and who remained in a rut of sectarianism, has suddenly found a platform against the Party running closely parallel to the attacks on Party by these before-mentioned groups.

It is interesting to note that during the whole of the Dies Committee frame-up, only such stool-pigeons as had already been discovered and expelled from the Party appeared and did their part in the dishonest procedure of the Dies Committee. But it would be very naive if we were to assume that their remain no further stool-pigeons, of Lovestoneite or other type, in the Party today. In that connection we can also see that the alertness of the Party must be exerted not only within the Party but within thw hole orbit of the Party's activities.

The case of Sam Baron, alternate member of the National Committee of the Socialist Party who went to Spain and there worked as a spy against the Spanish Government, is one we should study for the use it will be to us in this period in which war is in process. In Spain, Baron approached Comrades Minor and Ford, and made attempts which we now can see were the deliberate attempts of a provocateur. Mr. Baron was seen in conference with some questionable military persons, and his actions *were* reported in Spain to the proper persons.

Perhaps a mistake was made in not having exposed Mr. Baron as a military spy, which he surely was, in our Communist press. It is noteworthy that Mr. Baron's testimony before the Dies Committee against the whole cause of labor and progress and democracy in Spain and America did not have to go materially beyond the same stuff that he had written in the "Socialist Call" and which the "Socialist Call" continues to hold as its model for policy in regard to Spain.

Norman Thomas excuses Baron in such a way as to protect, not the victims of his espionage, but Baron himself. Perhaps this would not be so easily possible if we had, with sufficient energy and boldness, shown the character of the Trotskyist Baron more in the light of the Zinoviev-Trotsky-Bukharin type of military espionage than we did.

There are many other cases, which could be cited for other useful lessons, but, at this time, the National Control Commission wishes to emphasize the main task and make it stand out more sharply,—that the whole Party, from tops to bottom, and especially through every disciplinary committee and other leading committees, must be most vigilant and alert against the Trotskyites and Lovestoneites, as the most insidious agents of fascism and reaction among the workers; we must take active steps toward uncovering them (not merely passively waiting until they accidentally come to our attention), we must painstakingly trace all their connections, their associates, their directing centers. We must do this, in order to rid the Party and to protect the Party from this poison, this cancer; and we must do what we can toward exposing and crushing them also in other working-class and progressive organizations.

Another illustration of the party's grave concern with ideological deviation is **document 38**. This item is a transcription of two pages of the minutes of the New York State Executive Committee of the CPUSA for 28 December 1938. Under discussion is what to do about Comrade Herron, the party's organizer in Buffalo. Herron had recruited Mary Kelley into the CPUSA and married her. However, she was later expelled for Trotskyism. Document 38 says that Herron had "weakened. He had made a decision that he will have nothing to do with her. He broke the decision without the knowledge of the Party. He paid secret visits to her." These visits to his wife put his own position in jeopardy. The decision faced by the Communist leaders was whether to remove Herron as an organizer and member of the party's state committee for visiting his wife or only to "sharply" censure him if he mended his ways and if it looked as though his wife could be reclaimed for the party.

## Document 38

Excerpts from the fifteen-page "Minutes of New York State Executive Committee," CPUSA, 28 December 1938, RTsKhIDNI 495 14 102. Original in English. Israel Amter, Charles Krumbein, Hank Forbes, and Rose Wortis were party functionaries.

IV. HERRON CASE—Amter: Three or four months before going to school Herron married a young Irish Catholic girl—a member of the Socialist Party [SP]. About the same time she was taken into the Party. She was under the influence of Trotskyites and made vicious statements against the Party. She was expelled.

She had been corresponding with Herron at the school. He took a very fine position and sent a letter to the County. He took very firm bolshevik position and said he would have nothing further to do with her until she changed her position.

Before he returned from the school she decided to appeal. Told of her fainting in office, etc. Very weak, It was decided that she shall be expelled from the Party and shall have right to apply for readmittance to the Party provided that the work she was doing in a mass organization should be such as would make her material for the Party.

She was made branch secretary of the Workers Alliance Branch. But she could not do very much except on Saturday and Sunday, becayse of her work. Another motion was made that a leading member of the County should be assigned to work with her and try to reclaim her for the Party.

When Herron returned to Buffalo he evidently weakened. He had made a decision that he will have nothing to do with her. He broke the decision without the knowledge of the Party. He paid secret visits to her.

Just before the last State Committee the matter was taken up. Had a meeting with the leading comrades of Buffalo the day before the State Committee meeting and discussed it thoroughly. Herron admitted that he had double crossed the Party and was having relations with her and had visited her.

Abbott and Boyle took very firm position. One of the comrades was positively adamant—one of the old timers in the Party—who thought that the only thing to do was to be very harsh. That was why I proposed that Herron should be removed from the State Committee and removed from his position as County organizer. He asked if the State Committee would be willing to give him permission to visit her and try to bring her back to the Party. He decided to leave it for further discussion.

Comrade Steinberg made a trip recently to Buffalo. Comrade Herron made a report that showed he understood the political situation. Steinberg took up the question of what it would mean if Herron were removed as County Organizer. Everybody but this old timer agreed that although Herron had made a very serious mistake, to remove him would be a serious blow to the Party.

The proposal now made is that he be very sharply censured, and this be attached to his record, and to try and convince the comrades that he should not be removed. That when I go to Buffalo I should try to convince the Comrades in Buffalo to adopt this decision.

Proposal is that he shall have same relations with Mary Kelly as any other comrade, and none other. In so far as her readmission to the Party is concerned—she is very weak—and no time should be set.

KRUMBEIN: When Herron was in school he took a very good position. Meantime this developed while I was on vacation. When I got a letter from Rose, I expressed opinion that we were being too harsh. There has been one serious crime committed, and that is that he betrayed the confidence of the Party.

At the time Amter was up there she accepted the proposition that Amter put forth. Broke with SP and accepted responsibility in the Workers Alliance.

## Document 38 *continued*

When Herron got back there the situation was already different. She had broken with the SP.

While not organically connected with the Trotskyites, she was influenced by them and had put forth the position of the Trotskyites. Her Brother is a Trotskyite and she was very much influenced by him.

Feel that in view of the circumstance the proposal to remove Herron from the State Committee and from his position as County Organizer, is entirely too drastic. Being the type that she is, and having changed now and in so far as we know since she agreed, she has carried out the agreement. Think that under those circumstances a censure is sufficient on the basis of betraying the confidence of the Party. Think censure is necessary, but not the original proposal which is a very drastic action.

HANK: True that he took a good position in School, but much easier to take good position at school than after you get out. Certain things that have changed in the whole thing. Here it reflected a definite lack of political stability—has been reflected in the State Committee. This is the one thing that we should guard against and we should be very careful in a thing like this. Don't think we should lose what we have spent in the school and his ability, but have definite instance of political instability. While using him as county executive, but don't think there would be any harm in removing him from the State Committee. Should think it over a bit more on the face of it. What he would do as a state leader in politics, etc.

ROSE: Don't think the proposal of Hank very logical. If you decide to remove a comrade from the State Committee you have no justification in keeping him in the leadership of the county. Should take his record into consideration. Could not find any spot on his record in the past six or seven years that he has been in the Party. He has faced many tests. Should also take into consideration the impossible decision made by the comrades that everybody else was able to see her, but Herron was not. Considering all this, his background, etc., don't think we should be so drastic.

Before it was learned that Herron was seeing her there was a recommendation of the County to take her back into the Party.

---

Another facet of Communist hostility toward ideological deviationists is exhibited in a statement by an American leader of the Young Communist League (YCL) to the Comintern's Anglo-American Secretariat in 1930. After a discussion of the YCL's work,

Tony Minerich remarked: "One more point and I'll close, and that is on the fight against Lovestone. . . . When the youth section of the Lovestone group had a meeting the league [YCL] members went there and were able to break it up, beat up the Lovestoneites, chase them out of the hall, take over the hall and hold a meeting."[19]

Beyond breaking up a marriage and engaging in fisticuffs, there were more sinister aspects to this surveillance of enemies of the party. In document 27 Baker wrote of the "highly successful efforts" of the secret apparatus to "infiltrate the New York Trotskyist organization." The CPUSA's penetration of the American Trotskyist movement was used for more than just gathering political intelligence on an ideological enemy. Louis Budenz, who defected from the CPUSA in 1945, said that in 1937 and 1938 he had introduced Soviet NKVD officers to two secret Communists whom the CPUSA had asked to infiltrate the Trotskyist organization. One of the infiltrators was Sylvia Franklin, who eventually became secretary to James Cannon, the leader of the American Trotskyists. The Soviets later introduced Franklin to two of their covert agents who had penetrated the European Trotskyist organization for the NKVD, Jack Soble and Robert Soblen. Soble and Soblen moved to the United States in 1941 and later expanded their scope of operations to include espionage against the United States government. In the late 1950s, when Soble and Soblen were convicted of spying against the United States, Franklin was called before a federal grand jury and cited as an unindicted co-conspirator.

The second infiltrator whom Budenz introduced to the NKVD was Ruby Weil. Posing as a Trotskyist, Weil cultivated the friendship of Sylvia Ageloff, a Brooklyn social worker who devoted her vacations to Trotskyist work. The Soviets arranged for Weil to introduce Ageloff to a charming young man called Jacques Mornard, a student from Belgium. After a whirlwind romance, Mornard and Ageloff became lovers. In 1940 Mornard used Ageloff's standing as a trusted Trotskyist to gain access to Trotsky's home in Mexico, where he lived in exile. At a private meeting with Trotsky, Mornard killed him with a hand ax. Imprisoned for murder, he claimed to be a disillusioned Trotskyist, but after World War II he was identified

19. Minerich's statement to the American Commission of the Anglo-American Secretariat, 1 January 1930, RTsKhIDNI 495–72–118.

as Ramon Mercader, a Spanish Communist and NKVD agent. After twenty years in prison, Mercader was released; he retired to Moscow and, later, Cuba.[20]

Another example of the CPUSA's providing intelligence assistance to the Soviet Union can be found in **document 39**, a letter from Lapin to Randolph. Lapin was the pseudonym of Charles Dirba, head of the Central Control Commission, and Randolph was the generic pseudonym for the American representative to the Comintern. Dirba told Randolph, who would have relayed the information to the Comintern, that "a food worker here in New York reports that he has overheard Solomon Rechter's brother boasting to somebody else that Solomon Rechter, in Moscow, was carrying on underground work for Zionist 'black shirts'—the Zhabotinsky group."[21] What happened to Solomon Rechter is not known, but it is likely to have been grim. An accusation by a party official that someone was a Zionist usually meant arrest and either the gulag or execution.

---

# Document 39

Lapin to Randolph, 28 September 1933, RTsKhIDNI 515–1–3192. Original in English.

---

N.Y. City, 9/28/33.

Dear Comrade Randolph:—

We have received the following information which should be transmitted to the proper bodies at your end for whatever use they can and wish to make of it.

20. Louis Budenz affidavit, 11 November 1950, House Committee on Un-American Activities, *American Aspects of the Assasination of Leon Trotsky,* 81st Cong., 2d sess., 1950, v–ix; Issac Don Levine, *The Mind of an Assassin* (New York: Farrar, Straus and Cudahy, 1959); Romerstein and Levchenko, *The KGB against the "Main Enemy,"* 165–75; Christopher Andrew and Oleg Gordievsky, *KGB: The Inside Story* (New York: HarperCollins, 1990), 154–56. Franklin's grand jury testimony, which dealt with her infiltration of the Trotskyists as well as her role in the Soble-Soblen spy ring, was obtained by a Trotskyist group under an FOIA request and reprinted as *Confession of a GPU Spy* (London: New Park Publications, 1983). Franklin used the aliases Caldwell and Doxsee. When captured, Mornard carried a forged Canadian passport in the name of Frank Jacson.

21. Jabotinsky (here spelled Zhabotinsky) was one of the major figures in the history of modern Zionism. The contemporary Likud party of Israel is a successor to the Jabotinsky movement.

# Document 39 *continued*

Re: Solomon Rechter, who works in Moscow in some office as bookkeeper.

A food worker here in New York reports that he has overheard Solomon Rechter's brother boasting to somebody else that Solomon Rechter, in Moscow, was carrying on underground work for Zionist "black shirts"—the Zhabotinsky group.

Re: White Guard agents on Steamship "Skan City", which makes trips to Leningrad.

Lettish seamen here report that on this ship there are two cadets, who are engaged in smuggling plans and information about USSR. Radio services and apparatus out from Leningrad to white guards outside. One of them they know by the nick-name of "Black Mike", because he is of dark complexion. They have heard that this bird has gotten some plans or apparatus from somebody in Leningrad and delivered them to some white guards outside, for $1000.00. They could not give me anything more definite.

Re: Alexander Babalcin and Vorovski.

A comrade from Schenectady, N.Y., writes to us as follows:

"Alexander Babalcin, a white-guardist, some time ago left for Esthonia with the intention of afterwards going to Lithuania. He is a member of the "Bratski Soyuz" a white guardist organization, which had called some kind of a conference in Esthonia. From the information that I have received it seems that there is a concentration of white guardists in the small countries bordering the Soviet Union.

"This bird, who had been driven out of Russia during the Civil War was a rabid enemy of the Soviet Union and would go out of his way to make it as miserable as he could for Soviet technicians, who came to Schenectady in the past at different times. He was employed as a droughtsman by the General Electric and held his job despite inferior quality of work.

"The other person I want to write about is Vorovski, one of the leading figures of the Bratski Soyuz. This fellow is also a draoughtsman working in the International building of the plant (of the General Electric). He is the man who is charged by the Company to handle Soviet orders. At least he did this in the past. Anyway, this white-guardist is in charge of the affairs of the Company regarding the Soviet Union, including the care of Soviet technicians.

"If I can get any additional information about the activities of both these white-guardists, I'll send it along."

———

Comradely yours,
K.Lapin, Sec.CCC

Document 40 concerns a Russian immigrant named Dourmashkin who had come under suspicion for personal and political deviations. Officially, Dourmashkin worked for Amtorg (identified as "A." in the document); unofficially he was an editor of *Novy mir*, the CPUSA's Russian-language newspaper. Dourmashkin had apparently returned to the Soviet Union and Lapin/Dirba notes that "it was the idea from there [Amtorg] that Dourmashkin should be let go across (without arousing his suspicions), in order that he could not do any harm here and could be dealt with properly over there." Lapin/Dirba referred Randolph to "Comr. Murashoff," then in the USSR, for details on Dourmashkin's misbehavior. A Russian defector has identified Murashoff, a Soviet who had been an Amtorg official in the United States, as an officer of the GPU (the KGB of that era).[22]

---

## Document 40

Lapin to Randolph, 9 January 1933, RTsKhIDNI 515–1–3192. Original in English. "Let go across" meant returned to the Soviet Union. "A." refers to Amtorg, the Soviet trading agency headquartered in New York. The ICC in the letter's postscript was the International Control Commission, the Comintern's disciplinary agency.

---

N.Y. City, 1/9/33.

*Copy for Secretariat*

To Comrade Randolph,
Moscow, USSR.

Dear Comrade:—

In reply to your inquiries of Nov. 27th (on Zaitzeva and Ignatyuk) and the one on Dourmashkin, we can give you the following information.

Elizabeth Zaitzeva (Liza Borilenko). She was a member of the Party in Gary, Ind., for a short time before she left for the USSR. in the spring of 1932 without permission. For this reason she was dropped from Party rolls. Subsequently the comrades there learned that she had been bragging of 8 years in the Party (while she was in the Party only for a short while) and that she was in commu-

22. On Murashoff's GPU status, see Delgass testimony, 25 November 1930, House Special Committee to Investigate Communist Activities in the United States, *Investigation of Communist Propaganda*, 71st Cong., 2d sess., 1930, pt. 1, vol. 4:210; on Dourmashkin's work for *Novy mir*, see P. Fatoff's letter of 7 April 1930, ibid., pt. 3, vol. 2:26.

nication with N. Seledsow, who was some months ago expelled from the Party for dishonesty and misuse of trust in the Russian Cooperative Restaurant in Gary (strongly suspected of having stolen considerable amount of money). In these communications she is supposed to have shown a very bad approach to the Party.

B. Ignatiuk. You write that he was expelled from the Party here in 1926, and that you want to know the reasons for his expulsion. The records of the CCC. go back only to 1928, and, therefore, we have no records on the expulsion of Ignatiuk. We even do not know from what city he was here in USA., so that we could inquire about his record there. We have asked the Russian Buro to try to get some information on this matter, and when we get something we'll send it to you promptly.

Dourmashkin. When we wrote to you that his transfer was cancelled, we understood that full information about him was being sent across through other channels.

He was working at the A., and it was the idea from there that Dourmashkin should be let go across (without arousing his suspicions), in order that he could not do any harm here and could be dealt with properly over there.

Comr. Murashoff, who was here at the A. for some time before Dourmashkin went across, and who is now also in the USSR., should be consulted for full details on Dourmashkin.

What we can say off-hand is this: Dourmashkin maintained friendly relations with a relative of his, who was an editor (or pretty high in some other way) on the "Russky Golos" here (or some other white-guard Russian paper); in some instances it appeared that he was giving information out to this relative of his; Dourmashkin had other shady connections,—was constantly in touch and on the very best of terms with a dealer in books (riding around with him in taxis, going out to lunch, etc.); Dourmashkin was strongly suspected of stealing books from the store, of which he was manager (taking out packages, riding away in taxis, deliberately making all kinds of zig-zags apparently to throw off anybody who would try to trail him); in addition to this, he is supposed to have been on intimate (sexually) terms with girls employed by him in the store.

But we cannot give you these things as definitely established facts, because we ourselves did not conduct any investigation. It was conducted by others, and the whole record was supposed to have been sent across by others.

In all probability Comr. Murashoff will be able to give further details.

Comradely yours,

K. Lapin, Sec'y CCC.CPUSA.

P.S. I am sending herewith clippings from the Daily Worker of exposures of spies and unreliable elements (in two copies each): Cecil Ellis 11/5/32, Carmon Sipala 12/1, O.J. Jorgensen 12/22/32, Frank Note and Walter Smorag 12/28/32, and Milton Stone 1/6/33.

Please turn them over to the ICC.

K.L.

---

## Max, the Agent Who Wouldn't Go Home, 1939–1942

In addition to informing the Soviets about deviationists in Moscow, the CPUSA also dealt with Soviets who came to the United States and did not wish to return. **Documents 41, 42, 43, 44, and 45** concern a Comintern official who came to the United States as a representative of the Young Communist International, the Comintern's youth arm, and was known only by the pseudonym of Max. James Wechsler, later a well-known journalist and in the 1930s a Communist student leader, recalled Max's brooding presence at important YCL meetings: "I learned quickly that one did not ask about it [his name] or about him. He was just there." And, "When we faced any ideological quandary, he laid down the law."[23]

Max's real name was Boris Irmovich Daneman. Document 41 is a 1939 memo from Rudy Baker, head of the CPUSA secret apparatus, to Dimitrov, head of the Comintern, and Manuilsky, a senior Comintern official. Baker reported that "*Comrade M*" was demoralized but, after prior refusals, had agreed to return to the USSR accompanied by Mac Weiss, a CPUSA official. The memo, which was handwritten in English, was accompanied by a typed Russian translation upon which was a handwritten annotation in Russian identifying Comrade M as "Max" and "Daneman."[24] Baker noted that the American party had told Comrade Max that should he refuse to go back to the Soviet Union, he would be expelled from the CPUSA. Document 43 is a copy of a letter from Max to Browder, a distressed

---

23. James Wechsler, *The Age of Suspicion* (New York: Random House, 1953), 95. For more on Max's activity in the United States, see Harvey Klehr, *The Heyday of American Communism: The Depression Decade* (New York: Basic Books, 1984), 466.

24. R. Baker to Dimitrov, Russian translation, RTsKhIDNI 495–74–472.

and bizarre plea for help that amply demonstrates Max's demoralization. Browder sent the letter to Dimitrov in Moscow, Dimitrov forwarded it to Manuilsky (document 42), and Manuilsky wrote on it his recommendation: "Advise [Max's] immediate departure for the USSR."

Although Max was demoralized, he was not so confused as to return to the USSR. In 1942 General Fitin, the head of the foreign intelligence directorate of the NKVD, noted (document 44) that Max had been sent to the United States in the mid-1930s to work with young Communists and that he had failed to comply with the order to return home in 1939.[25] Document 45 is Dimitrov's cover note for the Comintern's report on Max.[26] How and why the foreign intelligence branch of the NKVD (predecessor to the KGB) came to take an interest in Max in 1942 is unknown, as is Max's ultimate fate.

---

## Document 41

R. [Rudy] Baker to Dimitrov and Manuilsky, 1939, RTsKhIDNI 495–74–472. Original in English. The ellipses are in the original.

---

*Dimitrov*

*Manuilsky*

*Comrade Browder requested me to convey the following information to you: comrade M . . . . . . . who up to now has refused to return to the Soviet Union, has now agreed to come. It was expected that he would leave New York on board the "Queen Mary" on January 10th 1939 bound for London and from there on boat to Helsingfors where he would take a train for Leningrad and Moscow. If he carries out this agreement he would be accompanied by comrade Mac Weiss who is coming to Moscow by the same route and on above date.*

*Comrade M . . . . . . is completely demoralized and sits in his rooms day and night. Should he once again fail to carry out the agreement to return to Moscow by the end of January the C.P.U.S.A. will expel him from its ranks and break all connections with him. In such an event his expulsion will not be*

---

25. General Pavel Mikhailovich Fitin was head of the foreign intelligence directorate of the NKVD from 1940 to 1946 and the Soviet Union's chief intelligence official.
26. A copy of the report on Max was not present in the file.

## Document 41 continued

published or made public. This procedure will be carried out by the end of January unless he departs for Moscow or unless comrade Browder is advised otherwise

I left New York January 3, 1939.

R. Baker

## Document 42

GD [Dimitrov] to Manuilsky, 21 March 1939, RTsKhIDNI 495–74–479. Original in Russian.

**27** File with No. <u>546/s</u>
20 March 193<u>9</u>

Letter
<u>from Daneman</u>

<u>to Browder!</u>

To be shown to
Com. Manuilsky
21 March 1939. GD.

## Document 43

Max to Browder, 27 February 1939, RTsKhIDNI 495–74–479. Original in Russian.

**27** File with No. <u>546/s</u>
20 March 193<u>9</u>
Feb. 27, 1939

Dearest Com. Browder!

Help me, my dear,

I can't take any more, it's bad I'm awfully bad off. I'm a wreck, I acted badly und [in]excusably in failing to follow your guidelines from the very beginning I'm willing to do any service at all to wash away my disgrace I am not an enemy my dear friend just a bad spineless nobody. that's failed to justify your confidence and the party's Help me don't ignore me tell me what I must do I'll do anything you tell me, anything, without question. Help me wash away my disgrace     I beg you

Your Max

I'm no stranger help me my dear friend help me.

Advise immediate departure
for the USSR
D. Man[uilsky]

Dimitrov
Manuilsky

2 A

Comrade Browder requested me to convey the following information to you: comrade M . . . . . . . who up to now has refused to return to the Soviet Union, has now agreed to come. It was expected that he would leave New York on board the "Queen Mary" on January 10th 1939 bound for London and from there on boat to Helsingfors where he would take a train for Leningrad and Moscow. If he carries out this agreement he would be accompanied by comrade Mac Weiss who is coming to Moscow by the same route and on above date.

Comrade M . . . . . is completely demoralized and sits in his room day and night. Should he once again fail to carry out the agreement to return to Moscow by the end of January the C.P.U.S.A. will expell him from its ranks and break all connections with him. In such an event his expulsion will not be published or made public. This procedure will be carried out by the end of January unless he departs for Moscow or unless comrade Browder is advised otherwise

I left New York January 3, 1939.

RWBaker

DOCUMENT 41. R. [Rudy] Baker to Dimitrov and Manuilsky, 1939.

# Document 44

Fitin to Dimitrov, 14 February 1942, RTsKhIDNI 495–73–124. Original in Russian.

E C C I

To Comrade D I M I T R O V.

inquiry

Please advise whether the ECCI knows of a certain MAX, currently living in New York. MAX was supposedly sent to the US 8 years ago through the Comintern network to work with young people. Three years ago, on being ordered by the center to return home, MAX refused to comply.

Fitin

(F I T I N)

14 February 1942

No. N21699

# Document 45

Dimitrov to Fitin, 24 February 1942, RTsKhIDNI 495–73–133. Original in Russian. The report referred to was not found.

To Comrade FITIN:

I am forwarding you a report from the ECCI personnel (cadres) department on the MAX (DANEMAN, Boris Irmovich) about whom you inquired.

(G. D I M I T R O V)

24 February 1942

No. 55

Encl.: three-page report.

## Fighting Deviationists and Bad Elements in the Spanish Civil War

American Communists also carried their fight against deviationists into the Spanish Civil War. In 1936 General Francisco Franco and a nationalist coalition of monarchists, conservatives, fascists, and the bulk of the Spanish army revolted against the Spanish Republic. The Republican government was backed by a Popular Front coalition that included Socialists, anarcho-syndicalists, Communists, and centrist democrats.

The Western democracies—France, Britain, and the United States—attempted to isolate the conflict by embargoing arms sales to both sides. Fascist Italy and Nazi Germany, however, supplied Franco with arms and troops, about 70,000 Italians and several thousand Germans. The Soviet Union sold arms to the Spanish Republic and through the Comintern raised 30,000 foreign volunteers who fought for the Spanish Republic in the so-called International Brigades. About 3,300 American volunteers fought with the International Brigades as soldiers in the Abraham Lincoln battalion, the George Washington battalion, the Mackenzie-Papineau battalion, and the John Brown Artillery Battery, or served with American medical units. The CPUSA organized the flow of American volunteers to Spain, but, in line with its Popular Front policy, it presented the effort as antifascist rather than Communist. For the same reason, the proportion of American volunteers who were Communists was also obscured.

In an influential history of Americans who fought with the International Brigades, Robert Rosenstone states that "Herbert Matthews [*New York Times* war correspondent] and John Gates [former American International Brigades officer] could claim that 80 per cent were Communists, Earl Browder 60 per cent, and Hans Amlie [Lincoln battalion commander] 25 per cent. But none of them really knew; none was making better than a guess, for there were no records of political affiliation ever kept by the battalions. When the men formally enrolled in the International Brigades at Albacete, their political party was put down as 'anti-fascist,' a designation that would at that time cover the political spectrum from Martin Dies [Texas congressman and anti-Communist] to Joseph Stalin, leaving a rather broad area for ideological differences." Rosenstone suggested that the Communist proportion was "perhaps half."[27]

The claim made to Rosenstone and other historians by International Brigades veterans that the brigades did not keep records of political affiliation can now be shown to be false. The International Brigades was a Comintern operation, and in the Comintern archives were numerous lists of American volunteers by political

27. Robert Rosenstone, *Crusade on the Left: The Lincoln Battalion in the Spanish Civil War* (New York: Pegasus, 1969), 113, 311.

affiliation. The most comprehensive list shows that of the 1,845 Americans on duty on 1 October 1937, exactly 65.6 percent were members of the Communist party and another 13.7 percent were members of the Young Communist League, a total Communist proportion of 79.3 percent, just short of the estimates made by Gates and Matthews.[28] So assiduous were the officers of the International Brigades in keeping records by political allegiance that even records of Americans killed in action listed their political affiliation.[29] The notion that the Communist leaders in the International Brigades submerged their concerns for ideological correctness by adopting a broad anti-fascist stance cannot survive an examination of the International Brigades archives in Moscow.

## The Surveillance of Bertram Wolfe, 1937

In March 1937, during the Spanish Civil War, the American representative to the Comintern, Randolph, received a report from his American comrades that Bertram Wolfe, a prominent Lovestoneist, was on his way to Spain. Randolph warned the Comintern in **document 46** that Wolfe was likely to act "as liaison man between Trotsky and the POUM or other Trotskyist elements in Spain" and urged the Comintern to "immediately notify our comrades in Spain to watch out for him and take appropriate measures." The POUM (Partido obrero de unificación Marxista) was an independent Marxist party in Spain. It was not Trotskyist, but some of its doctrines paralleled those of Trotsky. The POUM supported the Spanish Republic in its fight against Franco's nationalists, and the POUM's leaders were prominent in the anti-Franco government of the Catalonian region of Spain. Linking Wolfe to Trotsky made sense only in the paranoid world of Stalinist communism.

Wolfe, a Lovestoneist, had been expelled from the CPUSA in 1929 for sympathizing with Bukharin's "rightist" moderation. Trotsky had been purged for "leftist" extremism in 1927. In the mid-1930s Stalin insisted that the two heresies had combined, and Communist parties adhered to Stalin's position. In May 1937,

28. "American total tally as of Oct. 1, 1937," RTsKhIDNI 545–6–5. Original in English.
29. Killed in action list, RTsKhIDNI 545–6–21.

Spanish Communists, who by this point were the strongest force in the Spanish Republican government, suppressed the POUM and dispersed the POUM militia that had been fighting Franco. Hundreds of POUM leaders and militants were murdered after summary Communist courts-martial. Foreign volunteers attached to the POUM were also killed; George Orwell, the English writer who fought with the POUM militia, described the terror against the POUM and his escape from Communist death squads in his *Homage to Catalonia.*

The Comintern took Randolph's advice. Located in Comintern files is a surveillance report on Wolfe's visit to Spain.[30] Wolfe visited Catalonia, the POUM's stronghold, but had moved on to Madrid by the time of the Communist suppression of the POUM and avoided becoming a victim of "appropriate measures."[31]

---

## Document 46

Randolph to Comintern Cadre Department and Alichanov, 13 March 1937, RTsKhIDNI 495–14–81. Original in English.

---

13.3.37
SS/2

Strictly Confidential

Cadre Department ECCI.
Comrade Alichanov.

Dear Comrade:
Comrades travelling from the United States have reported that, on the boat, coming to Europe, they saw Bertram D. Wolfe.

In view of the possible significance of the visit, we believe you should immediately notify our comrades in Spain to watch out for him and take appropriate measures.

Bertram D. Wolfe is a very close friend and co-worker (in fact, co-author) with Diego Riviera, the host of Trotsky in Mexico. Wolfe speaks Spanish very fluently.

From a reasonably close knowledge of Wolfe, his connections and his activ-

30. Surveillance report on Bertram Wolfe, September 1937, from Barcelona, RTsKhIDNI 545–6–1015.
31. Wolfe in his later life became a renowned scholar of Spanish literature and of Soviet communism.

ities, it is my belief that he is on the way to Spain as liaison man between Trotsky and the POUM or other Trotskyist elements in Spain.

Wolfe is at present, by political affiliation, a Lovestoneite.

This note is intended for transmission to the proper comrades in Spain.

Comradely yours,

*Randolph*

Rep. CPUSA, ECCI.

*Done*
*To the archive*
25/IV/37

---

*The Death of Albert Wallach, 1938*

Bertram Wolfe was lucky; Albert Wallach was not. When the Spanish Civil War broke out, Wallach, then aged twenty-three, volunteered to fight fascism by joining the International Brigades. A fellow volunteer who met Wallach on the way to Spain described him as "a strikingly handsome young man with an ingratiating smile, a winning personality, and erect military bearing."[32] Most American volunteers entered Spain by hiking across the mountainous border between Spain and France. Wallach, however, had sustained a hernia while exercising on the ship to France. Because of his injury, the International Brigades sent Wallach with a group that traveled by a coastal steamer. Unfortunately, the ship was torpedoed. Wallach survived but was injured; a number of other American volunteers drowned. Once he was in Spain, his family heard little from him, and his father, Maxwell Wallach, urged the U.S. State Department to contact his son and try to get him out of the war. In March 1938, the State Department notified the elder Wallach that it had heard that his son would be leaving Spain shortly. But Albert Wallach never returned, and the International Brigades never provided his family with an explanation of what had happened.

Maxwell Wallach asked a number of International Brigades veterans about his son. None would talk to him on the record and most would not talk to him at all. Off the record, however, some told the

---

32. Sandor Voros, *American Commissar* (Philadelphia: Chilton Company, 1961), 286. Voros, a CPUSA functionary, became a political commissar on the staff of the XV International Brigade. He left the CPUSA after the Nazi-Soviet Pact.

elder Wallach a grim story. In 1940 Maxwell Wallach testified to the Special Committee on Un-American Activities (better known as the Dies committee after its chairman, Representative Martin Dies) that he had been told in confidence by several veterans that his son had been executed. "The man in charge of this prison was a fellow by the name of Tony De Maio, who I understand was the actual killer, not only of my boy but of six other American boys, whose remains to this very moment are in the courtyard of this prison camp, Castle de Fells."[33]

In August 1939 Maxwell Wallach received a letter from Edward Palega that said, "I must ask you not to show this letter to any one and above all not to use my name or quote me. I want no one to know I was in prison and I write this only because I promised Al I would." The story that Palega told was such that the distraught father ignored the request for confidentiality and read the letter to the committee:

> Your son Albert made me promise to let you know of his condition if and when I got out of Spain alive. . . . [H]e and I were in the International Brigade prison of Castle de Fells, about twenty-five kilometers south of Barcelona. . . . We were there together in June and July 1938. He was arrested in Barcelona in June while wearing civilian clothes and while carrying alleged forged papers from the American Consul, stating he was under protection of the United States Government. For that reason he was suspected of being a spy. . . . About a week after I entered that cell Albert was taken out in the nighttime. Though I inquired everywhere I could never learn what happened to him, but I am afraid he may have been killed that night.[34]

Palega surfaced to tell his story again in 1954 as a witness before the government's Subversive Activities Control Board.[35] Palega tes-

---

33. Testimony of Maxwell M. Wallach, 12 April 1940, House Special Committee on Un-American Activities, *Investigation of Un-American Propaganda Activities in the United States,* 76th Cong., 3d sess., 1940, 13:7732.

34. Edward Palega to Maxwell M. Wallach, 26 August 1939, quoted in testimony of Maxwell M. Wallach, ibid., 7733.

35. The Subversive Activities Control Board was charged with registering and making public certain information about Communist-controlled organizations. All of the organizations that it attempted to register fought the SACB's actions successfully in court, no organizations ever registered under the law, and eventually the SACB was abolished. While in existence, however, it conducted lengthy hearings about organizations that it felt were Communist controlled.

tified that he had been a member of the CPUSA in the early 1930s, joined the Lincoln battalion in 1937, and served until the American volunteers were withdrawn in late 1938. He also stated that from the time he joined the Communist party until he entered the U.S. armed forces in 1941 he had been an occasional and unpaid informant on Communist activities for the Chicago police department.

Palega testified that he was with the Lincoln battalion at Belchite in 1938. In this disastrous battle, the XV International Brigade (of which the Lincoln and Mackenzie-Papineau battalions were a part) was shattered and overrun by Franco's troops.[36] A majority of the Americans in the Lincoln and Mackenzie-Papineau battalions were killed or captured in the ensuing rout. The defeat was so devastating that several score American soldiers attempted to leave Spain, Palega among them. Hoping to reach the American consul, he fled to Barcelona but was arrested for desertion. His prior record got Palega out of prison, however, and he was reinstated in the International Brigades.

In 1954 Palega said that Wallach and he had shared a cell in Castle de Fells. Wallach

> had been with the Lincoln Battalion or the Fifteenth Brigade and had been in Barcelona and made contact with the C.N.T. They had given him a commission as a Lieutenant Colonel in a division that was commanded by C.N.T. personnel. . . . He also told me that he had been in the home of Mr. Flood [U.S. consul in Barcelona] and had had the run of the home to the extent that without the permission of Mr. Flood he had used Mr. Flood's typewriter and a letterhead that showed the seal of the United States, American Consul or something, across the letterhead, and had typed what he referred to as the salvo conducto [safe conduct pass]. . . . It was an identity and identified him as a American citizen and entitled him to privileges as an American citizen. He was working in the office of the C.N.T. or of the military branch that he had joined in Barcelona and was having coffee in a sidewalk cafe when he was picked up by several plain-clothesmen who recognized him. He was brought there and was accused of being an American spy. . . . Wallach didn't acknowledge being a spy of any kind.[37]

36. The Lincoln battalion fought at Belchite twice. In 1937 Belchite was the site of a major Lincoln battalion victory during a Republican offensive; in 1938 the site of the initial defeat in a disastrous retreat that sent Republican forces back behind the Ebro River.

37. Testimony of William Horan, transcript of proceedings held before the Sub-

The CNT (Confederación national del trabajo) was one of Spain's largest labor union federations, part of the coalition backing the Spanish Republican government, and maintained its own military formations fighting with the Spanish Republic's forces. The CNT was anarcho-syndicalist in ideology and hostile to communism.[38] Consequently, Communists sought constantly to isolate the CNT and weaken its position in the Spanish Republic. If, as Palega said, Wallach had attempted to shift from the Communist-led International Brigades to a CNT-aligned unit, Communists would have regarded it as a grave offense.

Palega went on to say that "Tony De Maio was the chief questioner of Albert Wallach. He had questioned Wallach before he had been brought to the Castillo. He had questioned Wallach again while Wallach was in the black hole [cell], taken out and talked to De Maio." Palega testified that one night Wallach was taken from their cell and "shortly later we heard machine gun fire and Albert Wallach has never been seen since."[39] The only significant differences between Palega's 1954 story and the letter he wrote to Maxwell Wallach in 1939 were the addition of a link between Albert Wallach and the CNT and his statement about De Maio's role. (Maxwell Wallach linked De Maio to his son in his 1940 testimony but did not give a source for the information.)

Also testifying to the Dies committee in 1940 was William C. McCuiston. McCuiston had been a prominent (although notoriously undisciplined) organizer in the Communist seamen's union in the early 1930s; his independent habits had once gotten him expelled, but his militancy as a labor organizer earned him readmission to the CPUSA before he went to Spain.[40] His experience in

---

versive Activities Control Board in the matter of *Herbert Brownell, Attorney General v. Veterans of the Abraham Lincoln Brigade*, 1954, 1250–51 (reprinted on microfilm in *Records of the Subversive Activities Control Board, 1950–1972*, pt. 2 [Frederick, Md.: University Press of America, 1988], reel 33). In 1940 Palega changed his name to Horan.

38. Anarcho-syndicalism envisioned the abolition of private property and the replacement of the political state by a voluntary association of labor unions and worker cooperatives. Hostile to communism because of Communist support for an all-powerful political state dominated by the Communist party, anarcho-syndicalists remained a significant force in France and Spain until the end of the 1930s.

39. Testimony of William Horan, 1250–1251.

40. A 1934 letter from Lapin/Dirba of the CPUSA Central Control Commission

Spain, however, irretrievably broke his relationship with the party. When he returned to the United States he became an aggressive organizer for anti-Communist maritime unions. McCuiston testified that while in Spain he had heard that Albert Wallach had been attempting to leave on a ship but was caught by Tony De Maio.[41]

Another International Brigades veteran who testified in 1940 was Humberto Galleani. Galleani had come to the United States in 1924 to escape Mussolini's fascism, joined the CPUSA in the 1930s, and became one of the first American volunteers to reach Spain. Galleani, who had served as an International Brigades staff officer, said that he had known De Maio as an officer at an International Brigades prison at Castle de Fells.[42] Anthony De Maio also appeared before the Dies committee. De Maio, an American Communist and International Brigades officer, had become an official of the United Electrical, Radio, and Machine Workers of America after his service in Spain.[43] He was uninformative about his Spanish activities, claiming that he had served with the infantry and knew nothing about any executions, and of Albert Wallach said, "Never heard of him. . . . No knowledge whatsoever."[44]

Historians have largely refused to treat as reliable the testimony of Palega, Galleani, and McCuiston about Wallach. In *The Odyssey of the Abraham Lincoln Brigade*, Peter Carroll questions the credibility of Palega's testimony but not of De Maio's, depicts Wallach himself as a liar, coward, and deserter, and, although agreeing that Wallach died in Spain, does not concede that he was executed. Rosenstone in *Crusade on the Left* suggests that Wallach and others suspected of being executed for ideological reasons "were simply

notes that "he has again become irresponsible, habitually drinking, etc.," and indicates that McCuiston was expelled from and readmitted to the party at least once (Lapin to Organizational Commission, 22 January 1934, RTsKhIDNI 515–1–3509).

41. Testimony of William C. McCuiston, 12 April 1940, House Special Committee on Un-American Activities, *Investigation of Un-American Propaganda Activities in the United States*, 13:7828.

42. Testimony of Humberto Galleani, 12 April 1940, House Special Committee on Un-American Activities, *Investigation of Un-American Propaganda Activities in the United States*, 13:7816.

43. In 1949 the CIO denounced the United Electrical, Radio, and Machine Workers of America as Communist controlled and expelled it.

44. Testimony of Anthony De Maio, 12 April 1940, House Special Committee on Un-American Activities, *Investigation of Un-American Propaganda Activities in the United States*, 13:7804, 7807.

killed in battle or executed for desertion."[45] There were about 3,300 Americans in the International Brigades, and assertions about the number of American volunteers executed for desertion by the International Brigades vary from none to several score. Although the United States executed deserters during the American Civil War, since that time executions have been extremely rare. American forces did not execute any deserters during the Spanish-American War, World War I, the Korean War, the Vietnam War, or the Gulf War. In World War II the American armed forces executed only one man for desertion out of the more than sixteen million serving.

Documents located in the International Brigades archives establish that Tony De Maio was not an infantryman but an officer with the SIM, the Servicio investigación militar, the military security police.[46] The International Brigades's SIM was autonomous from that of the Spanish Republican army and worked under the de facto control of the Political Commissariat of the International Brigades and was supervised by Alexander Orlov, a senior Soviet intelligence officer.[47]

A file on Albert Wallach was located in the Comintern archives. The documents in this file provide compelling evidence that Anthony De Maio lied to Congress when he denied knowledge of Albert Wallach. They also strongly support the conclusion that Wallach was executed. **Document 47,** dated 26 September 1938 and headed with Wallach's name, contains the statement "Report presented by Comrade DE MAIO." The document establishes De

45. Rosenstone, *Crusade on the Left,* 374. Rosenstone indicates that those executed, if any, were few. Peter Carroll puts the number executed at less than ten (Peter N. Carroll, *The Odyssey of the Abraham Lincoln Brigade: Americans in the Spanish Civil War* [Stanford, Calif.: Stanford University Press, 1994], 184–88).

46. Personal questionnaire filled out by hand and signed by Anthony De Maio, Comissariado de Guerra de las Brigadas Internacionales, 13 November 1938, RTsKhIDNI 545–6–880; biographical extract on Anthony De Maio, "Extractos de la biografia escrita el 20.9.38," 20 September 1938, RTsKhIDNI 545–6–880.

47. On the nature of the International Brigades' SIM, see R. Dan Richardson, *Comintern Army: The International Brigades and the Spanish Civil War* (Lexington: University Press of Kentucky, 1982), 161; Stanley Payne, *The Spanish Revolution* (New York: Norton, 1970), 346–47; Verle Johnston, *Legions of Babel: The International Brigades in the Spanish Civil War* (University Park: Pennsylvania State University Press, 1967), 105. Orlov later defected. See John Costello and Oleg Tsarev, *Deadly Illusions* (New York: Crown, 1993).

Maio's knowledge of Wallach. In it, Wallach is accused of deserting the International Brigades and of contacting American consuls in Valencia and Barcelona, and it is asserted that the consul in Barcelona gave Wallach false CNT credentials.[48] Until this document was found, the only evidence linking Wallach and the CNT was Edward Palega's 1954 testimony. Consequently, this document greatly enhances his credibility. **Document 48**, a 1938 list of "suspicious individuals and deserters" of the XV International Brigade, contains a note that Wallach had deserted and had "forged some documents at the US Embassy." The documents referred to may have been the safe conduct that, according to Palega, Wallach forged using the American consul's stationery.

Document 47 says that the American military attaché in Barcelona had asked Wallach to obtain military information. It concludes, ominously, "All evidence shows quite plainly that he was working as a spy." Another International Brigades document states bluntly that Wallach was an "agent of the U.S. espionage service."[49] There is no reason to believe that Wallach was an American spy. Only in the circumscribed world of the Comintern where one's first loyalty was to Moscow would an American citizen talking to the American consul be regarded as evidence of espionage. Although the documents found in the International Brigades records and discussed here do not prove that Wallach was executed, they do strongly point to a death sentence for him.[50]

48. This document also states that Wallach spent some time at Camp Lukas, an International Brigades rear area facility. McCuiston in his 1940 testimony stated that he had seen both De Maio and Wallach at Camp Lukas.

49. "Wallach, Albert, americano, periodista . . . ," 11 July 1938, RTsKhIDNI 545–6–1008.

50. When Wallach died is not clear. Palega in his 1939 letter quoted above stated he feared Wallace was executed in July 1938. However, document 47, De Maio's report on Wallach, is dated 26 September 1938 and is written in a way that implies he was alive at that time. If the latter is the case, he could not have been, as some defenders of the International Brigades have suggested, subsequently released from prison, sent to the front, and killed in combat. In September 1938 the Spanish Republic ordered its international volunteers to demobilize; the American battalions fought their last action on 24 September and withdrew from the front. The first large group of American volunteers left Spain in December, with the rest following in the next several months. Albert Wallach never returned.

# Document 47

"Report Presented by Comrade De Maio," 26 September 1938, RTsKhIDNI 545–6–1008. In the original the title is in Spanish and the main body of the text in English. F.A.I. is the Spanish acronym for the Federation of Iberian Anarchists, the political arm of the C.N.T. labor federation.

WALLACH Albert M. (Americano)

Sept. 26, 1938

(Report presented by Comrade DE MAIO)

Albert M. Wallach

American, age 24, came to Spain via the "COMMITTEE TO AID SPANISH DEMOCRACY" through France. He is a newspaperman and the son of a Lawyer. He left France on the "CITY OF BARCELONA" which was sunk of the coast of Spain, 29/5/37. he was sent to Tarazona where he remained until July and then went to the officers school at Pozo-Rubio later he went to the Medical Commission where he was found fit for auxiliary work in the rear. He was arrested and sent to CAMP LUKAS from which he deserted and visited the American consul in Valencia. In December 1937 he again contacted the American consul and the MILITARY ATTACHÈ this time in Barcelona.

He admits that he was often questioned and as often received money from the above mentioned consul. He said the military attaché asked the following type of questions. What type artillary have we, how much ammo, what are the markings, and reference to different members of the Brigade? To aid him he was given a document by the consul which showed that he worked as a newspaperman for the C.N.T.   F.A.I.

All evidence shows quite plainly that he was working as a spy.

W ALLACH Albert M. (Americano)

(Informe entregado por el camarada DE MAIO)    Sept. 26, 1938    57

### Albert M. Wallach

American, age 24, came to Spain via the "COMMITTEE TO AID SPANISH DEMOCRACY" through France. He is a newspaperman and the son of a Lawyer. He left France on the "CITY OF BARCELONA" which was sunk of the coast of Spain. 29/5/37. he was sent to Tarazona where he remained until July and then went to the officers school at Pozo-Rubio later he went to the Medical Commission where he was found fit for auxiliary work in the rear. He was arrested and sent to CAMP LUKAS from which he deserted and visited the American consul in Valencia. In December 1937 he again contacted the American consul and the MILITARY ATTACHE` this time in Barcelona.

He admits that he was often questioned and as often received money from the above mentioned consul. He said the military attache asked the following typo of questions. Hazdxxtxxxxx What type artillary have we, how much ammo, what are the markings, and reference to different members of the Brigade? To aid him he was given a document by the consul which showed that he worked as a newspaperman for the C.N.T. F.A.I.

All evidence shows quite plainly that he was working as a spy.

DOCUMENT 47. "Report Presented by Comrade De Maio," 26 September 1938.

# Document 48

"List of Suspicious Individuals and Deserters from the XVth Brigade," RTsKhIDNI 545–3–451. Original in Spanish. This document is undated, but in one section refers to deserters from operations at the end of July 1938. Consequently, the list was compiled after that date, probably in late July or August 1938. Albert Wallach appears in the list twice, and the entries appear here in boldface type. Personnel on the list are designated by unit. The XV Brigade of the International Brigades consisted at this time of four combat battalions, the 57th through the 60th, and various support units. The 57th battalion consisted chiefly of British volunteers reinforced by some Spanish soldiers. The 58th battalion was the Abraham Lincoln battalion, into which the remnants of the George Washington battalion had been merged. Most of the soldiers of the 58th were Americans, but by this time Spanish reinforcements were also present. The 59th battalion consisted almost entirely of Spanish soldiers. The 60th battalion was the Mackenzie-Papineau battalion; nominally the 60th was a Canadian battalion, but there were more Americans than Canadians in its ranks, along with Spanish reinforcements.

## LIST OF SUSPICIOUS INDIVIDUALS AND DESERTERS FROM THE XVTH BRIGADE

| Name | Battalion | Rank | Report |
|---|---|---|---|
| Bernard Abramofski | Ing. | Soldier | Deserted. Friend of White. |
| Acton | 57 | " | Deserted. Defeatist. |
| Aitken | 57 | " | Morally weak. Complainer. |
| Frank Alexander | 59 | — | Agitator against Spaniards. |
| Anderson | Muleteer | Officer | Follower of Wattis. |
| Sam Anderson | 59 | Soldier | Agitator against Spaniards |
| Henry Archibald | — | " | Detained near border. |
| James Arnot | 57 | — | Drunk, several times. |
| Stanley Baggerley | 57 | " | Deserter. Fascist friends. |
| Backell | 57 | " | Appears suspicious. Being watched. |
| Frank Bailey | 57 | — | Sent to disciplinary. |
| Baker | Auto-Park | — | Spoke in defeatist manner. |
| George Baker | 57 | " | Jailed 10 weeks in Castelldefels. |
| Baranowsky | 60 | — | Drunkard. Deserter. |
| Barker | — | " | Jailed 10 weeks in Castelldefels. |
| Barltrop | 57 | " | Arrested drunk. Bad conduct. |
| Leavit Barret | — | — | Suspicious. |
| Henry Barry or Barrie | 58 | " | Suspicious Trotskyist. Tried to desert. |
| Joseph Basan | — | — | Always far from the front. |
| Baxter (Frank) | 56 | — | Defeatist (insults government). |
| Ed. George Bee | 57 | Lieut. | Crazy. Lies and incites. |
| Joe Blar | 57 | — | Deserted. He was thought to be good. |

| Name | Battalion | Rank | Report |
|------|-----------|------|--------|
| Edward Boivin | 60 | — | Feigns illness. |
| Tahimon Bolislao | 59 | — | Fought. Very impulsive. |
| Jacob Bonnes | 57 | — | Sent for provisions then deserted. |
| Fristz Borer | 60 | — | Drunkard. Slept on guard duty. Arrested. |
| Boswell | 57 | — | Trotskyist. Being watched. |
| Max Bowers | Auto-Park | — | Deserted. Arrested. |
| Brickel | — | — | Arrested. Demoralized. |
| Harry Brooks | 57 | Soldier | Deserted 4-17-38. |
| William Brown | — | " | Deserted 4-2-38. |
| J. de Bruel | 57 | " | Spoke of deserting. Arrested. |
| Lawrence Bruton | 58 | — | Missing from battalion. Presumed deserted. |
| John Bubanicz | 60 | — | Deserted January 1938. |
| Joe Buckley | 57 | — | Imprisoned. Left without permission. |
| A. Burgess | — | — | Drunkard. Arrested for stealing food. |
| Robert Burns | — | — | Bad record in Spain. |
| Leonard Burton | 57 | — | Hit guard. |
| Frank Butler | 57 | Sergeant | Deserted. Claimed to be anti-Fascist. |
| Cains | — | — | Morally weak. |
| Archi[e] Campbell | 57 | — | Complainer. Previously arrested. |
| Ruben Carballo Gonzalez | 59 | Soldier | Deserted. Went abroad. |
| Carlisle | 57 | — | Suspicious. Inciter. |
| Peter Cassidy | 57 | Soldier | Drunkard. Incites and threatens. |
| Sidney Chapman | 57 | " | Tried to desert twice. |
| Albert Chishold | 58 | — | Missing from battalion. Presumed deserted. |
| Nathan Cohen | — | — | Weak. Politically suspicious. |
| Sidney Cohen | 60 | — | Missing from battalion since April [19]38. |
| Michael Collins | 60 | — | Drunkard. Scorns officers. |
| Julius Colman | 57 | — | Presumed deserted in Brunete. Seen in Planas. |
| Cornwallis | 57 | Sergeant | Believed to be arrested in Tarragona. |
| Constantino Covatis | 57 | Soldier | Very suspicious. Deserted. — |

| Name | Battalion | Rank | Report |
|---|---|---|---|
| Charles Cronin | — | Soldier | Said was arrested in error. |
| Cryer | 57 | Paymaster | Suspicious. Needs to be watched. |
| Alex Cummings | 57 | Lieut. | Bureaucrat, pretentious. Fearful. |
| Gus Daulsensheck | 57 | — | Suspicious. Tries to go home. |
| Albert Davies | 57 | Soldier | Bad individual. Deserted several times. |
| Dinners | — | — | Lazy, undisciplined. Suspicious. |
| James Donegan | 57 | — | Deserted, persuaded by other. |
| Donek | 58 | — | Suspicious. |
| Franklin Dow | — | — | Not suitable for the front. |
| Charles Downey | 57 | — | Mentally abnormal. Illiterate. |
| John Ducksberry | 57 | — | Disobeyed orders because of fear. |
| Henry Duffy | 60 | — | Arrested drunk. Left without — |
| William Duffy | 60 | Soldier | Drunkard. Bad individual. Keep watch. |
| Larry Dukes | 60 | — | Deserted. Thought to be in Corbera — |
| Dunbar | 57 | Soldier | Panicked. Riotous. |
| Dunne | 57 | — | Comes from Legión. Obedient. — |
| Durston | 57 | — | Dubious individual. |
| John Farmer | 57 | — | Deserter. Good record. |
| Wm. Henry Featherstone | 57 | Soldier | Wrote home calumnious letters. |
| Jerome Ferrojero | 58 | — | Mercenary soldier in several armies. |
| John Foyer | 57 | — | Deserted. Has missed everyone. |
| Clifford Garrow | 60 | — | Deserted in March of 1938. |
| Thomas Gleadhill | — | — | Deserted on retreat from Gandean. |
| Edwin Greening | 57 | — | Deserted. Has missed all very much. |
| Harry Greenwood | 57 | — | Deserted. |
| Hass (Andrie) | 60 | — | Deserted. |
| John Heaney | 60 | — | Deserted. |
| Herberry | Brigade | Quartermaster General | Deserted before holding the post. |

# Document 48 *continued*

| Name | Battalion | Rank | Report |
|---|---|---|---|
| Leonard Herert | — | Soldier | Tried to desert. Was jailed. |
| William Hewlett | 57 | — | Deserted. Presumably under influence. |
| James Hodgson | 57 | — | Deserted. Induced others. |
| Holtzman | 58 | — | Insubordinate. Tried to desert. |
| Wesley Howard | 58 | Soldier | Deserter. Weak and instigator. |
| Thomas Howie | 57 | " | Deserted several times. |
| Ben Hughes | 57 | " | Deserted. |
| Steve Hunrick | 58 | " | Deserted. |
| William Isaac | Auto-Park | — | Deserted. |
| Isobanni | 60 | Soldier | Very undisciplined. |
| John Jacques | 58 | — | Deserted. |
| James ----- | 57 | — | Very provoking. |
| I. - Jones | 57 | " | Provoking. |
| I. Kelly | — | — | Deserted. |
| Harry King | — | Corporal | Deserted. |
| George Kiranos | — | Soldier | Deserted. |
| Joseph Kierlein | 60 | Sergeant | Deserted. |
| Kremmer | 57 | — | Defeatist. |
| Charles Kuch | — | — | Deserted. |
| Alexander Lewis | 60 | Corporal | Swindler. |
| Chrise Litsas | 58 | Sergeant | Deserted. |
| Looser | 60 | Soldier | Demoralizer. Was demoted. |
| Louden | 57 | " | Deserted. |
| James Lucas or Dutton | 60 | " | Agitator. Aggressive. |
| Evan Lloyd | 57 | " | Deserted. |
| Richard McAleenan | — | " | Was in jail. |
| Lawrence McCallough | 58 | " | Deserted. |
| Patrick McGill | 57 | " | Recidivistic deserter. |
| Joseph McGill | 57 | " | Deserted. |
| Patrick Bryan McGuinness | 60 | " | Deserted. |
| John McLean | 57 | — | Deserted. |
| Robert McLean | Trans. Brigade | — | Deserted. |
| William McLennan | 57 | — | Deserted. |
| Francis MacMann | 60 | — | Deserted. |
| Hector Manning | 57 | Soldier | Deserted several times. |
| Alex Marcovitz | 57 | " | Defeatist. |
| Anthony Maresca Stephen | 59 | — | Supposedly tried to desert. |
| Rubin Markowitz | — | " | Tried to desert. Detained aboard |

# Document 48 *continued*

| Name | Battalion | Rank | Report |
|---|---|---|---|
| Dan Markovsky | 60 | — | Deserted. |
| Suarre Martinson | 60 | — | Disappeared from the company. |
| Chris Martin | 57 | — | Tried to desert. |
| William Mason | 58 | — | Defeatist and agitator. |
| Frank Middleton | 57 | Soldier | Accused of intent to desert. |
| Morris Mickenberg | 58 | — | Defeatist. Suspect Trotskyist. |
| Roland Mitter | — | " | Deserted. |
| Thompson Mochov | 57 | — | Presumed deserted. |
| Eugene Molte | 57 | Lieut. | Deserted. Suspect Trotskyist. |
| John Monks | 57 | — | Deserted in Brunete. |
| Joseph Moran | 57 | Soldier | Tried to desert. |
| James Muntin | 57 | — | Deserted. |
| O'Connor | 57 | — | Deserted. |
| Olson | 58 | — | Tried to desert. |
| James Oregan | 57 | Corporal | Deserted. |
| Frank Parsons | 60 | Soldier | Deserted. |
| Michael Pavlov | 57 | — | Arrested espionage suspect. |
| Tomás Paz Moreno | 59 | — | Deserted. |
| Peter Philips | — | — | Recidivistic deserter. |
| Frank Plumb | 58 | Soldier | Accused of desertion. |
| Erkki Poikalainen | 60 | " | Deserted. |
| Emil Portois | — | " | Intended desertion and suicide. |
| Evan Price | 57 | — | Disappeared. Presumed deserted. |
| Ronald Gordon Pulford | — | — | Deserted. |
| James Queen | 57 | — | Presumed deserted. Disappeared from company. |
| Juan Rafa | 57 | Lieut. | Immoral. Attempted to rape women in Darmes. |
| Peter Reiter | — | Soldier | Deserted. |
| John Reitz | 60 | " | Deserted. |
| Andrew Royce | 58 | " | Deserted. |
| Lewis Ruben | 57 | " | Would hide during combat, appearing afterward. |
| Walter Ryder | 57 | " | Tried to desert. |
| Aristides Saavedra | 59 | " | Tried to desert. |
| Saiman Saleman | 60 | " | Deserted. |
| George Sands | 58 | " | Accused of intent to desert. |
| Joseph Sands | 58 | " | Deserted. |
| Robert Schweinfest | — | " | Deserted. |

# Document 48 *continued*

| Name | Battalion | Rank | Report |
|------|-----------|------|--------|
| Roy Scuder | 58 | " | Suspected of intent to desert. |
| Ed Shaker | 58 | — | Accused of intent to desert. |
| Joaquin de Silva | 60 | " | Deserted. |
| Bernard Singer | — | — | Deserted. |
| Espil Spencer | 60 | " | Recidivistic deserter. Appears mentally ill. |
| John Spencer | 57 | — | Deserted. |
| Albert Stubs | 58 | " | Agitator. |
| Peter Sturgeon | — | Serg. Inte. | Presumed deserted. |
| John Takas | 58 | Soldier | Deserted. |
| Erkkila Tauno | 60 | " | Presumed deserted. |
| Patrick Tigue | 57 | — | Suspected intent to desert. |
| James Thompson | 57 | Sergeant | Presumed deserted. |
| Leonard Thompson | 57 | " | Very impulsive and aggressive. |
| Walter Tugwell | 57 | Soldier | Deserted. |
| George Turner | 58 | — | Missing from battalion. Presumed deserted. |
| Uedale | 58 | " | Demoralizer. |
| Robert E. Usher | — | " | Demoralizer and defeatist. |
| **Albert M. Wallach** | — | — | **Deserter. Forged documents.** |
| Gerald Ward | — | " | Tried to desert. Returned voluntarily. |
| James Wharmly | 60 | — | Defeatist and agitator. Hates Spaniards. |
| Milton White | 60 | — | Deserted. |
| Leslie Wiches Dair | 57 | — | Trotskyist. |
| Fish Wolf | 60 | — | Tried to forge permit and desert. |
| John Wood | E.M. | Soldier | Deserted. |
| John Wynne | 58 | " | Recidivistic deserter. |
| Archibald Yemm | 57 | " | Deserted. |
| John Young | — | " | Arrested on dock in Barcelona. |
| Sam Zackman | 58 | — | Deserted. Is in Paris. |
| P. Murphy | — | — | Demoralizer. |
| E. -. Rose | c. de E. Sanidad | | Withheld reports, insubordination, rumorist. |
| Jorgenson | 58 | Sergeant | Acted in suspicious manner in front of enemy. |
| Cyril Spencer | 60 | — | Said he was going for water. Hid and escaped. |
| Poward Taus | 58 | — | Presumed deserted. |

# Document 48 *continued*

| Name | Battalion | Rank | Report |
|---|---|---|---|
| Stanley Vernon | 58 | — | Deserted. |
| Robert Nelson | 58 | — | Deserted. |
| Adolf Bovaimen | 60 | — | Accused of self-inflicted wounds. |
| Vilfredo Mas | 59 | — | Presumed intent to desert. |
| McDowell | 60 | — | Anti-Spanish, promotes riots. |
| Jack Arnold | 58 | — | Suspected Trotskyist. |
| Edward Balchowsky | 58 | — | Defeatist. |
| Alejo Sanchez | 59 | — | Deserter. |
| Aniceto Alejardo | 59 | — | Deserter. |
| Peter Deenko | 60 | — | Deserter. |
| Lahte Vilpas | 60 | — | Disappeared. Presumed deserted. |
| Lu-atainen Vikko | 60 | — | idem. |
| Tugvinen Heik | 60 | — | idem. |
| Jose Pomroy | 60 | Soldier | Deserted from hospital. |
| Sam Echstein | 58 | " | Deserted. |
| M. Tyni Anderson | 60 | " | Receives foreign Fascist newspaper. |
| Andrew Flanagan | 57 | Sergeant | Deserted. |
| Alfred [illeg.] | 58 | Soldier | Extremely suspicious of being Nazi agent. |
| Joseph Keil | 58 | Transm | Has been inciteful lately. |

INDIVIDUALS DETAINED BY THE BRIGADES' DISCIPLINARY COMPANY

| Name | Rank | Report |
|---|---|---|
| Edwin Bee | Demoted Lieut. | Agitator, liar and defeatist. |
| Hillden Skinner | " " | Deserted several times. |
| Peter Phillips | Soldier | Deserted several times. Also agitator. |
| Robert Schweinfest | " | Three times deserter. |
| Joseph Klerlein | " | Deserted several times. |
| Frank Plumb | " | " " " |
| Robert McLean | " | Deserter. Bad individual. |
| Patrick Bryan McGuinness | " | Very bad individual. |
| Patrick Tihne | " | Defeatist. Bad individual. |
| John Mahler | " | Three times deserter. |
| Ronald Gordon Pulford | " | " " " |
| Milton Stillman | " | Bad individual. |
| Challis Escott | " | " " |
| Daniel Markowski | " | Deserted two times. |
| Sidney Silvent | " | Deserter. |
| William Rogers | " | " |

## Document 48 *continued*

| | | | |
|---|---|---|---|
| Frank Baxter | " | | Bad individual. |
| William Acton | " | | Bad individual. |
| James Queen | " | | Recidivistic deserter. |
| Ruben Lewis | " | | " " |
| Bernard Monten | " | | Deserter. |

PRESUMED DESERTERS FROM 58TH BATTALION DURING THE OPERATIONS
IN END JULY 1938

Roland Cleveland
Jack Liffland
Irving Wienshank

LIST OF SUSPICIOUS INDIVIDUALS FROM DIFFERENT BATTALIONS
OF THE XVTH BRIGADE

*57th Battalion*

| | | | |
|---|---|---|---|
| Actin | Soldier | 2nd | Bad individual. |
| Aiken | " | " | Morally weak. |
| Walter Anderson | " | — | Drunkard. |
| Stanley Baggerley | " | 1st | Somewhat rowdy. |
| Baikell | " | 4th | Appears suspicious. |
| Frank Barltrop | " | 1st | Drunkard. |
| Ed. George Bee | Lieut. | — | Provocation campaign. |
| Boswell | — | 4th | Supposed Trotskyist. |
| Harry Brooks | Soldier | 3rd | Deserter, detained in Figueras. |
| Brown | " | 4th | Under observation. |
| Cains | " | — | Morally weak. |
| José Calatayud | Lieut. E. Major | | Under observation. |
| Jack Carson | Soldier | 1st | Bad individual. |
| Henry McCaskill | " | — | (No details available) |
| Peter Cassidy | " | 2nd | Arrested drunk and threatening. |
| Juan Cots Fanca | " | — | (No details available) |
| Constantino Covatis | " | — | (No details available) |
| Alex Cummings | Lieut. | — | Very bureaucratic. |
| Albert Davies | Soldier | 1st | Deserted twice. |
| Gus Dausenbeck | — | 2nd | Tried to go home. Wattis sympathizer. |
| Charles Downy | — | — | Illiterate and mentally abnormal. |
| J. DeBrouell | Soldier | 4th | Tried to desert and afraid of the front. |
| Dunne | — | — | Under observation. |
| Durston | Soldier | 4th | Being watched. |

| | | | |
|---|---|---|---|
| Early | Soldier | 4th | Very weak morally. |
| Evant | Company Commander | | Exhausted and demoralized. |
| Miguel Fortuny Posta | " | 1st | Deserted in Calaceite. |
| John W. Fowlkes | " | 1st | Drunkard. |
| Rafael Garmendia | " | 3rd | Reactionary individual. |
| José Gars Alcovebre | " | — | Deserted in Calaceite. |
| Wam. Gaunlett | " | — | (No details available) |
| James Glavin | " | — | Drunkard and undisciplined. |
| Emery Griffith | Corporal | 4th | Tried to desert. Insolent. |
| Ernest Herbert | Soldier | 4th | Repeated protest over food. |
| Pilson    " | " | " | "      "      "      " |
| Thomas Howie | " | " | Deserter. Very demoralized. |
| Charles Humphreys | " | 1st | Arrested once for drunkenness. |
| Peter James | " | 4th | Provocateur. |
| James Jones | Sergeant | 1st | Drunkard and undisciplined. |
| Tom Jones | — | — | Disappeared in Calaceite and deserted in Brunete. |
| I. H. Jones | Soldier | 4th | Suspicious individual. |
| Kane | " | 2nd | Morally weak. |
| Kremmer | — | 4th | Demoralizer. |
| Lord | Soldier | 2nd | Morally weak. |
| Lowry | " | 2nd | Arrested in Mataró for escaping from hospital to brigade. |
| Lloyd | " | 4th | Under observation. |
| Evan Lloyd | " | — | Deserted and was arrested in the mountains. |
| Hector Manning | " | P. May. | Good conduct until Brunete, then demoralized. |
| Mazoni | " | 4th | Too much time in Spain. Little front. Bad background. |
| Marcovitch | " | 1st | Very bad individual. |
| Frank Middleton | " | 4th | Tried to desert. Bad individual in Company. |
| James Miller | " | 1st | Arrested for drunkenness in Tarrega. |
| John Mitcheson | " | 1st | Drunkenness in Tarrega. Under observation. |
| Moffat | " | 4th | Frightful. |
| Doming Morales | Lieut. | — | Drunkard. Sabotage in Garcín. |

| | | | |
|---|---|---|---|
| Nicholas A. (Trans) | Soldier | 2nd | Bad individual. |
| Noguer | Corporal | — | Ignorant, but also fakes it to see if he's evacuated. |
| Orte Carrillo | Corporal | — | Deserted in Calaceite. |
| Steve Palmer | Coc. | — | Demoralized. |
| Parra | Sergeant | — | Arrested for AWOL. |
| Michael Pavlov | — | — | Suspected of espionage. |
| J. Ant. Ponce | Commander. | Demoted | Is very afraid, confesses that he cannot help it. |
| Queen | — | — | Lazy, shameless scoundrel and drunkard. |
| Juan Rafa | Lieut. | 2nd | Tried to rape a woman in Darmós. |
| Alexander Reid | Soldier | — | Arrested for drunken behavior. |
| Benjamin Richardson | " | 1st | " " " and demoralizing behavior. |
| Maurice Ryan | " | [?] | Very bad and suspicious individual. |
| José Sanchez Mart. | (Trans) | | Under observation. |
| Cyril Scott | Soldier | 1st | Drunkard. |
| José Serrano | (Camil) | | Angered by a dispute. Threatened the International. |
| Leonard Thompson | Sergeant | 2nd | Quarrelsome and drunkard. |
| Miguel Torens Sala | Soldier | 4th | Deserted in Gandesa. |
| Manuel Termes | " | 2nd | Carries an unauthorized weapon. |
| Walter Tugwoll | Soldier | 4th | Deserter, detained in the Pyrenees. |
| Wakton | " | 3rd | Suspicious. |
| Elenio Valls | Sergeant | 3rd | Demoralizer. |
| D. Windline | Soldier | — | Coward. |
| Archibald Yimm | " | [?] | Deserter, detained in the Pyrenees. |
| Felix Saenz Rubio | Lieut. | — | His conduct in Calaceite was not good. |
| James McDonald | Soldier | — | Demoralized, drunkard, subversive, undisciplined. |
| Baldugs | — | — | Deserter, demoralizer, bad individual. |
| Malcolm Smith | — | — | Tried to desert, morally weak. |
| Andrew Oum | — | — | Possible agent on a small scale. |

| | | | |
|---|---|---|---|
| F. Thompson | — | — | Fascist family and very suspicious friends. |
| J. Cryer | Paymaster | — | Suspicious, possible agent intelligence service. |
| Glassey | — | 1st | Tried to desert. |
| Remy Goldmy | — | — | Demoted Commissioner. Goes around with Marcovitch. |
| Sydney Silver T. | — | — | Bad history, suspected of spying. |
| Jose Hughes | — | 3rd | Demoralized. |
| Kueddon | — | 3rd | Demoralized. |
| William Meeks | — | — | Undisciplined. |
| John Miller | — | — | Fearful. |
| Lobland | — | — | Panicky, drunkard, tried to desert. |
| Monks | — | — | Deserted in Calaceite. Panicky. |
| Simon | Sergt/Lieut. | 3rd | Belongs to the C.N.T. Claims to belong to the Communist party but does not. |
| Seutts | — | — | Deserted. Bad individual. |
| Ackwell | — | — | Demoralizer. |
| Gallagher | — | — | Tried to desert. |
| Harrington | — | — | Demoralizer. |
| Hanvey | — | — | Demoralizer. |
| Goldwin | — | — | Drunkard. |
| Archie Campbell | — | — | Complainer. Arrested. |
| Wickes, Leslie | — | — | Language professor. Trotsky sympathizer. |
| McEvoy | — | — | Drunkard. |
| Thomas Howie | — | — | (Already reported) |
| José Pasarols Pasarols | | | Speaks badly of the Internationals. |
| Jacobo Bonnes | — | — | Under observation. |
| Stubbs | — | — | Quarrelsome and disobedient. |
| Marks | — | — | Demoralizer. |
| Brickel | — | — | " |
| Dunbar | — | 2nd | Panicky. [?] |

*58th Battalion*

| | | | |
|---|---|---|---|
| Bernat Abramofski | Soldier | [?] | Deserter. |
| Henry Barrie | " | — | Provocateur and propagandist. Very suspicious. |
| Max Borvers | " | Auto-Park | Deserter. |
| Brutton | " | 3rd | Is head of a group that plans to desert. |
| Carlisle | " | 1st | Sanitary. Suspicious. |
| Claver | Lieut. | 4th | Rumored to belong to the P.O.U.M. |
| Vicente Coves Segarra | Sergeant | 1st | Suspicious. |
| Albert Chishold | Soldier | — | Tried to desert. |
| Emilio Esenders Gomez | " | 4th | Arrested for arguing with Sergeant. |
| García | Captain | 4th | Longtime military man. Suspicious. |
| Eduardo García | Soldier | — | Under observation. |
| Manuel García | Soldier | 2nd | Dubious friends. Family in other region. |
| Jaime Gilbert Perelló | " | 5th | Has belonged to Citizen Action. |
| Francisco Guillot | " | 3rd | Suspicious. |
| Walter Gunderman | " | — | Deserter. |
| William Halliwell | Lieut. | — | Improper conduct for a Lieutenant. |
| Hardy | Soldier | 5th | Protest demonstrations. |
| Howard Wesley | Soldier | [?] | Good conduct but deserted. Demoralized. |
| Kaminski | — | — | Follower of Wattis. |
| Nicolas Kurlikiotis | Major | 2nd | Very suspicious. |
| Massot | — | 2nd | Suspicious. Defeatist. |
| Elias Ortigas Villacampa | — | 2nd | Supposed Trotskyist. |
| José Remacho Jimenez | Lieut. | — | Good conduct but deserted on 10/3 |
| José Saltó | Soldier | (transferred to 60th Battalion) | Conduct in Battalion 5838 was very provocative, also wrote provocative letters. |
| George Sand | " | 3rd | Tried to desert with Brutton's group. |
| José Sand | " | [?] | Deserted in Mora la Nueva. |
| Hilario Sanz | Lieut. | (transferred) | Works towards the disunity of the International and the Spanish. |

| | | | |
|---|---|---|---|
| Roy Scudder | Soldier | [?] | Professional complainer. |
| Ed Shaker | " | — | Tried to desert on a ship. |
| Albert Stubbs | " | — | Arrested for insubordination and disobedience. Instigator. |
| Vig Swan | " | [?] | Suspicious. Suspicious friends in (?) |
| José Takats | " | — | Tried to desert but regretted having done so. |
| John Takats | " | — | " " " " |
| Updale | " | 1st | Demoralizer. |
| Rod Wigles | " | 3rd | Tried to desert with Brutton's group. |
| Samuel Zackman | " | 3rd | id. id. |
| Matias Lara Rodríguez | " | — | Protester and instigator. |
| Andrés Llansó | " | — | " " |
| Jaime Masa Vidal | " | — | " " |
| Luis Guerrero Portoles | " | — | (Lieut. demoted for desertion.) |
| José Remacho Jimenez | Lieut. | — | (Arrested. Deserter.) |
| Wesley Howard | — | — | Deserter. |
| Holtzman | — | — | Insubordination and attempt to desert. |
| Olson | — | — | " " |
| Jerome Ferrojero | — | — | Very suspicious character. |
| Andrés Pataghan | — | — | Arrested for drunkenness. Shady background. |
| | | | |
| *59th Battalion* | | | |
| Barrios | Sergeant | 4th | Is brutal with soldiers. |
| Castillo | Captain | 3rd | Became drunk and when reported he threatened the chief of the SIM and anyone else who reports him. |
| Emilio Diaz Moya | — | 1st | Insubordination. |
| Eugenio Fernández | — | 4th | Demoralized. |
| Luis Gonzalez | — | 4th | Instigator, defeatist, demoralizer. |
| Isovani | — | 1st | Very undisciplined. |
| Fco. Madrid Mellado | — | — | Demoted Commissioner. Very fearful. |
| José Mamporo | — | 3rd | Few morals, little discipline, and protester. |

| Name | Rank | Company | Notes |
|---|---|---|---|
| Mesa | — | 2nd | Under observation. |
| Antonio Muñoz | [?] | 3rd | Under observation. |
| Tomás Paz Moreno | — | — | Has deserted twice. |
| Crs. René Dios | — | 4th | Very demoralizing, adventurer, bad individual. |
| Salvador [?] Roger | — | 3rd | Has a Royal pistol. Not of good character. |
| Romero | Commissioner | 3rd | Not a very good Commissioner; threatens to give 25 bullets to whoever reports him. |
| Aristides Saavedra | Soldier | 4th | Has previously committed disastrous acts of provocation, but is behaving better now. |
| Salsaner | " | 1st | Very undisciplined. |
| Sianotoivoy | " | 1st | Very undisciplined. |
| Soriano | Lieut. | 4th | Military man from the old armed forces. His conduct leaves something to be desired. |
| Ugartividea | Soldier | 2nd | Suspicious. |
| Fco. Martínez Ortega | " | 2nd | It is not known if he is in the battalion. Signaled the Fascists. |
| Evelio Mesa Amarat | — | 3rd | Bad individual, undisciplined, defeatist. |
| Cosme Malero | Soldier | 3rd | Bad individual, undisciplined. |
| Antonio Castellano | — | 2nd | Headed a troop and in Calaceite abandoned his troop, alleging illness. |
| Ramón Barberá | — | — | Idiot playboy. |
| Domingo da Silva | — | — | Portuguese. Tired, demoralized. |
| Ashie Wolf | — | 1st | Translator. Tried to desert. |
| Teodoro Mañss Ruiz | Soldier | — | Has deserted twice. Is a coward and a scoundrel. |
| José Villar Orón | — | — | Deserted in Alcañiz. |
| Ricardo López Martínez | — | — | Deserted in Calaceite. |
| Francisco Gonzalez | Sergeant | — | In Calaceite he abandoned his people and gave up his weapon. |
| Domingo Quintana | — | — | Demoralizer. |

# Document 48 *continued*

| | | | |
|---|---|---|---|
| Luis Gonzalez | — | — | Demoralizer. |
| Heliodoro Perez Serra | — | — | Deserted in Gandesa. |
| Nicolás Altadilla Miguel | — | — | Deserted in Gandesa. |
| Camilo López Mondejar | — | — | Has been a gunslinger for the Fascists. Bad individual. |
| Ginés Perez Sosa | — | — | Deserted at the front. |
| Fernando Garcia | — | — | Individual of bad conduct. |
| Antonio Varela Gira | — | — | Demoted Sergeant. Bad conduct. |
| Antonio Perez Martínez | Lieut. (unconfirmed) | — | Instigator. Deserter. |
| Carmelo Marcos Palomero | — | — | Demoted Sergeant. Instigator. |
| Fco. Ibañez | — | — | Deserted the Brigade. No papers. |

*60th Battalion*

| | | | |
|---|---|---|---|
| Andrés Azor Mendes | Soldier | — | Deserted in Lagata. |
| John Bubaneez | — | — | Presumed deserted. |
| Bernardo Cano | Sergeant | — | Is very undisciplined and ridicules political rallies. Also creates discord between Cataluñas and rest of Spaniards. |
| Miguel Carpir Martinez | | — | Cannot be trusted. |
| William Duffy | Soldier | — | Drunkard. Threatens when he drinks. |
| Edward Engstron | Soldier | — | Hard drinker. |
| Erkilla Tauno | Soldier | — | Probably deserted other [?] |
| Robert Filler | Soldier | 4th | Speaks badly of our struggle. |
| Manuel García | — | 2nd | Reactionary tendencies. Suspicious. |
| Fco. García Gomez | — | 3rd | Instigator. |
| Clifford Garrow | " | 1st | Deserter. Bad conduct and instigator. |
| Glenn | " | 5th | Weak of character. Big talker, little doer. |
| Francisco Jara | — | 3rd | Is part of a group of complainers. |
| Lloyd Johnson | — | 2nd | Drunkard and insubordinate behavior. |

# Document 48 *continued*

| Name | Rank | Battalion | Notes |
|---|---|---|---|
| Jaime Latza | " | 2nd | Prominent instigator and complainer. |
| Alex Lewis | — | 2nd | Has not returned various sums of money. Arrested. |
| James Lucas or Dutton | " | — | Dangerous and insolent instigator. |
| Francisco McMann | — | — | Detained in the Pyrenees. |
| Ejdel Madsen | — | 3rd | Drunkard and careless. |
| Suerre Martinson | — | 1st | Arrested for drunken behavior. |
| Francisco Merino | — | 3rd | Suspected because of certain details. |
| Francisco Minana | Soldier | [?] | Instigator and defeatist. |
| Luis Naus | — | 3rd | Undisciplined, quarrelsome and complainer. |
| Armas Ojanen | — | 1st | Arrested for drunken behavior. |
| Frank Parsons | — | P.M. | Deserter. |
| Pelsilin | — | 5th | Suspicious and complainer. |
| Enrique Perez Vargas | — | Transferred | Under observation. |
| Ernesto Perillo | — | 3rd | Lazy, complainer, anti-Internationale. |
| Ernesto Perello | — | 5th | Somewhat dumb, but also fakes it for convenience. |
| Ekki Poikalainen | — | [?] | Deserter, detained in Figueras. |
| Ramón Ribo Alvarez | Soldier | 3rd | Under observation. |
| Ramón Rubio | — | 3rd | Is part of a group of complainers. |
| Juan Saiz | — | 5th | Tries to avoid being sent to the front. |
| William Sakti | — | 1st | Instigator and defeatist. |
| William C. Skinner | — | P.M. | Deserter twice. Coward. |
| Cyril Spencer | | 3rd | Deserter. Claims to have been crazy. |
| Cayetano (Bartonome) Torne | Soldier | — | Came from prison. Granted pardon from death penalty. |
| Toutlof | — | 1st | Continually complains and talks about strange things. |
| Ignacio Valls | — | 3rd | Suspicious and instigator. |
| Ricardo Diaz | Captain | — | Irresponsible and lacks interest in his unit. Fearful and cowardly. |
| Looser | — | — | Demoted from Lieut. to soldier. Dubious and undisciplined character. |

# Document 48 *continued*

| | | | |
|---|---|---|---|
| [illegible name] | — | — | Kitchen Commissioner. Fearful, good for nothing. |
| [illegible name] | — | — | Left Gadesa alleging illness. |
| Julio Valdes Rodríguez | — | — | Belongs to the "Ñáñigo" sect of Cuba and to the old Cuban armed forces. |
| Joseph Feller | — | — | Seems like he wants to desert. |
| Fritz Rorer | — | — | Hard drinker. |
| José Rodríguez | — | — | Ex-politician. Instigator, Trotskyist. |
| *Various Units* | | | |
| Anderson | Head Muleteer of Brigade | | Was a Wattis follower. Trotskyist. |
| William Brown | — | — | Deserted. Was detained in Figueras. Belonged to the 57th Battalion. |
| Thomas Glenhill | — | — | Deserted in Gandesa. Belonged to the 60th Battalion, Company 1. |
| N. Green (English) | — | — | Was Hospital Administrator in Valdeganga. Arrested for defending an instigator. Expelled from Spain and is now in this area again. (NOTE: This is a female). |
| Herberry | — | — | Ex-deserter. Is now quartermaster-general of Brigade. |
| George Kiranos | — | — | Deserter, detained in Seo de Urgel. Belonged to the 58th Battalion, 2nd Company. |
| Charles Kuch | — | — | Deserter. 60th Battalion, 4th Company. |
| Harry Lighter | — | — | Creates uprisings against the government. |
| Angel Mas Ballester | — | — | Deserted in Albacete. Is in hiding in the Pego mountains with several others. |
| William McKnight | — | — | Cook. Stole items from the kitchen to sell or exchange. |

| | | | |
|---|---|---|---|
| Juan Molines Soliveres | — | — | Deserted in Batea. |
| Pablo Monne Amenos | — | — | Presented himself without papers. Claims to have left with permission from the 60th Battalion, 2nd Company. |
| Ronald Gordon Pulford | — | — | Deserter. Detained in Olot. Belonged to the 57th Battalion, 3rd Company. |
| Bernard Singer | — | — | Deserter. Belonged to D.E.C.A.E.M.B.I. |
| Agustín Solsona Baldu | — | — | Classified as suspicious and instigator. Must be found. |
| Samuel Wren | — | — | Chauvinist, anti-Communist, anti-English. Imposed extremely strict discipline on others, while he got drunk. |

(Sent to the disciplinary unit because of desertion)
Harry King
Andrie Haas
Joseph Koran
Rubin Markowitz
John Heaney
John Wood
Robert Schweinfest
Joseph Klerlein
Chris E. Litsas
Lawrence McCallough
Evan Louden
Steve Hunrick
Ben Hughes

(Arrested in Castell de Fels for various reasons. Sent here.)

| | | |
|---|---|---|
| W. H. Featherstone | Bad individual. | Intercepted letter. |
| Charles Middleton | Bad individual. | |

(Presumed deserted)
Michael McLaughlin
Rose Madley
Joe Buckley
George Baker
S. Chapman
Peter Philips (Deserted in Teruel and then in Batea)
Joseph Magill

# Document 48 *continued*

(Arrested for various reasons)
Andrew Royce
John Travers
Thomas Kerr
Harry Leggett
John Lobban
Lance Rogers
Charles Watt
John Young
Frank Plumb
William Jones
Errik Hakamaki
Charles Cronin
William Haire
Paul Wirta

| | |
|---|---|
| **Albert M. Wallach** | **Deserted in Barcelona and forged some documents at the US Embassy.** |
| Alfred Litwin | Immoral. |

## LIST OF AMERICANS

| Name | Age | Causes |
|---|---|---|
| Bill Weber | | Suspicious |
| Brown Richard | 20 | Deserter |
| Bert Ahramberg | | Deserter |
| Cronin Charles | 33 | Drunkard |
| Ella Smith | 40 | Suspicious |
| Edouard Marquette | | Trotskyist |
| Fuller Henry | 23 | Demoralizer |
| Fishelson | | Deserter and thief |
| Howe William | | Deserter |
| Isenberg Robert | 25 | Deserter |
| Jacob George | 25 | Deserter |
| Johnson Lloyd | | Spy |
| Kolow Morris | | Undisciplined |
| Krupke Max | | Spy |
| Lecher Bencion | | Deserter and thief |
| Levinski Joseph | | Deserter |
| [?]otte Pierre | | Thief |
| Morrison Joe | | Deserter |
| Maurray Scheider | | Deserter |
| Montenaiolla Felice | 32 | Deserter |
| Murphy James | 37 | Deserter |
| Morris Virgil | 34 | Spy |
| Marquette Edward M. | | Thief |

| Name | Age | Causes |
|---|---|---|
| Piazacki Sigmund | | High treason |
| Peterson John | 37 | Deserter |
| Ramatowekin John A. | | Spy |
| Shapiro Larry | 27 | Undesirable |
| Siegal Joseph | | Deserter |
| Wildman Earl | | Spy |

*"Suspicious Individuals and Deserters" in the Abraham Lincoln Battalion*

Wallach is only one name in the lengthy "List of Suspicious Individuals and Deserters from the XVth Brigade" that constitutes document 48, dating from late July or August 1938. This list indicates that ideological deviation was regarded as a crime in the International Brigades and shows that the units of the XV Brigade were beset by serious problems of morale and discipline. The annotations on document 48 show a variety of charges against those listed. Morris Mickenberg, Lincoln battalion, is a "Suspect Trotskyist" while Lieutenant Claver, also of the Lincoln battalion, is "rumored to belong to the P.O.U.M.," the independent Marxist party that the Communists hated.[51] Others are accused of demoralization, malingering, indiscipline, and suspicious behavior.

Another indication of serious morale problems in the American battalions is document 49, an October 1937 letter to Bill Lawrence, the CPUSA's liaison to the International Brigades. Lawrence was stationed at Albacete, the supply base for the American battalions. The letter, from an unidentified officer with one of the American battalions, states:

> We have tried the first batch of twelve desertors you sent back to us. The results of the trial we are enclosing herewith. The effects on the men has been, in general, very good. The men feel that it is about time that we

51. Although Mickenberg was not a Trotskyist, he did justify, in Communist eyes, his designation as a "suspicious individual." After he returned from Spain he broke with the Communist party. In 1954 he testified to the Subversive Activities Control Board about Communist domination of the Veterans of the Abraham Lincoln Brigade (Testimony of Morris Maken [Mickenberg], transcript of proceedings held before the Subversive Activities Control Board in the matter of *Herbert Brownell, Attorney General v. Veterans of the Abraham Lincoln Brigade,* 1954 [reprinted on microfilm in *Records of the Subversive Activities Control Board,* reels 32–33]).

took such a clear cut position on the matter of desertion. Some questions may be raised in regard to the international complications which may arise. The trial here was conducted openly and the results are quite known. It appears to me inevitable that the international press will get hold of it.

In a 1969 book on American volunteers in the Spanish Civil War, Cecil Eby wrote that in the fall of 1937

a group of twenty-five disgruntled Americans left Aragon without permission and turned up in the office of Bill Lawrence in Albacete, where they claimed their "contracts" had expired and demanded repatriation. Since it was feared that if they got away with their high-handed demands massive desertions would follow among the remaining Americans, these men were . . . sent back to Aragon under guard. . . . According to three witnesses . . . , these men were later executed.[52]

---

## Document 49

"To Bill Lawrence," 9 October 1937, RTsKhIDNI 545–3–441. Original in English. The copy in Comintern files is unsigned. The M-P battalion referred to is the Mackenzie-Papineau battalion. Joe Dallet, an American Communist, was its political commissar. Robert Merriman, an American, and Vladimir Copic, a Yugoslav, were XV Brigade officers. Merriman commanded the Lincoln battalion for a period. Frank Ryan commanded the Irish company in the XV Brigade's British battalion. Both Dallet and Merriman died in action. Dallet's widow, Kitty, later married J. Robert Oppenheimer, who directed America's effort to build an atomic bomb.

---

9th. Oct 1937.

To Bill Lawrence,
ALBACETE.

Dear Bill,

We have tried the first batch of twelve desertors you sent back to us. The results of the trial we are enclosing herewith. The effects on the men has been, in general, very good. The men feel that it is about time that we took such a

52. Cecil Eby, *Between the Bullet and the Lie: American Volunteers in the Spanish Civil War* (New York: Holt, Rinehart and Winston, 1969), 174. Aragon was the region in which the American battalions were stationed at that time. The "contracts" were the six-month enlistments that many volunteers thought represented the extent of their obligation. The position of the International Brigades was that no matter what volunteers had been told in the United States, they were obligated to serve indefinitely. Eby does not cite any specific documents for this account, and one of the three witnesses given for the executions is the luckless Albert Wallach.

clear cut position on the matter of desertion. Some questions may be raised in regard to the international complications which may arise. The trial here was conducted openly and the results are quite known. It appears to me inevitable that the international press will get hold of it. We should, therefore, be prepared to answer. Meetings are being held in all battalions at the moment, where resolutions are being passed expressing full agreement with the sentences. All the Americans particularly are decidedly in favour of the sentences, the only doubt in their minds being that of international effects. It seems to me that if utilised properly the cases will serve to show the strength of the Americans in Spain and their ability to strike at weaker elements in their own ranks as well as serve to improve the quality of the people coming over here. I feel that as a result of these cases we shall have much less desertions in the entire Brigade. Of course we cannot leave the subject of desertions without commenting on the political work of the battalions, in which desertions have taken place. The low level of political work with very little education done is, without question, a big contributary factor towards desertions. Our commissars are taking full advantages of the educational value of the trial in order to improve the content of their political work.

You should continue sending deserters back to the Brigade, but please let us have a characterization of the people you are sending back, particularly in regards to whatever knowledge you may have about their arrest up to the point they leave you to come to the Brigade. Let us have your opinion on the trials.

With the completion of the deserters' trial, we feel here that we have clarified two basic problems for the Americans. One is repatriation, and the other is desertion. But there is still another which must be solved and a clear policy worked out. That is on the question of leaves. Lack of a clear policy on this creates much dissatisfaction amongst the men. It would be very good if you took it up with comrade [unreadable] to assign us a city which can now be close to Aragon, since we will be here, it seems, for quite a while. To such a city we can send a certain percentage of internationals for a ten or fifteen day leave. A struggle against desertion is impossible without the same time having a clear cut policy of regular leaves for the men.

I feel it is time to call to your attention the situation as regards Joe DALLET. It appears to me from a little contact with the M-P Battalion that we are approaching a critical situation. A percentage of the men openly declare that dissatisfaction with Joe and there is some talk of removal. We are taking energetic steps immediately to improve the situation. It will be necessary for us to involve the men in suggestions and improvements and changes of political work. I feel confident after an examination of the type of petty issues which the men raise that with a straight forward approach to the men instead of evasive defenses that we would be able to win the men's confidence. We will particularly use the organization of our friends to achieve this purpose. We are definitely against a removal and will not tolerate the suggestion of one. However it is well to bear in mind that this is rather a late date to do effective work in changing the situation prevailing in that Battalion. So, therefore, we have to resort to some changes which may include placing Dallet in another position if a change cannot be effective otherwise.

Frank RYAN is now on route to Madrid in order to revise and bring up to date the XV Brigade Book [unreadable] Combats. He was instructed to stop and see you. The value of general propaganda around this book is very great in America and England. We would, therefore, appreciate it if you would help Ryan as much as possible.

When Ryan is through with the book, which should be in about three weeks he should then go on tour to America. Please take the propor preparatory steps for his tour.

Those are the outstanding important questions of the moment. Our friends' organization is just getting under way, we are a bit dissatisfied about slowness and one or two other things. Our political commissariat is turning into a real propaganda department, the result of which will soon be evident. The brigade is now in a reserve position, very little action is taking place. We are utilising the time to develope political and cultural activity, a programme of which we will send you.

Robbie is feeling fine and sends you regards, Merriman, Copic, and all the comrades send their regards.

Antifascist greetings,

---

Document 49 and Eby's story agree about the date and Lawrence's role. Document 49 does not, however, confirm the executions, because a copy of the results of the trial, referred to in the letter, was not found in the International Brigades' records in Moscow.[53]

Several historians sympathetic to the International Brigades have written that most of the soldiers lived up to the Bolshevik ideal. For example, in *Crusade on the Left* Robert Rosenstone dismisses accounts of serious desertion by soldiers of the American battalions: "Men who were there have always insisted that there were 'few' desertions, and this seems to have been the case." He calculates the number of deserters for the entire war as thirty-three and concludes that "this total of 33, is about 1 per cent of the volunteers. Undoubtedly there were others, but the number does seem small enough to

53. Peter Carroll describes a trial of thirteen deserters in which all were found guilty: two were sentenced to death and the rest to combat duty without the opportunity for relief. Carroll believes that the executions were not carried out (Carroll, *The Odyssey of the Abraham Lincoln Brigade*, 164–65).

justify the insistence on 'few.'"[54] Document 49, however, refers to "the first batch of twelve desertors" in a single incident in October 1937, and document 48, from the summer of 1938, lists far more than thirty-three men as deserters from the Lincoln and Mackenzie-Papineau battalions.

The history of American volunteers in the Spanish Civil War has been romanticized as "the good fight" idealistic Americans bravely and nobly fought against fascism. No doubt most of the Americans volunteered, fought, and died to stop fascism. But the dark side of the Spanish Civil War, dramatically documented in these files, demands renewed attention. The severe problems with morale and desertion among the American volunteers in the Spanish Civil War and the ideological warfare and personal terror directed at some volunteers by their own comrades need to be honestly examined.

54. Rosenstone, *Crusade on the Left*, 300, 401.

# CHAPTER FIVE

# Other Faces of the Secret World

ALTHOUGH THE MAIN CHANNEL OF RECRUITMENT into the secret world of American communism was through the CPUSA underground, documents in the Comintern archives show other paths as well. Discussed below are a genteel Southern artist who volunteered for covert Comintern service and a New York school-teacher who became a Soviet radio propagandist. The training of American students at the International Lenin School in Moscow further documents the extent to which habits of secrecy, ideological militancy, and Soviet loyalty were inculcated.

## Ann Cadwallader Coles, a Southern Artist in the Secret World

In 1969 the *State,* the newspaper in Columbia, South Carolina, announced the death of Ann Cadwallader Coles, a local artist and portrait painter. The obituary read:

> Miss Ann Cadwallader Coles, Columbia artist, died Sunday at Columbia Hospital after an illness of several months.
>
> Born on August 2, 1882, in Columbia, Miss Coles spent a large part of her life here. Her parents were John Stricker and Helen Iredell Jones Coles.

Miss Coles' career as an artist began in Columbia when she was 8. She studied at Columbia College here until she was 16 when she entered Converse College at Spartanburg from which she received her B.L. degree in 1902. She studied in New York City at the Whipple School of Art and at the Art Students' League.

Miss Coles painted more than 100 commissioned portraits, and she exhibited at the Pennsylvania Academy of Fine Arts in Philadelphia, the Chicago Institute of Art, the Charlotte Mint Museum, the Columbia Museum of Art and the Florence Museum of Art. Her works are in the permanent collection here, in Florence, at Pierson College at Yale, at the University of North Carolina and at the State House in Columbia.

One of her last large projects was the painting of portraits of the founders, officers and directors of The State Company about a decade ago. These paintings included portraits of Ambrose Elliott Gonzales, Narciso Gener Gonzales, William Elliott Gonzales, Miss Harriet Elliott Gonzales and William Elliott, Sr.

Miss Coles' portraits are in many Columbia homes, and among her best works are portraits of Dr. Robert W. Gibbes (in the museum here), Associate Justice Daniel Edward Hydrick (in the State House), Judge George Bell Timmerman (in the U.S. Courthouse here) and Dr. J. Heyward Gibbes.

She was listed early in her career in Who's Who in Art and later in Who's Who of American Women. During World War II, then in her 60's, Miss Coles worked for the Merchant Marine making mechanical drawings of heat exchanges used by ships and oil companies. In 1953, she flew to Europe with a group of American artists sponsored by Artists Equity.

A small woman of spare frame, Miss Coles was an early advocate of health diets, some of which have recently come into vogue, and she was a believer in physical fitness. She walked almost everywhere she went in Columbia, and she attributed her ability to continue painting into her 80's to diet and physical exercise.

Although Miss Coles maintained a studio in New York for several years and painted and exhibited in many parts of the United States, Columbia was her home. She had lived here continuously since World War II.

Miss Coles had four brothers and three sisters, only one of whom, Mrs. Eliza (Ida) Coles Blythe of Saluda, N.C., survives. Among other survivors are a nephew, William Munro Shand, Jr.; and three nieces, Mrs. F. Barron Grier, Jr., Mrs. Emmett L. Wingfield and Mrs. James T. Green of Columbia.

MISS COLES

# Miss Coles, Artist, Dies In Columbia

Miss Ann Cadwallader Coles, Columbia artist, died Sunday at Columbia Hospital after an illness of several months.

Born on August 2, 1882, in Columbia, Miss Coles spent a large part of her life here. Her parents were John Stricker and Helen Iredell Jones Coles.

Miss Coles' career as an artist began in Columbia when she was 8. She studied at Columbia College here until she was 16 when she entered Converse College at Spartanburg from which she received her B.L. degree in 1902. She studied in New York City at the Whipple School of Art and at the Art Students' League.

Miss Coles painted more than 100 commissioned portraits, and she exhibited at the Pennsylvania Academy of Fine Arts in Philadelphia, the Chicago Institute of Art, the Charlotte Mint Museum, the Columbia Museum of Art and the Florence Museum of Art. Her works are in the permanent collection here, in Florence, at Pierson College at Yale, at the University of North Carolina and at the State House in Columbia.

One of her last large projects was the painting of portraits of the founders, officers and directors of The State Company about a decade ago. These paintings included portraits of Ambrose Elliott Gonzales, Narciso Gener Gonzales, William Elliott Gonzales, Miss Harriet Elliott Gonzales and William Elliott, Sr.

Miss Coles' portraits are in many Columbia homes, and among her best works are portraits of Dr. Robert W. Gibbes (in the museum here), Associate Justice Daniel Edward Hydrick (in the State House), Judge George Bell Timmerman (in the U.S. Courthouse here) and Dr. J. Heyward Gibbes.

She was listed early in her career in Who's Who in Art and later in Who's Who of American Women. During World War II, then in her 60's, Miss Coles worked for the Merchant Marine making mechanical drawings of heat exchanges used by ships and oil companies. In 1953, she flew to Europe with a group of American artists sponsored by Artists Equity.

A small woman of spare frame, Miss Coles was an early advocate of health diets, some of which have recently come into vogue, and she was a believer in physical fitness. She walked almost everywhere she went in Columbia, and she attributed her ability to continue painting into her 80's to diet and physical exercise.

Although Miss Coles maintained a studio in New York for several years and, painted and exhibited in many parts of the United States, Columbia was her home. She had lived here continuously since World War II.

Miss Coles had four brothers and three sisters, only one of whom, Mrs. Eliza (Ida) Coles Blythe of Saluda, N.C., survives. Among other survivors are a nephew, William Munro Shand, Jr.; and three nieces, Mrs. F. Barron Grier, Jr., Mrs. Emmett L. Wingfield and Mrs. James T. Green of Columbia.

Funeral services will be conducted at the graveside in Elmwood Cemetery at 4 p.m. Monday by the Rev. Charles Scott May, assistant rector of Trinity Episcopal Church of which she was a lifelong member.

Ann Cadwallader Coles's obituary from the *State*, Columbia, South Carolina, 31 March 1969.

Funeral services will be conducted at the graveside in Elmwood Cemetery at 4 p.m. Monday by the Rev. Charles Scott May, assistant rector of Trinity Episcopal Church of which she was a lifelong member.[1]

The obituary reflected an eminently respectable life. Documents in the Comintern archives show, however, that Ann Coles had a secret Communist life. **Documents 50 and 51** are the cover letter and an autobiographical application by Ann Coles for secret Comintern work. The material was addressed to an official in the eastern department of the Profintern, which had jurisdiction over Asia, and was found among papers dealing with East Asian activities; most likely the application was for work with the Pan-Pacific Trade Union Secretariat. Coles wrote that she had been a founding member of the Communist party. She said that in 1929 she was removed from open work in the New York District of the CPUSA "and given underground work to do." These assignments continued through 1935. She added: "I have never been re-connected with the open work of the Party since 1929. Have been very careful and I think was never exposed." Coles noted that several important party officials, including the membership director of the New York CPUSA district and Max Steinberg, a key party functionary, supervised her underground work.

---

## Document 50

"For Charlie Johnson," 3 September 1936, RTsKhIDNI 534–4–518. Original in English. Stamped "Secret" in Russian. The writer of this document is unknown. No information is available on <u>comrade Rock.</u> "A perfect book" means no police record.

---

September 3, 1936.

<u>FOR CHARLIE JOHNSON (Eastern Dept).</u>
     <u>Re: Comrade recommended in place of comrade Rock.</u>

Dear Comrade:
    Altho this comrade is 54 year old, she does not look more than forty years. In every respect she is well fit for the job. She can establish herself very well in

---

1. The *State*, Columbia, South Carolina, 31 March 1969.

## Document 50 *continued*

any place having a perfect book and a real profession, that of an accomplished artist. Her reliability is unquestionable.

Please reply by cable if she is accepted so that she can terminate her apartment lease, her place of employment and other personal matters. This cable should be sent even before other details are forwarded, if she is accepted.

## Document 51

"Name—Ann (Real—Cadwallader) Coles . . . ," August 1936, RTsKhIDNI 534–4–518. Original in English. C.L.P. is the Communist Labor Party.

August 1936.

Name—Ann (real—Cadwallader) Coles. Born August 4, 1882, at Columbia, S.C. U.S.A.

Second of eight children of bourgeois parents. Descended from early settlers of Maryland, Virginia, No. Carolina, South Carolina and Georgia. Mainly of English, Irish, Scotch and Welsh extraction. Ancestors fought in the Revolutionary War of 1776 and also Civil War of 1860.

My father owned in partnership a dock and warehouse in Georgia and was shipping cotton to Liverpool and Bremen when the Company went bankrupt in the panic of 1890. He then became a life insurance agent, traveling a great deal in eastern USA, my mother and eight children remaining in Columbia, S.C., where I graduated from High School and then from Converse College, Spartanburg, S.C. on a scholarship, in 1902.

My father then got a state agency in Jacksonville, Fla., moved the family there and later died in 1913 of caidiac trouble, leaving a little insurance and heavily mortgaged house.

On my own initiative and thru letters of recommendation from my College I got a job of bookkeeper in a samll New York City Art School which enabled me to study there for two years—1907–1908; teaching drawing also the second year. On account of parents' health, returned to Jacksonville for two years, teaching small art class, raising chickens and helping with the children.

In 1910, a college class mate who had inheritse some money gave me a year's study at the Arts Students League in New York City and a two months trip to France and England in the summer of 1911. I went with two young women, one an artist.

After a few months in Jacksonville, getting a few portraits to paint, I returned to New York City and shared an apartment with the aforementioned artist who soon afterwards married a Socialist. Thru his propoganda I began going to forums, campaign meetings and heard Socialist speakers. The first one was on a Sunday night in the Church of the Ascension on Fifth Avenue.

In the spring of 1913 I joined the Socialist Party. In the meantime for the past 18 months I had begun the difficult task of trying to be an artist and make a living in New York City. Walking the streets in search of work; occasionally selling a little picture; from time to time getting a portrait to paint; holding from time to time miserably paid jobs which required some drawing or color. At this time (1913) my activities in the Socialist Party diminished.

I was active in the Patterson Silk Strike, took in one of the striker's children for a few months when they were brought over to New York; helped in the unemployed agitation of the winter of 1914, but it was the World War which made me really a part of the working class movement and rid me of the remnants of Christian belief. (My family religion was Protestant Epescopal and as an adolescent I had been very active).

In 1915 I was financial secretary of Branch #1 for several years and later delegate to the Central Committee. Then the branches were re-organized along State Assembly District lines. I was ill for a while so that I was rather new in the 3rd, 5th and 10th A.D., when there began the first cleavage of the Left from the Right. We voted for the St. Louis Platform and the Left candidates. I was active in Peace demonstrations, especially of the Irish and street campaign meetings.

Later in 1918 or maybe early 1919 I was again delegate to the Central Committee. Both, Jim Larkin and Jack Reed were members of my branch, but on account of the strict Socialist rule of length of membership in the American Party they could not be delegates, but they trusted me. I know I was a delegate when the question was first launched as to which International we were to send delegates, and later in the Spring of 1919, when the Socialist Party officials called in the police and dispersed that last historical Central Committee which we attended. I was financial secretary of the new Left wing branch and helped to take with us the wavering and uninformed when the S.P. Executive tried to re-organize it.

If I remember correctly, our whole branch went over to the C.L.P. in September 1919. It was then that I had to stand worse taunts than during war when I was cursed and had fists shaken in my face. In NY city we were few; Socialists and CP numerous. We were accursed of being the arch splitters. Again, I was a delegate to the new C.L.P. Central Committee. Then came the arrests of Larkin and Gitlow, both of our branch and the Palmer raids in early 1920 and all over the States, from Coast to Coast it was the C.L.P. members who were arrested. They were the American Communist movement. I think that ours was the only branch which continued for a few months to meet openly until we were instructed to go underground. I was organizer for Unit and delegate to Section; lugging literature from one part of town to distribute in another, walking miles to avoid using a telephone. At this time I knew I. Amter and Wagenknecht. I was working in a studio for two artists, one a sister of Robert Minor. Comrade Minor drew cartoons while there when he first returned from Russia the first time, still not quite thru with being an anarchist and when he went to Cape Cod I mailed him all the underground literature all summer.

From 1919 to 1929 I lived as the wife (thru common law) of a comrade originally from Austria. However at the end of 1929 he married someone else with whom he still is living. I had no children as I have never had any economic security and at the time I might have had a child, any day we might both have been put to jail.

In 1922–23 he was sent to Cleveland Ohio, as District Organizer. I worked in a bindery factory there (the slogan then was "Every body into the factory") and for a few months after returning to New York.

In N.Y.—again financial secretary of West Side branch of the Workers Party, until 1925–6 when the branches were dissolved into street Nuclei. Sparks, the present Organizer in Pittsburgh, knew me thru this period.

I refused to belong to either organized faction; fought bitterly the Lovestone group (Gitlow, et al.) in our branch and while in sympathy and agreement on principal with the Fosterites, did not approve of their tactics, methods of work or some of their leaders. In 1928 I lived on the East side, vot [not] very active on account of ill health, only did drawing, stamps, buttons, posters, etc. Returned to West side and was Daily Worker agent in Needle Trades Unit.

In 1929 was arrested in a demonstration in Harlem with ten others. Was released that night (only two were held) did not have to appear in court and had not given my real name.

Soon after this, I was taken out of all open activity by the District; disconnected from the Unit and given underground work to do; filing, membership records, etc. Helen Allison and Jack Perilla knew me throughout this period. 1931–33 I lived with and did Party underground work with the present membership director of District #2, New York City. Also during 1934- and part of 1935 continued this under the direction of Max Steinberg, Org. Dept., District #2. I have never been re-connected with the open work of the Party since 1929. Have been very careful and I think was never exposed.

My membership in the organized Socialist-Communist workingclass movement has been unbroken since 1913. Never missed a dues payment until the spring of 1936 when I asked for three months unemployed stamps. When I had to barrow from friends and relatives for food and rent, I also barrowed enough to pay my Party dues and until 1928 I scarcely ever missed attending my Party Unit.

February 1936, I joined the Artists' Union (on account of the Party work I had been doing, could not join previously), became active in the unemployed group, arrested with the "sit-down" delegation. But again, I did not give my real name and the case was dismissed. In July I got a WPA job as an assistant mural painter which I now hold.

I am a painter, best at portraits, have had portraits and figure paintings accepted by juries in National exhibitions, but have made my living mostly thru many varieties of advertising art, struggling to keep on painting.

If I can serve the movement and still paint, I will be happy.

Altho I am 54 years old, I could pass for 15 years younger and am strong and in much better health than when I was young. I have never typed, but can learn it fast enough, I think. Although at college I have studied German, 2 years and French 4 years, I can speak neither now, but I think I could get back my ability to read French and learn to speak it.

My mother is quite old and had depended on her two small grandchildren and, except when I was out of work entirely, I tried to do my share by sending her $10.00 per month. It will be a blow to her that I go so far away and must promise her that regularly would help her. I also owe a debt of $75.00 which I borrowed in the early spring while out of work. If I stayed here on this job I probably would repay it in a few months and there really is no hurry, but I hate to go so far away, leaving it unpaid.

My apartment lease expires October 1st, 1936, so I would like to know as soon as possible whether I am accepted.

---

It is not known whether Coles was accepted for clandestine Comintern work, but her application illustrates the interchange between the American Communist underground and international Comintern covert activities. In any event, her friends and neighbors in Columbia, South Carolina, might well have been startled to learn that this respectable portrait painter had been engaged in secret work for the Communist party.

Coles's story illustrates that recruitment into the secret world was not confined to CPUSA cadre, those functionaries who spent a lifetime employed by the party or one of its allied institutions. Coles, an active Communist but not a party professional, responded willingly when the CPUSA called upon her to join the underground. Once acclimatized to the American Communist underground, she made herself available for international covert work.

## American Communists and Soviet Radio Propaganda, 1937–1942

Still another aspect of American Communist assistance to the Soviet cause was the effort to improve Soviet short-wave radio propaganda aimed at the United States. In **document 52**, Nat Ross, a CPUSA representative to the Comintern, criticizes current Soviet radio programing and suggests methods of improving it. In **document 53**, Pat Toohey, the chief CPUSA representative to the Comintern, reports

## Document 52 continued

2. Anglo-American Comrades in the C.I. must write regularly for the programme, specific comrades must be assigned to help draw up monthly programmes, and to help the comrades in radio to overcome the present shortcomings. The placing of responsibility upon Comrades from the C.I. apparatus should be accompanied by a certain amount of authority in helping to carry through improvements, etc.

3. It would be advisable to call together a group of comrades working in the C.I. who are connected in one way or another with the radio to meet and discuss the radio problems, exchange opinions on ways to help improve the radio programme and perhaps to draw up a collective report for the ECCI.

4. A number of suggestions contained herein were made directly to the radio comrades, including the Head of the Ino-Radio, as a result of my meetings with the Anglo-American radio comrades themselves.

Ross

## Document 53

Toohey to Ivanova, 7 February 1939, RTsKhIDNI 495–14–131. Original in English.

TO: Comrade Ivanova, Inoradio
FROM: Pat Toohey, Central Committee Representative, USA

1. As we agreed in the meeting held to discuss improvement of the American Radio Program, I am calling a meeting of all American and Canadian comrades employed in the Comintern apparatus at 12 o'clock, February 13th in the Comintern. This meeting will embrace ten responsible American and Canadian comrades. We hope to discuss the program, make assignments for necessary material and plan regularly for future programs.

2. At our meeting with you it was decided that further improvement of the American program exclusively depended upon capable cadres for this work. We came to the conclusion that we should request Comrade Browder to choose several politically responsible and developed comrades who understand radio and send them here for this purpose. I was on the verge of transmitting this message to Comrade Browder when I was informed by Comrade Stetzenko of the Comintern Cadres department that Comrade Gussev of the Radio informed him that with the possible exception of typists, no forces were required by the radio. I am, therefore, unclear on the entire matter and would deeply appreciate clarification before the message is sent to Comrade Browder.

Comradely yours,
Toohey

7/2/39

## Williana Burroughs, New York Teacher and
## Soviet Radio Propagandist

In any event, Soviet radio already employed at least one American. **Documents 54, 55, and 56** concern Williana Burroughs, who worked for Soviet radio as an announcer and as editor of its English-language propaganda broadcasts. Burroughs, a graduate of Hunter College, worked for a long time as an elementary-school teacher in New York City. She first came into contact with the Communist party in the early 1920s through the American Negro Labor Congress, the party's arm for organizing African Americans. She secretly joined the party in 1926 (her party name was Mary Adams), and by 1928 she was a delegate to the 1928 Comintern congress in Moscow. At that time she placed her two youngest sons (aged nine and five) in an elite Moscow school for the children of Soviet and foreign Communist cadre. She returned to America to undertake a variety of duties for the CPUSA, visiting Moscow from time to time to report to the Comintern and to see her sons.[3]

In the early 1930s Burroughs emerged as an activist in the Communist faction in the New York Teachers Union. She lost her teaching job, however, after a violent disruption at a Board of Education meeting. She publicly announced her Communist status in 1933 when she filed for election to public office on the Communist ticket. As document 54 shows, in 1937 the CPUSA recommended her for a position with Soviet radio. She was accepted and moved to Moscow. Document 55 states that Burroughs wanted to return to the United States in 1940 but was persuaded to stay because of a shortage of American personnel for Comintern duties at that time. Docu-

3. An example of a Burroughs report to the Comintern under the name of Mary Adams is her testimony to the Comintern's American Commission on the CPUSA's policy of inserting members into selected factories and on coordinating industrial organizing with organizing aimed at women: Mary Adams testimony, 8 September 1930, RTsKhIDNI 495–37–68. Williana Burroughs's husband, a United States Post Office employee, accompanied her to the 1928 Comintern congress but was not active in the CPUSA and remained in the United States when she moved to Moscow (Philip Sterling, "Communist Candidate for Comptroller," CPUSA biographical summary for Burroughs's 1933 comptroller campaign, copy in possession of the authors; "Charles G. Burroughs, DuSable Museum Co-Founder Passes," obituary notice released by the DuSable Museum, 1994; Phil Mellinger, "Charles Burroughs," *Chicago Journal* [10 June 1981]; Charles G. Burroughs's obituary notice, *Chicago Defender* [8 March 1994]. The authors thank Margaret Burroughs for providing these four items.).

ment 56 is a 1942 appeal from Burroughs to Dimitrov renewing her request to return to America. Her appeal was rejected, and she was not allowed to return to the United States until 1945. In poor health, Williana Burroughs died shortly after reentering the United States.[4]

# Document 54

Randolph to Cadre Department, ECCI, 4 May 1937, RTsKhIDNI 495–14–81. Original in English. This document incorrectly lists Burroughs's given name as Wilhelmina rather than Williana, as it is given in document 56.

May 4, 1937.

Confidential

Cadre Department
ECCI.

Re: BURROUGHS, Wilhemina (Mary Adams)

Please communicate to the Radio Centre, to Comrade Boyardsky, our recommendation for the post of editor of Comrade Mary Adams (Wilhemina Burroughs).

Comrade Burroughs is an old member of the CPUSA and has been active in a leading capacity in the New York District for many years. She is one of the leading members of our Teachers' fraction.

Comradely yours,<br>(s) RANDOLPH<br>Rep. CPUSA, ECCI.

SS/2.

---

4. Sterling, "Communist Candidate for Comptroller"; "Charles G. Burroughs, DuSable Museum Co-Founder Passes"; Mellinger, "Charles Burroughs"; Charles G. Burroughs's obituary, *Chicago Tribune* (14 March 1994). Burroughs's two youngest sons finished secondary school in Moscow. Charles Burroughs, the elder of the two, went to work as a toolmaker, then became a trapeze catcher in a Soviet circus, and finally drove a truck during World War II. Both sons retained their American citizenship, and in 1943 Charles Burroughs received a draft notice. Early in 1945 he reported to an American base in Teheran, Iran, and was inducted. His younger brother, Neal, returned to the United States with his mother the same year. After his military service, Charles Burroughs returned to the United States and graduated from Roosevelt University. In 1961 he co-founded the DuSable Museum of African American History in Chicago and served as its curator until 1980. In 1987 Charles Burroughs described himself as "pro-Soviet" and stated that "you could say I'm pro-Communist" although not a member of the CPUSA (Jack Houston, "Chicagoan Returns to Boyhood Residence after 42 Years," *Chicago Tribune* [17 May 1987]). Charles Burroughs died in 1994; a Chicago high school is named after him.

# Document 55

N. [Nat] Ross to Dimitrov, 14 September 1942, RTsKhIDNI 495–73–152. Original in Russian.

Comrade
Burroughs

To Comrade DIMITROV
Explanatory note on the enclosed letter
from Com. Burroughs, member of CP USA.

Com. Burroughs came to me with a request to forward you the enclosed letter, written by her on her own initiative.

Com. Burroughs is a Negro woman, a member of the CP USA for fifteen years, in the past a member of the CCC of the CP USA. For the last several years she has been working for the Radio Committee as an announcer.

In the spring of 1940, Com. Burroughs asked permission to return to the US together with her two grown sons, but in view of the fact that numbers of American comrades in Moscow were then negligible, she was asked not to go, and she stayed.

Throughout her stay in Moscow, especially during the last two years, she has been dissatisfied with her financial situation, and in the last year she has suffered from impaired health. (She is 61 years old.) During the last several months she has applied personally to the Comintern for help, and to a certain degree Comrades Belov and Sukharev have met her halfway.

I do not know what reasons compelled her to turn directly to you, but I believe that one of her motives is the fact that her financial situation is unsatisfactory, that that is affecting her health, and is therefore applying to you for help. Of course, it is not excluded that she has been moved to do this by other reasons that are unknown to me.

Comradely regards,
(N. ROSS)

14 September 1942
*P.S. Com. Belov knows something about this matter.*
*N. Ross.*

# Document 56

Burroughs to Dimitrov, 8 September 1942, RTsKhIDNI 495–73–152. Handwritten. Original in Russian. The V.R.K. is the Soviet radio agency.

*8/ix/42*
*Com. Dimitrov!*
*For over five years I have been working in the V.R.K. as an announcer and editor. I am a Negro woman, a U.S. citizen, member of the U.S. Communist*

*Party, and former member of the CC of the American Comparty. In the U.S. I worked as a propagandist.*

*I have questions connected with my work, as well as personal concerns that require your attention.*

*I urgently request that you appoint a time that will be convenient for you to meet with me.*

> *Comradely regards,*
> *Williana Burroughs*
> *(the Anglo-American editorial office of the V.R.K.)*

---

## American Students in the International Lenin School

Over the years, hundreds of American Communists passed through the International Lenin School (ILS) in Moscow. The school trained Communist cadre in a variety of areas, including Marxist-Leninist theory, organizational techniques, and Soviet history. The school also functioned as a means of linking foreign Communists to the Soviet Union. As document 35 shows, many American students at the ILS were admitted into the Communist Party of the Soviet Union. Graduates of the Lenin school held influential positions within the party; among them were such noteworthy figures in the party's secret apparatus as Rudy Baker and Steve Nelson.

Much of what went on at the ILS was secret. In 1930, William Weinstone, the CPUSA's representative to the Comintern, rebuked the CPUSA's Secretariat for publishing an article about the school. Weinstone told his comrades that the article "has aroused the School Administration and the students because THERE MUST BE ABSOLUTELY NO PUBLICITY GIVEN IN REGARD TO THE SCHOOL OR ANY OF ITS ACTIVITIES. . . . Nothing like this must be repeated." He also reminded the party not to send material to the students using an ILS address.[5]

5. Weinstone to Secretariat, CPUSA, 6 March 1930, RTsKhIDNI 515–1–1870.

*American Communists in Red Army Uniforms, 1936*

One of the ILS secrets was that its students received military training. **Document 57** is a 1936 letter from Randolph, the CPUSA's representative to the Comintern, to two senior Comintern officials, Dmitry Manuilsky and André Marty. Randolph said, "Our students were sent for 2 weeks to a military training camp where they received instructions in military tactics, jiu-jitsu rifle practice, etc. I would strongly urge that the question should be considered that this part of the school curriculum should be abolished. . . . Because of the nature of the training and especially because military uniforms are worn by the students." In 1936 the CPUSA was implementing its Popular Front strategy, which included an insistence on the Americanness of the party and the adoption of previously eschewed American patriotic symbols. Randolph was concerned about possible adverse publicity in the United States if it leaked out that American Communists were getting military training and wearing Red Army uniforms.

---

## Document 57

Randolph to Manuilsky and Marty, 28 June 1936, RTsKhIDNI 515–1–3968. Original in English.

---

Confidential

June 28, 1936.

Comrades Manuilsky and Marty.

Regarding Military Training Camps.

Dear Comrades:

Although the American Section of the International Lenin School is being transferred for the coming year, yet because it may affect other sectors, I would like to call the following to your attention:

Our students were sent for 2 weeks to a military training camp where they received instructions in military tactics, jiu-jitsu rifle practice, etc. I would strongly urge that the question should be considered that this part of the school curriculum should be abolished for the following reasons:

1—Especially for countries as the United States, it gives the comrades a wrong idea as to how to fight back against terror.

2—Because of the nature of the training and especially because military uniforms are worn by the students, a renegade or an enemy spy can utilise it diplomatically against the Soviet Union on the basis that the Soviet Union is giving military training to individuals to organise a military uprising against the American government and for physical attacks upon the police.

3—The physical self-reliance which is the only real use these two weeks of training has, can be easily supplied by an ordinary physical culture camp where without uniforms, students are taught boxing, wrestling, shooting and other athletic activities.

The last mentioned is my proposal for substituting the present two weeks camp.

> Comradely
> *Randolph*
> Rep. CPUSA. ECCI.

It is not known whether all the Americans who passed through the Lenin school received Red Army training. A number of the CPUSA cadre who were officers in the International Brigades were ILS graduates, however, and this may have been the extent of their preparation for military service.

The party's clandestine activities touched many Communists beyond its top leadership. Rudy Baker was a professional revolutionary, but Ann Coles was a portrait painter, and Williana Burroughs was a New York schoolteacher who became a propagandist for Soviet radio. Other American Communists at the Lenin school found themselves wearing Red Army uniforms, practicing jujitsu, and firing rifles. Baker left his covert work to become a minor official in Tito's government in Yugoslavia. Coles returned from her clandestine work to life as an artist in Columbia, South Carolina. Some of the Americans who went through the Lenin school would call upon its brief lessons in military tactics when they fought and died in Spain. Those entering the secret world could not predict where they might be led.

# CHAPTER SIX

# The American Communist Party, the Secret Apparatus, and the NKVD

THE AMERICAN PARTY'S CLANDESTINE WORK and the secret apparatus that it had created in the 1930s provided Soviet intelligence with a bountiful harvest during World War II.

## The Brother-Son Network in World War II

The Comintern's files include two documents proving that the secret apparatus of the CPUSA had integral links to Soviet espionage against the United States during World War II. In document 58 General Pavel Fitin, head of the foreign intelligence directorate of the NKVD, conveys the text of a 1942 message transmitted through NKVD channels to Dimitrov; the message is signed "Son." In his cover note to Son's message, Fitin says, "We are forwarding a telegram we received from New York addressed to you from <u>Rudy</u>." Son, thus, was Rudy Baker. Son's message to Dimitrov was "Reception is good [from] 8 to 9. One of your new drivers is often lax in his work." This is a report on short-wave radio exchanges between Baker's secret apparatus and Moscow. Short-wave radio operations were referred to as "auto work" or "automobile work," and the radio operators were called "drivers." The "8 to 9" referred to the quality of radio reception on a ten-point scale. In the message,

Son/Baker appears to be complaining about the inefficiency of one of Moscow's radio operators.[1]

---

## Document 58

Fitin to Dimitrov, enclosing Son to Dimitrov, 22 May 1942, RTsKhIDNI 495–74–484. Original in Russian. The English word *Son* is in Cyrillic letters; *son* in Russian is a noun that can mean either "sleep" or "dream."

TOP SECRET

To Comrade D I M I T R O V:

We are forwarding a telegram we received from New York addressed to you from Rudy:

"Reception is good [from] 8 to 9. One of your new drivers is often lax in his work. Son." No. 452.

P. Fitin
F I T I N

No. 294/Ru
22 May 1942
*Shown to comrades Sorkin, Nikolaev, Egorov*
*22 May 1942 GD*

---

**Document 59** is a year-end report on the 1942 activities and financing of an espionage network. The report is addressed to "Brother" and is signed by "Son," the head of the CPUSA secret apparatus. Son/Baker reported that for security purposes his network was "kept strictly isolated from party as before. . . . Periodically all questions are discussed and considered by son and father. While the party generally is functioning on the war efforts entirely openly and enjoy greater legal freedom than ever, the F.B.I. and military intelligence has not decreased its surveillance. . . . This requires that we . . . maintain our contacts with father and other vital comrades with greatest care." Father is thus identified as the link between the network and the CPUSA leadership.[2]

1. Direct short-wave radio contact between the CPUSA and Moscow continued to be problematic. In 1944 Soviet military intelligence forwarded to Dimitrov a Browder message delivered through one of its American agents. The message stated that the CPUSA's short-wave radio had picked up a recent Dimitrov message but reception was so poor that the message was not understood (Bolshakov to Dimitrov, top secret, 29 February 1944, RTsKhIDNI 495–74–486).

2. In 1944 Dimitrov received confirmation from Soviet military intelligence that it had delivered his message to "Rudy's boss" (*khoziain*). This was probably "Father" (Bolshakov to Dimitrov, top secret, 23 April 1944, RTsKhIDNI 495–74–486).

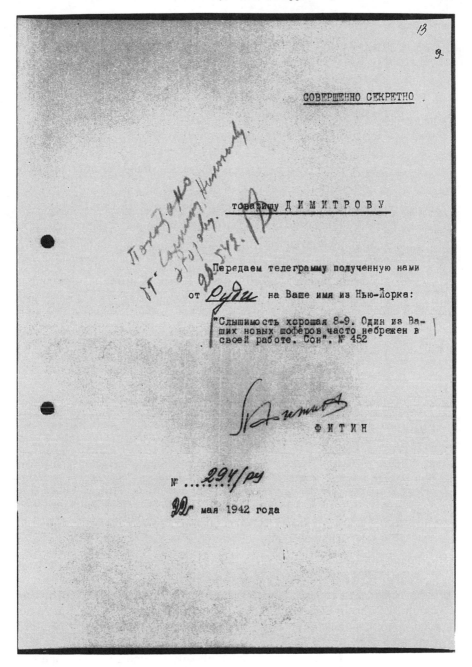

СОВЕРШЕННО СЕКРЕТНО

товарищу ДИМИТРОВУ

Передаем телеграмму полученную нами

от _Руди_ на Ваше имя из Нью-Йорка:

"Слышимость хорошая 8-9. Один из Ваших новых шоферов часто небрежен в своей работе. Сон". № 452

ФИТИН

№ 294/ру

22 мая 1942 года

DOCUMENT 58. Fitin to Dimitrov, enclosing Son to Dimitrov, 22 May 1942.

Son devotes one paragraph to an agent code-named Merton and to relations with an agent called Cooper. Son/Baker says, "We have again recently given substantial aid to Merton which will grow in volume and importance as time goes on. We can consider this problem solved and will be in position to improve from time to time due primarily to assistance from Father. We are also cooperating very closely with Cooper which accounts also for his helpfull aid in communication with you." In other sections of the report, Son/Baker states, "We began sending mail through Cooper and Merton" and that a member of the network had been temporarily loaned to Cooper for "auto building work," which refers to setting up a radio station. In addition to Merton and Cooper, a lengthy paragraph is given to an agent code-named Louis and his expensive "auto" (radio) work and a proposal that he set up operations in an unknown location called Gilla. The report also notes that Father, the network's link to the CPUSA, is concerned about Louis's next assignment.

Document 59's discussion of Cooper and Louis connects the Brother-Son network directly to Soviet intelligence, because the two were important figures in Soviet espionage in the United States.

---

# Document 59

Son to Brother with attached "Son Financial Statement for 1942," RTsKhIDNI 495–74–480. Original in English. The document in the Comintern archives is a print from microfilm. Son's remark that "several drivers went to sea or the army" refers not to the loss of men who can drive cars but to the loss of radio operators, or "drivers." Gilla and A. America are code names for unknown locations. The references to Argentina and Cuba may refer to those nations or may be code words for other locations.

---

*Brother 5 pages*

### GENERAL REPORT

Brother: Year 1942 has been characterized by difficulties arising from the war, difficulties we were not equipped to cope with and on the whole have not solved up to this time.

Normal legal mail facilities which were already limited in 1941 came to a virtual stop in 1942. Military conscription and labor registration has effected our cadres while stringent war regulations have added new difficulties to auto work and travel to South American countries.

<u>Mail</u>: This year we began sending mail through Cooper and Merton regularly. We have been informed that two packages have been lost by ship sinking in April. Since you never acknowledge receipt of our mail it is impossible to indicate what was lost.

We have made full arrangement for sending mail with seamen as per your suggestion. This method is irregular but will be used to full possibility. We also use seamen to deliver our printed materials to England, Iceland, N. Africa, India, S. Africa, South American countries, New Zealand and Australia. Seamen also bring to us printed materials from England, India, South Africa, New Zealand, Algeria and Australia, much of it has been sent to you. We are striving to organize special correspondence with parties in these countries through seamen. This task of course is more complicated than simple transfer of printed literature. We maintain regular and reliable communications only with Cuba, Mexico, Spanish Center in Mexico and Cuba and with Canada. Our Communications with Chilli and Argentine are irregular and unsatisfactory. It is virtually impossible to send courier to South American countries during war. Seamen communications to A. America are also unpredictable because all ship schedules have been cancelled and are always changing. We can send visitors to Gilla and Cuba only—at this time.

<u>Cadres</u>: All our cadres with exception of George and Mike were under 45 years of age at the time of registration for army service. This meant either being called into army or find such vital war work which is ground for exemption from army. In New York this situation created no serious problem. Our best and most reliable driver has gone to sea on a ship but he has been replaced. Son is no longer subject to military call due to lowering of age limit recently. Our difficulties in this respect are mainly felt in California where several drivers went to sea or the army. We cannot send anyone there. Trained girls with former experience are no longer available. We are training one now and more later. We have asigned one responsible person in California (Mack) to be responsible for all our work from there. Cannot predict how soon we shall be ready to begin work from there. We are trying to solve this constantly.

<u>Louis</u>: Your suggestion of more than year ago that he set up auto in Argentina has been conveyed to him and 5,000 sent to him as per your suggestion. We also invited him to come to Gilla but he informed us that if he left he could not return. Now your present suggestion that he organize auto in Gilla is very much along same lines. Insofar as his trip to Gilla will mean that he loses his connection in South American countries and cannot return Father is firmly opposed to his leaving. More than one year ago son reported to you that our comrades in Gilla investigated problem of auto and reported that it would cost

about $4000 which is over five times its cost here. We reported this to you but you never commented on this matter. We will send person to Gilla to work on this problem from here again. Generally communications with Louis are extremely difficult. We cannot send a visitor to him. We can only wait until someone From Chili or Cuba receives permission to travel and send message to Louis.

<u>Merton</u>: We have again recently given substantial aid to Merton which will grow in volume and importance as time goes on. We can consider this problem solved and will be in position to improve from time to time due primarily to assistence from Father. We are also cooperating very closely with Cooper which accounts also for his helpfull aid in communication with you.

Generally our apparatus is kept strictly isolated from party as before. We have had to make a number of replacements and adjustments of personell due to changing conditions. Political attention is given to everyone. Periodically all questions are discussed and considered by son and father.

While the party generally is functioning on the war efforts entirely openly and enjoy greater legal freedom than ever, The F.B.I. and military intelligence has not decreased its surveillence and still sends spies into party ranks. This requires that we must increase our vigillence and maintain our contacts with father and other vital comrades with greatest care. This necessarily results in great delays and postponements of numerous tasks and problems and creates many disappointments.

Son

### JAPANESE CADRES

Relative to your request for Japanese comrades. Our most developed and experienced Japanese comrades have been funktioning on the West Coast (San Francisco and Los Angeles.) The best ones are well known to Okano. During May and June of 1941 the entire Japanese population of California, Oregon, Washington, Arizona and Utah have been interned by the government in special camps. This includes both American born (Nissei) and Japanese born (Issei) Up to this time they could not be visited by others than immediate relatives. We do not have direct contact with them at present. Prior to their internment they had the option of moving to the central or eastern part of the country and thus avoid internment. We made the decision that Joe and Saito should move to Colorado and publish our paper Doho, from there. We arranged for a trade union committee to help them and furnished them with funds to make this possible. Our decision was rejected at the last minute and the comrades went to the camps. Saito has been released and hired by the O.W.I. (Office of War Information) which is a government department of propoganda that among other functions prepares radio broadcasts to Japan and similar propoganda materials for Axis countries and occupied countries. While we have no contact with Saito it does not necessarilly follow that he has betrayed the party by accepting such a post. There are reliable Chinese comrades and others who have been invited by O.W.I. for such work. Saito and others have been cooperating with government agencies ever since Dec. 7. 1941 in exposing Japanese fascists and their organizations with our direct approval and under our steady guidence. We now learn that the internment conditions are being relaxed and some internees are permitted to leave camps for non-military districts provided they can get jobs and living quarters. At present we do not know if this applies to both Issei and Nissei. We are striving to get this information in order to make efforts to release Joe and perhaps some others.

We do not at this time discount the possibilities of making West Coast comrades available for your purposes.

Japanese comrades living in New York are living under relatively normal conditions but subject to some restrictions. But N.Y. Japanese are very few and little developed and but little known to the party because the center of J. populations and party work among them has always been in california. We have already taken steps to make full inquiries about them and will inform you.

In the meantime we should be informed whether you are primarily interested in the Jap comrades born in Japan (Issei) or also in American born Japanese (Nissei)

There are 105,000 Japanese in government camps. Of these two thirds are Nissei. At present Nissei are being conditionnally released at the rate of 10,000 per month principally for jobs on the farms in non military arreas.

Son

SON FINANCIAL STATEMENT FOR 1942.

Balance Jan.1, 1942 ............................... $30.145

EXPENDITURES FOR 1942.

| | | |
|---|---|---|
| Son. | | 2.090 |
| Mike | | 1.560 |
| George. | (2 1/2 months) | 433 |
| Tom | (10 months) | 1.125 |
| Eve. | (6 months). | 625 |
| Goldie | (2 months). | 250 |
| Steve | (6 months). | 300 |
| Mack | (3 1/2 months) | 350 |
| Gilla | (Technical work) | 600 |

## Document 59 *continued*

Cuba ................ (Technical work) .......... 300
Rents ................ (4 places) ................ 556
Japanese work ......... (6 months) ............... 1.400
Miscellaneous .................................... 1.722
　　　　GRAND TOTAL FOR 1942 ..................... $11.311

SUMMARY

Balance Jan.1,1942 .............................. $30.145
Expenditures for 1942 ........................... 11.311
Balance Jan.1,1943 .............................. $18.834

Notes on 1942 Expenditures:
We have arranged for a defense job for George and subsequently loaned him to Cooper for auto building work and will soon take him back. Tom is gone to sea on a ship temporarily. Eve has been released due to illness and after some delay has been replaced by Goldie. Steve has been released but continues to cooperate with us. Mack has been placed in charge of all our Pacific coast communications and specially charged with preparing auto work with you from there.

We sent you our 1941 Financial report through Merton facilities last January but you have never acknowledged receipt of it. Please do so now. Please also acknowledge receipt of this report so that we may destroy our copy.

Japanese work involves usual $150. per month, special for publications, moving expenses and fares for Joe and Saito to Colorado to continue issuing "Doho". This plan was not carried out but funds used to liquidate debts of Doho and pack and store all its equipments.
　　END

　　　　　　　　　　　　　　　　　　　　　　Son

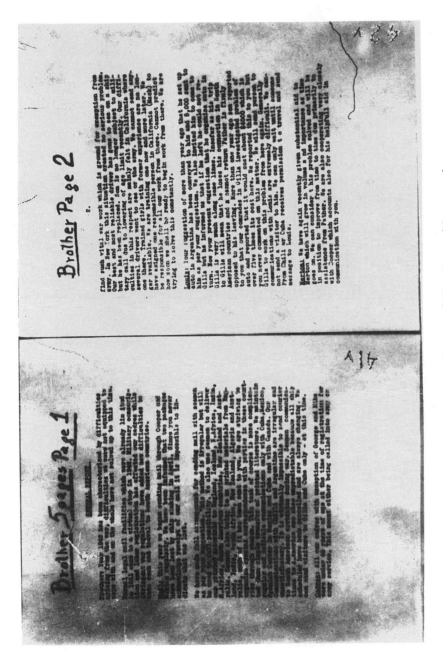

DOCUMENT 59. Son to Brother with attached "Son Financial Statement for 1942."

213

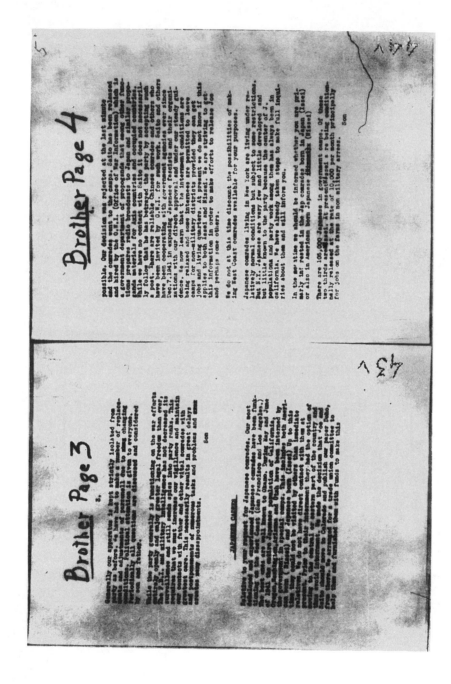

## Brother Page 4

possible. Our decision was rejected at the last minute and hired by the O.W.I. (Office of War Information) which is a government department of propaganda that among other functions prepares radio broadcasts to Japan and other countries. While we have no contact with Saito it does seem particularly to follow that he has betrayed the party by accepting a post. There are reliable Chinese comrades and others who have been invited by O.W.I. for such work. Saito and others have been cooperating with government agencies and organizations with our direct approval of their practices. We now learn that the internment conditions are being relaxed and some internees are permitted to leave camps for non-military districts provided they can get jobs and living quarters. At present we do not know if this applies to both Issei and Nisei. We are striving to get this information in order to make efforts to release so and perhaps some others.

We do not at this time discount the possibilities of making West Coast comrades available for your purposes.

Japanese comrades living in New York are living under relatively normal conditions but are subject to some restrictions. But N.Y. Japanese are very few and little is developed but little known to the party because the center of J. populations and party work among them has always been in California. We have already taken steps to make full inquiries about them and will inform you.

In the meantime we should be informed whether you ?? ?? marly int rested in the Jap comrades known ?? ?? or also in American born Japanese comrades (Nisei)

There are 105,000 Japanese in government camps. Of these two thirds are interned. At present Nisei are being continually released at the rate of 10,000 per month principally for jobs on the farms in non military areas.

Con

## Brother Page 3

s.

Generally our apparatus is kept strictly isolated from mass ?? as before, we have had to make ?? number of replacements and adjustments if personnel will due to many changing conditions. All organization is given to everyone if we can gather.

This is the party generally to functioning on the war efforts in ?? way and with only greater legal freedom than ever before. Our ?? intelligence had not decreased its ?? and ?? duties. ?? into party ranks. This means that we must increase ?? and month by month ?? with father and other vital ?? and with great care. This necessarily results in great delays in our ?? tasks and problems and some ?? many disappointment.

Con

### Japanese Canadians

Relating to the Japanese comrades. Our most ?? of Japanese comrades have been found ?? in ?? in the West Coast (San Francisco and Los Angeles) and ?? well known to Ottawa. Dept. they ?? ?? with the evacuation of California. Then ?? in ?? ?? them been ?? held ?? ?? ?? (Nisei) up to add ?? to be related to their ?? contact with the immediate ?? to do ?? no ?? ?? that ?? ?? southern part of the country who ?? us ?? the decision that the ?? of ?? ?? ?? and publish our Paper whose ?? ?? ?? found ?? ?? ?? ?? ?? ?? them and consider that ?? to make this

SON FINANCIAL STATEMENT FOR 1942.

Balance Jan.1,1942..........................$30.145

EXPENDITURES FOR 1942.

```
Son......................................................2.090
Mike...................................................1.560
George......(2½ months)............................  433
Tom.........(10 months)............................1.125
Eve.........( 6  months)...........................  625
Goldie......(2 months )............................  250
Steve.......( 6  months)...........................  300
Mack........(3½ months)............................  350
Gilla.......(Technical work).......................  600
Cuba........(Technical work).......................  300
Rents.......( 4 places)............................  556
Japanese work..(6 months).........................1.400
Miscellaneous.....................................1.722
            GRAND TOTAL FOR 1942...............$11.311
```

S U M M A R Y

```
Balance Jan.1,1942........................$30.145
Expenditures for 1942.....................  11.311
Balance Jan.1,1943........................$18.834
```

Notes on 1942 Expenditures:
We have arranged for a defense job for George and subsequently loaned him to Cooper for auto building work and
will soon take him back. Tom is gone to sea on a ship
temporarily. Eve has been released due to illness and
after some delay has been replaced by Goldie. Steve has
been released but continues to cooperate with us. Mack
has been placed in charge of all our Pacific coast communications and specially charged with preparing auto
work with you from there.

We sent you our 1941 Financial report through Merton
facilities last January but you have never acknowledged
receipt of it.Please do so now.Please also acknowledge receipt of this report so that we may destroy our copy.

Japanese work involves usual $150. per month,special for
publications, moving expenses and fares for Joe and Saito
to Colorado to continue issuing "Doho".This plan was not
carried out but funds used to liquidate debts of Doho
and pack and store all its equipments.

## END

Son

## The Brother-Son Network and Soviet Atomic Espionage

Since the collapse of the Soviet Union, the Russian Foreign Intelligence Service, successor to the foreign intelligence directorate of the KGB, has released selected documents to the Russian press. These documents and the stories that have accompanied them from retired Soviet intelligence officers have highlighted successful intelligence operations and appear to have been aimed at demonstrating the value of intelligence operations at a time when many former Soviet institutions were under attack as unneeded or inefficient. One of the operations praised for its success was the Soviet penetration of the American atomic bomb project (the Manhattan project) during World War II.

In 1991, Colonel Vladimir Chikov, a KGB officer, wrote a lengthy article about Soviet atomic espionage.[3] Chikov identified the intelligence officer in the United States who supervised Soviet atomic espionage as Vasily Zubilin, nominally third secretary in the Soviet embassy in Washington but actually a senior NKVD officer. Chikov quoted a 1942 message from Zubilin to General Pavel Fitin describing the isolation and elaborate security measures of America's atomic bomb facility at Los Alamos, New Mexico. Zubilin assured Fitin, head of the NKVD's foreign intelligence directorate, however, that "we are taking further measures to plant our reliable sources in Los Alamos."[4] Zubilin and the Cooper mentioned in document 59 are one and the same person. The FBI identified Zubilin as Cooper when its hidden listening devices recorded a 1943 meeting in California between Zubilin and Steve Nelson, a senior CPUSA official discussed in chapter 4.[5]

---

3. Vladimir Chikov, "How the Soviet Secret Service Split the American Atom," *Novoe vremia*, nos. 16 and 17 (23 April and 30 April 1991); the material quoted below from this article is translated from the Russian edition of *Novoe vremia* and not directly quoted from the English edition entitled *New Times*.

4. Maxim [Zubilin] to Alexandrov [Fitin], reply to Fitin message of 14 June 1942, reproduced in Chikov, "How the Soviet Secret Service Split the American Atom." Zubilin's real name was Zarubin.

5. The FBI summary of the surreptitiously recorded 1943 conversation is found in Senate Subcommittee to Investigate the Administration of the Internal Security Act, *Interlocking Subversion in Government Departments*, 83d Cong., 1st sess., 6 May 1953, pt. 15:1050–51. The FBI did not reveal that its report was based on bugging, stating instead that the report stemmed from "a highly confidential source of complete reliability." This euphemism was used and the actual transcript withheld, it appears, in order to obscure FBI methods of investigation and because the

## Morris Cohen, Atomic Spy

Chikov also wrote that an American code-named Morton assisted Soviet atomic espionage. Chikov quoted a message from a Soviet intelligence officer in America to Moscow stating: "Means for advancing 'Morton' to one of the production centers in the state of Maryland are being worked out. It is beginning production of new types of weapons for the American army."[6]

Chikov's article singled out another American, code-named Louis, as a key figure in the success of Soviet atomic espionage, stating that Louis had recruited an American physicist who became the chief Soviet source within the Manhattan project. Chikov published a 1942 message from an NKVD officer in the United States that said: "The physicist . . . contacted our source 'Louis,' an acquaintance from the Spanish civil war. . . . We propose to recruit him through 'Louis.' 'Louis' has already carried out a similar task, and very successfully."[7]

Although Chikov did not identify Morton, he identified Louis as an American named Morris Cohen and released parts of Cohen's KGB file. Chikov also wrote that Morris's wife, Lona, was an active participant in the penetration of the Manhattan project. Included in the material released in Chikov's article was Cohen's own account of his training in covert radio operations at a secret Russian-run school in Spain during the Spanish Civil War and his recruitment as a Soviet agent at that time.[8]

---

bugging was done without a court order. That the report was based on listening devices was confirmed in 1980 by the FBI agent who recorded the Cooper/Zubilin conversation (Comments by William Branigan on Herbert Romerstein's "Soviet Intelligence in the United States," in *Intelligence Requirements for the 1980s: Counterintelligence,* ed. Roy Godson, vol. 3 [New Brunswick, N.J.: National Strategy Information Center and Transaction Books, 1980], 201).

6. Chikov, "How the Soviet Secret Service Split the American Atom." Although not clearly dated, the essay places this message in 1942 or 1943.

7. Ibid.

8. Ibid. John Costello and Oleg Tsarev (*Deadly Illusions* [New York: Crown, 1993], 275–77) name Alexander Orlov, a senior Soviet intelligence officer mentioned in chapter 4, as Cohen's recruiter. Chikov does not name Cohen's recruiter, and his description of the recruiter matches Orlov in some respects but not in others. Costello and Tsarev's book, like the Chikov article and the Yatskov interview (below), was prepared with the cooperation of the Russian Foreign Intelligence Service and made use of documents chosen and released by the intelligence service from Soviet intelligence archives that are closed to independent researchers. These factors must be kept in mind when weighing these accounts.

Document 59 goes well beyond Chikov's account by showing that Louis, an American who was part of the Soviet penetration of the Manhattan project, was also a member of the CPUSA's secret apparatus and the Brother-Son network and that the apparatus was working with Vasily Zubilin (Cooper), the NKVD officer who supervised Soviet atomic espionage. In this connection between the CPUSA, the Brother-Son network, and the NKVD, we see substantiated for the first time that the CPUSA was doing much more to undermine the American political process than simply pilfering State Department documents. Through its secret apparatus, it was, in fact, also engaged in stealing the secrets of America's atomic bomb project.

Document 60 is a 1937 questionnaire filled out by Cohen, then an American Communist serving in the Mackenzie-Papineau battalion. Cohen, who used the name Israel Altman while in Spain, states that he was born in New York City in 1910. A high school football star, Cohen later coached football at Mississippi State College and joined the CPUSA in 1935 when he *realized that the CP is the vanguard of the working class which is directing the path toward revolution and an International Soviet, i.e., the building of a better world for the masses.* Even while serving in Spain he remained an active party worker; an International Brigades Communist committee praised his "great initiative and activity in our political work."[9]

---

# Document 60

Personal questionnaire of Morris Cohen (Israel Pickett Altman), "Historical Commission of the International Brigades—Mackenzie-Papineau Battalion—August 1937," RTsKhIDNI 545–3–509. Original in English. Partly handwritten.

---

### HISTORICAL COMMISSION OF THE INTERNATIONAL BRIGADES
#### —MACKENZIE-PAPINEAU BATTALION—

August, 1937

COMRADE: It is important for the records of our Battalion and of the International Brigades, that you cooperate in answering the following questions both exactly and as completely as possible. If there is not sufficient space opposite

9. Unit party committee to Communist Party of Spain Central Committee, 14 November 1938, evaluation of Morris Cohen, RTsKhIDNI 545–6–874.

# Document 60 *continued*

any question, use the other side of this sheet or another sheet of paper to complete your answer or remarks. This information is confidential, so please do not ask to see the answers given by other comrades, and feel secure that your own comments will be treated likewise.

FULL NAME   *Israel Pickett Altman (name in U.S. Morris Cohen)*
Company   *4*      Section   *3*      Rank or function   *Section Political Leader*
National Origin   *American*      Home (City, State)   *[at] Harry Cohen -*
*1244 Grand Concourse New York, N.Y.*
Birth Place   *New York, N.Y. U.S.A.*
Birth Date (Month, day, year)   *July 2, 1910*
Parents' Occupation   *Produce Peddler*
Married?   *No*      Divorced?   *No*      Number of Children   *None*
Political affiliation?   *Communist Party Branch Org. & Section Com*
When joined and Why   *Dec. 1935. Realized that the CP is the vanguard of the working class which is directing the path toward revolution and an International Soviet, i.e., the building of a better world for the masses*
Unions, Fraternal organizations, Clubs you belong to, and positions held
*Writers' Union & Local autonomous unions formed for the summer's duration in hotels*
Schooling   *Six years of college incl. B.S. degree & 2 years of graduate work*
Military experience and previous rank   *No military experience*
Trade   *Journalist—Reporting & advertising sales*
Age started to work   *9 years old*
Employment Record (Types of work and where)   *2 years news reporting in Mississippi, 9 years as a waiter at N.Y., Urbana, Illinois, Mississippi & N.J., 4 years as football coach & athletic trainer at Mississippi State College, N.Y. University, & James Monroe H.S., camp manager in NY State for 2 summers, then filled in at odd manual jobs.*
If unemployed, how long?   *2 periods, for 9 months & for 4 months*
What was your most outstanding experience in the labor movement of the U.S. or Canada?   *1. Building a co-operative restaurant for negroes & white students while in a college YCL unit; this work I led and felt in the progress thereby 2. Participating in local strikes at summer hotels in 1933, 1935, & 1936 3. Broadening the influence of the CP in my local neighborhood where we led the assistance for Spanish Democracy.*
Ever arrested? What charges? Sentences?   *Never*
What finally decided you to come to Spain?   *I realized the necessity from the outbreak of the uprising. It was principally a question of leaving my parents. But when I heard Phil Bard speak at a meeting of Bronx County functionaries, I decided that my duty lie where liberty was in greatest danger in Spain. I feel that as Dimitrov said, the central commission of the CI is my highest judge and its analysis of world events points to where our highest duty lies.*

## Document 60 *continued*

On the reverse side, please answer the following two questions: What is the most outstanding thing you've noticed or experienced since leaving the US or Canada; and, What do you intend to do after this war is finished? Please add any other comments, opinions or suggestions you wish, also, either for the Battalion or IB leadership, or specifically on the work of the Historical Commission. Notes on other comrades will also be appreciated.

Question #1 *The most outstanding thing I have noticed since leaving the U.S. is the maturity of the People's Front and the labor movement in France & Spain as compared with the U.S. This is even reflected in the education of the little children, in their conduct on the streets or at the stations when our train approached as well as in the progress of their parents and the latter's organizations. This is coupled with the change in the institutions of Spain. Here is a former church, shorn of every ecclesiastical vestige, transformed into a House of the People with union meeting halls at the sides, a platform for speakers, posters depicting pictures and slogans reflecting the historical events of the day, the bust and name of the founder of the Socialist Party of Spain, Pablo Iglesias, proudly spread over the top of the platform, union announcements on the walls outside, and the agricultural worker leaving a meeting at this "House" of theirs at 3 A.M. to start the day's labor. Alongside this ideological transformation is the economic hangover, the primitive manner of threshing wheat, dependant upon the wind, still prevailing as a heritage from the feudalistic reign of King Alfonso and his reactionary successors. But when ideology and culture are revolutionized, the mechanical way of doing things, the methods of production will follow in the wake. It is these parallel rails of progress whose course can never be stopped, which struck me most powerfully.*

On Ques. #2. *When the war is finished, I would like to return to activity in the American Labor movement. However, if circumstances require my presence elsewhere, similar to the Spanish struggle against fascism, then I would go there.*

On #3, suggestions & opinions:

1. *If a little Spanish could be learned by the members of the American, Canadian, English Battalions, then every phase of life here would benefit by it; greater co-operation and progress would result.*

2. *A Battalion newspaper reflecting our life here and connecting it with the front would liven up things.*

3.

August, 1937

COMRADE: It is important for the records of our Battalion and of the International Brigades, that you cooperate in answering the following questions both exactly and as completely as possible. If there is not sufficient space opposite any question, use the other side of this sheet or another sheet of paper to complete your answer or remarks. This information is confidential, so please do not ask to see the answers given by other comrades, and feel secure that your own comments will be treated likewise.

*(name in U.S.)*

FULL NAME **ISRAEL Pickett ALTMAN** (**MORRIS COHEN**)

Company **4** Section **3** Rank or function **Section Political Leader**
*to Harry Cohen - 1244 Grand Concourse*

National Origin **American** Home(City,State) **New York, N.Y.**

Birth Place **New York, N.Y. U.S.A.** Birth Date(Month, day, year) **July 2, 1910**

Parents' Occupation **Produce Peddler**

Married? **No** Divorced? **No** Number of Children **None**

Political affiliation? **Communist Party** *Branch Org. + Section Comm.* When joined and Why **Dec. 1935. Realized** *that the C P is the vanguard of the working class which is directing the path toward revolution and a international Soviet, i.e., the building of a better world for the masses*

Unions, Fraternal organizations, Clubs you belong to, and positions held *Writers' Union + Local autonomous unions formed for the communists denotation in hotels*

Schooling *Six Years of College incl. B.S. degree + 2 years of graduate work*

Military experience and previous rank **No military experience.**

Trade **Journalist - Reporting + Advertising Sales** Age started to work **9 years old**

Employment Record (Types of work and where) *2 years reporting in Mississippi, 9 years office a writer of N.Y., Urbana, Illinois, Mississippi + N.J. 4 years as football coach + athletic trainer of Mississippi State College, N.Y. University, + games, Monroe H.S. Camp manage in NY State for 2 Summers,* If unemployed, how long? *2 periods, for 9 months then filled in odd manual jobs. 4 for 4 months.*

**What was your most outstanding experience in the labor movement of the U.S. or Canada?**
1. *Building a co-operative restaurant for Negroes + white students while in a college YCL unit; this work I later felt in the progress therein*
2. *Participating in local strikes at Summer hotels in 1933, 1935, + 1936*
3. *Broadening the influence of the CP in my local neighborhood where we led the assistance for Spanish Democracy.*

Ever arrested? What charges? Sentences? *Never*

What finally decided you to come to Spain? *I realized the necessity for the...*

On the reverse side, please answer the following two questions: What is the most outstanding thing you've noticed or experienced since leaving the U S or Canada; and, What do you intend to do after this war is finished? Please add any other comments, opinions or suggestions you wish, also, either for the Battalion or IB leadership, or specifically on the work of the Historical Commission. Notes on other comrades will also be appreciated.

DOCUMENT 60. First page of the personal questionnaire of Morris Cohen (Israel Pickett Altman), August 1937.

The questionnaire asked about postwar plans, and Cohen wrote, *"When the war is finished, I would like to return to activity in the American Labor movement."* Questionnaires were filled out by many Abraham Lincoln and Mackenzie-Papineau battalion members. Many of the soldiers' responses were very similar to Cohen's, and they expressed a desire to work in the labor movement, for the Communist party, or for a left-wing cause. Cohen, however, added a sentiment that was unusual among those found in the Comintern's files. He added, *"However, if circumstances require my presence elsewhere, similar to the Spanish struggle against fascism, then I would go there."* Many of the Lincoln and Mackenzie-Papineau veterans would fight again when World War II came. But in the midst of difficult and harrowing duty, few went out of their way to volunteer for another such fight.

Cohen's answer illustrates why Soviet intelligence officers spotted him as a potential recruit. They approached him and recruited him; his later service to the Communist cause put him in the center of Soviet atomic espionage against the United States.

In 1992 Anatoly Yatskov, another senior retired KGB officer, discussed with the press his leading role in uncovering the American atomic bomb project, stating, "No other intelligence service in the world succeeded in penetrating the wall of secrecy around the Manhattan Project." Yatskov, as had Chikov, credited Morris Cohen with making the initial contact between Soviet intelligence and an American physicist who eventually supplied the Soviets with the most important American nuclear secrets. Yatskov, who operated in the United States from 1941 to 1946 as one of Zubilin's colleagues, said that Morris Cohen and his wife, Lona, were among his chief links to sources inside the Manhattan project. He noted that Lona undertook two vital courier missions to pick up material from an unnamed source working at the Los Alamos, New Mexico, facility where the first atomic bombs were built.[10]

10. Michael Dobbs, "How Soviets Stole U.S. Atom Secrets," *Washington Post,* 4 October 1992; Ronald Radosh, "Ending the Myth," *New York Post,* 18 June 1993. Yatskov used the name Yakolev in the United States. Yatskov did not name the American physicist, and the document that Chikov released used a pseudonym. Lona Cohen may have taken on courier duties when Morris entered the U.S. Army and had less freedom to perform such missions. Morris served as an army cook in the United States and Canada (Sanche de Gramont, *The Secret War* [New York: Dell, 1962]).

Chikov and Yatskov felt free to identify Louis as Morris Cohen because Cohen's identity as a Soviet agent was no longer in question. In 1950 Klaus Fuchs, a physicist on the joint Anglo-American atomic bomb project who had worked at Los Alamos, confessed to British authorities that he was a Communist and Soviet spy. His confession led the FBI to an American named Harry Gold.[11] Gold confessed and led the FBI to David Greenglass, an American soldier who had worked as a skilled machinist in one of the sensitive sections of the Los Alamos project. Greenglass confessed and said he had been recruited into Soviet espionage by his brother-in-law, Julius Rosenberg, a Communist who had quietly dropped out of open party work in the early 1940s.

On the day Greenglass's arrest was announced in the press, Joel Barr, a close friend of Julius Rosenberg, a fellow engineer who had worked on military electronics, and a secret Communist, disappeared from his Paris apartment. He did not reappear until forty years later, when he turned up under the name Joseph Berg working on microelectronics at a Soviet military laboratory in Leningrad.[12] When Barr disappeared, the FBI questioned Alfred Sarant, another military electronics engineer, Rosenberg associate, and secret Communist, about Barr. Sarant denied all but a casual relationship with Barr. A few weeks later he crossed the border into Mexico and disappeared. He surfaced in the Soviet Union in the 1980s, working, like Barr, on military electronics. On the day Barr disappeared, Morton Sobell, another friend of the Rosenbergs and an engineer who had worked on military radar, procured emergency leave from his employer and flew to Mexico. Sobell made plans to take his family to Europe but was delayed by the lack of passports, which had not been needed to enter Mexico. Before he could make arrangements, Mexican police seized Sobell and turned him over to the FBI. Meanwhile, the FBI arrested Julius Rosenberg and, later, his wife, Ethel.

Julius Rosenberg's arrest triggered yet another flight. Morris Cohen and his wife quietly vanished from their New York apart-

11. Anatoly Yatskov also named Gold, along with the Cohens, as his couriers to a Soviet source at Los Alamos (Dobbs, "How Soviets Stole U.S. Atom Secrets"; Ronald Radosh and Eric Breindel, "Bombshell," *New Republic*, 10 June 1991; Radosh, "Ending the Myth").

12. Since the collapse of the Soviet Union, Barr has returned to the United States for visits. He denies any participation in Soviet espionage.

ment. Both were associates of the Rosenbergs.[13] The Cohens reappeared a few years later in London as antiquarian book dealers using the names Peter and Helen Kroger and holding fraudulently obtained New Zealand passports. In 1961 British security officials arrested the two as part of a Soviet spy ring that had penetrated the British navy. The Cohen residence housed the ring's elaborate radio and microfilming equipment. A British court convicted and imprisoned the Cohens for espionage. In 1967 the Soviet intelligence services obtained their release by exchanging them for British spies held by the Soviet Union.[14]

Harry Gold and David Greenglass, who confessed, and Morton Sobell, who did not, were imprisoned for their role in the Rosenberg operation. Julius and Ethel Rosenberg, who denied even being Communists, much less spies, were convicted, their appeal to the Supreme Court failed, and in 1953 they were executed for espionage.[15] Lona Cohen died in Moscow in 1993. Morris Cohen lives in retirement in Moscow on a pension provided by Soviet, now Russian, intelligence.

In 1992, Anatoly Yatskov, the NKVD officer who assisted in penetrating the Manhattan project, said that "the information we acquired enabled us to gain time in building our own bomb. . . . How much time we gained is hard to tell, but a few years at least." Also in 1992, the journal of the Russian Academy of Science, *Voprosy istorii estestvoznaniia i tekhniki* (Questions about the history of natural science and technology) reprinted a series of memoranda, spanning the period 1941 to 1946, written by NKVD officials or by Igor Kurchatov, the chief scientist directing the Soviet atomic bomb project. These documents, released from the archives of the KGB, show that Soviet intelligence provided Kurchatov with

13. The Cohens' link to the Rosenberg case is discussed in Ronald Radosh and Joyce Milton, *The Rosenberg File: A Search for the Truth* (New York: Holt, Rinehart and Winston, 1983), 425–26, 571n; Ronald Radosh, "More Evidence against the Rosenbergs," *Washington Post*, 31 October 1992; Radosh, "Ending the Myth."

14. The Cohens' role in espionage against Great Britain is described in Rebecca West, *The New Meaning of Treason* (New York: Viking, 1964), 281–88.

15. As with the Hiss case, there remains an energetic group of partisans who deny that the Rosenbergs were involved in espionage. The evidence against them, however, was overwhelming. Radosh and Milton's *The Rosenberg File*, the definitive history of the case, confirms their guilt but suggests that imposition of the death penalty on Ethel Rosenberg was an effort to force her or Julius to confess in return for a reprieve.

a massive amount of high-quality technical intelligence on the Anglo-American atomic project. Kurchatov's reports show that the information allowed the Soviet atomic project to proceed much faster and at much lower cost than would otherwise have been possible.[16]

The Brother-Son network was not an organization formed by the NKVD to recruit various Americans, some of whom just happened to be American Communists; the network was part of the American Communist party's own secret apparatus. The head of the Brother-Son network, "Son," and the head of the CPUSA's secret apparatus, Rudy Baker, were one and the same person. The network also had a direct link to the CPUSA's leadership through "Father." The role of Louis/Cohen, an American who spied for the Soviets, in the Brother-Son network, along with the link between the network and Cooper/Zubilin of the NKVD, demonstrate the network's, and through it the CPUSA's, direct connection to Soviet atomic espionage against the United States.

It is difficult to overstate the importance of Soviet atomic espionage in shaping the history of the Cold War. World War II had ended with Americans confident that the atomic bomb gave them a monopoly on the ultimate weapon, a monopoly expected to last ten to twenty years. The Soviet explosion of a nuclear bomb in 1949 destroyed this sense of physical security. America had fought in two world wars without suffering serious civilian deaths or destruction. Now it faced an enemy led by a ruthless dictator who could wipe out any American city with a single bomb.

16. Dobbs, "How Soviets Stole U.S. Atom Secrets." The documents reprinted in *Voprosy istorii estestvoznaniia i tekhniki,* 1992, no. 3:107–34, are reprinted in translation in an appendix to Pavel A. Sudoplatov, Anatoli P. Sudoplatov, Jerrold Schecter, and Leona Schecter, *Special Tasks: The Memoirs of an Unwanted Witness* (New York: Little, Brown, 1994), 436–67. The Foreign Intelligence Service of Russia, which released the documents, evidently had second thoughts about its action, and this issue of *Voprosy istorii estestvoznaniia i tekhniki* was hastily withdrawn from public circulation and removed from Russian libraries. *Special Tasks* also reproduces in translation similar documents from Igor Kurchatov's papers held by the archive of the Ministry of Atomic Energy in Moscow (Sudoplatov, *Special Tasks,* 468–73). Other accounts bearing on the importance of intelligence in speeding up the Soviet atomic project are Feliks Ivanovich Chuev, *Molotov Remembers: Inside Kremlin Politics, Conversations with Felix Chuev* (Chicago: I. R. Dee, 1993), 55–59, 341; and the Associated Press's 31 March 1993 obituary of Anatoly Yatskov based on an Itar-Tass report from Russia.

Had the American nuclear monopoly lasted longer, Stalin might have refused to allow North Korean Communists to launch the Korean War, or the Chinese Communists might have hesitated to intervene in the war. Had the American nuclear monopoly lasted until Stalin's death, the restraint on Soviet aggressiveness might have alleviated the most dangerous years of the Cold War.

As it was, the widespread frustration and fear caused by America's loss of its nuclear monopoly turned to rage when the trial of the Rosenbergs demonstrated that American Communists had assisted Soviet intelligence in stealing nuclear weapons technology. Part of the harshness of government and popular anticommunism in the 1950s is attributable to anger at the assistance American Communists provided to Soviet atomic espionage. Revisionist historians have portrayed that anger as misdirected, denying any significant Communist assistance to Soviet espionage efforts and insisting that the CPUSA was itself innocent of any taint of espionage. The documents in this volume prove for the first time that the CPUSA's own covert arm was an integral part of Soviet atomic espionage.

### Recruiting Japanese Cadre for the Comintern

The longest section of document 59 deals with "your request for Japanese comrades." There is no indication why Moscow wanted the names of Japanese Communists in the United States, but Son's network was a natural source for this information in view of Baker's earlier work with the Pan-Pacific Trade Union Secretariat (chapter 2) and a 1939 Comintern request (document 67, discussed later in this chapter) that his apparatus assist a broken Japanese network.[17]

Son/Baker said that Okano had identified a number of reliable cadre. Okano was the pseudonym for Sanzo Nosaka, a leading

17. Because of the difficulty of direct Soviet-Japanese communications and the existence of a sizable Japanese population in America, the Comintern often used the CPUSA as an intermediary. Sen Katayama and Eizo Kondo, two of the principal founders of Japanese communism, began their work while in exile in the United States in 1918. Katayama, later a prominent Comintern official, also assisted in the founding of the American movement in 1919. During World War II, owing to intense Japanese patriotism and the efficiency of the security police, the Japanese Communist party ceased to exist for all practical purposes. The Comintern may have asked for Japanese cadre in preparation for rebuilding the Japanese Communist movement in the postwar period. On the ties between the American and Japanese Communist parties, see Rodger Swearingen and Paul Langer, *Red Flag in Japan: International Communism in Action, 1919–1951* (New York: Greenwood Press, 1968).

Japanese Communist who had spent part of the 1930s in the United States.[18] Unfortunately, noted Son, the wartime detention of West Coast Japanese and Japanese-Americans had cut off communications with Okano's contacts. Son said two reliable comrades, "Joe" and "Saito," were originally ordered to move to Colorado to avoid internment and to publish a Communist Japanese-language paper. Saito was the Comintern pseudonym for Shuji Fuji, editor of the Japanese-language CPUSA newspaper, *Doho*. Joe was Joe Koide, whose work editing the Japanese-language section of the Pan-Pacific Trade Union Secretariat's journal, the *Pan-Pacific Worker*, was discussed in chapter 2. Son/Baker reported that the plan to establish a Colorado paper was canceled at the last minute, and Saito and Joe went into the government internment camps for Japanese. Another 1942 Comintern report, **document 61**, also discusses Joe Koide's and Saito/Shuji Fuji's work among Japanese and Japanese-Americans. According to this report, Saito and Joe may have produced one issue of a Japanese-oriented paper from Denver. Document 61 also refers to Rudy Baker using his old Pan-Pacific Trade Union Secretariat code name, Betford.

---

## Document 61

Excerpt from Plyshevsky to Dimitrov, 5 November 1942, RTsKhIDNI 495–74–479. Original in Russian. In this document it is noted that Joe Koide had the code name Nisi. In the discussion of the *Pacific Citizen* the Russian word *no* (but) is so faint that it cannot be distinguished from *ne* (not); consequently the sentence may in fact read: "The newspaper is in English, not exclusively devoted to Japanese issues." The second item in the list of suggestions is marked "3)" as here.

---

(Regarding materials that have arrived from the US through special channel[s]) . . .

18. After World War II, Nosaka became one of the chief figures in the rebuilt Japanese Communist party, and under his leadership it came to play a lively role in Japanese politics, although it never won more than a handful of parliamentary seats. In 1993 he was one hundred years old and the most senior and respected member of the Japanese Communist party; nonetheless, he was dismissed as the party's honorary chairman. The dismissal came after researchers found in the Comintern's archives a letter that Nosaka wrote in 1939 falsely accusing a fellow Communist leader, Kenzo Yamamoto, of being a spy for the Japanese military government of that era. A few weeks after Nosaka wrote his letter, Yamamoto, in exile in the Soviet Union, was arrested by the NKVD and secretly executed (David E. Sanger, "Top Japanese Communist Dishonored at the Age of 100," *New York Times*, 23 September 1993).

3. A number of documents on the work of Japanese Communist groups in the US since the beginning of the Japanese-American war:

a) CPUSA Central Committee member Comrade Betford reports that leading Japanese Communists, specifically, Comrades Nisi (Joe) and Saito (Fuji, publisher of the newspaper "Doho"), have analyzed the Japanese-American war situation well and adopted the correct line. Com. Betford gives Com. Nisi's activities extremely high marks: "Throughout the entire crisis Joe held up splendidly; Nisi and Saito are now the clearest thinkers around on the whole situation." Contact between Joe and Com. Nelson (the member of the CPUSA CC responsible for work among the Japanese) has been well set up; their work is now proceeding in full coordination. The major issue in the work of the Japanese comrades has been evacuation to the interior of the country (evidently, the Salt Lake region). On the issues of evacuation and general support for the war, the Japanese Communists have acquired mass influence in the Japanese immigrant community in the US; however, as Com. Betford notes, "they are reluctant to expand the scope of their work to include developing prospects for a democratic Japan and the concrete, progressive aspects of the United Countries." On that issue, as well as the issue of coverage of the Soviet Union in "Doho," as the letter indicates, the necessary guidelines have been provided. Betford writes: "I am certain that with time Joe will work these issues out, just as he has the others." Joe contributed the proposal to airdrop democratic literature, "Doho," etc., over Japan. In Com. Betford's view, this proposal "is today completely feasible and practical and shows his (Joe's) determination to reach the popular masses of Japan."

In connection with the evacuation to the interior of the US, Joe considers the critical task to be the creation of a unified, democratic Japanese-language newspaper. The closing of many reactionary Japanese-language newspapers in the US is conducive to the implementation of this measure.

b) Five letters by Com. Nisi with reports on the work of Japanese Communist groups. These letters are in reply to our inquiry of April 1942.

In the letter dated 29 April 1942, there is a general description of the mood of Japanese immigrants in the US in connection with the onset of the Japanese-American war. The letter is of some general interest (an abridged version of the letter is attached). The letter dated 30 April 1942: the main focus of the letter is on the issue of creating a democratic newspaper (an abridged version of the letter is attached).

The letter dated 1 May 1942: the principal directives for Japanese Communist work in the US. These directives demonstrate a correct understanding of the tasks faced by Japanese Communists (the complete text of the letter is attached).

The letter dated 8 May 1942: written before departing for the new resettlement point, an analysis of the latest parliamentary elections in Japan. The argumentation is sound. The Japanese comrades are evidently following all developments in Japan closely and analyzing the situation in the country well. (An abridged version of the letter is attached.)

The fifth letter, dated 30 May 1942: this letter is devoted chiefly to the reaction of Japanese Communists in the US to the situation that has arisen as a result of the Japanese-American war. The letter is of great interest for the study of Japanese Communist cadres.

Suggestions regarding the given materials:

1) Transmit abridged versions (attached) of the letters dated 29 April 1942, 30 April 1942, 1 May 1942 and 8 May 1942 to Com. Li Kuyu one section at a time.

3) Use Com. Betford's letter and Com. Nisi's second letter, dated 30 April 1942, to study Japanese party cadres in the US.

4) The remaining material is a sheaf of issues of "Doho," its run from July 1941 through 10 April 1942. It is interesting to note that whereas before the war the motto beneath the newspaper's masthead read, "For equality, peace, and progress," since the war began the motto has read, "For total victory over Japanese militarism and German fascism." The newspapers have not yet been examined for their content.

There is one issue of the newspaper "Pacific Citizen," dated 9 July 1942, published in Salt Lake City. The newspaper is in English but is devoted exclusively to Japanese issues; it began publication recently (issue no. 6 came out on 9 July 1942). It is possible that this is in fact the unified democratic newspaper of which Com. Nisi wrote, for the emblem of the "Japanese-American Citizens' League" appears on it. (Com. Nisi wrote that he would try to have a newspaper come out sponsored by the "Japanese-American Citizens' League.")

Moreover, the newspaper includes an article reprinted from the Communist "Peoples' World."

However, it is difficult to reach a definite conclusion on the basis of a single issue.

ENCLOSURE: 4 letters.

*Plyshevsky*
(PLYSHEVSKY)

5 November 1942

In document 59, Son/Baker wrote that Saito was later hired by the Office of War Information (the chief U.S. propaganda agency in World War II) to work on Japanese-language radio propaganda. Although the apparatus had lost contact with Saito, Son reported that "it does not necessarily follow that he has betrayed the party by accepting such a post." Joe was still in the camps. Son said, "We should be informed whether you are primarily interested in the Jap comrades born in Japan (Issei) or also in American born Japanese (Nissei)."

Several of the issues brought up in the report were also discussed by Steve Nelson and the NKVD's Zubilin/Cooper when they met at Nelson's California home in April 1943. The FBI summary of the secretly recorded conversation between Zubilin and Nelson states, "The principal activities which were not being conducted to Nelson's satisfaction were contacts with Japanese Communists in the relocation centers and the handling of literature and other documentary material which was being transmitted to points in the South Pacific by Communist seamen couriers."[19] Nelson and Rudy Baker had often worked together; both were Yugoslav immigrants, and they had shared an apartment in the 1920s. Document 61 also described Steve Nelson as "the member of the CPUSA CC responsible for work among the Japanese."

There is another link between Baker and Nelson and the Brother-Son network. Although Nelson was never indicted for espionage, after World War II U.S. officials charged that he was involved in Soviet spying, including atomic espionage. The FBI summary of its bugging of Nelson's meeting with Zubilin stated, "Nelson advised Zubilin that his work on behalf of the apparatus had been predicated upon a note from Moscow which had been brought to him by a courier from New York and that Earl Browder was fully cognizant of the fact that he, Nelson, was engaged in secret work for the Soviets."[20] In the early 1940s, Nelson met with several physicists involved in the atomic bomb project at the Lawrence-Livermore Laboratory in Berkeley, California, and with Soviet diplomats. When questioned about this under oath, he invoked the Fifth Amendment and refused to answer.[21] In his memoirs, Nelson denied any connection with or knowledge of Soviet espionage.

Rudy Baker, the hitherto unheralded and almost unknown coor-

19. Senate Subcommittee to Investigate the Administration of the Internal Security Act, *Interlocking Subversion in Government Departments*, 1050.
20. Ibid. Nelson is an obvious candidate for the Brother-Son network agent codenamed Mack. In document 59 Son/Baker reported that "we have assigned one responsible person in California (Mack) to be responsible for all our work there." There is, however, no direct evidence that Nelson was Mack.
21. The government's charges against Nelson are summarized in Herbert Romerstein and Stanislav Levchenko, *The KGB against the "Main Enemy"* (Lexington, Mass.: Lexington Books, 1989), 214–17.

dinator of this extensive and valuable espionage ring, lived during the 1940s as "a gentleman farmer near Peekskill," New York.[22] He returned to his native Yugoslavia after World War II and worked for a state publishing house as a translator and for a government research institute. Baker sided with Tito after Tito's split with Stalin in 1948, and in the early 1950s began a correspondence with Browder, who had been deposed as head of the CPUSA on Moscow's orders in 1945.[23] The letters, found in the Earl Browder papers, are largely reworkings of Marxist theory and discussions of where the Soviet Union had gone wrong.

Baker, who was then using the name Rudy Blum, passed some of Browder's writings on to high officials in the Yugoslav government. Blum probably was Baker's original family name. His Comintern biography, document 34, does not give his birth name but does note that his brother's name was Blum. Baker's FBI file gives his birth name as Rudolf Blum. Browder, following his wife's death, sent Lilly Blum (Baker's wife and the former wife of J. Peters) some of her clothing, and he regularly sent books to the Blums' son Daniel. Apart from a letter Browder provided in 1952 certifying that Blum was a charter member of the CPUSA and from 1922 to 1945 had done "responsible and leading work in the higher cadres of the Party"—a letter prepared to help Blum get pension credit—the two did not reminisce about their party experiences.[24]

The close relationship between Browder, the CPUSA's general secretary, and Baker, head of its underground, suggests but does not prove that Earl Browder was "Father" in Baker's network.[25] It

22. Louis Budenz, *Men without Faces: The Communist Conspiracy in the U.S.A.* (New York: Harper, 1950), 19.

23. After being ousted from the leadership of the CPUSA in mid-1945, Browder was expelled from the party in 1946. He traveled to Moscow and unsuccessfully appealed his ouster in a meeting with Soviet Foreign Minister Molotov. The Soviets, however, did give Browder a franchise to sell Soviet books in the United States. The venture proved financially disastrous for Browder. Browder asked for readmission to the CPUSA during the Stalin-Tito split. Rebuffed, he slowly moved away from communism and retired to Princeton, New Jersey. Despite his having led the CPUSA for fifteen years during the era of its greatest growth and dynamism, the Communist press failed to acknowledge his death in 1973 with an obituary.

24. The Browder-Blum correspondence is found in series 1–11, reel 1, of the Earl Browder papers on microfilm (Glen Rock, N.J.: Microfilm Corporation of America, 1976). Rudy Baker's FBI file is #100–258542, FOIA document.

25. Son's report, labeled the "Brother, General Report" in Comintern files, is literally addressed to "Brother." Brother is likely the code name for the Comintern controller of the network.

strains credulity that Baker would have so deeply implicated the CPUSA in Soviet espionage without approval from his party's superiors. And, as the next section will demonstrate, Earl Browder was himself no stranger to Soviet intelligence.

## Earl Browder and the NKVD

Earl Browder dominated the Communist Party of the United States of America during its heyday, and in his career we can see how the underground became central to the mission of the CPUSA. When he became its general secretary in 1934, the party was still a small sectarian movement on the margins of society. By the time he was purged in 1945, it had become a major power in the labor movement and a significant factor in liberal politics. Born in Kansas in 1891 to a family of old American stock, Browder joined the Socialist party as a young man and quickly gravitated to its radical wing. He opposed American participation in World War I and spent time in prison for refusing to register for the draft; he moved to New York and joined the newly formed Communist party upon his release in 1920. After working for several years for the American Communist party's trade union arm, he was sent to Moscow in 1926 for Comintern duty. He spent 1927 and 1928 in China heading the Pan-Pacific Trade Union Secretariat and proving himself in clandestine work.

Moscow ousted Jay Lovestone from the leadership of the CPUSA in 1929 and Browder was ordered back to the United States to help form the party's new leadership. Browder's stay abroad had allowed him to miss much of the party's bitter factionalism of the late 1920s, his clandestine work with the Pan-Pacific Trade Union Secretariat had earned him the Comintern's trust, and his administrative competence and methodical style were attractive qualities in an organization needing both. In 1934 he became general secretary of the CPUSA, and for the next decade his policies dominated the American Communist movement and he himself was the object of a personality cult that depicted him as an all-wise leader.

The question of Browder's involvement in Soviet espionage is an important historical issue. The U.S. government attacked the Communist party in the late 1940s and 1950s because it believed the

CPUSA functioned as an auxiliary to Soviet intelligence. If Earl Browder, who controlled the CPUSA from 1930 to 1945, was involved in espionage, that belief was well founded.

Two former Communists claimed direct knowledge of Browder's espionage role. Louis Budenz asserted that on a number of occasions he had heard Browder and other CPUSA leaders discuss cooperation with Soviet intelligence and the usefulness of the informants the party maintained inside the U.S. government. Elizabeth Bentley stated that Browder not only knew about but assisted the espionage operations she and Jacob Golos (Bentley's lover and espionage superior) conducted by providing funding for Golos's cover businesses (World Tourists travel agency and U.S. Service and Shipping Corporation). Browder always denied any participation in or knowledge of Soviet intelligence operations.[26]

### Earl Browder as an NKVD Talent Spotter, 1940

In November 1940 Dimitrov received a memo, **document 63,** from General Fitin. Conveying the memo was a cover note, **document 62,** from Lavrenti Beria, overall head of the NKVD, of which Fitin's foreign intelligence division was a part.[27] Handwritten on Beria's note was the comment "*Comrades Stalin and Molotov were informed about this.*" Fitin's memo contains the text of a Browder report to the Comintern sent through NKVD channels, establishing, obviously, his use of Soviet intelligence as his link to Moscow. One section in the memo also shows that Browder was sufficiently intimate with the NKVD to ask that his wife's birth certificate (she was born in Russia) be sent to him through Soviet intelligence channels rather than through the less secure regular mail.[28]

26. Budenz, *Men without Faces,* 247–81; Elizabeth Bentley, *Out of Bondage* (New York: Ivy Books, 1988), 85–87, 128–29, 134, 140, 145, 154–56, 159.

27. The foreign intelligence directorate of the NKVD was its most prestigious division, but most employees of the NKVD, and later of the KGB, dealt with internal Soviet security.

28. Points one and two in the memo deal with internal factional problems in the Mexican and Canadian Communist parties. The CPUSA had close relations with the Communist parties of Mexico and Canada and often acted as a channel for Comintern contacts with and financial subsidies for them. Browder, in particular, took an avuncular attitude toward the Mexican party. In his discussion of the Mexican situation, Browder suggests that the Comintern consider using "channels of influ-

More important, however, the memo indicates that Browder was acting as a talent spotter for Soviet intelligence. He reported on a meeting he had held with the French politician Pierre Cot. A member of the French Radical party, Cot had served in more than half a dozen of the short-lived cabinets of the French government in the 1930s. He was a passionate supporter of a Franco-Soviet alliance against Germany. During the Spanish Civil War, hostile sections of the French press accused Cot, then aviation minister, of handing over French aviation secrets to the Soviets in his enthusiasm for a Soviet alliance. In 1937 Walter Krivitsky, a senior Soviet military intelligence officer in Europe, defected and named Cot as a Soviet source inside the French government.[29] After the fall of France in the summer of 1940, Cot refused to support the French Vichy regime that signed a peace accord with Hitler, and fled. Cot initially tried to join General Charles de Gaulle's Free French in London, but de Gaulle regarded Cot as an embarrassment and rebuffed him.[30]

Cot arrived in the United States in September 1940. Browder reported that Cot had asked him to notify the USSR that he continued to work "for a full alliance between France and the Soviet Union," a coalition that could "be achieved only through the French Comparty." Cot also reportedly said that he supported Britain's hostile stance toward the Vichy regime. But, Browder noted, Cot "wants the leaders of the Soviet Union to know of his willingness to perform whatever mission we might choose, for which purpose he is even prepared to break faith with his own position."

---

ence on CAMACHO," the newly elected president of Mexico, to promote Mexican diplomatic recognition of the USSR. It is not clear what Browder meant by "channels of influence." This may have referred to the political influence of Mexican Communists or may have been a reference to the considerable ability of the CPUSA and its friends in the United States to generate newspaper stories and press coverage about causes it supported.

29. In which case, Browder was part of re-recruiting an agent with whom the Soviets had lost contact.

30. De Gaulle's attitude toward Cot is discussed in Jean Lacouture, *De Gaulle* (New York: New American Library, 1966), 79, 90.

# Document 62

Beria to Dimitrov, 29/30 November 1940, RTsKhIDNI 495–74–478. Original in Russian.

### E C C I

#### To Com. DIMITROV

A telegram received from New York from the secretary of the CC of the American Comparty, BROWDER, addressed to the leadership of the ECCI, is [herewith] forwarded to you.

L. Beria
(L. BERIA)

29/30 November 1940
No. 5/70/b [?]
*Comrades Stalin and Molotov were
informed about this. 3 December 1940*
GD

---

# Document 63

Fitin, "The Secretary of the CC of the American Comparty Has Asked Me . . . ," attached to Beria to Dimitrov, 29/30 November 1940, RTsKhIDNI 495–74–478. Original in Russian.

"The secretary of the CC of the American Comparty has asked me to convey the following to the Comintern leadership:

1. a) Before concluding some sort of agreement with America, the newly elected president of Mexico, CAMACHO, met with the general secretary of the Mexican Communist organization, Dionisio Encinas, whom he assured that the Mexican Communist organization will not be banned. CAMACHO said that it would be easier for him if the Mexican Communist organization changed its name, but irrespective of that, CAMACHO repeated that Communists will not be persecuted.

b) The CC of the Mexican Communist organization is experiencing difficulties. PAVON, who was elected to membership in the CC at the last congress, has left the party. Another member of the CC, SALGADO, is making trouble.

NOTE: if we have any interest in pressuring Mexico to recognize the Soviet Union, we could make use of channels of influence on CAMACHO.

2. The Communist organization of Canada is also undergoing difficulties. The leader of one of its centers, STEWART, has adopted ultra-left positions. Despite the CC decision that is on record, STEWART has postponed convening a congress and is waging a struggle against the leaders Tim Buck and Sam Karr,

taking advantage of the fact that the latter are in the US. STEWART ignores their instructions and is insubordinate.

3. Regarding his wife, Irina's, birth certificate, the secretary of the CC of the American Comparty, BROWDER, requests that the ECCI not send the birth certificate that has been prepared through the conventional mails; rather, he asks that it be delivered to him through the NKVD.

4. At the recent meeting between the secretary of the CC of the American Comparty, BROWDER, and Pierre COT, the latter asked [Browder] to inform the Soviet Union that he is campaigning for a full alliance between France and the Soviet Union, which, in his view, can be achieved only through the French Comparty, since, as he stated, there is currently no other force in France defending the interests of the French people.

Pierre COT also supports England's struggle against the Vichy government. COT wants the leaders of the Soviet Union to know of his willingness to perform whatever mission we might choose, for which purpose he is even prepared to break faith with his own position."

Accurate.

HEAD OF THE FIFTH DEPARTMENT OF [illegible, perhaps State Security] USSR NKVD

FITIN

---

Browder continued to cultivate Cot as a source of diplomatic intelligence. In 1943 General Fitin of the NKVD sent a message to Dimitrov: "We are sending you Pierre Cot's report on the international situation with perspectives on its development. We received it by telegraph in compressed form. The report was made on comrade Browder's initiative, based on the materials and personal observations of Pierre Cot. As soon as we have the complete text we will forward it to you."[31]

The Soviets followed up on Browder's messages about Cot. During World War II, U.S. intelligence agencies kept copies of coded cables leaving the United States, including thousands of coded NKVD and GRU messages sent to Moscow from Soviet diplomatic

---

31. Fitin to Dimitrov, 21 February 1943, quoted in Thierry Wolton, *Le Grand Recrutement* (Paris: Grasset, 1993), 248.

offices in America. The NKVD used a code based on "one-time pads," a type of cipher that, when properly used, is nearly impossible to break because the code is changed so frequently that the small volume of text under any one code gives little opportunity for code breakers. However, one-time pads were laborious to produce, and the Soviets' need for coded material during the war led to compromises. In a number of cases, the same one-time pad was sent to different locations rather than being used only once. During World War II, Finnish agents obtained a partially destroyed Soviet codebook governing use of the one-time pad code and other Soviet cipher material. Late in the war, the Finns sold the material to the OSS. The Roosevelt administration, at the urging of Secretary of State Edward Stettinius, returned the codebook and other material to the Soviets as a gesture of goodwill. The OSS, however, kept a copy. After World War II, cryptographers of the U.S. Army Security Agency (forerunner of the National Security Agency) put the damaged codebook together with information provided by Igor Gouzenko, a Soviet cipher clerk at the Soviet embassy in Canada who defected, and some cipher messages the FBI had secretly photographed in a New York office housing an NKVD message center. The combination allowed American cryptographers to decode, with great difficulty and often only partially, a number of World War II Soviet intelligence messages. The "Venona" intercepts, as they were known, led to the identification of Soviet agents in the British, French, Australian, and American governments. In the 1960s the cryptographers broke the code for some World War II messages from the NKVD in the United States to Moscow indicating that Vasily Zubilin, the NKVD officer discussed earlier in relation to the Brother-Son network, had recruited Cot as a Soviet agent. After World War II, Cot successfully reentered French politics, becoming once again aviation minister for a time. He championed French-Soviet friendship and in 1953 received the Stalin Peace Prize. By the time the code was broken, Cot had retired from active politics. Because use of the Venona intercepts in court would expose the National Security Agency's cryptographic techniques, the individuals identified as Soviet agents were often quietly pushed out of the government and not prosecuted. The National Security Agency has never released the Venona intercepts, and only a sketchy outline and a few details have ever been made public, usually by retired officers of other agencies.[32]

### Margaret Browder, NKVD Agent, 1938

Browder's ties to the NKVD were familial as well. In 1939 Benjamin Gitlow, briefly CPUSA general secretary in 1929 before being expelled along with Jay Lovestone, charged that Browder's sister Margaret (sometimes spelled Marguerite) was a Soviet intelligence agent.[33] The same year, Walter Krivitsky wrote that Margaret, using a passport under the name of Jean Montgomery, had been one of his agents.[34] In interviews with the FBI, Krivitsky noted that Margaret had played a key role in establishing a secret Soviet radio station in Berlin. In 1937, according to Krivitsky, she was transferred from his control to that of Mikhail Shpigelglas, deputy director of the NKVD's foreign intelligence division, for operations in France. Shortly thereafter, Shpigelglas supervised the abduction of General Yevgeni Miller, an exile in Paris who headed the tsarist White Guard veterans' association, and the murder of Ignace Reiss, a defecting Soviet intelligence officer suspected of Trotskyism. Reiss was lured to a meeting in Switzerland and shot. Miller was kid-

32. Peter Wright, *Spy Catcher: The Candid Autobiography of a Senior Intelligence Officer* (New York: Viking, 1987), 239–41; Christopher Andrew and Oleg Gordievsky, *KGB: The Inside Story* (New York: HarperCollins Publishers, 1990), 373–76, 446–47. According to Wright, although American cryptographers of the National Security Agency decoded the messages regarding Cot, it was Wright and his British MI5 (security service) that identified the references to Cot. On the OSS's purchase of the code material from the Finns and on the Venona decryption project, see Bradley Smith, *The Shadow Warriors: O.S.S. and the Origins of the C.I.A.* (New York: Basic Books, 1983), 353–55; Robert J. Lamphere and Tom Shachtman, *The FBI-KGB War: A Special Agent's Story* (New York: Random House, 1986), 80–86; Wright, *Spy Catcher*, 239–41; Andrew and Gordievsky, *KGB*, 373–76, 446–47; and David Martin, *Wilderness of Mirrors* (New York: Ballantine Books, 1981), 46.

33. Gitlow testimony, 7 September 1939, House Special Committee on Un-American Activities, *Investigations of Un-American Propaganda Activities in the United States*, 76th Cong., 1st sess., 1939, 7:4681. See also Benjamin Gitlow, *The Whole of Their Lives* (New York: Scribner's, 1948), 358.

34. Walter G. Krivitsky, *Inside Stalin's Secret Service* (New York: Harpers, 1939), 258–59. Krivitsky defected in late 1937. He described Margaret Browder as an agent who first worked for Soviet military intelligence before she was assigned to the NKVD. Relations among Soviet intelligence agencies were complicated, and in 1937 and 1938, the period under question here, Soviet military intelligence reported to the chief of the NKVD, as did the NKVD's own foreign intelligence branch.

napped, taken to the Soviet Union, and executed after questioning. Although Krivitsky did not have direct knowledge of Margaret's role, he suspected that she was part of Shpigelglas's operation against Reiss and Miller.[35] In addition to Gitlow and Krivitsky, two other former Communists, Elizabeth Bentley in 1946 and Joseph Zack Kornfeder in 1951, told the FBI that they had heard from colleagues who had been involved in CPUSA secret work that Margaret had herself been involved in espionage in Europe in the 1930s but had left that work by the 1940s.[36]

A congressional committee questioned Browder and his brother William about their sister in 1939, but their responses were carefully phrased. When asked if she was employed by either the Comintern or the Soviet government, Earl Browder answered, "I think not. . . . To the best of my knowledge, she is not now and has not in the past been officially connected with any government institution." William Browder testified that "to the best of my knowledge and belief," his sister did not work for the Soviet government.[37]

Later government investigators determined that the photograph for an American passport issued to "Jean Montgomery" was a picture of Margaret Browder and that the signature on her passport application purporting to be that of Jean Montgomery's brother was in the handwriting of William Browder.[38]

Margaret Browder left the CPUSA after her brother's expulsion in 1946. In the 1950s she admitted to FBI agents that she had used the name Jean Montgomery for an American passport and met with Vasily Zubilin. She denied, however, being employed by the Soviet

35. New York FBI report on Margaret Browder, 16 July 1946, #100–59645, FOIA document. The Miller and Reiss affairs are summarized in Andrew and Gordievsky, KGB, 160–64. Reiss was the pseudonym for Ignace Poretsky.

36. New York FBI report on Margaret Browder, 16 July 1946, #100–59645, and Hennrith to Belmont, 29 May 1951, #100–287645, FOIA document; Detroit FBI report on Kornfeder interview, 6 August 1951, #100–20202, FOIA document.

37. Earl Browder testimony, 5 September 1939, and William Browder testimony, 12 September 1939, House Special Committee on Un-American Activities, Investigations of Un-American Propaganda Activities in the United States, 7:4439, 4830.

38. U.S. Department of State Passport Division brief of a conspiracy charge against World Tourists and the CPUSA, reprinted in Senate Subcommittee to Investigate the Administration of the Internal Security Act, Scope of Soviet Activity in the United States, 85th Cong., 1st sess., 1957, app. 1, pt. 23-A:A8, A93–A94, A107.

government or knowing that Zubilin was an officer of the foreign intelligence bureau of the NKVD. When a U.S. grand jury asked her about her activities, she refused to answer on the grounds that her testimony might incriminate her.[39] Her refusal was well advised, because files in Moscow confirm that Margaret Browder was a Soviet agent. In **document 64,** a memo dated 19 January 1938, Earl told Dimitrov:

> For about 7 years my younger sister, Marguerite Browder, has been working for the foreign department of the NKVD, in various European countries. I am informed that her work has been valuable and satisfactory, and she has expressed no desire to be released. But it seems to me, in view of my increasing involvement in national political affairs and growing connections in Washington political circles, it might become dangerous to this political work if hostile circles in America should by any means obtain knowledge of my sister's work in Europe and make use of this knowledge in America.

Browder suggested that "steps can be taken by you to secure my sister's release from her present work." In response, Dimitrov in **document 65** wrote to Nikolai Yezhov, then head of the NKVD, the following: "In forwarding you [this] note from Com. BROWDER . . . I, for my part, consider it politically expedient to relieve his sister of her duties in the foreign department of the NKVD." These documents show that Gitlow, Krivitsky, Bentley, and Kornfeder were correct about Margaret, that Earl Browder was well aware of his sister's status as an NKVD agent, and that Earl and his brother perjured themselves in their 1939 testimony to Congress.

39. Report on New York FBI interview with Margaret Browder, 10 July 1951, #100–59645, FOIA document; New York FBI synopsis of interview with Margaret Browder, 29 October 1957, #100–287645, FOIA document; Special Agent in Charge New York to FBI Director, report on interview with Margaret Browder, #100–59645, FOIA document; Special Agent in Charge of New York to FBI Director, 15 December 1952, Report on Margaret Browder's Grand Jury Testimony, #100–59645, FOIA document.

# Document 64

Browder to Dimitrov, 19 January 1938. Original in English. All documents transcribed in this volume are from the Russian Center for the Preservation and Study of Documents of Recent History (RTsKhIDNI) except for this one. A note on document 65, Dimitrov's cover letter, said that the original Browder letter was forwarded to the NKVD and no copy was kept. The independent researcher Herbert Romerstein, after examining the cover note, asked for and received a copy of Browder's letter from the Foreign Intelligence Service of Russia. The authors thank him for making this letter available.

*Confidential*

Memorandum to Comrade Dimitroff:

Another personal question I must raise, because of its possible future political importance. For about 7 years my younger sister, Marguerite Browder, has been working for the foreign department of the NKVD, in various European countries. I am informed that her work has been valuable and satisfactory, and she has expressed no desire to be released. But it seems to me, in view of my increasing involvement in national political affairs and growing connections in Washington political circles, it might become dangerous to this political work if hostile circles in America should by any means obtain knowledge of my sister's work in Europe and make use of this knowledge in America. The political implications of such possible danger will be clear to you, being directly connected with the relations between USSR and USA, as well as to the work of our Party in America. I raise this question, so that if you agree to the existence of this danger, and consider it of sufficient importance, steps can be taken by you to secure my sister's release from her present work and her return to America where she can be used in other fields of activity.

> Fraternally
> *Earl Browder*

Moscow, Jan. 19, 1938

*Confidential*

Memorandum to Comrade Dimitroff:                              187

Another personal question I must raise, because of its possible future political importance. For about 7 years my younger sister, Marguerite Browder, has been working for the foreign department of the NKVD, in various European countries. I am informed that her work has been valuable and satisfactory, and she has expressed no desire to be released. But it seems to me, in view of my increasing involvement in national political affairs and growing connections in Washington political circles, it might become dangerous to this political work if hostile circles in America should by any means obtain knowledge of my sister's work in Europe and make use of this knowledge in America. The political implications of such possible danger will be clear to you, being directly ~~connected with~~ the relations between USSR and USA, as well as to the work of our Party in America. I raise this question, so that if you agree to the existence of this danger, and consider it of sufficient importance, steps can be taken by you to secure my sister's release from her present work and her return to America where she can be used in other fields of activity.

Fraternally

Earl Browder

Moscow, Jan.19, 1938

DOCUMENT 64. Browder to Dimitrov, 19 January 1938.

# Document 65

Dimitrov to Yezhov, 24 January 1938, RTsKhIDNI 495–74–465. Original in Russian.

To Com. YEZHOV, N. V.

In forwarding you [this] note from Com. BROWDER (General Secretary of the CPUSA), I, for my part, consider it politically expedient to relieve his sister of her duties in the foreign department of the NKVD.

With comradely regards,

p.p. [Original signed by] (G. DIMITROV)

24 January 1938

No. 153/ld [sheets of file]

Com. Browder's note in English has been sent to Com. Yezhov, no copy was kept.

## Irene Browder, Commissar with "Emergency Powers"

Browder also had close contact with Soviet authorities through his wife, Raisa. Born in Russia in 1895, Raisa Borisovna Luganovskaya grew up in Lithuania, then part of the Russian Empire. She was trained as a lawyer, married an early Bolshevik, and joined the Bolsheviks herself in 1917 in Kharkov, Ukraine. According to a Comintern biography, **document 66,** she was very active in the Bolshevik Revolution and served as "Provincial Commissar of Justice, with emergency powers." A commissar of justice in Bolshevik practice supervised trial court judges, heard appeals from trial courts, and had the power to change trial court actions. After the revolution, she became a member of the presidium of the Soviet state court in Moscow. She held a variety of responsible Communist party and Soviet state positions during the 1920s, traveled to Germany and France on unspecified missions, and in 1933 entered a program of advanced studies at the International Lenin School specializing in American studies.[40]

40. Two earlier autobiographies of Raisa Browder were also found. Both contain substantially the same information, including that she held "emergency powers" as a commissar of justice (R. Luganovskaya 1932 AUCP(b) autobiography, 17 June 1932, RTsKhIDNI 495–261–3264; R. Luganovskaya 1933 ILS autobiography, 19 March 1933, RTsKhIDNI 495–261–3264).

# Document 66

Belov report on "Luganovskaya, Raisa Borisovna," 21 January 1938, RTsKhIDNI 495–74–469. Original in Russian. Luganovskaya was Raisa Browder's name from her first marriage. Her maiden name was Berkmann.

---

3 copies m. kh. [?]

21 January 1938

LUGANOVSKAYA, Raisa Borisovna (the wife of Com. Browder).

Born 31 December 1895 in Mariumpole, Suvalkovsk region.[1] A Jewess. Father a German citizen, native and permanent resident of Prussia, a white-collar worker. According to questionnaire data furnished in 1925 and 1933, her elderly parents lived in Berlin (she lists them as dependents). According to her 1933 autobiography, her mother divorced her father in 1897, and she was raised by her father's parents until the age of 8, at which time her mother took her and, with her four children, settled in Kovno.[2] In the materials we have available, there is no information on the fates of the other three children.

In Kovno she completed public primary school and secondary school [gimnaziya] (she earned a gold medal); in Leningrad she enrolled in the Bestuzhev Higher Women's courses, in the law department; married the director of the "Pravda" publishing house; lived in Kharkov, where her husband had been exiled, starting in 1914; in 1917 she took her graduation exams in Leningrad. She has an advanced legal education. Her husband of the time, a Bolshevik since 1902, was a baker by trade and a professional revolutionary. She divorced him in 1924.

A member of the AUCP(b) since March of 1917 (joined in Kharkov).

Work record: before the Revolution she was a typist, a translator of French in Leningrad, a tutor in Kharkov, since May of 1917 a member of the Bolshevik Party City Committee in Kharkov, in the days of the October Revolution she was a hospital detachment organizer and head of medical detachments with the Red Guard.

In 1918—the retreat from the Germans—she worked in Moscow in the area of cultural services for the Red Army.

In 1918—in Kharkov, Provincial Commissar of Justice, with emergency powers; after the retreat from Kharkov, a member in Moscow of the presidium of the Council of People's Judges [Sovnarsud] and secretary of [party] fraction of people's judges; from fall 1920 to fall 1922, head of the agitation sub-department of the AUCP(b) Moscow Committee; from fall 1922 until 1924, a Moscow Council representative in all foreign famine-relief [Pomgol] organizations[3] (the American Relief Administration, [Fridtjof] Nansen, the Catholic mission, etc.); she was in Germany and in places bordering France; in 1925/26 secretary of the executive bureau of the Profintern [Red International of Labor Unions]; from 1927 to 1929 was secretary of [both] the presidium and [the party] fraction of the Central Committee of the Workers in the Chemical Industry [Union] within the All-Union Central Council of Trade Unions [VTsSPS];

244

starting in 1930, on the faculty of the Trade Union Movement Department of the International Lenin School; starting in 1932/33, studied history of the West at the Institute of the Red Professorate; starting in 1933, enrolled in graduate program of the ILS, concentrating on the US.

In 1922 and 1926 was in Germany and France.

(Source: 3 personal files—archives of the ECCI, the Profintern and the ILS.)

*Belov*

(BELOV).

1. The Russian typescript has *Mariumpole* and the *Suvalkovsk* region, which are errors evidently repeated from the 1932 AUCP(b) autobiography. The 1933 International Lenin School autobiography has *Mariampole* and the *Suvalksk* region. Mariampole is in Lithuania (the city bore the name Kapsukas from 1955 to 1989), about 30 miles due northeast of Suwałki, the city in the extreme northeast of Poland from which, presumably, the Suvalksk region derives its name. The city of Mariupol (named Zhdanov from 1948 to 1989) is in the Donetsk region of Ukraine, on the north coast of the Sea of Azov, about 750 miles southeast of Mariampole. There is a faint penned correction of *Mariupol* to *Mariumpole* on the 1933 AUCP(b) autobiography. The words *Mariumpole* and *Suvalkovskoi* on the present Russian typescript are both errors (the first is likely a hasty copying of *Mariupol* with its penned correction on the 1933 AUCP(b) autobiography). Both autobiographies are in RTsKhIDNI 495–261–3264.

2. Kovno (Kóvno) was until 1917 the official name of Kaunas, in central Lithuania, a river port where the Niaris river flows into the Niemen.

3. Luganovskaya specifies in her 1933 autobiography that she worked with these organizations until 1924, "the end of the existence of foreign famine-relief [pomgol] agencies here"; the term *pomgol* evidently persisted past September 1922, when the Soviet official aid committee known as Pomgol was outlawed (it had existed since July of 1921, chaired by M. I. Kalinin). The American Relief Administration was expelled from the USSR in 1922. Other foreign relief efforts (e.g., by the Norwegian arctic explorer Fridtjof Nansen) continued after the abolition of the "local" Pomgol and the expulsion of the American Relief Administration.

---

Benjamin Gitlow described Raisa Browder as "a woman who, during the early stages of the revolution, sat as supreme judge of a revolutionary tribunal that meted out death sentences to so-called counter-revolutionists and opponents of the Bolshevik party. When Browder met her, she was assigned by the OGPU to watch over the affairs of the Lenin University and to ferret out anti-Bolshevik elements that might have crept into the student body."[41] This Comintern biography does not confirm Gitlow's assertion but is compatible with it. In 1918, during the civil war that followed the Russian Revolution, Kharkov's Bolsheviks, facing isolation, aban-

---

41. Gitlow, *The Whole of Their Lives*, 358–59.

doned the city. The column of retreating Bolsheviks, moving through hostile territory, developed a reputation for ruthless methods. Was document 66's observation that in 1918 Raisa Browder was "Provincial Commissar of Justice, with emergency powers" a delicate version of Gitlow's description of her as a "supreme judge of a revolutionary tribunal that meted out death sentences to so-called counter-revolutionists"? Document 66 also puts Raisa at the International Lenin School and the Institute of the Red Professoriat from 1930 to 1933. Was she an OGPU ferret, as Gitlow says? The earlier autobiographies in the Comintern's files do not confirm Gitlow's assertion, but they do not preclude it either.[42]

Raisa was known as Irene when she came to the United States. Divorced from her first husband in 1924, she married Earl Browder in 1926. She was active in the CPUSA during the last half of the 1930s, assisting the party with its work among East European ethnic groups. She was the recipient of at least one coded letter from Pat Toohey, the CPUSA's Moscow representative, in February 1939. Typed drafts in both Russian and English of Toohey's letter, **document 67**, were found in Comintern files. They are couched in the form of a family note and addressed to Irene. The drafts are marked "<u>Confidential</u>" and "approved," and the Russian draft has two annotations: "the letter will be handwritten in English" and "Mail to J.N. Golos c/o World Tourists, 175 Fifth Avenue, New York, New York." Golos, for whom Elizabeth Bentley worked, was a senior member of the CPUSA and also headed a Soviet spy ring that used World Tourists as its front.

While ostensibly a family letter, document 67 has less innocent overtones. The precautions taken in its writing, its confidential stamp, and the disguised language make it clear that Pat Toohey is not chatting about his family. Moreover, the Russian-language version has a handwritten note across the top, in German, identifying it as a "conventional letter to Browder about Japanese cadres." Al-

---

42. Nor do the earlier autobiographies state that she worked for the OGPU, but this is not definitive. The OGPU co-opted many people whose principal activity was in a nonintelligence area but who also worked, part-time, as OGPU agents in their main field of employment. The identity of these co-opted agents, particularly those used for internal security tasks, was closely held by the OGPU and would not necessarily or even likely show up in a Comintern biography.

though many of the references are obscure, these clues help decipher its meaning.

Rudy Baker had been in Moscow in January 1939 and had returned to the United States. Toohey notes that Rudy's old friend Tom had suffered a series of setbacks. Tom's "father, mother and several brothers" had been "badly incapacitated" by an automobile accident. This suggests that Tom ran a Comintern network, likely a Japanese-related one, that had collapsed or at least lost its communications links. Toohey suggested that Rudolph (Rudy Baker) "might immediately locate some of his relatives" and discuss whether they could help this group of agents. There is the suggestion that the agents should be relocated, given new work, and supported during the transition: Tom could contact "all members of his family in your country" and Rudy and Irene (or perhaps Earl) ought to "help them finish school to learn their trades." Tom's identity is not known. However, the letter does suggest that Irene Browder, like her husband, was involved in secret Comintern work in the United States.

---

## Document 67

Pat [Toohey] to Irene [Browder], 19 February 1939, RTsKhIDNI 495–14–128. Original in English. All the words on the line beginning with "(Draft-" have been crossed out, with the exception of the word *approved*. In the accompanying Russian version, beneath this line is the following: "Draft—After it is drawn up, the letter will be handwritten in English." Also in the Russian version is a handwritten note in German at the top of the page that states, "Conventional letter to Browder about Japanese cadre."

---

"8"

1513 '1                                                           Confidential

vt/transcription

19.ii.39

(Draft- to be handwritten after approved)

Dear Irene:

We were glad to receive your Christmas message and ask you to pardon us for not answering you sooner. It is good to learn that the children are well despite the bad winter. We are all feeling well. Patsy had a slight case of measles which she soon got rid of. I have been working since around

## Document 67 *continued*

Christmas, and although have to lose some time in the mornings receiving treatments, I am feeling very well and taking on more and more work.

My brother and his wife came to see me yesterday and he immediately found a job. About ten days ago my son and daughter-in-law and their baby also decided to move near me. They are well, except Sadie, who is having some stomach troubles.

I was glad to hear that Rudolph finally returned home and decided to settle down. It will do him good to be near you. His old friend Tom asks about him now and then, and of course, I tell him what I know of Rudolph's affairs. Rudolph will regret to know that Tom is also having his own family troubles. He has been most morose and sad for the past several weeks. It seems that his father, mother, and several brothers, who are the main support of the family, suffered a terrible automobile accident. They were badly incapacitated, apparently for some time to come. Tom doesn't know how he can carry the whole burden of supporting the family now alone. I thought Rudolph might immediately locate some of his relatives there and discuss with them the imperative need of their doing something about helping the family. If he could persuade several of Tom's brothers to go home as soon as possible and see what they could do about easing their dad's uncomfortable position, maybe that would help a great deal. It was a sad blow to Tom and he is not going to get over it so soon. In face of that he is thinking about reaching all members of his family in your country and take up with them the matter of completing their education as quickly as possible so that they also, in due course, could help carry the burdens which result from this terrible thing.

If you and Rudolph could help Tom in that way, I am sure he would be ever grateful. You probably know all the different members of Tom's family— uncles, cousins, and the like. It will not be possible for many of them to immediately break off their studies, because even if necessary you and Rudolph ought to help them finish school to learn their trades so that steady employment will be waiting for them.

Anyway, everything else is fine. Chris decided to look elsewhere for work and he was in fairly good health when I saw him last. From the proceeds of his last book he received sufficient royalties to give him an opportunity for at least a year's peaceful study and work.

Give my kind regards to all the family and tell them I appreciate hearing from them whenever they can get around to remembering me. Love to the children and the family as a whole.

Pat

*Handwritten copy given to S. 23/III/39*

## Earl Browder's "Back Channel" to the White House

Earl Browder not only had direct ties with the NKVD but thought he had ties with the White House. The Communist leader believed that he was in frequent and candid political contact with President Roosevelt through a discreet third party and that he was functioning as a "back channel" link between the White House and the Kremlin. **Documents 68 and 69** are the NKVD cover note and the actual Browder report concerning this back channel.

---

# Document 68

Fitin to Dimitrov, 23 July 1943, RTsKhIDNI 495–74–484. Original in Russian.

---

Top Secret/Personal Only

To Comrade DIMITROV:

I am forwarding you the enclosed report we received from New York concerning the following issues:

1. Com. Browder's appeal to Roosevelt on the Codovilli affair and Roosevelt's reply.

2. Certain political views that Roosevelt expressed to Com. Browder (specifically, concerning the activity of the CPUSA).

3. A letter from Encino (the CP of Mexico) on the CC session.

Enclosure: According to a text of 1 sheet (2 pages).

(FITIN)<br>P. Fitin

23 July 1943
No. 1/3/3163

---

# Document 69

NKVD report "On 14 June of This Year, Com. [Comrade] Browder . . . ," attached to Fitin to Dimitrov, 23 July 1943, RTsKhIDNI 495–74–484. Original in Russian.

---

Top secret

1. On 14 June of this year, Com. Browder sent Roosevelt a telegram in which he asked the latter to intervene in the case of Codovilli, who has been slated for exile to Spain by the Argentine government.

In his reply, a telegram dated 23 June of this year, Roosevelt informed Com. Browder that he cannot interfere in the internal affairs of Argentina, but that he had directed the American ambassador to Argentina, Armor, to follow the progress of the Codovilli case.

# Document 69 *continued*

On 26 June of this year, Roosevelt informed Com. Browder that, according to reports US Ambassador Armor had received from the Argentine Ministry of Foreign Affairs, Codovilli will not be exiled but will remain in custody in Argentina.

2. Roosevelt conveyed the following verbally to Com. Browder:

In his opinion, at the present time the CPUSA is conducting its political line skillfully, furthering US military efforts.

He, Roosevelt, is mistrustful of Willkie, who, in his opinion, is seeking power, and once he has it, he will again revert to Republican tactics.

The CPUSA should understand that the Sicilian campaign is only the prelude to a major invasion of the European continent during this summer; however, Churchill objects to that invasion and is the major obstacle in its way.

Roosevelt agrees that some sort of prohibitive (limiting) tax must be introduced for voters, since, in his view, only by breaking the "Southern political machine" will he be able to garner the potential support of the majority of the population in the Southern states.

Roosevelt is particularly pleased with the conduct of the New Jersey Communists, designed to unify the factions of the Democratic party, and with their struggle against the growth of the US Labor party in the other states. Roosevelt believes that that party will strengthen the Republicans in 1944, if it is not already doing so.

3. Com. Browder received the following report from the CP of Mexico:

"We have held a session of the CC to discuss the resolution of the ECCI. The resolution was approved unanimously. The decisions reached together with Jim were also discussed. A lengthy discussion followed on criticism by Velasco, who together with Olivo, Carnero Cheka, Torres, and Simon Gonzales has formed a bloc opposing his withdrawal from the PB and 'La voz.' This group defended the syndicalist political line to which it adhered before the STM congress and which we considered incorrect.

"The withdrawal of Velasco from the PB and 'La voz' was decided with a vote of 12 against 5. They proposed convening a congress in August for a discussion of the party's situation. This proposal was rejected, and it was decided to hold a session of the CC in August.

"The political struggle against the Comparty is continuing. A campaign against me is currently being readied in Mexico City and Monterrey.

"Carlos Contreras quit his post at 'La voz.'

"We will keep you informed.

"Encino"

Accurate:

Apresian
(Apresian)

21 July 1943.

On its face, document 69 is a sensational item that requires a significant historical reevaluation of President Roosevelt. Although such vitriolic critics of the New Deal as Joseph McCarthy have implied that President Roosevelt maintained intimate political contacts with Earl Browder, most historians of the New Deal era have dismissed the possibility.

Browder wrote that he had appealed to President Roosevelt by telegram to intervene in the Codovilla affair in Argentina, referring to the slated exile of Argentine Communist leader Vittorio Codovilla by the newly installed dictatorship of Juan Perón. Browder said that Roosevelt had told him that although he could not interfere in Argentina's internal affairs, he would have the U.S. ambassador keep informed. That the head of the CPUSA would telegraph the president regarding an international incident is of no particular interest, nor that the president should make a formal reply. But Browder's report goes well beyond that.

Browder further stated that Roosevelt had "verbally" told him that the recent invasion of Sicily by American and British forces was a prelude to a larger invasion of the European mainland later in the year; however, Roosevelt stated, Churchill opposed such an invasion. In addition to these foreign policy matters, Browder also said Roosevelt offered his views on a number of domestic political questions. According to Browder, Roosevelt told him that he did not trust Wendell Willkie. Willkie, the Republican presidential candidate in 1940, emerged in 1942 and 1943 as the most prominent Republican backer of Roosevelt's war policies. Browder reported that Roosevelt told him that he recognized the need to do something about the poll tax on voting in the South in order to enhance the political strength of New Deal supporters. (The poll tax, a fee charged to vote in some Southern states, acted to reduce voter turnout among low-income farmers, workers, and blacks. The Communist party as well as liberal groups had called for a federal government attack on the poll tax for years.)

In addition, Browder said Roosevelt had praised the CPUSA's political conduct and congratulated the party for opposing the development of an independent labor party in New Jersey, where Communists used their influence in the CIO and in liberal political circles to block a strong attempt to create a third party for New

Jersey modeled on the successful American Labor Party in neighboring New York. Even though the New Jersey Democratic party was dominated by the corrupt Jersey City political machine of Frank Hague, the White House opposed the attempt by liberal reformers and labor activists to form a new party. Roosevelt's political advisers feared that a disruption of the New Jersey Democratic party might weaken Roosevelt's ability to carry the state in the 1944 presidential election.[43]

The import of document 69, however, is less dramatic than it appears. Although the document is authentic and reflects Browder's honest beliefs, the impression it conveys is misleading. The most likely explanation concerning the meaning of document 69 lies in another memo, **document 70**. This 1944 memo to Dimitrov from Soviet military intelligence requests confirmation that "an American citizen, Josephine Treslow, on instructions from Browder, is meeting systematically with the president of the US, Roosevelt."

---

## Document 70

Bolshakov to Dimitrov, 21 August 1944, RTsKhIDNI 495–74–485. Original in Russian.

---

TOP SECRET
Copy No. 1

CENTRAL COMMITTEE OF THE ALL-UNION
COMMUNIST PARTY (BOLSHEVIK)

PERSONALLY TO COM. D I M I T R O V

According to information we have received, an American citizen, Josephine Treslow, on instructions from Browder, is meeting systematically with the president of the US, Roosevelt.

---

43. John Earl Haynes, *Dubious Alliance: The Making of Minnesota's DFL Party* (Minneapolis: University of Minnesota Press), 112; Harvey Klehr and John Earl Haynes, *The American Communist Movement: Storming Heaven Itself* (New York: Twayne, 1992), 99.

## Document 70 *continued*

Please advise whether this is in fact the case, and whether you have any information on this issue.

*Bolshakov*
(BOLSHAKOV)

21 August 1944
No. _360426 ss_
2 copies printed
1st: to Com. Dimitrov
2d: for file
    pv

---

The Josephine Treslow referred to in document 70 is Josephine Truslow Adams, born in Brooklyn in 1897. (Truslow is misspelled Treslow in the document.) From 1934 to 1941 she taught art at Swarthmore College and, while not openly acknowledging her Communist loyalties, joined a remarkable number of Communist-led organizations. Her public enthusiasm for Communist causes during the period of the Nazi-Soviet Pact probably contributed to Swarthmore's decision not to rehire her after 1941. Adams's contact with the Roosevelt family began when a friend of Eleanor Roosevelt's commissioned Adams to paint a picture for Mrs. Roosevelt. That in turn led to an occasional correspondence between the artist and the First Lady. They met in 1941 when Eleanor Roosevelt visited Swarthmore. After this encounter, Adams sent her another painting and began bombarding her with innumerable long letters.[44]

Among the subjects Adams stressed in her letters was freeing Earl Browder from federal prison. During the period of the Nazi-Soviet Pact, the CPUSA's unrelenting attacks on Roosevelt's policy of aid to the anti-Hitler belligerents prompted Roosevelt to crack down on the party's covert activity. One result was Browder's sentencing in 1941 to a four-year term for using a false passport during his many secret trips to the Soviet Union.[45] Communists were eager to free

44. For a full discussion of Josephine Truslow Adams, see Harvey Klehr, "The Strange Case of Roosevelt's 'Secret Agent': Frauds, Fools, and Fantasies," *Encounter* [Great Britain] 59, no. 6 (1982). See also Joseph P. Lash, *Eleanor and Franklin: The Story of Their Relationship, Based on Eleanor Roosevelt's Private Papers* (New York: W. W. Norton, 1971), 702–4.

45. U.S. authorities discovered evidence of Browder's use of a false passport when they seized the records of World Tourists, Jacob Golos's business front.

their leader and thought Roosevelt might be amenable because of their shift to support of his foreign policy after the Nazi invasion of the Soviet Union. Adams quickly became a mainstay of the Citizens' Committee to Free Earl Browder, a Communist front group.

Although Adams later claimed to have met personally with President Roosevelt to discuss freeing Browder, there is no record of her having been at Hyde Park, the president's New York home, at the times she claimed. Nor is there any record in the Roosevelt papers of her ever having met with him. What can be found among those papers are her many letters to Eleanor Roosevelt, which received polite but often perfunctory replies.

Roosevelt released Browder in May 1942, in part as a goodwill gesture toward the Soviet Union at the time of Molotov's arrival in Washington and in part, no doubt, to reward Communists for their recent support of his war policies. There is no evidence that Josephine Truslow Adams's lobbying had any effect on the president's decision. Earl Browder, however, thought otherwise. He knew of Adams's long association with the Communist party and of her active role in the campaign to get him released. He met with her at a Communist gala in July 1942 and believed her story that she had met with President and Mrs. Roosevelt on many occasions, had successfully lobbied for his release, and had become an intimate family friend. Browder also believed that his release was a sign that Roosevelt recognized the potential value of Communist support for his policies.

Adams misled Browder because she suffered from mental delusions. An FBI agent who interviewed her described her as "in an emotional and intellectual state of unbalance."[46] Later when she offered to assist the FBI, J. Edgar Hoover rejected her as a confidential source due to her unreliability. By 1956 she was receiving psychiatric treatment for paranoia and delusions and was in and out of hospitals. In 1943, however, her mental delusions were less apparent, and Browder believed he had a private pipeline to the White House.

Browder gave Adams material on various political matters to discuss with President Roosevelt during their, he thought, frequent

46. Klehr, "The Strange Case of Roosevelt's 'Secret Agent,' " 88.

chats. Actually, Browder's political advice and information became the texts of the letters with which Adams continued to deluge Mrs. Roosevelt, who recognized the political interest of some of Adams's letters and forwarded them to her husband—noting on one, however, that "I know nothing of her reliability." Mrs. Roosevelt sent polite responses to Adams, the most encouraging being a note that "I think you should know that your letters go directly to the president. What then happens I do not know."[47] That is not what Josephine Adams told Earl Browder. She told Browder that she met in person with Roosevelt and then gave Browder substantive messages that she said were the president's responses to Browder's messages. Adams simply made up Roosevelt's responses, basing them on the speculation and analysis of various political commentators and journalists and often telling Browder what he wanted to hear.[48]

After Earl Browder was expelled from the CPUSA, Adams also drifted away from the party. The FBI interviewed her several times and examined her papers but concluded that she was unreliable. While in a New York hospital in late 1956, she wrote to the staff of the Senate Internal Security Subcommittee and said she wanted to reveal her role as the secret link between President Roosevelt and the Communist party. She also said that "Communist doctors" were giving her shock treatments, drugs, and lobotomies to convince her she was mentally ill. Despite this, she was invited to Washington and testified in executive session in January 1957. Excerpts of her testimony were released in February and provided a sensation for those who believed that the New Deal was essentially a Communist conspiracy. In the excerpts, Adams claimed to have met with the president personally nearly forty times at Hyde Park or the White House. In addition to communicating Browder's views and Roosevelt's responses, she said she also brought Roosevelt documents from the Chinese Communist party and requested governmental favors for various Communists. According to her testi-

47. Adams to Eleanor Roosevelt, January 1944, and Eleanor Roosevelt to Adams, 13 July 1944, Eleanor Roosevelt papers, Franklin D. Roosevelt Library, Hyde Park, New York.

48. Even in the 1950s, when Adams's mental instability was apparent, Browder had difficulty believing that he had been hoodwinked. He insisted that Adams was not politically sophisticated enough to make up the messages that she delivered to him.

mony, Josephine Adams established so solid a relationship with Roosevelt that he jokingly called her Dr. Johnson, after the famous conversationalist.[49]

The sensation, however, was brief because there was no follow-up. Her complete testimony was never released, probably because, as one FBI agent who examined the complete account noted, much of it was "rambling and unorganized." After giving testimony, she signed a book contract with Isaac Don Levine, a veteran anti-Communist journalist, as her ghost writer. When Adams sent to Levine a file of what she said were letters between herself and President Roosevelt, he became suspicious. Included in Adams's material were more than twenty letters from Roosevelt to Adams, sprinkled with the irreverence and flightiness that characterized Adams's style, not Roosevelt's. Moreover, of the twenty-one dates on which Roosevelt supposedly wrote from Washington, Levine discovered the president was not there on ten. In addition, some of the Adams to Roosevelt letters were so prescient about future events that Levine concluded they had been written after the fact. Adams eventually admitted that the letters were forgeries. The planned book, tentatively entitled *I Was Roosevelt's Secret Emissary,* was dropped and the publisher's advance returned. Adams drifted deeper into her delusional world, and in 1958 she was committed to Norristown sanitarium in Pennsylvania and remained there under care for her mental illness until her death in the 1960s.

Although Browder was deceived about his links to the White House, these documents raise several important points. In the period from 1943 to 1945, Earl Browder thought that he and the CPUSA were being accepted as legitimate and respected, although as yet not publicly acknowledged, participants in mainstream American politics. He saw his link to the White House through Adams as proof both of his importance and of the influence of the American Communist movement.[50] Browder would often hint at

49. Excerpts of Adams's testimony are in Senate Subcommittee to Investigate the Administration of the Internal Security Act, *Scope of Soviet Activity in the United States,* pt. 54:3590–3600.

50. This is discussed more fully in Klehr, "The Strange Case of Roosevelt's 'Secret Agent.'" See also Maurice Isserman, *Which Side Were You On? The American Communist Party during the Second World War* (Middletown, Conn.: Wesleyan University Press, 1982), 131, 146–47, 201, 207.

his relationship with Roosevelt. Rumors of Browder's back channel to the White House circulated among the upper echelons of the CPUSA and from there seeped out to liberal allies of the party whom the CPUSA wished to impress. The news that Roosevelt communicated secretly with Browder reassured Popular Front liberals that there was nothing improper in their own relationship with the CPUSA.

Not surprisingly, these rumors of the political intimacy between Roosevelt and Browder also reached anti-Communists; in some cases, Communists who had become disillusioned and quit the party carried with them what they thought was inside knowledge of a Browder-Roosevelt relationship.[51] Many anti-Communists discounted these rumors, but some conservative anti-Communists who intensely disliked both Roosevelt and the CPUSA found the rumors believable. These right-wing anti-Communists were wrong, but their convictions were based on credible sources from within the Communist party itself. This belief in President Roosevelt's conspiratorial relationship with the CPUSA contributed to the partisan divisiveness concerning the nature of the domestic Communist problem in the postwar period.[52]

What is not known is the extent to which Browder's messages containing Adams's fantasies influenced Stalin's or Molotov's thinking. Document 70 suggests that Soviet intelligence was aware of Browder's claim of a back channel to the White House and was considering how seriously to take his information. If it was taken seriously, then the political fantasies of a mentally unstable artist may have had some influence on Soviet foreign policy.

These last few documents demonstrate the importance of histori-

51. John Lautner and Frank Meyer, two prominent defectors from the CPUSA, reported that they had heard of a secret Browder communications link with President Roosevelt.

52. An example of the sour nature of the divisiveness is the congressional handling of Adams's story. Adams was in a clinic receiving care for her mental delusions when she contacted the Senate Internal Security Subcommittee, a situation that should have suggested that her story might be flawed. The FBI had also informed the committee of its reservations concerning Adams. The committee did not inform anyone of her serious psychiatric problems and released an edited version of her testimony that minimized the disorganization of her story. Nor did the committee act to correct the record when Isaac Don Levine discovered her fraud. The committee's action indicates that its leadership was willing to use dubious evidence to suggest that Roosevelt had secretly dealt with the CPUSA.

cal context in understanding archival material. The significance of these documents differs from their apparent, surface meaning. They do not demonstrate that Earl Browder had a covert relationship with President Roosevelt. Rather, Browder's involvement in the secret world, with its atmosphere of intrigue, conspiracy, and danger, misled him into believing that President Roosevelt would conspire with him.

# CHAPTER SEVEN

# The American Communist Underground Fights World War II

THE RELATIONSHIPS FORGED in the Pan-Pacific Trade Union Secretariat, on the battlefields of Spain, in Washington's Communist underground, and in the party's secret apparatus allowed the CPUSA and Soviet intelligence to penetrate America's chief intelligence agency in World War II.

## The CPUSA, the OSS, and Soviet Intelligence

*Recruiting Veterans of the International Brigades for the OSS, 1941–1945*

In May 1942 General Pavel Fitin of the NKVD sent a memo, originally in code and labeled "Top Secret" and "Personal" to Dimitrov, head of the Comintern. This memo, **document 71**, and its companion, document 74, implicate Eugene Dennis, the man who succeeded Earl Browder as general secretary of the CPUSA, in Soviet espionage. Fitin stated that one of his NKVD officers in the United States had met with Comrade Ryan. Ryan was Dennis's pseudonym.[1]

Dennis, then a member of the CPUSA's ruling Political Bureau, was born Francis X. Waldron in 1905 in Seattle, Washington. He

1. That Ryan was Dennis's Moscow pseudonym was acknowledged by his wife in Peggy Dennis, *The Autobiography of an American Communist: A Personal View of a Political Life, 1925–1975* (Westport, Conn.: Greenwood Press, 1977), 54.

joined the Communist party in 1926 and became a full-time party organizer. He arrived in Moscow in 1930 after his work for the CPUSA's Trade Union Unity League led to an indictment for criminal syndicalism. In Moscow he changed his name to Tim Ryan. A veteran of the Pan-Pacific Trade Union Secretariat, he served as a covert Comintern agent in the Philippines, South Africa, and Shanghai. He returned to the United States in 1935 with the name he would use in America thereafter—Eugene Dennis. After serving as a Communist leader in Wisconsin, Dennis returned to Moscow in 1937 as the CPUSA's representative to the Comintern. He came back to America in 1938 to join the party's national leadership. By 1940 he was a member of the Political Bureau and was marked as a potential successor to Browder. In recognition of Dennis's potential as a future party leader, he was ordered underground in 1940 to avoid arrest in a government crackdown, which never occurred.[2]

---

## Document 71

Fitin to Dimitrov, 13 May 1942, RTsKhIDNI 495–74–484. Original in Russian.

---

TOP SECRET.

PERSONAL

*A directive has been given to New York for the discontinuation of this work. GD 13.5.42*[1]

### To Comrade DIMITROV

Regarding the activities of WOLFF, commander of Lincoln Brigade veterans and a member of the US Comparty, in the area of recruiting [such] veterans for diversionary work in the interior of the Axis countries and Axis-occupied territories under instructions from British and American intelligence, our representative in America has met with a member of the Politburo of the American Communist Party, Com. RYAN, who conveyed the following:

In November of 1941 WOLFF met with a representative of American intelligence, Colonel DONOVAN, ostensibly to work on arranging the release of a member of the Italian Comparty CC, LUIGI GALLO, a former inspector of an international brigade, from a French concentration camp.

At that meeting Colonel DONOVAN expressed the opinion that using participants of the Lincoln Brigade as soldiers in the American army was ill-advised, since some of them are officers of the Spanish Republican Army with modern battle experience. DONOVAN proposed selecting dependable veterans and put-

2. Bernard K. Johnpoll and Harvey Klehr, *Biographical Dictionary of the American Left* (New York: Greenwood Press, 1986), 108–11.

ting them at the disposal of the British for deployment in the interior of the Axis countries for diversionary work. WOLFF conveyed this proposal by the intelligence service to the Comparty leadership and was given a sanction for it. Afterward, Colonel DONOVAN put WOLFF in touch with Colonel BAILEY of British intelligence, and WOLFF began to operate along the indicated lines. At first, people were selected for the Balkans and Greece, and by the time the US entered the war, WOLFF had provided the British with 12 Yugoslavs, 3 Czechs, and 1 Italian. The volunteers selected were to be instructed, trained, and sent to Malta for further conveyance to their destination countries. To date, only a single Yugoslav has left for England.

After the United States entered the war, and in connection with laws on the registration of conscripted contingents and of foreign agents (this category included the people selected by WOLFF), the British and the Americans drew up an accord providing for the sharing of information with American intelligence, with which WOLFF is to date maintaining a tie parallel with his tie to British intelligence.

In the recent period, WOLFF has provided American intelligence with 10 Americans, 1 Greek, and 3 Yugoslavs, who are [officially] considered on active duty in the army and undergoing training in special ("commando") groups. Apart from the party members indicated, WOLFF has provided 6 nonparty Hungarians and 4 Czechs to American intelligence.

WOLFF was recently summoned by American intelligence, which advised him to leave immediately for Canada and Mexico to carry out the same sort of work. That trip is currently being delayed in connection with your inquiry concerning this matter.

Analogous work is also being carried out by the Italian antifascist POKARDI, who has also established contact with WOLFF and is recruiting, through the latter, Italians for special groups.

POKARDI has the right to recall Italians of American descent from the army if they are suitable for "D" [diversionary?] work.

At approximately the same time, the British approached Canada with a request for recruitment of personnel for this same work, addressing this request to a member of the Italian Comparty CC, VERDI. VERDI replied that he could not decide the issue on his own and that he would consult with comrades in the US. Another member of the Italian Comparty CC, known by the nickname YAKOPOV, learning of the request the British had made in the US, spoke in favor of cooperating with the British.

American intelligence has also raised the question of using Spaniards. An inquiry was directed to the Spanish Comparty CC in Cuba, which approved the idea of cooperating with the British and Americans, seeing that cooperation as its only possible means of infiltrating Europe, creating its own outposts and bases of operation in Marseilles and Lisbon, and organizing its radio propaganda.

## Document 71 *continued*

The intelligence [branch] of the US Ministry of War has given the Spanish a detailed questionnaire ascertaining the presence of insurgent organizations, partisan detachments, fighting groups, and individuals in Spain. Answers have been prepared for the majority of the questions, but their transmission has been delayed in connection with your inquiry.

Colonel DONOVAN has approached RYAN with a request for a connection to the party organization in France. DONOVAN was answered that they have no such connection.

In December of last year, the leadership of the Comparty of the United States of America discussed the question of a connection with American intelligence for the purpose of organizing antifascist radio propaganda. RYAN himself was chosen for permanent contact and negotiations. As a result of [RYAN's (?)] meeting [with the intelligence service (?)], an agreement was reached on the selection of Italian and German immigrants for the compilation of propagandistic materials and radio broadcasting.

Moreover, RYAN provided the intelligence service with information on the "fifth column" in the US and South America. According to a statement by RYAN, this was for the most part official information drawn from the "Daily Worker."

Apart from what has been indicated above, we have further established that WOLFF's introduction to Colonel DONOVAN was organized by the wife of a former correspondent in Spain, VINCENT SHEEAN; it was SHEEAN's wife who invited WOLFF to travel to Washington, supposedly in connection with the freeing of GALLO. SHEEAN himself is anti-Soviet, and his wife, according to our information, is an agent of British intelligence.

It is also reported that the veterans are very mistrustful of this entire enterprise and its leaders. WOLFF is continuing this work; he has organized a secret staff in New York and receives 60 dollars a week plus expenses from the intelligence service.

In conclusion, RYAN has submitted his own proposals for your consideration and final decision, which can be summarized as follows:

1. a) We must agree to the intelligence service's using American party members of draft age as "commandos," since people are being drafted into army service.

b) No more people should be provided for use in the Balkans, and this work should be curtailed.

c) The question of whether to use Spanish comrades should be decided based on the fact that the Spaniards have no connections with Europe whatsoever, and this is the only opportunity they have for an opening into Europe and [for] infiltrating Spain to establish connections and operations.

For our part, we regard this entire matter as a political mistake by the leadership of the US Comparty, thanks to which the American and British intelligence services have been given the opportunity to infiltrate not only American Comparty channels but also the Comparty organizations of other countries.

## Document 71 *continued*

Com. RYAN asks that we provide the leadership of the American, Spanish, Italian, and Canadian Comparties with instructions on all of these issues as soon as possible.

Please inform us of your decision on the given issue.

Fitin

(F I T I N)

13 May 1942
1/3/4160

1. Dimitrov's initialed notation in the upper left, dated 13 May 1942, seems to read: "A directive has been given to New York for the discontinuation of this work." However, (1) Dimitrov's handwriting of the word *discontinuation* (*prekrashchenie*), although unobscured photographically, is difficult to decipher, so the word cannot be identified as *prekrashchenie* without reservation; and (2) the case endings of "this work" are incorrect no matter what verbal noun is found for the word tentatively identified as *prekrashchenie*. Dimitrov has "this work" in the accusative, whereas the genitive is obligatory, "*of* this work." This is grammatically wrong but may be explained as the mistake of a Bulgarian speaker of Russian.

---

Dennis, then, was a top-level CPUSA leader with experience in clandestine work. His meeting with the NKVD officer dealt with the activities of Milton Wolff, the last commander of the Abraham Lincoln battalion in the Spanish Civil War.[3] In 1942 Wolff headed the Veterans of the Abraham Lincoln Brigade (VALB), the veterans' organization for Americans who had served with the International Brigades.[4] In document 71 Fitin describes Wolff as a "member of the US Comparty." When asked about Fitin's description in 1992, Milton Wolff denied having been a Communist, asserting as he has done over the years that although he had been a member of the Young Communist League before he went to Spain, he never joined the Communist party itself.[5] However, **document 72** is a biographical questionnaire from the International Brigades, filled out by hand and signed and dated 1 November 1938 by Milton Wolff. In answer to a question about his political affiliations, Wolff wrote, "*Communist Party of Spain.* [and] *Y.C.L. of America.*" The authors of another document, a 1938 evaluation of Wolff's political work

3. Milton Wolff should not be confused with Bertram Wolfe, discussed in chapter 4.

4. There was no Abraham Lincoln *Brigade* in the Spanish Civil War. Most Americans served in one of three battalions, the Lincoln, Washington, or Mackenzie-Papineau of the XV Brigade of the International Brigades, or in several smaller units. The Lincoln battalion was the best known, however, and the veterans' organization adopted the title Veterans of the Abraham Lincoln Brigade.

5. John Haynes's phone interview with Milton Wolff, 4 August 1992.

prepared by the XV Brigade's Communist party committee, call him "a good Party member," compliment his work as "an organizer propagandist," and comment that "he worked hard in executing a correct Party line with Bon [battalion]."[6] Also recorded in his file was his Spanish Communist party (P.C.E., Spanish acronym) membership card number: "Carnet del P.C.E. 1938/303267."[7] Wolff was a Communist.[8]

---

## Document 72

Excerpts from a six-page questionnaire for the Comisariado de Guerra de las Brigadas Internacionales, 1 November 1938, RTsKhIDNI 545–6–1015. Original in Spanish and in English. Milton Wolff signed it by hand.

---

COMISARIADO DE GUERRA

DE LAS

BRIGADAS INTERNACIONALES

Pasaje Méndez Vigo, 5

BARCELONA                Fecha   1-XI-38

Apellidos   *Milton*                Nombre   *Wolff*                Edad   23
Nacionalidad   *American*                Oficio
Organización política y sindical a la que perteneces   *Communist Party of Spain. Y.C.L of America.*
Grado y función en fecha 1.e de octubre de 1938   *Major—Commander of Lincoln-Washington Battalion*
Fecha de tu llegada a España   *March 7.—1937*
Unidad a la que has sido enrolado   *XV Brigade*
Batallón   *Washington*                Compañía   *Machine Gun.*
Otras unidades a las que perteneciste durante tu estancia en España (la Brigada, Batallón, Compañía o lugar de formación y duración de tu afectación)
Ultima unidad   *Lincoln-Washington Bon. XV Brigade*

*Milton Wolff*

---

6. Brigade Party committee to Communist Party of Spain Central Committee, Milton Wolff evaluation, partly illegible date 1938, RTsKhIDNI 545–6–1015. The evaluation is signed by Jim Bourne, John Gates, A. Donaldson, and a fourth person whose signature is illegible. Bourne and Gates were high-ranking political commissars.

7. Milton Wolff, "Extractas de la biografia Escrita el 6 de Junio 1938," RTsKhIDNI 545–6–1015.

8. These documents refute Wolff's testimony to the Subversive Activities Control Board (SACB) in 1954 that he had never observed any organized Communist

In document 71 Dennis reported that, in November 1941, Wolff met with Colonel (later General) William Donovan, recently appointed head of the Office of the Coordinator of Information by President Roosevelt. Donovan's agency, later renamed the Office of Strategic Services (OSS), was the chief intelligence and clandestine operations arm of the United States during World War II and the predecessor to the Central Intelligence Agency. Dennis explained that the meeting had been arranged by Diana Sheean, the wife of the journalist Vincent Sheean. Sheean had covered the Spanish Civil War from the Republican side, and both he and his wife were acquainted with Wolff. Fitin noted that the NKVD believed Diana Sheean, British by birth, was a British intelligence agent. Ostensibly, Donovan wanted to discuss Wolff's interest in the release of the high-ranking Italian Communist and International Brigades officer Luigi Gallo from a French internment camp.[9] In a 1992 interview, Wolff confirmed that this meeting had taken place and stated that he, too, felt that Diana Sheean had some link to British intelligence.[10]

Dennis reported that Donovan had asked Wolff to recruit veterans of the International Brigades for British covert operations against the Nazis or the Italian fascists. Donovan, the report said, "put WOLFF in touch with Colonel BAILEY of British intelligence."

---

political activity in the Lincoln battalion. They also confirm the testimony of Leo Hecht, a former Communist and Lincoln battalion veteran, who told the SACB that Wolff had joined the Spanish Communist party. Wolff, when asked about this by the SACB, refused to answer, citing his Fifth Amendment right not to testify against himself. (Testimony of Milton Wolff and testimony of Leo Hecht, transcript of the proceedings held before the Subversive Activities Control Board in the matter of *Herbert Brownell, Attorney General, v. Veterans of the Abraham Lincoln Brigade,* 1954 [reprinted on microfilm in *Records of the Subversive Activities Control Board, 1950–1972,* pt. 2 (Frederick, Md.: University Press of America, 1988), Hecht testimony, reel 34; Wolff testimony, reels 35 and 36]; and Subversive Activities Control Board, *Herbert Brownell, Attorney General, v. Veterans of the Abraham Lincoln Brigade, Recommended Decision,* 18 May 1955, pp. 28, 47). Wolff testified to the Dies committee in 1940 that he was not and had never been a member of the Communist party or the Young Communist League. He later admitted that his denial of membership in the Young Communist League was false, and these documents show that his statement about Communist party membership was also false. That Wolff joined the Spanish rather than the American Communist party is of little import. See Testimony of Milton Wolff, 12 April 1940, House Special Committee on Un-American Activities, *Investigations of Un-American Propaganda Activities in the United States,* 76th Cong., 3d sess., 1940, 13:7785.

9. Gallo was the nom de guerre of the Italian Communist Luigi Longo.

10. John Haynes's phone interview with Milton Wolff, 4 August 1992.

This would have been Colonel S. W. Bailey, a recruiter for the Special Operations Executive, the British commando force. America was not at war at this time and was officially neutral. Donovan's acting as a recruiter for British commandos illustrates the extent of President Roosevelt's policy of all-out aid to Britain short of actual belligerency. Dennis told the NKVD that "WOLFF conveyed this proposal by the intelligence service to the Comparty leadership and was given a sanction for it." Wolff established an office in New York, engaged a staff, and "receives 60 dollars a week plus expenses from the intelligence service." Dennis reported that "WOLFF had provided the British with 12 Yugoslavs, 3 Czechs, and 1 Italian."

### Eugene Dennis, William Donovan, and the Infiltration of the OSS and OWI

The next month Pearl Harbor was bombed and America entered the war. Dennis reported that Donovan then wanted such men for his own agency and ordered Wolff to redirect his recruits to the OSS. As a consequence, Dennis reported that "in the recent period, WOLFF has provided American intelligence with 10 Americans, 1 Greek, and 3 Yugoslavs, who are [officially] considered on active duty in the army and undergoing training in special ("commando") groups. Apart from the party members indicated, WOLFF has provided 6 nonparty Hungarians and 4 Czechs to American intelligence."[11]

11. Fragments of the story in document 71 and recounted here have appeared earlier based on participants' memories, but other documentation was missing. In a 1989 autobiography, the International Brigades veteran Milt Felsen described how Wolff asked him to volunteer for British commando work in late November 1941. Felsen understood that British intelligence had approached Wolff through Diana Sheean. After America entered the war, Felsen said he and other Lincoln veterans recruited by Wolff were diverted from the British to the American OSS (Milt Felsen, *The Anti-Warrior* [Iowa City: University of Iowa Press, 1989], 151–52). In a 1964 interview with Robert Rosenstone, Irving Goff, another Lincoln veteran, said that Donovan had recruited him for OSS work shortly before Pearl Harbor and that he had also recruited other Lincoln veterans for the OSS. Rosenstone does not report Goff's mentioning Wolff's role or that of the CPUSA (Robert Rosenstone, *Crusade on the Left: The Lincoln Battalion in the Spanish Civil War* [New York: Pegasus, 1969], 350). In 1982 the historian Maurice Isserman reported that Eugene Dennis's widow, Peggy, and the veteran Communist Gilbert Green told him that Dennis had met with and furnished Donovan with information on possible OSS recruits. Their account, however, does not mention Milton Wolff's role or Dennis's checking with Moscow (Maurice Isserman, *Which Side Were You On? The American Communist Party during the Second World War* [Middletown, Conn.: Wesleyan University Press, 1982], 183).

In 1992 document 71 was read to Milton Wolff, and although he insisted on his independence from the CPUSA, he verified its major points. In addition to the November meeting with Donovan and Diana Sheean's role, he confirmed that his activities were financed first by the British and then by the OSS, that Colonel Bailey was his link to the British, and that he had recruited a few dozen veterans for commando duty. While continuing to deny that he had been a Communist or that the CPUSA had supervised his activity, Wolff allowed that it had been necessary for him to work with and through Eugene Dennis because of the Communist party's influence among International Brigades veterans.

Wolff also stated that although the meeting with Donovan occurred as described, he had already been working for British intelligence well before the Nazi invasion of the Soviet Union in June 1941 and prior to Donovan's contact. He said that he did this because as an antifascist, he supported any nation fighting Nazi Germany. This story, however, is implausible. During the period of the Nazi-Soviet Pact, Wolff's stance was one of unwavering opposition to any assistance to Great Britain or the other nations fighting Hitler.

Wolff was elected national commander of the Veterans of the Abraham Lincoln Brigade at its convention in December 1939 and retained that position into the 1960s. At the 1939 convention, Wolff personally stressed the slogan, originated by the Communist party, "The Yanks Are Not Coming"—a reversal of the World War I American slogan that was a promise to the French and British to hold on because the "Yanks are coming" to fight the Germans. The VALB convention passed a "main resolution," adopted unanimously, stating that "this war is an Imperialist War and we are opposed to it, and we are more strongly opposed to the United States taking any part in it, on either side. We condemn the actions of the American press in giving support to the war-mongers of this country in their war-inciting editorials. . . . Let our slogan be: KEEP AMERICA OUT OF THIS IMPERIALIST WAR! THE YANKS ARE *NOT* COMING!"[12] Under Wolff's leadership, the VALB joined the American

12. Proceedings of the Third National Convention of the Veterans of the Abraham Lincoln Brigade, 23–24 December 1939, New York, New York, pp. 2, 33. Emphasis in the original. Reprinted as Petitioners' Exhibit 59, proceedings held before the Subversive Activities Control Board in the matter of *Herbert Brownell, Attorney General, v. Veterans of the Abraham Lincoln Brigade*, 1954.

Peace Mobilization, the CPUSA's front group that campaigned against Roosevelt's program of assistance to the anti-Hitler belligerents.

There were International Brigades veterans who rejected the Nazi-Soviet Pact and supported those fighting Hitler. Milton Wolff, however, did not allow these men to remain in the Veterans of the Abraham Lincoln Brigade. Wolff announced that all members must be in "agreement with our present program and policies" and expelled members who criticized the Nazi-Soviet Pact.[13] A few of those expelled attempted to form a Veterans of the Abraham Lincoln Brigade, Anti-Totalitarian as an alternative to the Communist-aligned VALB, but the effort failed for lack of support from the veterans who, after all, were predominately Communists and supported the Nazi-Soviet Pact.[14] In May 1941 Wolff delivered the keynote speech at a convention of the Veterans of the Abraham Lincoln Brigade. At this point in the war, Nazi Germany had conquered most of Western and Central Europe. Yet Wolff mentioned Hitler only once, in a sentence that denounced as equally evil "Roosevelt, Hitler, Churchill and Mussolini." His chief target was President Roosevelt's policy of providing assistance to Great Britain in its fight against Nazi Germany. Wolff told the convention:

> Under the dishonest slogan of anti-fascism, he [President Roosevelt] prepares the red-baiting, union-busting, alien-hunting, anti-Negro, anti-Semitic Jingoistic road to fascism in America: we accuse him. Turning with cynical calculation on his own lies and false promises, he drags the American people, despite their repeated expressed opposition, closer and closer to open participation in the imperialist slaughter, in which the youth of our country will, if he has his way, join the 1,000 British seamen of the H.M.S. Hood, the 30,000 German bodies floating in the Mediterranean, the bloody and bloated corpses on battle fields the world over, for the greater glory of foreign trade and the brutal oppression of free people at home and abroad: we accuse him. Franklin

13. Ibid., Membership Reports, 23.

14. The attempt to form the VALB, Anti-Totalitarian is discussed in testimony of Morris Maken, transcript of the proceedings held before the Subversive Activities Control Board in the matter of *Herbert Brownell, Attorney General, v. Veterans of the Abraham Lincoln Brigade,* 1954, 890–92; Subversive Activities Control Board, *Recommended Decision,* 18 May 1955, p. 120; Robert Rosenstone, *Crusade on the Left,* 345; and Cecil Eby, *Between the Bullet and the Lie: American Volunteers in the Spanish Civil War* (New York: Holt, Rinehart and Winston, 1969), 270.

Demagogue Roosevelt we accuse; tirelessly and until the people hear and understand, we accuse him. . . . We fight against the involvement of our country in an imperialist war from which the great majority of the American people can derive only misery, suffering, and death. We stubbornly oppose every move of Roosevelt and the war-mongers in this direction, and call on the American people to organize and make vocal their deep and sincere opposition to any program of convoys and an A.E.F.[15]

If Wolff had doubts about the Nazi-Soviet Pact and was working for British intelligence prior to the Nazi invasion of the Soviet Union in June 1941, he hid it well.

Wolff's 1992 claim that he had worked for the British prior to the Nazi invasion of the Soviet Union and prior to Donovan's contact is also discredited by his own testimony to the Subversive Activities Control Board in 1954. Wolff testified to the board as a witness for the Veterans of the Abraham Lincoln Brigade in its objection to the SACB's proposed listing of it as a Communist front organization. In his testimony, Wolff mentioned that he had worked for British military intelligence and the OSS in 1941 and 1942, although he refused to describe the nature of the work. He testified, however, that his work for the British had been at the initiative of General Donovan and that, while his memory was unclear on the precise timing, he placed his work for the British in the latter half of 1941, perhaps starting in July, after the Nazi invasion of the USSR.[16]

In document 71 Dennis told his NKVD contact that Donovan

15. Keynote speech of Milton Wolff to May 1941 convention of the Veterans of the Abraham Lincoln Brigade, reprinted as Petitioners' Exhibit 98, proceedings held before the Subversive Activities Control Board in the matter of *Herbert Brownell, Attorney General, v. Veterans of the Abraham Lincoln Brigade*, 1954. The *Hood* was a British ship sunk with a huge loss of life. The reference to the German dead recalls the sinking of German troop transports during the conquest of the Greek islands. Roosevelt was considering plans to provide armed convoys to protect Allied ships taking supplies to Britain, hence the reference to convoys. A.E.F. stands for American Expeditionary Force, the term used for American troops sent to Europe in World War I.

16. Testimony of Milton Wolff, transcript of the proceedings held before the Subversive Activities Control Board in the matter of *Herbert Brownell, Attorney General, v. Veterans of the Abraham Lincoln Brigade*, 1954, 3695, 4119, 4123, 4272, 4275, 4323–28. Peter Carroll in *The Odyssey of the Abraham Lincoln Brigade: Americans in the Spanish Civil War* (Stanford, Calif.: Stanford University Press, 1994), 244–47, accepts Wolff's story that he worked for British intelligence prior to the Nazi invasion but provides no documentation other than Wolff's claim.

had also asked Wolff to recruit International Brigades veterans in Canada and Mexico. Dennis noted that Wolff was prepared to do so, but "that trip is currently being delayed in connection with your [Dimitrov's] inquiry concerning this matter." Fitin's report also noted that in December 1941 "RYAN [Dennis] himself was chosen for permanent contact and negotiations" between the CPUSA and U.S. intelligence to organize antifascist propaganda for radio broadcasts. Further, Dennis reported that Donovan had met with him and had asked him "for a connection to the party organization in France," but Dennis had claimed to possess no such contacts. In addition, Dennis described Donovan's contacts with exiled Italian Communists and relayed queries from Spanish Communist party leaders, exiled in Cuba after their defeat in the Spanish Civil War, about what they should do in response to requests from American intelligence for recruits and information on Spanish matters.

Dennis, clearly uneasy about these matters, told the NKVD officer that he wanted "instructions on all of these issues as soon as possible." General Fitin concluded the memo with his own comment that the NKVD regarded "this entire matter as a political mistake by the leadership of the US Comparty, thanks to which the American and British intelligence services have been given the opportunity to infiltrate not only American Comparty channels but also the Comparty organizations of other countries."

That Georgi Dimitrov shared Fitin's worry is demonstrated by his handwritten note on document 71, "A directive has been given to New York for the discontinuation of this work," as well as by two other documents. **Document 73** is the actual order sent to American Communists to shut down Wolff's recruiting operation. Dimitrov tells Fitin, "On the matter of Wolff, the following advisory has been sent to our American friends: 'We consider allowing Wolff to recruit people for English and American intelligence a mistaken policy. This gives intelligence the opportunity to infiltrate the American and other Comparties. We advise serious discussion of the most effective measures and forms of curtailing that recruitment and all connection with the indicated intelligence services.'"

# Document 73

Dimitrov to Fitin, 13 May 1942, RTsKhIDNI 495–73–188. Original in Russian.

TOP SECRET.

PERSONAL.

<u>TO COMRADE FITIN.</u>

On the matter of Wolff, the following advisory has been sent to our American friends:

"We consider allowing Wolff to recruit people for English and American intelligence a mistaken policy. This gives intelligence the opportunity to infiltrate the American and other Comparties. We advise serious discussion of the most effective measures and forms of curtailing that recruitment and all connection with the indicated intelligence services. Warn the Spanish and Italian comrades about this as well."

(G. DIMITROV)

13 May 1942

No.

---

**Document 74** is a coded "TOP SECRET. Personal Only" telegram, delivered through NKVD channels, from Ryan/Dennis in response to Moscow's orders. Dennis reported that he and other CPUSA leaders "fully agree with your proposals regarding the activities of *Wolff* and we have taken all necessary measures for its discontinuation." Moreover, Dennis noted that "we have discussed the matter with *Earl*." Earl Browder, the CPUSA's chief, had been out of active leadership while serving a prison sentence for passport fraud. On 16 May 1942, just prior to Dennis's message, Roosevelt commuted Browder's sentence to time served and released him.

When this episode was discussed with Wolff in 1992, he acknowledged that he had shut down his OSS recruiting operation in mid-1942 but was reluctant to attribute this to CPUSA orders. He noted that without the Communist party's help it was very difficult to continue to recruit International Brigades veterans, but he stressed that the decision was a personal one stemming from his irritation with the OSS because it was not, as he had expected, planning to operate against the Franco regime in Spain. Wolff said he had then quit the OSS and joined the U.S. Army. Because of his Communist connections, however, he was assigned to longshore work at an Indian port rather than to the combat duty he wanted. Even so,

Wolff succeeded in getting into combat by volunteering for General Stillwell's Burma offensive; there is no doubting Wolff's courage and willingness to fight. Displeased by his treatment in the regular army, Wolff asked for reinstatement in the OSS. Donovan agreed, and in 1943 he received a commission and found himself working in Italy with a number of Lincoln Brigade veterans whom he had originally recruited for the OSS.[17]

Although the matter of Wolff's recruitment efforts had been settled, Dennis, in his June 1942 telegram to Dimitrov (document 74), asked on behalf of himself and Browder for "your instructions" on other issues. First, Dennis said that the exiled Spanish Communists had asked that they be allowed to cooperate with Donovan because they no longer had reliable communications to the European continent and needed American intelligence help to get Spanish Communist agents into Lisbon and Marseilles. Second, Dennis noted that American Communist party leaders in Chicago and Detroit had given the FBI information on people suspected of pro-Nazi "fifth-column" activity, and American Communists wanted permission to continue to hand over "certain selected materials . . . to government organizations." That Dennis discussed both these matters with the OSS is confirmed in a memo Donovan sent President Roosevelt.[18]

---

## Document 74

Ryan to Dimitrov, enclosed in Fitin to Dimitrov, 1 June 1942, RTsKhIDNI 495–74–484. Original in Russian.

---

**TOP SECRET**
<u>Personal Only</u>

E C C I—
To Com. D I M I T R O V

Here are the contents of a telegram sent to you from New York:
"We fully agree with your proposals regarding the activities of *Wolff* and we

17. John Haynes's phone interview with Milton Wolff, 4 August 1992. Lt. Col E. C. Huntington, Jr., of OSS security office to Commander Vanderbilt, 18 June 1942, COI/OSS Central Files, record group 226, entry 92, box 69, folder 47, National Archives. The Huntington memo confirms that Wolff had stopped recruiting for the OSS and was entering the regular armed forces.

18. Donovan said he gave the information about fifth columnists to the FBI

# Document 74 *continued*

have taken all necessary measures for their discontinuation, as well as exerting influence on leftist organizations to do likewise. We have discussed the matter with <u>Earl</u> and request your instructions on the following matters:

1) Upon receiving your instructions, our Spanish friends consider that their situation is different and request that we attempt directly and indirectly to influence the <u>Donovan</u> Committee or other American institutions to assist in getting the two Spaniards sent <u>to Marseilles and Lisbon.</u>

2) The party secretary in Chicago and Detroit has provided the <u>FBI</u> with information on Nazi[1] agents and their activities.

In general, we believe that information pertaining to the activities of the <u>fifth column</u> should not only be published in our press <u>but also thoroughly</u> <u>studied, and certain selected materials could be passed on to government</u> <u>organizations.</u>

3) We are in contact with the department of foreign propaganda and with the information coordinator of the US. That department is one of three departments in the so-called <u>Donovan</u> Committee and is directly controlled by the White House. We also <u>have several persons working in the Czech and Italian</u> <u>radio-broadcast sections of that department and influencing certain broad-</u> <u>casts in Germany, although not in the overall program. We consider it expe-</u> <u>dient to prolong that contact and keep these persons in the radio-broadcast</u> <u>section, if, of course, you are in agreement. We have a similar contact with the</u> <u>Inter-American Committee.</u>

EARL sends his greetings. He is in a splendid mood, and will assume active leadership duties in about two weeks. <u>Ryan.</u>"

F I T I N.

P. Fitin

No. 302/ru

1 June 1942

<u>Answer given</u> 4 June 1942 GD

1. The last letter in the four-letter word taken to be *Nazi* is quite faint, but the first three letters, n-a-ts, do not leave a more likely possibility than *i* for the fourth in this context. Standard Russian, however, uses either a noun form, *natsist*, as in *agent-natsist*, or an adjectival form, *natsistskii*, as in *natsistskie agenty*; the form *agenty natsi*, which is used in this document, is the third instance of non- or substandard language on this page. The first is the syntactically "orphaned" noun *vozdeistviia* (influences); the second is *po polucheniiu* instead of *po poluchenii* (upon receiving) under point 1. Under point 3, *peredachakh* (broadcasts) in the prepositional case must be read as genitive, and *vozdeistvuemykh* (influenced) must be read, evidently, as *vozdeistvuiushchikh* (influencing).

СОВ. СЕКРЕТНО

Только лично

И К К И -

тов. ДИМИТРОВУ

Сообщаем содержание телеграммы полученной для Вас из Нью-Йорка:

"Мы полностью согласны с Вашими предложениями относительно деятельности *Вульфа* и приняли все необходимые меры к ее прекращению, а также воздействия на левые организации поступать точно также. Обсудили вопрос с *Эрлом* и просим Ваших указаний по следующим вопросам:

1) испанские друзья по получению Ваших указаний считают, что их положение различное и требуют, чтобы мы непосредственно и окольным путем попытались воздействовать на комитет *Донована* или другие американские учреждения, чтобы содействовать посылке двух испанцев *с Марсель и Лисабон*.

2) партийный секретарь в Чикаго и Детройте передал Ф.Б.И. данные на агентов наци и их деятельности.

DOCUMENT 74. Ryan to Dimitrov, enclosed in Fitin to Dimitrov, 1 June 1942.

2.-

Вообще мы считаем, что информация, относящаяся к деятельности 5-й колоны, не должна только опубликовываться в нашей печати, но тщательно изучаться и отдельные отобранные материалы могут быть передаваемы правительственным организациям.

3) Мы находимся в контакте с департаментом иностранной пропаганды и с координатором информации США. Этот департамент один из трех департаментов в так называемом комитете *Донована* и контролируется непосредственно белым домом. Мы имеем также несколько человек работающих в отделах чешской и итальянской радиопередачах этого департамента и воздействуемых на отдельные передачи в Германии, хотя и не в общей программе. Мы считаем целесообразным продолжать этот контакт и оставить людей в отделе радиопередач, конечно, если Вы с этим согласны. Мы имеем такой же контакт с Интер Американ Коммити.

ЭРЛ шлет привет. Он прекрасно настроен, приступит к активному руководству недели через две. *Рамн.* ".

Ф И Т И Н .

№ .. *302/84*
" *1* " июня 1942 года

DOCUMENT 74. continued

These Dennis/Ryan documents show more than the intermixing of CPUSA operations with Soviet intelligence activities. They also demonstrate that top party leaders were not only aware of such operations but also directly involved in them. Dennis, after all, was second in the CPUSA hierarchy and was shortly to succeed Earl Browder as general secretary. The messages also make very clear where the loyalty of Eugene Dennis, Earl Browder, and other Communists lay. Dennis noted that he and Browder awaited Comintern "instructions"—instructions about whether the CPUSA should cooperate with American authorities to mount campaigns against Nazi Germany. These two American citizens were also in agreement with the Comintern's orders to halt Wolff's recruitment for the OSS because it might jeopardize the security of Communist apparatuses.

These messages also document another point. American Communist contact with the OSS was initiated by the OSS. Not only did Donovan approach Wolff, but he remained in contact with Dennis specifically because of Dennis's role as the CPUSA liaison with American intelligence. William Donovan once remarked to an aide, "I'd put Stalin on the OSS payroll if I thought it would help us defeat Hitler."[19] And, indirectly, Donovan did put Stalin on the payroll: researchers have identified Communists in the Russian, Spanish, Balkan, Hungarian, and Latin American sections of the OSS's Research and Analysis Division and in its operational Japanese, Korean, Italian, Spanish, Hungarian, Indonesian, and German divisions.[20] In the midst of World War II, when Hitler was the main enemy, General Donovan's approach was pragmatic, but it was also

---

without disclosing its source. Donovan got Roosevelt's approval, contingent on the State Department's not objecting, to insert exiled Spanish Communist agents into Lisbon and Marseilles. It is not known, however, whether this project was carried out (Donovan to Roosevelt, 22 April 1942, and Roosevelt to Donovan, 23 April 1942, OSS Report #439, box 149, President's Secretary's File, Franklin D. Roosevelt Library, Hyde Park, New York). See also Bradley Smith, *The Shadow Warriors: O.S.S. and the Origins of the C.I.A.* (New York: Basic Books, 1983), 97–98.

19. Robert Hayden Alcorn, *No Bugles for Spies* (New York: David McKay, 1962), 134.

20. OSS Communists are identified and their roles are discussed in R. Harris Smith, *OSS: The Secret History of America's First Central Intelligence Agency* (Berkeley: University of California Press, 1972); Barry M. Katz, *Foreign Intelligence: Research and Analysis in the Office of Strategic Services, 1942–1945* (Cambridge: Harvard University Press, 1989); Earl Latham, *The Communist Controversy in Washington: From the New Deal to McCarthy* (Cambridge: Harvard University

fraught with risk. Although this arrangement allowed the OSS to make use of Communists, it also allowed Communists to make use of the OSS.[21]

After the OSS disbanded at the end of World War II, its officials did not deny that they had recruited Communists, explaining that they used Communists when the individuals in question had the appropriate skills, did not conceal their Communist background, and were willing to subordinate themselves to OSS policies. In line with this policy, Donovan had discharged a number of OSS personnel for concealing Communist membership or for carrying on party activities while working for the OSS.[22]

While the OSS was operational, however, Donovan steadfastly denied that he ever recruited Communists. In 1945 a congressional committee, concerned about Communists holding military commissions, asked Donovan about four OSS officers it had identified as probable Communists. The four were Milton Wolff, Vincent Lossowski, Irving Fajans, and Irving Goff, all Lincoln Brigade veterans then serving with the OSS in Italy.[23] Donovan praised their

---

Press, 1966); Christopher Andrew and Oleg Gordievsky, *KGB: The Inside Story* (New York: HarperCollins Publishers, 1990); Peter Wright, *Spycatcher: The Candid Autobiography of a Senior Intelligence Officer* (New York: Dell Publishing, 1988); Robin W. Winks, *Cloak and Gown: Scholars in the Secret War, 1939–1961* (New York: Quill, 1988); Anthony Cave Brown, *The Last Hero: Wild Bill Donovan* (New York: Times Books, 1982); and Stewart Alsop and Thomas Braden, *Sub Rosa: The OSS and American Espionage* (New York: Reynal and Hitchcock, 1948).

21. In 1943 Donovan visited Moscow and proposed to General Fitin that the OSS establish a liaison mission in Moscow and the NKVD establish a similar office in Washington. Fitin's reaction was favorable, but nothing came of the idea because of the fierce opposition of FBI director J. Edgar Hoover. Hoover argued that an official NKVD presence would exacerbate his counterespionage problems. See Smith, *Shadow Warriors*, 335–46; and Andrew and Gordievsky, *KGB*, 322–24.

22. Among these was Stephen Dedijer, a Croatian immigrant recruited for OSS work in Yugoslavia. The OSS released Dedijer when it concluded that Moscow had sent him to the United States to edit a Croatian-language Communist newspaper and discovered that his brother was an aide to Yugoslav Communist leader Tito. OSS officials decided Stephen Dedijer's Communist partisanship was so blatant that he could not work successfully with noncommunist Yugoslavs. After leaving the OSS, Dedijer joined the U.S. Army, became a paratrooper, and, to the amusement of his fellow troopers, insisted on shouting "Long live Stalin!" when jumping, rather than the then-customary U.S. airborne shout of "Geronimo!" After World War II, Dedijer directed atomic energy research for the Yugoslav government but later broke with Tito and left the country. See Smith, *OSS*, 135.

23. William Herrick, a Lincoln battalion veteran, testified to the Subversive Activities Control Board in 1955 that he had procured a job with the Communist-led Furriers union when he returned from Spain. After the Nazi-Soviet Pact, however, he

OSS records, saying, "These men I've been in the slit trenches with and have been in the muck with, and I have seen what they have done and I would measure them up against any man in their loyalty." If Donovan had left it at that, his remarks would have been simply a commendable defense of soldiers who were then serving the nation well regardless of their politics. General Donovan went on to testify, however, that he had investigated all four and "did not find that they were Communists. I found that they were not." Donovan was also asked if any of the four had been in the Young Communist League. Donovan testified that "they were not."[24] In fact, two of the four, Wolff and Fajans, had been open members of the Young Communist League in the 1930s.

Donovan assured the Congress that everyone in the OSS had been thoroughly investigated: "I try to determine whether a man is or is not a Fascist or a Communist—I have never taken a man of whom I had any doubt." One congressman asked if perhaps because of special qualifications needed for some types of OSS work Donovan had recruited someone with those special qualifications even though "he had been a member of the Communist Party . . . or a contributor to . . . some Communistic magazine." Donovan, refusing the opportunity to gain some wiggle room, replied unequivocally, "I should say right here no such case has ever happened."[25]

There is now no doubt that Donovan deceived Congress when he denied knowledge of the Communist links of Milton Wolff and other OSS personnel or that, given his negotiations with Dennis, he concealed from Congress the extent of OSS dealings with the CPUSA. If a senior intelligence official were to so mislead a congressional committee today, the deception would be regarded as worthy of a criminal charge.

---

became disillusioned with the CPUSA and attended meetings of a Lovestoneist group. Herrick said that Irving Fajans had attended one of the meetings as a Communist informant, spotted Herrick, and reported him to the union; Herrick was fired (Testimony of William Herrick, transcript of proceedings held before the Subversive Activities Control Board in the matter of *Herbert Brownell, Attorney General, v. Veterans of the Abraham Lincoln Brigade,* 1954, 543–45).

24. Donovan testimony, unpublished report of proceedings of hearings held before the Special Committee of the Committee on Military Affairs, vol. 3, 13 March 1945, pp. 189–90, Record Group 233, Center for Legislative Archives, National Archives, Washington, D.C.

25. Ibid., 179, 182.

Unbeknownst to Donovan, while he was praising the four officers under question, senior OSS officers in Italy instituted an inquiry into Irving Goff's work, and U.S. Army security officers were raising questions about Fajans, Wolff, and Lossowski. Goff ran an OSS radio network for Italian Communist partisans, a powerful force in Italy's antifascist resistance. Milton Wolff, who worked with Goff, said that OSS operatives in Italy referred to Goff's network with some amusement as the Moscow Chain. The OSS established the network under an agreement that it would be used only for messages related to the fight against the Nazis and not for messages dealing with Communist preparation for a postwar Italian political struggle with noncommunists. Senior OSS officers reviewing the message traffic thought the agreement had been broken and suspected that Goff's Communist loyalties had led him to allow the partisans to misuse the OSS network. In addition, Fajans and Wolff had angered an OSS colonel in Italy by proselytizing for communism among OSS personnel.[26]

Donovan was not pleased when he learned of the inquiries. His angry message to OSS commanders in Italy said: "I do not understand why all the facts of this matter were not reported to me before this day. You will have in mind that I appeared before a Congressional Committee inquiring into loyalty of American officers who were charged with having been members of that party. Relying upon my own observations as well as available information from your theatre, I sincerely defended these men and testified as to their loyalty and their efficient service. I want now to have full information. . . . This is not a matter which can be handled by cable. . . . Pouch direct to me in Washington."[27] Cable traffic passed through the hands of a number of U.S. services. By directing that further information about the Goff affair be transmitted by courier (pouch), Donovan was reducing the likelihood that knowledge of the affair

26. John Haynes's phone inteview with Milton Wolff, 4 August 1992; Smith, *OSS*, 99; J. J. Monigan, Jr., to Donovan, 11 May 1945, "Report of Traffic over Circuits to Communist Party Partisan Bands," OSS field files, record group 226, entry 190, box 734, on microfilm reel 127 (micro 1642), National Archives.

27. Donovan to OSS headquarters, Italy, 17 April 1945, General William J. Donovan OSS Documents on microfilm, record group 226, reel 18, National Archives. See also Maj. William P. Madoon to Commanding Officer, "Reports on Lts. Goff, Lossowski, Fajans and Wolff," 24 April 1945, Donovan OSS Documents on microfilm, reel 18. Brown, *The Last Hero*, 706–27, discusses the Goff inquiry in detail.

would pass outside his control. Ultimately an internal OSS investigation determined that the evidence was too ambiguous to hold Goff responsible for Italian Communist misuse of the OSS radio net. Indeed, it may have been so, but one cannot help observing that any other outcome would have been an embarrassment to Donovan.

Goff, Wolff, Fajans, and Lossowski were ordered out of Italy as soon as hostilities ceased in order to avoid the possibility that they might become involved in what were expected to be (and were) bruising political battles between Communists and anti-Communists for control of postwar Italy. Donovan sent all four OSS officers letters of praise for their work, promoted Goff to captain, and awarded him the Legion of Merit. After the war, Goff became a full-time organizer for the CPUSA, serving as head of the Louisiana Communist party and as an official in the New York party. In 1953 Fajans and Wolff were asked while testifying to a congressional committee whether they had been Communists when in the OSS. Both refused to answer, citing their right not to provide information that might be used against them in a criminal prosecution.[28]

In the June 1942 message to Dimitrov, document 74, Dennis noted that the American Communists had "contact with the department of foreign propaganda and with the information coordinator of the US. That department is one of three departments in the so-called _Donovan_ Committee and is directly controlled by the White House." Dennis went on to report that "we also have several persons working in the Czech and Italian radio-broadcast sections of that department and influencing certain broadcasts in Germany. . . . We consider it expedient to prolong that contact and keep these persons in the radio-broadcast section, if, of course, you are in agreement. We have a similar contact with the Inter-American Committee." The latter was Nelson Rockefeller's Inter-American Coordinator's Office, to which President Roosevelt had given jurisdiction over propaganda activity in Central and South America.

Dennis's boast about Communist influence in the OSS confirms

28. Maj. J. J. Monigan to Donovan, report of Special Investigation Committee on Wolff, Fajans, Lossowski, and Goff, 10 May 1945, Donovan OSS Documents on microfilm, reel 18; testimony of Irving Fajans and testimony of Milton Wolff in Senate Subcommittee to Investigate the Administration of the Internal Security Act, _Interlocking Subversion in Government Departments_, 83d Cong., 1st sess., 6 May 1953, pt. 12:765–72, 787–92.

postwar claims made by several Communist defectors. After Louis Budenz left the CPUSA, he accused Dennis of "directing the agents in the Office of Strategic Services" and made specific reference to OSS radio propaganda.[29] Elizabeth Bentley, the former Soviet spy, said several Communists in the OSS had furnished her with information, and she described the infiltration of a Communist into Rockefeller's Inter-American Coordinator's Office.[30] Many historians have hitherto dismissed Bentley's and Budenz's testimony about CPUSA espionage activity.[31]

In June 1942 President Roosevelt pulled most propaganda operations out of Donovan's Coordinator of Information agency and placed them with the newly created Office of War Information (OWI). Donovan's agency, renamed the Office of Strategic Services, retained intelligence, commando, and other clandestine operations, as well as propaganda operations aimed at enemy nations. Part of Dennis's network went to the OWI with this transfer. In 1943, Representative John Lesinski, a Michigan Democrat with a Polish-American constituency, denounced a number of OWI employees as pro-Soviet and warned OWI head Elmer Davis that members of the OWI's Polish-language section were Communists. Davis received a similar but private warning from Ambassador Jan Ciechanowski of the Polish government-in-exile. Davis, a popular liberal radio commentator whom Roosevelt had selected to head the OWI, dismissed Lesinski's speech as containing "more lies than were ever comprised in any other speech made about the Office of War Information" and rebuked Ambassador Ciechanowski for interfering with internal American matters.[32]

Ciechanowski and Lesinski, however, were not alone. In 1944,

29. Louis Budenz, *Men without Faces: The Communist Conspiracy in the USA* (New York: Harper and Brothers, 1948), 252.

30. Elizabeth Bentley, *Out of Bondage* (New York: Ivy Books, 1988), 107.

31. Evaluations of Budenz and Bentley range from the skeptical (Herbert L. Packer, *Ex-Communist Witnesses: Four Studies in Fact Finding* [Stanford, Calif.: Stanford University Press, 1962]) to the dismissive (Athan G. Theoharis and John Stuart Cox, *The Boss: J. Edgar Hoover and the Great American Inquisition* [Philadelphia: Temple University Press, 1988]; and Robert Justin Goldstein, *Political Repression in Modern America: 1870 to the Present* [New York: Schenkman Publishing, 1978]) to the contemptuous (David Caute, *The Great Fear: The Anti-Communist Purge under Truman and Eisenhower* [New York: Simon and Schuster, 1978]).

32. Remarks of Representative Lesinski, *Congressional Record,* 78th Cong., 1st sess., 17 June 1943, vol. 89, pt. 5:5999–6003; testimony of Elmer Davis, House

Vanni Montana, an official of the International Ladies' Garment Workers' Union and a former Communist, visited liberated Italy and reported finding a number of American Communists on the staff of Radio Italy, a propaganda station operated by the Office of War Information. Montana complained that Radio Italy's programs, beamed toward Nazi-occupied northern Italy, supported the political ambitions of Italian Communists in postwar Italy.[33]

After the war, several members of the OWI Polish-language section emerged as defenders of the Communist takeover of Poland and as close relatives of officials in the new Polish Communist regime; one official of the OWI's Polish-language section became editor of *Robotnik* (Worker), a Communist-aligned newspaper in Warsaw. In addition, the head of OWI's Czechoslovakian desk in New York emerged as a high-ranking Czechoslovak Communist and became the Czechoslovakian ambassador to France.[34]

In 1952 a congressional committee investigated the murder of nearly fifteen thousand captured Polish officers at Katyn. The committee questioned Davis about the OWI's endorsement of the Soviet story that the Nazis had executed the Poles and about OWI pressure on several domestic radio stations to stop carrying commentaries suggesting that the Soviets were responsible for the Katyn massacre. Davis explained that although in 1952 evidence of Soviet guilt was clear, in the midst of the war he had had every reason to believe the Soviet explanation. (Davis was not alone. During the war most American journalists accepted the Soviet version.) When asked about the complaints of Communist influence in the OWI, Davis refused to give any ground, saying that his opinion of Lesinski's charges and of Ciechanowski's warning was unchanged. Davis stated that during the war he had fired about a dozen OWI employees, including the head of the OWI's labor news desk and its

---

Select Committee, *Hearings before the Select Committee to Conduct an Investigation of the Facts, Evidence and Circumstances of the Katyn Forest Massacre* (Washington, D.C.: GPO, 1952), 1991–94.

33. Ronald L. Filippelli, "Luigi Antonini, the Italian-American Labor Council, and Cold-War Politics in Italy, 1943–1949," *Labor History* 33, no. 1 (Winter 1992): 102–25.

34. House Select Committee, *Hearings before the Select Committee to Conduct an Investigation of the Facts, Evidence and Circumstances of the Katyn Forest Massacre*, pp. 1987–88, 1991–94.

Greek desk in New York, when evidence surfaced that they were involved in Communist party activities while working for the OWI. Despite this, he dismissed as unimportant the matter of other OWI employees who later emerged as Communists.[35]

Some historians have taken the view that the surprisingly large number of Communists in the OSS and the OWI was accidental, merely the happenstance of these agencies recruiting people with the appropriate skills, some of whom were Communists. They have disregarded or denied that any of these secret Communists were reporting to the CPUSA or to Soviet intelligence.[36] Given Eugene Dennis's statement in document 74 that he had placed Communists in the OSS and OWI and was monitoring their work, that benign view is no longer tenable.

The discovery in the Comintern files of a stolen OSS document further undermines the view that Communist affiliation was insignificant. This report, **document 75,** is a classified OSS report on Spain dealing with the strength of the Communist party in Catalonia. Most information from Communist agents in the OSS would have gone to and been retained by the two chief Soviet intelligence agencies, the NKVD and Soviet military intelligence.[37] This report was probably forwarded to the Comintern because its subject, the activities of the Communist party in Catalonia, was a matter of Comintern interest and jurisdiction.

35. Ibid., Transcript of Davis Radio Broadcast of 3 May 1943.

36. Among the historians who have taken a complacent or dismissive stand in regard to the presence of Communists in the OSS are Smith, *Shadow Warriors*; Alsop and Braden, *Sub Rosa: The OSS and American Espionage*; Smith, *OSS*; and Katz, *Foreign Intelligence*. Winks, *Cloak and Gown*; Brown, *Last Hero*; Latham, *Communist Controversy in Washington*; and Andrew and Gordievsky, *KGB*, take the Communist presence in the OSS much more seriously, but they were unable to cite direct evidence of contact between individual Communists in the OSS and either CPUSA or Soviet intelligence services. The documents discussed in this chapter and documents 78, 88, 89, and 90 presented in chapter 8 provide that evidence.

37. In 1993, the archives of these agencies were still closed to research.

# Document 75

OSS report "Spain, Communist Party of Catalonia," 8 July 1943, RTsKhIDNI 495–74–481. Original in English. Stamped "Secret."

Office of Strategic Services
Washington, D.C.

| | |
|---|---|
| Dissemination/WELN No. | A–10880 |
| # pages | 8 |
| evaluation | A–3 |
| distributed | Sept. 3, 1943 |

Country:        Spain
Subject         Communist Party of Catalonia
Date of origin  July 8, 1943
Place of origin Spain

This Communist Party in Catalonia is practicing infiltration tactics on such a wide scale as to become a menace, if not for the present, for the future.

They have established the following services:

When a Communist or mere Communistic sympathizer is arrested for political reasons or for ordinary infractions of the law, pressure is applied until his liberty is obtained. The same thing occurs when a Communist escapes across the Franco-Spanish frontier and is arrested. In order to understand the wide scope of the organization, it should be pointed out that in the jails and penitentiaries, only three percent of the political prisoners belong to the Communist Party, although there were the strongest reasons for detaining them. This is because of their activities, as set forth here.

They infiltrate into firms of all sorts, and give jobs and means of support to brother-Communists. They have also established machine shops and millinery establishments where Party members and their families are given employment. These firms, which operate at a deficit, are supported by the organization.

Thanks to this, and the constant aid given to their needy, the Communists have become the most powerful working class element. Although some of the members are sincere Communists, the majority follow them only for reasons of self-interest and aggrandizement.

They have infiltrated into the syndicates of the F.E.T. of the J.O.N.S. and even into the Falange, which permits them to gain the upper hand on many operations. So firmly entrenched are they that they even reveal their identity and offer aid and assurance of immunity for the future to Flanagist members and leaders. This is possible because panic is beginning to invade the ranks of the Falange. In many instances, the Communists consider themselves supreme authorities, thanks to this fact.

There organization and activities are widespread. They give the Communist Party a position of superiority and effectiveness. At a time of disorganization and chaos or weakening of authority, the Communist Party has the means to impose itself upon the country.

The situation is much more significant if one remembers that no other well organized party exists to oppose the Communists. There is not even a badly organized one. There is nothing. Except for the Nationalist Party in the Basque Provinces and a small group of Republicans in Madrid, there exists absolutely nothing of an organized nature which might operate as a counter-balance or check to the Communists in the future. All this constitutes a grave peril.

The Republicans cannot be counted upon to remedy the situation. They are disillusioned and incapable of effective action at any given moment.

On the other hand the scattered force of the C.N.T. (Confederacion Nacional del Trabajo) are of some importance. This organization which heretofore has disdained politics for direct action and revolution, has changed its tactics to become more constructive. Far from being an anarchistic organization, it aspired to be a political force. In Catalonia the C.N.T. has a great number of members and sympathizers. It can well be said that there is no firm where members of the C.N.T. are not employed. They are able to control entire factories and shops. In addition, they are persons who know how to plot, because that is what they have been doing for the last twenty years. Moreover, they have boldness and sufficient determination to meet any situations and to undertake any act.

Their forces are totally without organization. The members are known to one-another, but they have made no preparations. Misery and poverty prevent them from undertaking any kind of special work. In Barcelona there are several leaders, loved and respected by the masses (of C.N.T.) who have a record of meritorious political activity within the organization.

The possibility of organizing these forces can readily be envisioned, in order to obtain the following results:

1. To weaken the Communist organization and its position among the work-

ing classes. It should not be forgotten that the Communist has always hated and feared the C.N.T. because under any conditions the letter has surpassed him in shrewdness, force, and audacity.

2. To obtain control over Catalonian industrial enterprises and information on their activities.

3. To form a bold and well-prepared organization ready for any undertaking at any given moment.

SECRET

---

## Reporting on the American Embassy in Moscow, 1942–1943

During World War II, the American Communist party provided the Soviet Union with a channel not only into the OSS but also into the American embassy in Moscow.

For a long time, large segments of the American press and many governmental bodies refused to treat the reporters of the Communist party newspaper, the *Daily Worker,* as legitimate journalists. Instead, *Daily Worker* writers were generally put in the same category as publicists for private trade associations, special interests, or political advocacy newsletters. The *Daily Worker* complained of this treatment and demanded that its reporters receive the same access as reporters for other newspapers to press briefings, interviews, and informal conversations with government officials. After America entered the war as a Soviet ally, the *Daily Worker*'s complaint was echoed by Popular Front supporters who attributed the lesser status given *Daily Worker* reporters to anti-Communist prejudice. They maintained that the *Daily Worker* was a newspaper just like other American papers and that the CPUSA was an American political organization just like the Democratic or the Republican parties.

This view won acceptance at the American embassy in Moscow, where there was an eye to the Soviet alliance. In 1942 and 1943 Janet Weaver, the Moscow correspondent of Intercontinental News, the *Daily Worker*'s foreign press arm, was accorded the same press privileges given to the Moscow correspondents of regular American newspapers. This included admittance not only to on- and off-the-record press briefings but also to interviews with American diplomats and invitations to "Americans only" dinners and cocktail parties where the American press socialized with embassy officials. The "Americans only" social events were highly popular with American correspondents and U.S. diplomats because they could relax and talk more freely than was possible in the presence of Russians. It was generally assumed that anything said in the presence of a Russian was reported to the Soviet government.

Janet Weaver, however, was not a normal reporter. Although known to the American embassy in Moscow as Janet Weaver, back in the United States she was better known as Janet Ross, the wife of Nat Ross. Nat Ross was the head of CPUSA activities in the Deep South in the early 1930s, a physically dangerous assignment, and later head of party activities in Minnesota, North Dakota, and South Dakota. Ross's success as an organizer gained him a spot in the party's national leadership, and in 1939 he was rewarded with the prestigious and responsible position of CPUSA representative to the Communist International in Moscow. Officially, the CPUSA withdrew from the Comintern after the passage of the Voorhis Act in 1940, but unofficially nothing had changed.[38] Janet Ross was herself a veteran Communist, the sister of Don West, a full-time CPUSA functionary, and had been a partner to her husband in his assignments. She accompanied him to Moscow, and one of the assignments she received was that of *Daily Worker* correspondent under the name of Janet Weaver.

In this position Ross did more than act as the Moscow correspondent for the *Daily Worker*. She used her access to the American embassy to prepare secret reports for the Comintern about what she heard in the embassy. Dimitrov then forwarded her reports to Molotov, the Soviet foreign minister. These documents span the period from August 1942 to June 1943. In some cases the documents

38. Nat Ross, in a report to the Presidium of the Executive Committee of the Comintern, said that despite American law, "in essence and in fact the entire Party membership . . . will be drawn still more closely under the banner of the Communist International" (Nat Ross's statement, Presidium of ECCI on the American Question, 21 November 1940, RTsKhIDNI 495–20–540).

found in the Comintern's archives were Ross's original signed reports in English. In other cases, only the Russian translation was on file. Ross's reports are numerous, some are lengthy, and together they amount to a considerable volume. Only one, **document 77,** concerning the informal remarks of U.S. Ambassador William Standley, is reproduced in this book, along with Dimitrov's cover note to Molotov, **document 76.**[39]

---

# Document 76

Dimitrov to Molotov, 26 August 1942, RTsKhIDNI 495–73–173. Original in Russian.

---

<u>Top secret</u>

**TO COMRADE MOLOTOV**
I am forwarding you the enclosed memorandum from our American correspondent comrade Janet Ross concerning the reception in honor of the American ambassador Standley, which took place on 23 August 1942.
I believe that this information may be of some interest to you.
Comradely regards,

/G. DIMITROV/

26 August 1942

---

# Document 77

Ross to Dimitrov, 24 August 1942, RTsKhIDNI 495–73–173. Original in English. Ross signed it by hand.

---

August 24, 1942
To Comrade Dimitrov:
Report on party for American Ambassador Standley:
Sunday afternoon, from 6:00 to 8:00 p.m., the Associated Press correspondent Cassidy gave a party in his apartment in honor of the Ambassador who is leaving for Kuibyshev today. Present were all the 13 American correspondents, the Ambassador, Captain Duncan of the U.S. Navy, Colonel McKellar,

---

39. In addition to Ambassador Standley's remarks, Ross also reported on the informal remarks of Wendell Willkie (the 1940 Republican presidential candidate, then visiting Moscow), Joseph Davies (former U.S. ambassador to the USSR), British Ambassador Clark-Kerr, American Generals James H. Burns and Omar Bradley, Arthur H. Sulzberger of the *New York Times,* the journalist Quentin Reynolds, and other American correspondents and embassy officials. All of the Ross reports are in RTsKhIDNI 495–73–173.

Military attache, Henderson of the Eastern European department of the U.S. State Department, who is on a visit here, and Mr. Thompson and Mr. Page of the embassy staff. The party was an informal, intimate affair.

During the course of the evening the Ambassador came to sit by me for a few minutes and asked what I thought of the movie evening held by the Soviet Cinema Committee on Friday and Saturday, *August 21 and 22* and which the Ambassador attended on Friday night. He was very enthusiastic about it and said he was particularly impressed by the interest of the Soviet movie people in American movies, and by the friendship they feel for the American people. He said he finds the same friendly feeling among Russians everywhere, and that he is trying to foster this friendship. Then he said the following: "But our people at home don't seem to understand the importance of this. For instance, I tried to get Walt Disney's "Fantasia" for this affair, and asked them to send it. They refused on the basis that it took up too much space in the diplomatic pouch. America must foster this friendship, because when this war is over Russia is going to need America, for we are going to be the country that sends materials to them. The entire country will have to be rebuilt. Every house in Moscow will need rebuilding. The plumbing is bad and they will need materials to fix it up. The people here will demand consumers' goods, because before the war they were just beginning to be able to get such things, but after the war it will be impossible for Russian industry to produce them. America cannot consume all the consumers' goods she produces, and Russia will be an ideal market for us. Therefore we must foster this friendship, because we will be able to sell millions of dollars worth of goods to the Soviet Union."

I would like to add that on Friday night he talked to one of the translators from the Movie Committee, a Russian girl who is a friend of mine, something along the same line about friendship. And to her he said, "It seems to me that there are differences between the Americans and the British and between the British and the Russian people, but there is very little difference and a considerable similarity between the Americans and the Russians."

I was told by one of the correspondents that as a result of the decision last week on the Stalin-Churchill communique, that the British correspondents should send it from Moscow at 7 o'clock and the Americans at 8:00, the American Ambassador went to see Clark Kerr and had a sharp talk with him. When BBC released the communique before anyone else, Standley condemned this action and told Clark Kerr that from now on in such cases he would "take care of *his* boys" (meaning American correspondents.)

I should add that the sentiment among the American correspondents is that there will not be a second front in Europe soon, which was indicated in the interview with Standley who said no promise had been made, but the correspondents cannot understand why the British Ambassador indicated that there will be a second front when he told them at his interview on Churchill visit that it was "an epoch making event."

With regard to Willkie: I learned from the correspondents that about two months ago in Kuibyshev, Gilmore of A.P., Hindus of the Herald Tribune, and Robertson of the P.M., all of whom know Willkie very well, sent him a telegram asking him to come to the Soviet Union on a so to speak good will visit. These correspondents were of the opinion that the British embassy was more active here than the American embassy under Standley, and that Willkie's visit would, so to speak, counteract the British activity. Willkie replied at that time, thanking them, and saying that he would go into the matter. When they learned he was coming they wired him again. Yesterday they received a cable from Willkie, saying, "Thanks for cable. Save one drink for me," indicating that he expects to spend some time with them when he comes.

Perhaps I should add one word about Willkie. It is a fact and generally recognized in the U.S. that Willkie is financially connected with J.P. Morgan and is generally considered a political spokesman for the Morgan company. At the same time Willkie tries to pose as a liberal, and has written articles for the liberal magazine, the New Republic, in one of which, about two years ago, he condemned the arrest of Browder as political persecution. At the present time he is counsel for defense of Comrade William Schneiderman, secretary of the C.P. of California, whose case has been appealed to the U.S. Supreme Court against deportation because of his Party membership at the time he received his citizenship papers.

Comradely yours,
Janet Ross

P.S: I forgot to say that at the party when someone asked about the position of Turkey at present, the Ambassador said he doesn't know. He said the Turkish ambassador here is very haughty to him and refused to have a confidential talk.

---

Ross's reports do not convey secret information. She was an informant, not a spy in a technical sense. She was not given access to classified embassy information and did not steal any files. Nor would any conscientious embassy official have given any reporter highly classified information. Even so, the information Ross conveyed was of a type and quality that the Soviets had difficulty getting. Her reports on what American diplomats told fellow Americans in informal "Americans only" settings provided the Soviets with background, nuances of meaning, and checks on what they learned through more formal, direct exchanges. The reports were of sufficient interest to Dimitrov that on occasion he summarized them in a secret, personal diary he kept.[40] He also regarded Ross's

40. One such entry dealt with a Ross report of conversations between American

reports as sufficiently important to be sent to Molotov. He would probably not have done this if Molotov, burdened as he was with wartime diplomacy, had not shown some interest.

From time to time during the Cold War, American intelligence agencies interviewed American reporters returning from Moscow about what they had learned. Some reporters cooperated; others refused, regarding the interviews as incompatible with their journalistic role. Those who did cooperate with American intelligence were American correspondents assisting the American government. By contrast, Janet Ross was an *American* correspondent assisting the *Soviet* government. She was in reality a Soviet patriot. As Dimitrov told Molotov in document 76, Ross was "*our* American correspondent comrade Janet Ross."[41]

---

correspondents and Wendell Willkie (Georgi Dimitrov's diary entry of 14 September 1942). Dimitrov kept this diary during his tenure in Moscow as head of the Comintern. Written in his own hand, Dimitrov's diary is more than two thousand pages long and contains a wealth of information. Yale University Press will be publishing the Dimitrov diary as part of its Annals of Communism series.

41. Emphasis added. Ross was not the only correspondent to provide the Comintern with information. The Comintern records also contain reports by John Gibbons, a British correspondent, that Dimitrov sent on to Molotov. For example, see Dimitrov to Molotov, 29 April 1943; and Gibbons's report to Dimitrov, "On Monday 19/4/43 I lunched with British Ambassador, Sir Archibald Clark Kerr" (RTsKhIDNI 495–73–173). Gibbons was a member of the British Communist party.

CHAPTER EIGHT

# Soviet Intelligence and American Communists, 1942–1945

BY WORLD WAR II the Comintern was past its prime. Once the Soviet Union's chief foreign intelligence and covert action arm, it was displaced by the foreign intelligence directorate of the NKVD and by the military intelligence service (GRU) of the Red Army in the 1930s. Even as an agency to promote Communist ideology and revolution around the world, it had become a much reduced organization. Externally, the Soviet Union's acceptance as a legitimate nation-state in the 1930s forced the Comintern to take a much lower profile. There was, after all, considerable contradiction between the government's exchange of ambassadors and pledges of mutual respect for national sovereignty with various nations and its support for an organization whose goal was to overthrow the governments of those nations.

When the United States recognized the Soviet Union in 1933, for example, the Soviets made promises to refrain from promoting Communist propaganda in the United States. America's first ambassador to the Soviet Union, William Bullitt, soon judged that the Soviets had broken their pledge and regarded the continued activity of the Communist International as evidence. Although Bullitt was correct, the Comintern had scaled back its activity somewhat and had reduced its public profile.

The Comintern's usefulness as an institution was further reduced by World War II. Wartime dislocations cut off the Comintern's direct communications with foreign Communists, and it often had to communicate with its client-parties through covert channels provided by the NKVD and the official Soviet diplomatic service. Moreover, the USSR desperately needed the cooperation and aid of the United States and Great Britain in its fight against Nazi Germany. In these circumstances, the Comintern, with its revolutionary history, was a diplomatic liability. These considerations led Stalin to dissolve the Comintern officially in 1943, although it continued to function for two more years while its various activities were transferred to Soviet government or Soviet Communist party departments. As an organization, the Comintern effectively ended in 1945 when Georgi Dimitrov, head of the Comintern since 1935, left Moscow to become the leader of the new Communist regime in Bulgaria.

Even as the Comintern was phased out of existence, however, it retained one major asset: its files. The records of its dealings with foreign Communists provided a vast storehouse of information. After the Nazi attack on the Soviet Union, General Fitin, chief of the NKVD's foreign intelligence directorate, and Dimitrov met to discuss how their relationship might change to accommodate the new situation. In his diary entry for 20 August 1941, Dimitrov noted that they had "agreed concerning contact and mutual cooperation in the area of liaisons with foreign countries in the interest of intensifying operations in all spheres. Commissioned Fit[in] and Sorkin to work up the concrete issues and make a report."[1] Following this meeting, Fitin frequently requested information about foreign Communists and others with Comintern links. Both NKVD and GRU exchanges with the Comintern regarding Americans will be examined in this chapter.

Various considerations prompted these inquiries. The NKVD and Soviet military intelligence both used foreign Communist parties as recruiting grounds for agents and had foreign parties act as talent spotters for potential sources. For security reasons, however, both agencies regarded it as desirable for intelligence recruits to sever ties with the Communist party. By contrast, when the Comintern was in operation, Communists had shifted back and forth between Communist political activity and underground work. Dur-

---

1. Georgi Dimitrov's diary entry of 20 August 1941.

ing World War II, the NKVD and the GRU took over the Comintern's various intelligence networks. When the NKVD absorbed a Comintern operation, it reexamined the agents in order to bring the network into compliance with the NKVD's standards of intelligence work. In revetting the networks, the NKVD called upon the files of the Comintern itself for information.

Reproduced here are NKVD and GRU inquiries sent to the Comintern and Comintern replies containing substantive information. The Comintern did not maintain files on ordinary Americans, and the NKVD knew this. Only Americans who had significant contact with some Comintern activity or with the CPUSA would have had a Comintern file. Although an NKVD inquiry alone is not proof either of Communist party membership or of involvement in espionage, it does suggest that the NKVD had some reason to believe that the individual might have had some Communist link. In a number of cases the Comintern reported that it could not find any records about the individual. These negative replies are not reproduced. The Comintern did not maintain files or lists of CPUSA members or even cadre below the level of the CPUSA Central Committee and its major subsidiary bodies, so the number of negative replies is not surprising.

## NKVD and GRU Inquiries about Americans

### Judith Coplon, Soviet Spy

Although mere mention in an NKVD inquiry is not proof that someone was an intelligence agent, it does signify NKVD interest and, when combined with other evidence, may be persuasive. For example, **document 78** is a 1944 NKVD message requesting Comintern data on "*COPLON (Kompid) Judy* works in the US Justice Department." In 1948, American cryptographers in the Venona project (discussed in chapter 6) decoded an NKVD message indicating that a female employee of the FBI was a Soviet agent. The message did not identify the woman by name, but it supplied enough information to enable the FBI to identify the most likely candidate as Judith Coplon in the Justice Department's Foreign Agents Registration Division, an office that worked with FBI counterintelligence. After the FBI turned its attention to Coplon, it discovered that a background security check conducted in 1944 when

Coplon had first gone to work for the Justice Department had shown that she had been a member of a Young Communist League student club as an undergraduate at Barnard College. In 1944 that was not a bar to employment, however, and her personnel file was not even flagged for attention when she transferred to a job giving her access to Justice Department and FBI internal security investigative data regarding Soviet espionage activities.[2]

The FBI placed Coplon under surveillance, and early in 1949 she was arrested when she handed over notes on counterintelligence operations to a Soviet citizen, Valentine Gubitchev, who worked for the United Nations. Coplon was tried and convicted, but her conviction was overturned on a legal technicality that prevented use in court of most of the evidence against her. There was, however, not the slightest doubt of her guilt. Fitin's 1944 inquiry about Coplon suggests that her relationship with Soviet intelligence was of some years' standing.[3]

---

## Document 78

Fitin to Dimitrov, 19 October 1944, RTsKhIDNI 495–74–485. Original in Russian. Helen Tenney is discussed later. Nothing is known of Gerta and Hans Poper. The Comintern had no information on any of the four (Gullaev to Dimitrov, 30 October 1944, RTsKhIDNI 495–74–485).

TOP SECRET.

### To Com. D I M I T R O V

We urgently request any information you have on the following American citizens:

1. *COPLON* [Kompid] *Judy* works in the US Justice Department.
2. *TENNEY Elena* [Helen] works in the Office of Strategic Services.
3. *POPER* [Popper] *Hans* and *POPER* [Popper] *Gerta* living in Dallas.

1/3/18161                                                      (F I T I N)
19 October 1944                                         *Pavel Fitin*
   *To Com. Gulyaev*
   *20 October 1944*
   *GD*

---

2. Robert J. Lamphere and Tom Shachtman, *The FBI-KGB War: A Special Agent's Story* (New York: Random House, 1986), 97–125.

3. Gubitchev was also convicted, but because of his quasi-diplomatic status he was allowed to return to the USSR.

## Albert Feierabend, Soviet Agent

**Document 79**, a 1942 message to Dimitrov from GRU officials, deals with another Soviet agent. It reads: "Please advise us of what data you have at your disposal on the CP USA member Com. FEIERABEND, Albert Ivanovich, who worked on your line from 1928 to 1929 in London and from 1930 to 1932 in Japan, China, and India." Dimitrov's staff could not locate any information on Feierabend in the Comintern's files and, consequently, noted that Bolshakov, the military intelligence official who made the request, "will check on his own network in the USA" about Feierabend.[4] However, located in the American party's own records was a hand-written letter, **document 80**, from A. Brigadier, a Comintern official who served in the Anglo-American Secretariat, confirming Feierabend's engagement in *"special work"* (Communist idiom for clandestine duties) in the mid-1930s.[5]

Albert Feierabend, a Lettish American, had been arrested in 1930 in New York for smuggling. Found in his possession was a small white ribbon upon which was written a note that he was trustworthy and to be accorded all help in his mission. It was signed by Max Bedacht for the CPUSA Secretariat. At the time, Bedacht was one of the CPUSA leaders who worked with the secret apparatus. In 1933 Feierabend was arrested again, this time for using a false passport. On this occasion, he was carrying $28,700 in cash. The State Department, in a later investigation of the CPUSA's use of fraudulent passports, concluded that Feierabend was a courier delivering Comintern funds.[6]

4. Handwritten annotation, "Bolshakov will check on his own network in the USA," Belov memo, 15 July 1942, RTsKhIDNI 495–73–191.

5. As described by Wolfgang Leonhard in chapter 1, the Comintern kept the CPUSA records, but they were not well organized and they became further disordered when they were shipped from Moscow to Ufa in 1941. Leonhard did not reorganize the collection until 1943. It is not surprising that Brigadier's letter did not come to the attention of Dimitrov's staff in 1942.

6. Max Bedacht's role in secret work is discussed in chapter 2. Nicholas Dozenberg, a confessed Soviet spy, said that he had recruited Feierabend to assist him in his work. See Theodore Draper, *American Communism and Soviet Russia* (New York: Viking Press, 1960), 482n.

# Document 79

Bolshakov and Yegorov to Dimitrov, 7 July 1942, RTsKhIDNI 495–73–191. Original in Russian. "Line" was Soviet jargon for a network.

Top secret.
Copy No. 1

E. C. C. I.

—To Com. D I M I T R O V

*To Com. Belov*
*9 July 1942.*
     *G.D.*

Please advise us of what data you have at your disposal on the CP USA member Com. FEIERABEND, Albert Ivanovich, who worked on your line from 1928 to 1929 in London and from 1930 to 1932 in Japan, China, and India.

*Bolshakov* (BOLSHAKOV) *Yegorov* (YEGOROV)

"7" July 1942
No. 66424 pp.
G.Sh.K.A.

*Read. Belov*
*10 July.*

released 2 copies
1st address
2d to file
 ab[?]

# Document 80

Brigadier to Randolph, 3 June 1936, RTsKhIDNI 515–1–3968. Original in English. CCC is the Central Control Commission.

June 3, 1936.

*Com. Randolph:*
   *In your next letter please inform K. Lapin CCC that Albert Feierabend is out on special work. According available information A.F. did not promise to communicate or arrange for his wife going accross when he left the U.S.A., vice versa he informed her that she could look upon herself as "free" and that he made some sort of a money arrangement before leaving. As far as I can gather she is what is called a "gold digger." As there are no children concerned, and as his former wife is not an invalid, I do not understand why it is necessary to make such a fuss over the question.*

*A. Brigadier*

June 3, 1936.

Dear Randolph:

In your next letter please inform K. Lapin CCC that Albert Feierabend is out on special work. According available information A. F. did not promise to communicate or arrange for his wife going accross when he left the U.S.A, vice versa he informed her that she could look upon herself as "free" and that he made some sort of a money arrangement before leaving. As far I can gather she is what is called a "gold digger." As there are no children concerned, and as his former wife is not an invalid, I do not understand why Lapin it is necessary to make such a fuss over the question.

A. Brigadier

41

DOCUMENT 80. Brigadier to Randolph, 3 June 1936.

*Edmund Stevens, Pulitzer Prize–Winning Reporter*

Several of the messages between the Comintern and the NKVD concern an American journalist. Edmund Stevens arrived in the USSR in 1934, a recent graduate of Columbia University. He found work as a translator and editor for a Soviet publishing house and in 1935 married a Soviet citizen. He also began to write for the American-Russian Chamber of Commerce and became a part-time Moscow correspondent for various British newspapers and magazines. He was allowed to purchase a traditionally styled but luxuriously equipped log cabin in Moscow, an extremely unusual privilege granted to only a handful of foreigners. In 1939 he returned to the United States with his Russian wife. That was unusual as well, because in the Stalin era the Soviets rarely allowed Russians, even those who married foreigners, to leave the country. He attributed his success to his friendship with American Ambassador Joseph Davies. Davies, then leaving his post, asked the Soviet foreign minister to grant Nina Stevens an exit visa as a personal going-away gift. Stevens was also allowed to retain ownership of the residence he had bought. Once in the United States, his wife became an American citizen.

Stevens, meanwhile, became a successful war correspondent for the *Christian Science Monitor*. In the latter half of 1942, he took a temporary position as an adviser on Soviet matters to General Russell Maxwell, an American officer accompanying W. Averell Harriman, one of President Roosevelt's most trusted aides, to an August 1942 Moscow conference with Stalin and British Prime Minister Winston Churchill. After the Moscow conference, Stevens returned to reporting and undertook lengthy tours in Russia in 1943 and 1944. In 1945 he published *Russia Is No Riddle,* in which he lavished praise on Stalin, described the USSR governing structure as "a form of democracy, elementary if you will, but more genuine and pure within its limited scope than any American institution except the town meeting, to which in many ways it closely corresponds," and insisted that the Soviet Communist party had "a large degree of inner-Party democracy."[7] Stevens also defended the

7. Edmund Stevens, *Russia Is No Riddle* (New York: Greenberg, 1945), 176.

Nazi-Soviet Pact of 1939 and denounced in harsh terms those Eastern Europeans who resisted Soviet occupation in 1945.

Stevens returned to Moscow in 1946 as resident correspondent for the *Christian Science Monitor*. He left the Soviet Union in 1949 and published a series of forty-four articles, reprinted in book form in 1951 as *This Is Russia—Un-Censored,* that won a Pulitzer Prize.[8] In striking contrast to his 1945 book, this was a highly critical portrait of the last years of Stalin's rule as a harshly oppressive dictatorship in which government-sponsored suspicion and anti-Semitism permeated and degraded society. He added, however, that the Soviet Union had achieved permanence and that the United States needed to offer friendship to its people and reach an understanding with its government. Stevens returned to the USSR after Stalin's death and continued to work as a Moscow correspondent, publishing in a wide variety of Western newspapers and magazines. He retired in Moscow and died there in 1992.[9]

In *The Moscow Correspondents: Reporting on Russia from the Revolution to Glasnost,* Whitman Bassow, himself a former Moscow correspondent, wrote that Stevens's fellow Moscow correspondents

> speculated on Nina's ability to send underground art out of the country for exhibition and sale in New York. They could not understand when the log cabin was demolished by the Moscow municipality to make way for a housing development, Stevens was given a three-story mansion that formerly served as the embassy for an African country. Nor did they comprehend why, during all his years in Moscow, Stevens, unlike most correspondents, was rarely attacked by the Soviet press. . . .
>
> Despite the lack of proof, several correspondents over the years believed that Edmund Stevens had in some way compromised himself with the Soviets and had worked out an arrangement.[10]

Stevens, of course, vehemently denied that his reporting favored the regime or that he was given special treatment.

In July 1942 General Fitin sent a message to Dimitrov regarding

8. Edmund Stevens, *This Is Russia—Un-Censored* (New York: Eaton Books, 1951).

9. Edmund Stevens entry, *Current Biography,* ed. Anna Rothe (New York: H. W. Wilson, 1950), 546–48.

10. Whitman Bassow, *The Moscow Correspondents: Reporting on Russia from the Revolution to Glasnost* (New York: William Morrow, 1988), 320–21.

Stevens, marked "Please do not delay with your reply!" At this time Stevens had become an adviser to General Maxwell and was to accompany Maxwell and Ambassador Harriman to Moscow in August 1942. Fitin's inquiry, **document 81**, was probably prompted by the NKVD's having learned that Stevens would be entering the Soviet Union as part of the Harriman delegation. The Comintern's reply, **document 82**, states that Stevens had been a member of both the Young Communist League and the American Communist party. The Comintern even quoted from a letter of recommendation written by Earl Browder, who considered Stevens's work in the American youth movement "to be satisfactory."

Stevens concealed his membership in the CPUSA throughout his journalistic career. Whether Stevens had an understanding with the Soviet government may never be known, but these documents greatly strengthen the suspicion that he was not a neutral journalist.

---

## Document 81

Fitin to Dimitrov, 8 July 1942, RTsKhIDNI 495–74–485. Original in Russian. Stevens's first name is given as Edward. The Comintern in its reply properly corrects this to Edmund. Comsomol is the Russian term for the Young Communist League. Note NKVD irritation at Stevens's use of Ambassador Davies's influence to get his wife, Nina, out of the Soviet Union. Nothing is known of Gluck, the second Hungarian mentioned in this document. Fitin's reference to Gluck's having "worked on your line" indicates that the NKVD believed Gluck had been employed by the Comintern. Roy Hudson, whom Edith Emery married after divorcing Stevens, was a high-ranking leader of the CPUSA. The Comintern's replies about Emery and Gluck were not found. Emery is discussed later.

---

TOP SECRET

8 July 1942
*To Comrade Belov:*
*Immediately give information*
GD

To the ECCI
To Com. DIMITROV

Please inform us of whatever you may know concerning the following persons:

1. Edward Stevens [name repeated typed in Latin letters], 30–32 years of age, purportedly a former leader of the American Comsomol, currently chairman. Around 1932 was in the USSR, where he married a Soviet citizen whose

## Document 81 *continued*

name is unknown. In view of the latter's being denied legal exit from the USSR, STEVENS organized her illegal passage to the U.S.

2. Edith (Ondra) EMERY, a.k.a. EMERVY [name repeated typed in Latin letters], 40–43 years of age, Hungarian, former wife of STEVENS. Was in the USSR. While in Hungary purportedly led a Catholic women's organization. Currently married to a member of the CPUSA CC Politburo, Roy B. HUDSON.

3. GLUCK [name repeated typed in Latin letters], male Hungarian, a close acquaintance of Edith EMERY. Purportedly worked in your network in a number of European countries and the U.S.

All the above-named persons currently reside in the U.S.

Please do not delay with your reply!

Fitin

(F I T I N)

8 July 1942
1/3/6346

---

## Document 82

Vilkov memo on Stevens, Edmund, 21 July 1942, RTsKhIDNI 495–74–485. Original in Russian. Vilkov's memo was conveyed to the NKVD in Dimitrov to Fitin, 5 August 1942, RTsKhIDNI 495–74–485. Original in Russian. Stevens was the subject of Comintern scrutiny again in 1943 (Belov to Dimitrov, 16 May 1943, RTsKhIDNI 495–74–485).

Top Secret

INFORMATION

STEVENS, Edmund Edmundovich, b. 1910, Denver (USA). American, U.S. citizen, higher education. By profession an editor and translator, knows English, Italian, French and Russian.

A member of the CPUSA since 1938, member of YCLUSA since 1931. In 1926 he belonged to a school organization of Italian fascists for 2 months in Rome.

Comrade Earl Browder, the general secretary of the CPUSA, wrote in a letter dated 26 [?] January 1938: "I knew Edmund Stevens when he was working in the American youth movement, and I found his work to be satisfactory. For our part there are no objections to his being given work in Moscow, where he could be useful."

He arrived in the USSR in 1934 on the invitation of the Foreign Language Literature Publishing House, through Trachtenberg, and worked for the publishing house as an editor in the English section until 30 January 1937; dismissed because of staff cuts.

We have no more recent information about him.

Source: personal file materials.

K. *Vilkov*

(K. V I L K O V)

21 July 1942

---

*Veterans of the International Brigades*

Several of the NKVD inquiries deal with American veterans of the Spanish Civil War. **Documents 83 and 84** are inquiries about Alfred Tanz and Fred Thompson, **document 85** about Paul Burns, and **document 86** about Samuel Krafsur. There is no evidence that these people worked for the NKVD, but two of the names in this group, Alfred Tanz and Paul Burns, also appear in a document found in the International Brigades records. **Document 87** is an excerpt from the 1937 memo, labeled top secret and written in Russian, regarding nine Americans, one Canadian, and one Dutchman who were judged to be politically reliable and qualified for unspecified organizational-technical work.[11]

Frederick Thompson provides another dramatic example of how the most unlikely people could become enmeshed in the secret world of American communism. He was the scion of an old and distinguished California family; his father, a wealthy banker, was an early president of the elite Bohemian Club in San Francisco. His sister was the novelist Kathleen Norris; a brother-in-law was the writer William Rose Benét. Fred Thompson fought with Pancho Villa, built ships during World War I, was elected as a supervisor in Marin County, California (he resigned to attend the coronation of George VI of Great Britain), and described himself in the 1930s as a retired capitalist and Bohemian Club member. When the Spanish Civil War broke out, his son David joined the International Brigades and was wounded in Spain. Thompson then went to Paris and organized a distinguished committee of Americans to arrange the return of wounded and demobilized Lincoln battalion veterans to

---

11. On the activities of Tanz and Burns in the Spanish Civil War, see Arthur Landis, *The Abraham Lincoln Brigade* (New York: Citadel Press, 1967), for Tanz: 18, 33, 38, 242, 500; for Burns: 34, 66, 162, 193, 206, 207, 242.

the United States, a task he portrayed as a spontaneous human-
itarian action.[12]

Document 84 makes clear, however, that Thompson was a secret
member of the CPUSA and his activity in France had been an assignment from the party. Whether the NKVD inquiry in 1943 means
that he took on other secret assignments is not known. In any event,
his fellow capitalists in the Bohemian Club would surely have been
startled to learn about their colleague's secret life.

---

## Document 83

Dimitrov to Fitin, 27 March 1943, RTsKhIDNI 495–74–485. Reply to Fitin to Dimitrov, 23
February 1943, RTsKhIDNI 495–74–485. Original in Russian. MOPR is the Russian acronym for International Red Aid, an organization that provided assistance to jailed Communists and radicals.

Top Secret

To Comrade FITIN:
    In reply to your inquiry dated 23 February of this year, No. 1/2/2234, our
information on Alfredo TANZ is as follows:
    TANZ, Alfredo—b. in 1906 in America. American. By profession a lawyer.
Member of the CPUSA since 1935. Was a member of the American Workers'
Alliance and a member of MOPR. In January of 1937 voluntarily joined the
ranks of the Inter[national] Brigades in Spain. Served in the quartermaster's
department of the Lincoln Brigade. Took part in battles on the Jarama, Bru-
nette, and Ebro. Wounded in battle in the Sierra Kanallo. Consequently transferred out of the battalion for health reasons and recommended for other work
in the rear.

(G. Dimitrov)

27 March 1943
No. 236

---

12. Frederick Thompson obituary, *San Francisco Chronicle*, 11 August 1965.

# Document 84

Fitin to Dimitrov, 6 May 1943, RTsKhIDNI 495–74–485. Original in Russian. The Comintern had no substantive information about Thompson (Belov and Plyshevsky to Dimitrov, 8 May 1943, RTsKhIDNI 495–74–485).

To the ECCI
To Com. DIMITROV

Please inform us of whatever you may know concerning a covert member of the CPUSA, Fred Thompson, b. 1883, American national, residing in San Francisco.

From 1937 to 1939, on assignment from the American Comparty, Thompson headed a commission in Paris for the evacuation of American fighters who had been in action in Spain.

Please do not delay with your reply.

(FITIN)
Fitin

1/3/5354
6 May 1943
6 May 1943
*To Comrades Belov and Plyshevsky:*
*Investigate immediately and give information*
*GD*
8 *May 1943 Plyshevsky*
*On this issue also make inquiries of Comrades Marty and Andrei [?]*
*GD*

---

# Document 85

Fitin to Dimitrov, 19 August 1944, RTsKhIDNI 495–74–485. Original in Russian. No reply to this message was located. Nothing is known about Louis Horvitz. "Conspiritized" (*zakonspirirovannykh*) is an unusual term suggesting someone initiated into a secret order, not merely a secret member of the CPUSA.

To Com. DIMITROV:

Please report immediately whatever information you have on the conspiritized members of the Comparty of the USA, Louis D. Horvitz (works in a judicial office), and *Paul Burns* (social worker). Both reside in New York.

(Fitin)
Fitin

19 August 1944
No. 1/2/14082

# Document 86

Fitin to Dimitrov, 12 September 1944, RTsKhIDNI 495–74–485. Original in Russian. The Comintern had no information about Krafsur (Guliaev to Dimitrov, 22 September 1944, RTsKhIDNI 495–74–485; Dimitrov to Fitin, 23 September 1944, RTsKhIDNI 495–74–485).

To Com. DIMITROV:

Please report immediately whatever information you have on the worker in the New York division of Tass, Krafsur, Samuel, b. 1913, a native of Boston, member of the Communist party since 1934, in the Lincoln Brigade in Spain in 1937.

1/3/15593 (FITIN)

12 September 1944

# Document 87

Excerpts from "Report on Americans," 27 September 1937, RTsKhIDNI 545–3–453. Original in Russian.

## Report on Americans

BURNS, PAUL. American, 31. In Spain since 14 January 1937. A CP member for many years, a writer and teacher by profession. Was active in the CP and Writers' Union in America. Single.

This comrade was in the Lincoln battalion on the Jarama front and has taken part in all battles since February. Took part in Madrid offensive. Wounded. Rank of company commander.

Respected by all in the Lincoln battalion. Politically he is sound. A reliable and honest member of the party.

Suitable for organizational work.

Currently in Roseville in an American hospital.

. . .

TANZ, ALFREDO L. American, 31. Member of CP USA since 1935. Arrived in Spain 6 January 37. A quartermaster for the whole time in the quartermaster service of the Lincoln battalion. He was withdrawn from the battalion and recommended for other work in the rear because of physical exhaustion.

This comrade is reliable and will do well in organizational-technical work. He is now in Albacete.

## OSS and State Department Employees

In **documents 88 and 89,** General Fitin asks for Comintern records on three employees of the United States government: Lillian Hoell of the OSS, Marion Davis of the American embassy in Mexico, and "(female) TRAUGOTT, . . . employed by the American mission in Stockholm." Nothing is known of Davis and Hoell. Traugott, however, was Lillian S. Traugott, an officer in the labor division of the OSS, which worked with underground labor unions and left-of-center political bodies in occupied Europe. She served in OSS offices in New York, London, and, at the time of this message, Stockholm. In mid-1945 she received orders to establish OSS contact with Norwegian labor leaders, who were engaged in rebuilding unions suppressed during the German occupation. Traugott's assignment was to learn the extent of and attitudes "toward local Communist Party efforts to increase its influence in trade unions," an assignment she was unlikely to have received had her OSS superiors been aware of her Communist background.[13] Lillian Traugott, due to her background and in light of what the documents in this volume show, must be considered a likely target for a Soviet recruitment attempt. There is, however, no evidence that she, Davis, or Hoell were ever approached by the NKVD.

---

## Document 88

Fitin to Dimitrov, 29 September 1944, RTsKhIDNI 495–74–485. Original in Russian. The Comintern did not have any information about Hoell, Davis, or Stoklitsky. It did have information about Davidovskaya. Because she was a Soviet citizen with no apparent American connection, however, the information is not included here (Dimitrov to Fitin, 17 October 1944, RTsKhIDNI 495–74–485).

---

To Comrade Tunov
GD
30 September 1944                                    TOP SECRET

To Com. DIMITROV:

Please report immediately whatever information you have on the [following] American citizens:

1. Lillian Hoell, an employee of the Office of Strategic Services.

13. George Pratt to Lillian Traugott, Oslo assignment, 11 June 1945, OSS field

## Document 88 *continued*

2. <u>Marion Davis</u>, an employee of the American embassy in Mexico, and on the Soviet citizens <u>Sof'ia DAVIDOVSKAYA</u> a physician by profession, residing in Moscow, and <u>Leonard STOKLITSKY</u>, who works on the editorial board of the "Moscow News."

Fitin

(FITIN)

No. 1/3/16895

<u>29 September 1944</u>

---

## Document 89

Fitin to Dimitrov, 17 November 1944, RTsKhIDNI 495–74–485. Original in Russian. Dimitrov did not have any information on Traugott (Guliaev to Dimitrov, 30 November 1944, RTsKhIDNI 495–74–485).

---

$N=897$      TOP SECRET

<u>To Comrade DIMITROV</u>

Please report whatever you know about the American citizen (female) TRAUGOTT, currently employed by the American mission in Stockholm.

TRAUGOTT, supposedly a member of the Comparty since 1937, in the spring of 1942 worked in the Secretariat of the Quakers in Philadelphia. Her brother is an active member of the Comparty in New York.

FITIN

<u>17 November 1944</u>

No. <u>1/2/19697</u>

*To Com. Guliaev*

<u>19 November 1944</u>

<u>GD</u>

<u>Prepare a report</u>

20 Nov.

[illegible signature]

---

files, record group 226, entry 190, box 326, folder 545, National Archives. Pratt told Traugott that later she would go to Paris as one of the OSS's contacts with the founding convention of the World Federation of Trade Unions. Other information on Traugott's OSS work is in Traugott to Sydney Clarke, 28 January 1943, Donald Downes OSS papers, record group 226, entry 136A, box 5, folder 95; Traugott to William Carlson, 27 August 1945, record group 226, entry 190, box 326, folder 538; I. S. Dorfman to William J. Casey for Lillian S. Traugott of Kitten Mission, 28 June 1945, record group 226, entry 190, box 326, folder 538, National Archives.

## Elizabeth Bentley and the Perlo Group

Several of the NKVD inquiries strongly support Elizabeth Bentley's stories of espionage by secret members of the American Communist party. History has not been kind to Bentley. When the brown-haired, somewhat plump, unfashionably dressed forty-year-old testified to a congressional committee in 1948, a newspaper headline, with more concern for drama than accuracy in regard to her hair color, read: "Red Ring Bared by Its Blond Queen." Her critics ever after mocked Bentley as the "Blond Spy Queen." The *Nation*, a Popular Front liberal journal of the era, denounced her testimony as "smears" and as "such wanton charges as hardly seem worth the dignity of denial." In the *New Yorker*, A. J. Liebling denounced the press for even noticing this "Nutmeg Mata Hari." *Newsweek* patronized her, dismissing her as a "New England spinster . . . wearing slinky black silk."[14]

Nor have historians been much more generous. Although allowing that some of her story might be true, Herbert Packer said, "No witness's story is better calculated to inspire mistrust or disbelief than Elizabeth Bentley's. The extravagance of her claims about her espionage contacts, the vagueness of her testimony about the content of the secret material that she allegedly received, the absence of corroboration for most of her story, and above all, her evasiveness as a witness, all combine to raise serious doubts about her reliability."[15] David Caute painted her as unbelievable.[16] Although Earl Latham found Bentley's story credible, he presented the consensus view: Bentley's charges were the "imaginings of a neurotic spinster."[17]

14. *New York World Telegram,* 21 July 1948; "The Shape of Things," *Nation,* 7 August 1948, 141; A. J. Liebling, "The Wayward Press," *New Yorker,* 28 August 1948, 42; *Newsweek,* 9 August 1948, 19–20.

15. Herbert L. Packer, *Ex-Communist Witnesses: Four Studies in Fact Finding* (Stanford, Calif.: Stanford University Press, 1962), 222.

16. Caute underscored his doubt about Bentley's veracity by injecting skeptical qualifiers such as "at least, this is what she said happened" in his description of her story (David Caute, *The Great Fear: The Anti-Communist Purge under Truman and Eisenhower* [New York: Simon and Schuster, 1978], 56).

17. Earl Latham, *The Communist Controversy in Washington: From the New Deal to McCarthy* (Cambridge: Harvard University Press, 1966), 160. In a reissue of Elizabeth Bentley's autobiography, *Out of Bondage* (New York: Ivy Books, 1988), the writer Hayden Peake included a 112-page afterword that brought together evidence supporting Bentley's story and rebutted attacks on her testimony.

Bentley's saga, told first to the FBI in 1945, then to congressional committees in 1948 and in her autobiography, *Out of Bondage,* was an extraordinary one. After attending Vassar and doing graduate work at Columbia, she joined the Communist party in 1935— or "so she said," to use Caute's ever distrustful phrasing.[18] In 1938 she took a job at an Italian information center with links to Italy's fascist government and began to inform on its activities to Jacob Golos, a high official of the American Communist party and secretly a Soviet intelligence agent. In 1940 the U.S. government charged that Golos and his firm, World Tourists, were fronts for the Soviet government. Golos escaped with a plea-bargain conviction for failing to register as an agent of the USSR.

Bentley, who had become Golos's lover, also became courier to his agents. In late 1943, Golos died of a heart attack. Bentley then became the link between his several rings of informants in Washington and the CPUSA. The NKVD, however, put the Golos-Bentley espionage rings under direct NKVD control in 1944 and 1945. The Golos-Bentley networks typified the type of trade craft the NKVD mistrusted. The Golos-Bentley agents were secret members of the American Communist party employed by various government agencies. Bentley both collected intelligence information from them and supervised their secret participation in the Communist party by collecting dues, delivering party literature, and even allowing them to meet together to discuss party policies. To the NKVD, this practice was unnecessarily risky.

Pushed out of secret work by the NKVD, her lover dead, and fearing that the FBI was closing in, Bentley turned herself in to the FBI in August 1945. She named more than forty persons employed by a wide variety of government agencies who had given her information of varying sensitivity. Unlike Whittaker Chambers, who validated his story about Alger Hiss by producing microfilm and papers he had hidden, Bentley could provide only her testimony. In a number of cases, she also described a secondhand relationship, noting that she had received information directly from key members of a ring of agents who had received it from other members of the ring who did not deal directly with her. The FBI produced circumstantial evidence that corroborated Bentley's story but little direct

18. Caute, *Great Fear,* 56.

evidence of espionage—nothing like Chambers's production of U.S. State Department memoranda that had crossed Hiss's desk, documents in his handwriting, or copies of confidential government documents that, according to experts, had been typed on Hiss's typewriter. Chambers had saved the documents as insurance against Soviet retaliation when he decided to break with Soviet intelligence in 1938. Apart from these documents, the case against Hiss came down to Chambers's word against Hiss's. But the documentary evidence was persuasive, and Hiss was convicted. Bentley, however, had kept no documents.

Most of those named by Bentley refused to answer questions under oath about her story, standing on their constitutional right not to make statements that might incriminate themselves. With such limited evidence, only two persons named by Bentley were imprisoned, Edward J. Fitzgerald and William Remington. Fitzgerald is a special case. The government gave him immunity from prosecution when he was questioned. He still refused to testify but, being unable to make use of the Fifth Amendment, was jailed for his refusal. Therefore, Fitzgerald's conviction did not provide a clear test of Bentley's claims.

William Remington did not use the Fifth Amendment. He admitted meeting with Bentley and Golos but described the information he gave them as innocuous. He was convicted and imprisoned for perjury. Yet, according to Bentley, Remington was not a very important source, so the espionage aspects of his case were not dramatic, and his perjury conviction in large part revolved around his testimony that he had not been a Communist and the willingness of his ex-wife to testify against him. Further, serious procedural irregularities in Remington's original indictment and first trial resulted in a retrial. He was convicted once more, but in the eyes of Bentley's critics the original irregularities tainted the entire enterprise.

The fact that Bentley named dozens of government employees as Soviet intelligence sources, yet only two convictions resulted from her evidence, undercut her credibility. Various activities that she undertook after making the accusations also enraged her critics and were seen as signs of her untrustworthiness. Her autobiography, *Out of Bondage*, was ghostwritten, sensationalistic, and aimed at a quick commercial return on her notoriety. It contained a number of minor chronological or factual errors and verbatim conversations that, on examination, proved to be reconstructions of conversations rather than real quotations. (According to her critics the conversations were fiction.) Many of her critics also found Bentley's conversion to Roman Catholicism offensive; Caute, in his influential *The Great Fear,* called Bentley one of the "most conspicuous" of the church's "publicity-conscious converts."[19]

Three of the memos from Fitin to Dimitrov, however, support Bentley's story. In her autobiography, Bentley asserted that in the late fall of 1944 she met with her NKVD contact, who told her, "We have at last decided what to do about all the contacts that Golos handled. You cannot, obviously, continue to handle them; the setup is too full of holes and therefore too dangerous. I'm afraid our friend Golos was not too cautious a man, and there is the risk that you, because of your connection with him, may endanger the apparatus. You will therefore turn them over to us; we will look into their backgrounds thoroughly and decide which ones we will keep."[20] Documents 90, 91, and 78, all dating from September and October of 1944, fit precisely with the story Bentley told in *Out of Bondage.*

**Document 90** is a "TOP SECRET" memo in which General Fitin wrote, "Please provide any information at your disposal on the following members of the Comparty of America." Fitin then listed seven names, "1. *Charles . . . Flato,* in 1943 worked in the US Office of Economic Warfare 2. *Donald Wheeler . . . ,* works in the Office of Strategic Services. 3. *Kramer / Kreimer,* works in a government institution in Washington. 4. *Edward Fitzgerald,* works on the WPB [War Production Board]. 5. *Magdoff,* works on the WPB. 6. *Harold Glas[s]er,* currently on assignment outside the U.S. 7. *P[e]rlo,* works on the WPB." All seven men were employed as Fitin said. Glasser worked for the Treasury Department and was on assignment in various foreign nations during World War II. Charles

---

19. Her conversion was one of the items that inspired Caute to denounce the Roman Catholic church in America for producing "not so much poets, scholars, scientists and artists as security officers, immigration officers, policemen, customs officers and prison wardens"; the latter professions were apparently unsavory in Caute's view (Caute, *Great Fear,* 108–9).

20. Bentley, *Out of Bondage,* 184.

Kramer was on the staff of the U.S. Senate Subcommittee on War Mobilization.[21]

Of the seven names in this message, Elizabeth Bentley named six of them, Wheeler, Kramer, Fitzgerald, Harry Magdoff, Glasser, and Victor Perlo, as sources from whom she received espionage material. The six were members of a ring of eight agents that Bentley called the Perlo group after its chief figure. A seventh member of Bentley's Perlo group was Allan Rosenberg. Bentley also said that she had taken over supervision of the Perlo group from John Abt. Both Rosenberg and Abt are discussed in chapter 3 in regard to secret Communists who worked for the La Follette committee and the NLRB. Charles Flato, about whom Fitin also inquired in document 90, was not named by Bentley as a Soviet source, but he had also been a secret Communist working for the La Follette committee.[22]

---

## Document 90

Fitin to Dimitrov, 28/29 September 1944, RTsKhIDNI 495–74–485. Original in Russian. The Comintern had no information on Flato, Wheeler, Fitzgerald, Magdoff, Glasser, or Perlo (Dimitrov to Fitin, 18 October 1944, RTsKhIDNI 495–74–485; and Guliaev to Dimitrov, 17 October 1944, RTsKhIDNI 495–74–485). Fitin did not provide a first name for Kramer, so the Comintern provided information on a Myron Kramer. This Kramer, however, immigrated to the USSR in 1934 and worked in a tractor factory in Cheliabinsk (Vilkov and Kozlova report on Myron Kramer, 7 October 1944, RTsKhIDNI 495–74–485). This was not the Kramer whom Fitin identified as working in a government institution in Washington. "WPB" for War Production Board is a translation of the Russian acronym UDVP (Upravlenie delami voennogo proizvodstva [Board of War Production Affairs]).

---

TOP SECRET.

### To Com. D I M I T R O V

Please provide any information at your disposal on the following members of the Comparty of America:

1. _Charles Floto / Flato /,_ in 1943 worked in the US Office of Economic Warfare
2. _Donald Wheeler / Veeler /,_ works in the Office of Strategic Services.
3. _Kramer / Kreimer,_ works in a government institution in Washington.
4. _Edward Fitzgerald,_ works on the WPB [War Production Board].
5. _Magdoff,_ works on the WPB.

21. Kramer was born Krivitsky and changed his name in 1935.
22. Charles Flato, not named by Bentley or anyone else as a spy, testified to Congress that he had never passed information to the Soviets, but he refused to

# Document 90 *continued*

6. *Harold Glas[s]er,* currently on assignment outside the US.
7. *P[e]rlo,* works on the WPB.
1/3/16796

F I T I N.
*P. Fitin*

<u>28/29 September 1944</u>

<u>To Comrade Guliaev</u> *29 September 1944 GD*

answer questions about Communist party membership or participation in secret Communist caucuses while a government employee (Flato testimony, 19 May 1953, Senate Subcommittee to Investigate the Administration of the Internal Security Act, *Interlocking Subversion in Government Departments,* 83d Cong., 1st sess., 6 May 1953, pt. 8:487–544).

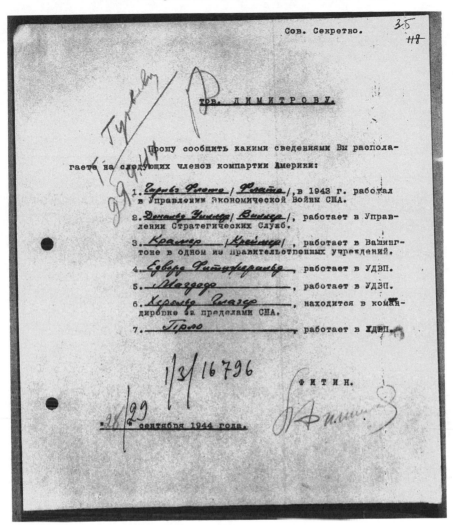

Сов. Секретно.

тов. ДИМИТРОВУ.

Прошу сообщить какими сведениями Вы располагаете на следующих членов компартии Америки:

1. *Гарвэ Флэто* / *Флэта* /, в 1943 г. работал в Управлении Экономической Войны США.

2. *Дональд Уиллер* / *Вилер* /, работает в Управлении Стратегических Служб.

3. *Крамер* / *Креймер* /, работает в Вашингтоне в одном из правительственных учреждений.

4. *Эдвард Фитцджеральд*, работает в УДВП.

5. *Магдофф*, работает в УДВП.

6. *Хэролд Глэссэр*, находится в командировке за пределами США.

7. *Перло*, работает в УДВП.

1/3/16796

Ф И Т И Н.

28/29 сентября 1944 года.

DOCUMENT 90. Fitin to Dimitrov, 28/29 September 1944.

In **document 91** Fitin asked for information about "*Bursler, Norman,*" a former member of the CPUSA, currently working in the U.S. Ministry of Justice." Document 78, introduced earlier, includes a request for information on "TENNEY *Elena* [*Helen*] works in the Office of Strategic Services." Bentley named Bursler as a member of a second spy ring, the Silvermaster group, and named Tenney as a singleton agent whom she ran directly.[23]

## Document 91

Fitin to Dimitrov, 5 November 1944, RTsKhIDNI 495–74–485. Original in Russian. The Comintern had no information on Bursler (Dimitrov to Fitin, 21 November 1944, RTsKhIDNI 495–74–485).

TOP SECRET

To Com. DIMITROV:

Please check and report whatever information you have on *Bursler, Norman,* a former member of the CPUSA, currently working in the U.S. Ministry of Justice.

Fitin<br>(FITIN)

5 November 1944
No. 1/3/19142
*To Comrade Guliaev*

GD
*5 November 1944*

Fitzgerald, Glasser, Kramer, Perlo, Magdoff, Wheeler, and Tenney were called by congressional committees to testify about Bentley's charges. All refused to answer, citing their right under the Fifth Amendment not to give testimony that might incriminate themselves.[24] Perlo, who refused to answer questions about Communist

23. Tenney worked in the Spanish and Balkan division of the OSS, the division in which the stolen OSS report, document 75, originated.

24. Fitzgerald testimony, 1 May 1953, pt. 5:241–86; Glasser testimony, 14 April 1953, pt. 2:53, 90, 99; Kramer testimony, 6 May 1953, pt. 6:327–79; Perlo testimony, 12 May 1953, pt. 7:383–459; Magdoff testimony, 1 May 1953, pt. 5:286–326; Tenney testimony, 16 June 1953, pt. 12:772–86, all in Senate Subcommittee to Investigate the Administration of the Internal Security Act, *Interlocking Subversion in Government Departments;* Wheeler testimony, House Committee on Un-American Activities, *Investigations of Communist Activities in San Francisco Area—Part 1* (1 December 1953), 83d Cong., 1st sess., 1954, 3138–53.

party membership, told a congressional committee that he had only been "helping in my humble way to carry out the great New Deal program under the leadership of Franklin D. Roosevelt," a description later echoed by a prominent critic of Bentley's, Victor Navasky of the *Nation,* who called Perlo a "New Deal economist." Some years after the Bentley controversy died down, however, *Political Affairs,* the theoretical journal of the American Communist party, proudly described Perlo, not as a New Deal Democrat, but, instead, as "chairman of the Economic Commission of the CPUSA."[25]

These three Fitin memos do not verify all of Bentley's story. They name only eight of the more than forty persons Bentley named as her informants within the U.S. government. Nor do the memos standing alone show that the eight provided information to Soviet intelligence. They do indicate, however, that the NKVD regarded seven of those named by Bentley as Communist party members (as she had said), that the NKVD had an interest in eight of those she named, and that the NKVD's interest coincided with the period in which Bentley said the NKVD was taking over and revetting the Golos espionage networks. Assuredly, the NKVD was not asking the Comintern for information about American government employees chosen at random. It could not be mere coincidence that in 1944 the head of the foreign intelligence directorate of the NKVD instituted inquiries about eight persons whom Elizabeth Bentley named as Soviet sources in secret testimony to the FBI a year later. Despite her dismissal as a "New England spinster . . . wearing slinky black silk," Elizabeth Bentley knew what she was talking about.

## The Credibility of Whittaker Chambers

Bentley's story, as sensational as it was, was overshadowed by Whittaker Chambers's accusation that Alger Hiss, a high-ranking State Department official, had engaged in espionage. The stories of Elizabeth Bentley and Whittaker Chambers overlap. The underground

25. Perlo testimony, 9 August 1948, House Committee on Un-American Activities, *Hearings Regarding Communist Espionage in the United States Government,* 80th Cong., 2d sess., 1948, 699–700; Victor Navasky, "The Case Not Proved against Alger Hiss," *Nation,* 8 April 1978, 395–96; Victor Perlo, "Imperialism— New Features," *Political Affairs* (May 1981): 3.

Communists whom Chambers knew in the mid-1930s were working for Soviet intelligence in the early 1940s, according to Bentley. In fact, Chambers was initially called to testify only to corroborate part of Bentley's testimony.

Chambers's allegations concerning J. Peters and the Communist underground in Washington, D.C., in the 1930s were true, as documents 24–33 show. Several of these Fitin messages provide support for other aspects of Chambers's story as well. Chambers first brought his story to the attention of government officials in 1939. After the Nazi-Soviet Pact, the anti-Communist journalist Isaac Don Levine arranged a meeting between Chambers and Adolph Berle, assistant secretary of state. Berle handled many internal security matters for President Roosevelt at the time. Chambers warned Berle that there was a network of secret Communist informants in Washington, and he named Alger Hiss and, among others, Charles Kramer and Marion Bachrach. Chambers also later identified Kramer as a member of the Ware group of secret Communist professionals at the Agricultural Adjustment Administration in 1933 and 1934. Document 90 identifies Kramer for the first time as a CPUSA member and lends credence to Chambers's claim.

Marion Bachrach was John Abt's sister. In 1937 and 1938 she was the personal secretary to Representative John T. Bernard, a Farmer-Labor party congressman from Minnesota and an avid supporter of the Popular Front alliance of a segment of liberals with the Communist party. After Bernard's defeat in 1938, Bachrach worked as a journalist, including a stint as the Washington correspondent for *PM*, a liberal New York City newspaper. In **document 92** Dimitrov replies to an earlier Fitin inquiry about Bachrach, stating that she is a party member—again corroborating Chambers's statements.[26]

26. Hope Hale Davis, a former Communist and member of the party's Washington underground in the 1930s, also later identified Bachrach as one of the secret Communists with whom she worked. See Hope Hale Davis, "Looking Back at My Years in the Party," *New Leader*, 11 February 1980. In his 1993 memoir, John Abt said that Harold Ware had recruited his sister Marion into the CPUSA (John Abt, with Michael Myerson, *Advocate and Activist: Memoirs of an American Communist Lawyer* [Champaign: University of Illinois Press, 1993], 40–41). Abt married the widow of Hal Ware.

# Document 92

Dimitrov to Fitin, 20 November 1942, RTsKhIDNI 495–74–484. Original in Russian. This is in reply to a Fitin to Dimitrov message of 2 November 1942 that was not found.

Top Secret.

To Com. FITIN.

In reply to your No. 1/3/11315, of 2 November 1942:

Here is the information we have received from our American comrades on BACHRACH, Marion.

BACHRACH, Marion—American, approximately forty years of age, born into a wealthy Washington family, an American citizen, member of the CPUSA. Has a disabled husband and a grown son.

Until 1938, Marion Bachrach worked as personal secretary to Barnard, a progressive US congressman. In 1938, due to Barnard's losing his re-election bid, she was dismissed from this position and began working as the Washington correspondent for the newspaper "PM." After "PM" began taking a more conservative line, she was dismissed from her position at the newspaper on the grounds that her correspondence during the Soviet war with Finland had been "too radical." [Afterward] she nevertheless wrote occasionally for that newspaper.

In 1940 Marion Bachrach published a weekly, "Letters from Washington."

According to the comments of [her] American comrades, Marion Bachrach is a good and politically competent journalist.

(G. DIMITROV)

20 November 1942

N 663

When Chambers described the Washington Communist underground of the mid-1930s to the FBI, he mentioned one woman whose name he remembered as Andre Embrey. (Her name never came up in public testimony.) Chambers remembered Embrey as a Hungarian and the girlfriend of Communist labor leader Roy Hudson. He recalled that she was a secret Communist, who worked for the Bureau of Indian Affairs in 1933–1934. Embrey's female roommate, whose name Chambers could not remember, took over his role as the courier between J. Peters and the Ware group. In document 81, General Fitin asks the Comintern for information about a woman named "Edith (Ondra) EMERY," a Hungarian once married to Edmund Stevens but now the wife of Roy Hudson. Clearly, Fitin's

"Ondra Emery" and Chambers's "Andre Embrey" were one and the same.[27]

In addition to Kramer, Bachrach, and Emery, two other individuals named by Chambers are also the subjects of Fitin's inquiries: Victor Perlo and Harold Glasser, both listed in document 90. Chambers identified Perlo as a member of the Ware group and Glasser as a secret party member whom the Washington Communist underground placed in the Treasury Department. In total, five people named by Chambers either in 1939 or after World War II as members of the Washington Communist underground in the mid-1930s are the subjects of NKVD inquiries in 1942 or 1944.[28]

The overlap between the stories told by Chambers and Bentley is vividly illustrated by a passage from Bentley's confidential statement to the FBI in 1945, in which she names three of those who played prominent roles in Chambers's story:

> Referring again to Harold Glasser, I recall that after his return from his assignment in Europe, probably in Italy, for the United States Treasury Department, Victor Perlo told me that Glasser had asked him if he would be able to get back in with the Perlo group. I asked Perlo how Glasser happened to leave the group and he explained that Glasser and one or two others had been taken sometime before by some American in some governmental agency in Washington, and that this unidentified American turned Glasser and the others over to some Russian. Perlo declared he did not know the identity of this American, and said that

27. The FBI showed Chambers a photograph of Emery, and he identified her as the woman he remembered as Embrey (Chambers, "Statement to the Federal Bureau of Investigation," 11 May 1949, reproduced in Edith Tiger, ed., *In Re Alger Hiss: Petition for a Writ of Error Coram Nobis* [New York: Hill and Wang, 1979], 79–80). Emery divorced Edmund Stevens in Moscow in 1935 and married Hudson in 1936. After World War II, she functioned as an open party member (House Committee on Un-American Activities, *Exposure of the Communist Party of Pennsylvania*, 81st Cong., 2d sess., 23 February 1950 and 28 September 1950, 1257–59, 3057). Hudson was close to Earl Browder and failed to disavow him quickly enough when Moscow turned against Browder in 1945. He was banished from the national leadership and assigned first to Pittsburgh and then to San Francisco. After Stalin's 1949 purge of the Hungarian Communist leadership, California Communists demanded that Hudson disassociate himself from his wife on the grounds that her aristocratic Hungarian family background made her suspect. Hudson refused and was expelled from the CPUSA (Dorothy Healey and Maurice Isserman, *Dorothy Healey Remembers: A Life in the American Communist Party* [New York: Oxford University Press, 1990], 131).

28. Three persons (Perlo, Kramer, and Glasser) were identified by both Chambers and Bentley.

Charley Kramer, so far as he knew, was the only person who had this information. Sometime later I was talking with Kramer in New York City, and brought up this matter to him. At this time Kramer told me that the person who had originally taken Glasser away from Perlo's group was named Hiss and that he was in the U.S. State Department.[29]

The evidence against Alger Hiss was sufficient to convict him in 1950; subsequent documentation has further substantiated the case that Hiss was a spy.[30] Nevertheless, Hiss's defenders have continued to attack Whittaker Chambers's credibility and have clung to the belief that there was no Communist underground in Washington or that, if one did exist, it was not involved in espionage. Documents 81, 90, and 92, taken together with documents 24–33, demonstrate the existence of a long-standing Communist party underground with direct ties to the NKVD. It had also managed to penetrate America's own intelligence service (documents 71, 74, and 75) and to assist in stealing America's atomic secrets (documents 58 and 59). These documents do not prove that Alger Hiss was engaged in espionage; indeed, his name never occurs. What these documents do demonstrate, however, is the accuracy of the story told by the chief witness against Hiss, thus greatly strengthening the credibility of that witness. Hiss's guilt may never be unequivocally proved to everyone's satisfaction, but this new documentation provides a dramatically new standpoint from which to assess the evidence against him.

29. Elizabeth Bentley, "Statement to the Federal Bureau of Investigation, 30 November 1945," FOIA document.

30. Allen Weinstein, *Perjury: The Hiss-Chambers Case* (New York: Knopf, 1978), has written the definitive history of the case, in which he concludes that Hiss was guilty.

# CHAPTER NINE

# Conclusion

IN THE PARABLE OF THE CAVE in *The Republic,* Plato suggests that most people are like prisoners in a cave, chained and confined so that they cannot turn around. Behind them is a fire, and between them and the fire, a puppet show is taking place. The prisoners see the shadows reflected on the walls of the cave, but they are unable to see the puppets themselves, nor can they see the fire. They assume that the images they see on the walls are real. For these people, "truth is nothing other than the shadows of artificial things." How, Plato asked, would people react when they were released from their chains and allowed to turn around, if they were told that now they "see more correctly"? They would, says Plato, be at a loss and would think that the shadows they had seen before were more real. If compelled to look at the light itself, would their eyes hurt and would they flee, turning away to those things they are able to make out and consider them to be clearer than what is shown? And if someone taken out to see the sun were to be brought back into the cave, "wouldn't he be the source of laughter and wouldn't it be said of him that he went up and came back with his eyes corrupted, and that it's not even worth trying to go up? And if they were somehow able to get their hands on and kill the man who attempts to release and lead [them] up, wouldn't they kill him?"[1]

1. *The Republic of Plato,* trans. Allan Bloom (New York: Basic Books, 1968), 193–96.

The history of the CPUSA's secret apparatus and espionage in America has parallels with this story. Most people saw only the shadows on the walls. Many Americans believed the stories told by defectors like Bentley, Chambers, and Budenz, but the characters were faint, obscure, and often misunderstood. Particularly after the Vietnam War destroyed the anti-Communist consensus in American politics, other Americans questioned the evidence that did exist and dismissed what seemed to be only shadows without substance. Many academic historians discounted the testimony of Communist defectors who claimed to have acted in the drama and who insisted that they had been freed from the cave and had seen real things in their true light. The opening of the Comintern's archives frees all of us from the cave. No longer must we argue about the meaning of obscure reflections on a wall; these documents allow us to see things as they really were.

The documents in this book demonstrate with unmistakable clarity that the common perception that "American communism was a Soviet weapon in the Cold War"[2] was indeed well founded, and they reveal the process through which the CPUSA became an instrument of Soviet espionage. Because so many of the party's activities required secrecy and subterfuge, not only to launder Soviet money but also to avoid government prosecution, the CPUSA very early developed the habits and customs of conspiracy. And this conspiratorial organization later assisted Soviet intelligence and placed loyalty to the Soviet Union ahead of loyalty to the United States.

To say this is not to claim that every American Communist was disloyal. Americans became Communists for a wide variety of motives, many of them entirely honorable and decent. Perhaps a quarter of a million people passed through the American Communist party between 1919 and 1960; the overwhelming majority had nothing to do with espionage. Most who joined left the party within two years, because they lost interest, did not have enough time or energy to devote to it, or concluded that it was ineffective or undemocratic, or because the party itself had changed its policies and they no longer agreed with its goals or views. But the people

2. M. J. Heale, *American Anticommunism: Combating the Enemy Within, 1830–1970* (Baltimore, Md.: Johns Hopkins University Press, 1990), 189.

who passed through the CPUSA did not define its character or mission: that was done by its hard core of permanent cadre who devoted their lives to the movement.

There were many worlds of American communism. The CPUSA, for much of its history, devoted its energies to organizing workers into trade unions, opposing segregation, leading demonstrations, and pursuing a myriad other causes and crusades. Most party members lived in that public world of American communism. They had no connection with, or even knowledge of, another world, although even the most obtuse party member knew that there was no room for criticizing the Soviet Union. And some American Communists concealed their political affiliations, the better to advance their own careers and increase party influence. Although all party functionaries may not have known the details of the special relationship with the Soviet Union, "special work" was part and parcel of the Communist mission in the United States, and this was well known and discussed openly in the CPUSA's Political Bureau.

Participants in the Communist party's secret apparatus came from all sectors of the party. In addition to the party's top leaders, the documents in this collection tell of a number of other high-ranking party officials, some of whom quietly retired behind the Iron Curtain after World War II. But the apparatus could not have functioned without the obscure men and women who were willing to devote their lives to its service: it was the intense devotion to the Communist cause of the Morris Cohens and Ann Coleses that enabled the secret apparatus to carry out its mission.

And it was these ordinary Communists whose lives demonstrate that some rank-and-file members were willing to serve the USSR by spying on their own country. There but for the grace of not being asked went other American Communists. The CPUSA showered hosannas on the USSR as the promised land. In Communist propaganda the survival of the Soviet Union as the one bright, shining star of humankind was a constant refrain, as in the 1934 American Communist poem that described the Soviet Union as "a heaven . . . brought to earth in Russia."[3] When given the opportunity to serve the Soviet Union, is it any surprise that some American Communists said yes?

3. Tillie Olsen, "I Want You Women Up North to Know," *Partisan*, March 1934.

During its history, the CPUSA pursued many goals in many different ways. At times, party members not only believed that a revolutionary upheaval was possible in the United States but also entertained fantasies that it was imminent. More often, they recognized that American capitalist democracy was so firmly entrenched that only modest reforms in its operation were possible. During the ultra-revolutionary periods, they scorned alliances with noncommunist groups; during conciliatory eras, they worked cooperatively with other radicals and liberals. Throughout the shifts and zigzags in policies, however, one thing remained constant—the belief that the society being created in the Soviet Union marked a progressive stage in human evolution that ought to be emulated in the United States. But behind the party's public facade, there was a more sinister and less innocent world. The inhabitants of that secret world gave more than rhetorical loyalty to the Soviet Union; they worked with and for Soviet intelligence agencies.

During the late 1940s and early 1950s, anti-Communist sentiment was broad, deep, and passionate in the United States, particularly when patriotic feelings were inflamed by the Korean War. Whether or not American Communists were perceived as agents of the Soviet Union, there would have been an aversion to communism. Many of the doctrines and beliefs central to Communist ideology were fundamentally hostile to American democratic values. But the peculiar and particular edge to American anticommunism cannot be severed from the CPUSA's allegiance to the Soviet Union; the belief that American Communists were disloyal is what made the Communist issue so powerful and at times poisonous. Both Democrats and Republicans declared American Communists to be illegitimate participants in the democratic polity, a wide range of private organizations eliminated Communists from their ranks, and although the CPUSA was never outlawed, the U.S. government exposed its activities, jailed some of its leaders, and removed its adherents from federal jobs.

Like other popular movements, anticommunism produced oversimplification and exaggeration and attracted both opportunists and fanatics. The internal Communist threat to the United States was often wildly exaggerated. It is difficult to regard Senator Joseph McCarthy's assault on political civility as much more than the vicious partisanship of a political bully. For many politically aware

Americans, endorsing the view that espionage and conspiracies were central to the Communist enterprise in America was akin to joining the ranks of the demagogues and paranoid extremists or to entering that uncomfortable world where the John Birch Society added Dwight Eisenhower to the ranks of the conspirators, where anti-Semites and paranoids spun elaborate tales of secret Zionist or Masonic bands plotting with Moscow to subvert white Christian America.[4]

Many of the recent historical accounts of this period have accepted the revisionist view that concern about domestic communism in the late 1940s and 1950s was without justification and constituted an authoritarian, antidemocratic attack on a movement whose only sin was to dissent from prevailing norms. Indeed, the predominant view among scholars is that the notion that American Communists maintained a secret underground or assisted Soviet intelligence is without any credible basis. Consequently, the prevailing academic consensus paints America in the late 1940s and 1950s as a "nightmare in red"[5] during which Americans were "sweat-drenched in fear"[6] of a figment of their own paranoid imaginations.

As the documents in this volume show, however, the belief that the American Communist movement assisted Soviet intelligence and placed loyalty to the Soviet Union ahead of loyalty to the United States was well founded. American communism was certainly a radical political movement—a heretical dissent from the American tradition. But the Communist Party of the United States of America was also a conspiracy financed by a hostile foreign power that recruited members for clandestine work, developed an elaborate underground apparatus, and used that apparatus to collaborate with espionage services of that power. The situation in America in the later 1940s and 1950s was much more complicated than is suggested by the view that an idealistic, innocent Communist movement was persecuted by a paranoid security apparatus. Although

4. The John Birch Society is an extremist anti-Communist organization. The description of Eisenhower as a Communist traitor appears in Robert Henry Winborne Welch, *The Politician* (n.p., 1959).

5. Richard M. Fried, *Nightmare in Red: The McCarthy Era in Perspective* (New York: Oxford University Press, 1990).

6. David Caute, *The Great Fear: The Anti-Communist Purge under Truman and Eisenhower* (New York: Simon and Schuster, 1978), 11.

many innocent people were harassed, the secret world of the CPUSA made such excesses possible. Without excusing these excesses, historians need now to take into account the CPUSA's extensive covert activities and collaboration with Soviet intelligence.

The sentimental and ideological attachment of the American Left to its origins in the CPUSA has been enshrined in an edifice of scholarly monographs, reference works, journals, and popular histories. Communism has or had a mythic quality in the minds of some Americans precisely because it allowed them to imagine a better world and envision a way of achieving it. Yet the dreams and aspirations of people who were drawn to the party because it represented, they supposed, a chance for social justice, equality, and freedom, have little place among the documents contained in this volume. Revisionist historiography has often simply encouraged a continued belief in mythic thinking by attempting to "set the record straight" and eliminate the problem of American communism by demonstrating that it was merely a normal part of American political life. This attitude has contributed to a significant misunderstanding of American culture and politics in the late 1940s and 1950s. It is a misunderstanding based on denial, which is as detrimental to the life of a society as it is to the psychic life of an individual. Whatever prevents us from accepting the past will also prevent us from making reasoned decisions in the future. In this regard, the history of American communism represents as deeply conflicted a phenomenon as the Vietnam War does.

For more than a generation, the lack of adequate documentation concerning Communist activity in the United States has hampered scholars' ability to realistically evaluate the politics of the 1930s, 1940s, and 1950s. Misunderstandings about the nature and activities of the American Communist movement have led to distortions in the history of both liberal and conservative politics. The ambiguity of the available evidence has allowed concern for protecting this or that political view to shape scholarly interpretation or has offered the opportunity for scoring ideological points.

Now we have entered a new era: the Soviet Union is gone, communism is moribund, and the Cold War is over. The political and ideological positions of that era are sliding rapidly into history. With the opening of Soviet archives, the opportunity exists for scholars to come to a clearer understanding of the role of communism and anticommunism in American society. We are no longer chained in place, forced to look at the shadows on the wall. We need only turn around to examine the secret apparatus created by the CPUSA to carry out its clandestine operations and to assist Soviet intelligence agencies in their efforts to penetrate American political and military institutions.

# The Archival Record

## The Comintern Archive

From 1919 until 1943, the Communist International, headquartered in Moscow, supervised the activities of Communist parties throughout the world. After the Comintern (from its Russian acronym) dissolved in 1943, its records were stored in an archive that became the Russian Center for the Preservation and Study of Documents of Recent History, RTsKhIDNI, in late 1991. This archive, formerly known as the Central Party Archive of the Institute of the Theory and History of Socialism of the Communist Party of the Soviet Union Central Committee and before that as the Institute of Marxism-Leninism of the Central Committee of the Communist Party, holds the bulk of the records of the central bodies of the Communist Party of the Soviet Union (CPSU) from the early 1920s until Stalin's death in 1953.

The Comintern's records on foreign Communist parties are extremely detailed, and these archives constitute an immensely rich resource for studying the politics of the twentieth century. Comintern records include reports and cables from Comintern agents sent to the United States to supervise the activities of the Communist Party of the United States of America (CPUSA) and transcripts or summaries of the deliberations of the CPUSA's Political Bureau and Central Committee, its ruling bodies.

Throughout the 1920s and 1930s, American Communist officials traveled to Moscow to report on their activities to the Comintern. CPUSA officials made their reports and were questioned, often sharply, by Comintern committees, sometimes by a specially designated American Commission or by the Anglo-American Secretariat, a standing Comintern body that supervised the Communist parties of the United States, Great Britain, Canada, and several other English-speaking nations. The transcripts of testimony by CPUSA officials to the Anglo-American Secretariat and other Comintern bodies total many thousands of pages.

The Anglo-American Secretariat interrogated not just CPUSA officials but also American students attending the International Lenin School, a training institution for Communist cadre. The CPUSA, moreover, stationed in Moscow an official representative to the Executive Committee of the Comintern to provide the Comintern with information on and explanations of CPUSA activities. The American representative to the Comintern also sent frequent letters back to the CPUSA explaining the current policy directives of the Comintern or conveying Comintern orders. In addition to the CPUSA's standing representative, at any one time several other CPUSA cadre were usually in Moscow for one- or two-year tours in various Comintern offices. Copies of letters and memoranda prepared by these Americans are in the Comintern's files.

## American Communist Party Records

In addition to the records of the Comintern's various agencies, the RTsKhIDNI houses a separate CPUSA collection of more than 4,300 files that span the years 1919 to 1944. Each file contains between ten and several hundred pages of documents. The files include the records from the national headquarters of the American Communist party: the original incoming mail, carbons of outgoing correspondence, reports from regional and local organizers, and internal memoranda produced by officials and offices of the national headquarters. In addition to CPUSA records produced in America, these files also contain some documents created in Moscow by CPUSA representatives to the Comintern. Most of the material in the CPUSA records is in English, although in many files key documents are accompanied by Russian translations. In a few cases, the English original is not present and only the Russian translation is extant. The presence of these Russian translations shows that these files were sent to Moscow for Comintern review as well as for safekeeping. The records of the CPUSA's myriad foreign-language bureaus for immigrants also contain material in the appropriate language (Finnish, Yiddish, German, Hungarian, and so on).

The CPUSA collection is not complete. Records are spotty for the period

1919–1922, when American communism was first being organized, several competing Communist parties existed, and government officials on occasion arrested Communist organizers and seized their papers. The records for the period 1923–1936 appear to be largely intact. After 1936 the records grow spotty once more. Because records were retained in the United States for several years for use by the CPUSA itself, the reduced volume after 1936 likely reflects the start of World War II in 1939 and the increasing difficulty of ensuring secure shipment of records between the United States and the USSR. Prior to 1940, most of the records are originals shipped to the Soviet Union, not copies. In 1940 and thereafter, however, not only are there fewer documents, but a significant portion consist of prints made from microfilm. This suggests that the originals were kept in the United States and the film sent to Moscow to reduce the problem of bulk shipments during wartime. This judgment is reinforced by a Comintern cover memo attached to copies of CPUSA memoranda regarding party membership and Young Communist League activities in 1942. The cover memo notes that the attached material is difficult to read because "the film was visibly wet at the time of mailing."[1]

After the Comintern dissolved, its functions were split among various agencies of the Soviet government and the Communist Party of the Soviet Union. The CPUSA collection in the Comintern archives stops in 1944. It is not known whether records were no longer routinely sent to Moscow after 1944 or whether the 1944 cutoff simply reflects the Comintern's 1943 dissolution and the placement of post-1944 CPUSA records elsewhere in a still-closed depository. Scattered post-1944 documents dealing with American Communist activities have been found in other CPSU files at the RTsKhIDNI.

Some especially sensitive material is known to have been transferred in recent years from RTsKhIDNI to a depository known as the Archive of the President of the Russian Federation that was still closed to research in 1993. The presidential archive is said to hold selected CPSU Political Bureau and foreign intelligence records, including some dating back to the 1920s and 1930s. Some sensitive material from the Stalin era is held in the Center for the Preservation of Contemporary Documentation, formerly the archive of the Central Committee of the CPSU. This archive holds the bulk of the post-1953 CPSU material, and access to this depository is more restricted than is access to the RTsKhIDNI.

---

1. Plyshevsky to Dimitrov, 5 November 1942, "Regarding material coming via our special channels in the US," RTsKhIDNI 495–74–479.

## Records on Intelligence Activity

In regard to espionage matters, the most significant Soviet material is not yet available—indeed, some of it may never be. The Foreign Intelligence Service of Russia has not opened the archive of its institutional predecessor, the foreign intelligence directorate of the KGB. The KGB was the chief internal security service of the USSR as well as its chief foreign intelligence agency. The KGB has a complex organizational history; its predecessor organizations include, to use their acronyms, the Cheka, the NKVD, the GPU, the OGPU, the NKGB, the GUGB, the MGB, and the MVD. In some periods the foreign intelligence organization was separate from the much larger internal security apparatus.

In the past several years, the Foreign Intelligence Service has released selected historical documents, but researchers have not been allowed to examine the files from which these documents came, and it is difficult to judge whether the documents are distorted by being wrenched out of context. In addition, the files of the Soviet military intelligence agency, a powerful separate organization often called the GRU, remain completely inaccessible. The foreign intelligence operations of the GRU were extensive, although smaller than those of the KGB. Military intelligence records are held by the Historico-Archival and Military-Memorial Center of the General Staff of the Armed Forces of the Russian Federation and the Central Archive of the Ministry of Defense of the Russian Federation.

Even though the intelligence archives are closed, the records of the Comintern are open, and the predecessors of the KGB and the GRU communicated with the Comintern about matters of mutual interest. Although most sensitive intelligence-related material was removed when the Comintern was dissolved or at some later date, the Comintern records contain a significant amount of KGB and, to a lesser extent, GRU material that illuminates hitherto hidden activities.

In the Comintern archives, documents about clandestine activities do not announce themselves with explicit labels; nor are they found in special files entitled "intelligence" or "espionage." Instead, these documents are mixed in with files dealing with the Comintern's political, organizational, and propagandistic activities. Only a prior knowledge of the personalities and events connected with various intelligence operations allows a number of the documents reproduced in this book to be identified as involving clandestine work.

The authors of this volume also located documents whose content or origin strongly suggests that they concern clandestine work. Because nothing or very little is known of the personalities or the events discussed, however, it remains unclear whether covert activities are their subject; their explication must be left to future researchers. The authors examined the most likely files in the Comintern archives, but the Comintern's holdings are immense. Files not yet examined may well contain other documents that concern clandestine work.

The documents in this book greatly advance knowledge of clandestine Communist activity in the United States. Nevertheless, because Soviet intelligence archives remain closed, the activities described are but the tip of the iceberg, the now-visible part of a much larger and still obscure secret world of American communism.

# Organization of the American Communist Party

In 1919, the American Communist movement looked very much like the Socialist party out of which it had emerged. The majority of Communists belonged to language federations, and business was conducted in a foreign language. The relatively few English-speaking party members belonged to clubs based on electoral districts. In 1925 the Comintern instituted a Bolshevization campaign to turn the Communist party into a disciplined, cohesive, and centralized Marxist-Leninist vanguard organization. The language federations were downgraded. Communists were transferred into street or shop nuclei, which were organized by residence or place of employment. Several nuclei formed a section or subsection; large cities had a number of sections. Depending on their size, one or several states formed a district. New York, with the largest number of party members, was divided into two districts. A district organizer was the ranking party official.

In theory, the party was organized from the bottom up. Beginning in the nuclei, party members chose delegates to local and state gatherings. The highest body was the National Convention, which, ostensibly, chose the members of the Central Committee; they, in turn, selected the members of the Political Bureau, or Politburo. In fact, Politburo members were approved by the Comintern in Moscow. The Politburo, in turn, selected Central Committee members, although states and districts could include prominent party figures from their areas.

Since the Central Committee met infrequently, the smaller Politburo wielded more power. Politburo meetings took place at least weekly. At various times, Politburo members were given specific assignments, such as overseeing agitation and propaganda or trade union affairs. At certain times, particularly when factional warfare was under way or recently concluded, a small Secretariat, composed of three or four people, might be responsible for day-to-day operations. In 1934 Earl Browder became general secretary of the CPUSA. For the next decade, he exercised enormous power over the party's direction, although he did regularly consult with the Politburo.

Discussion, debate, and even disagreements occurred in the Politburo but rarely in the Central Committee. When the Politburo found itself in conflict, the participants would consult with the Communist International. From the early 1920s until the late 1930s, Comintern representatives were stationed in the United States to serve as the eyes, ears, and voice of Moscow. These "Comintern reps" were never American citizens; their primary loyalty was to Moscow. In addition, American representatives to the Comintern served in Moscow and regularly advised their American comrades on current issues being discussed in the USSR. In communications with the United States, these American delegates often used the generic code name Randolph. Top leaders of the CPUSA also traveled regularly to Moscow to seek advice, resolve disputes, or seek clarification of Comintern orders.

# Selected Readings

Bentley, Elizabeth: Elizabeth Bentley, *Out of Bondage* (New York: Ivy Books, 1988); Earl Latham, *The Communist Controversy in Washington: From the New Deal to McCarthy* (Cambridge: Harvard University Press, 1966); Gary May, *Un-American Activities: The Trials of William Remington* (New York: Oxford University Press, 1994); Herbert L. Packer, *Ex-Communist Witnesses: Four Studies in Fact Finding* (Stanford, Calif.: Stanford University Press, 1962).

Clandestine Funding of American Communism: John Earl Haynes and Harvey Klehr, "'Moscow Gold,' Confirmed at Last?" *Labor History* 33, no. 2 (Spring 1992) and 33, no. 4 (Fall 1992).

Communist International: Standard histories include Franz Borkenau, *World Communism: A History of the Communist International* (New York: Norton, 1939); Julius Braunthal, *History of the International, 1914–1943* (London: Nelson, 1967); Jane Degras, ed., *The Communist International, 1919–1943: Documents*, vol. 1: *1919–1922* and vol. 2: *1923–1943* (London: Oxford University Press, 1956 and 1960); Gunther Nollau, *International Communism and World Revolution* (London: Hollis and Carter, 1961); and Milorad Drachkovitch and Branko Lazitch, eds., *The Comintern: Historical Highlights* (New York: Praeger, 1966). In the future these and other histories of the Communist International will be substantially supplemented or supplanted by works based on the newly opened Comintern archives. New publications and research based on the newly opened archives are announced in the *Cold War International History Project Bulletin* and the *International Newsletter of Historical Studies on Comintern, Communism and Stalinism* (Germany).

Communist Party of the United States of America: Harvey Klehr and John Earl Haynes, *The American Communist Movement: Storming Heaven Itself* (New York: Twayne Publishers, 1992); Irving Howe and Lewis Coser, *The American Communist Party: A Critical History, 1919–1957* (Boston: Beacon Press, 1957); Theodore Draper, *The Roots of American Communism* (New York: Viking Press, 1957); Theodore Draper, *American Communism and Soviet Russia: The Formative Period* (New York: Viking Press, 1960); Harvey Klehr, *The Heyday of American Communism: The Depression Decade* (New York: Basic Books, 1984); Maurice Isserman, *Which Side Were You On? The American Communist Party during the Second World War* (Middletown,

Conn.: Wesleyan University Press, 1982); Joseph R. Starobin, *American Communism in Crisis, 1943–1957* (Cambridge: Harvard University Press, 1972); and Louis Budenz, *Men without Faces: The Communist Conspiracy in the USA* (New York: Harper and Brothers, 1948).

**Hammer, Armand:** Steve Weinberg, *Armand Hammer: The Untold Story* (Boston: Little, Brown, 1989).

**Hiss-Chambers Case:** Allen Weinstein, *Perjury: The Hiss-Chambers Case* (New York: Knopf, 1978); Whittaker Chambers, *Witness* (New York: Random House, 1952); Alger Hiss, *In the Court of Public Opinion* (New York: Knopf, 1957).

**McCarthyism and Post–World War II Anticommunism:** Earl Latham, *The Communist Controversy in Washington: From the New Deal to McCarthy* (Cambridge: Harvard University Press, 1966); Stephen J. Whitfield, *The Culture of the Cold War* (Baltimore, Md.: Johns Hopkins University Press, 1990); David Oshinsky, *A Conspiracy So Immense: The World of Joe McCarthy* (New York: The Free Press, 1983); Thomas C. Reeves, *The Life and Times of Joe McCarthy* (New York: Stein and Day, 1982); David Caute, *The Great Fear: The Anti-Communist Purge under Truman and Eisenhower* (New York: Simon and Schuster, 1978); and Richard M. Fried, *Nightmare in Red: The McCarthy Era in Perspective* (New York: Oxford University Press, 1990).

**OSS:** Bradley Smith, *The Shadow Warriors: O.S.S. and the Origins of the C.I.A.* (New York: Basic Books, 1983); R. Harris Smith, *OSS: The Secret History of America's First Central Intelligence Agency* (Berkeley: University of California Press, 1972); Barry M. Katz, *Foreign Intelligence: Research and Analysis in the Office of Strategic Services, 1942–1945* (Cambridge: Harvard University Press, 1989); Robin W. Winks, *Cloak and Gown: Scholars in the Secret War, 1939–1961* (New York: Quill, 1988); Anthony Cave Brown, *The Last Hero: Wild Bill Donovan* (New York: Times Books, 1982).

**Reed, John:** Robert Rosenstone, *Romantic Revolutionary: A Biography of John Reed* (Cambridge: Harvard University Press, 1990); Eric Homberger, *John Reed* (Manchester: Manchester University Press, 1990); John Reed, *Ten Days That Shook the World* (New York: Boni and Liveright, 1919).

**Rosenberg Case:** Ronald Radosh and Joyce Milton, *The Rosenberg File: A Search for the Truth* (New York: Holt, Rinehart and Winston, 1983).

**Smedley, Agnes:** Janice R. MacKinnon and Stephen R. MacKinnon, *Agnes Smedley: The Life and Times of an American Radical* (Berkeley: University of California Press, 1988); Charles Andrew Willoughby, *Shanghai Conspiracy: The Sorge Spy Ring, Moscow, Shanghai, Tokyo, San Francisco, New York* (New York: Dutton, 1952).

**Sorge Ring:** F. W. Deakin and G. R. Storry, *The Case of Richard Sorge* (New York: Harper and Row, 1966); Gordon W. Prange with Donald M. Goldstein and Katherine V. Dillon, *Target Tokyo: The Story of the Sorge Spy Ring* (New York: McGraw-Hill, 1984); "The Case of Richard Sorge," in *Covert Warfare*, ed. John Mendelsohn, vol. 7 (New York: Garland, 1989); Chalmers Johnson, *An Instance of Treason: Ozaki Hotsumi and the Sorge Spy Ring* (Stanford, Calif.: Stanford University Press, 1990).

**Soviet Intelligence Agencies:** Christopher Andrew and Oleg Gordievsky, *KGB: The Inside Story* (New York: HarperCollins Publishers, 1990); Raymond G. Rocca and John J. Dziak, *Bibliography on Soviet Intelligence and Security Services* (Boulder,

Colo.: Westview Press and Consortium for the Study of Intelligence, 1985); John Barron, *KGB: The Secret Work of Soviet Secret Agents* (New York: Reader's Digest Press, 1974); David J. Dallin, *Soviet Espionage* (New Haven: Yale University Press, 1955); Sanche de Gramont [pseudonym of Ted Morgan], *The Secret War: The Story of International Espionage since World War II* (New York: Putnam, 1962); George H. Leggett, *The Cheka, Lenin's Political Police: The All-Russian Extraordinary Commission for Combating Counter-Revolution and Sabotage, December 1917 to February 1922* (Oxford: Oxford University Press, 1981); and Simon Wolin and Robert M. Slusser, eds., *The Soviet Secret Police* (Westport, Conn.: Greenwood Press, 1974).

**Spanish Civil War; American Volunteers in the International Brigades:** R. Dan Richardson, *Comintern Army: The International Brigades and the Spanish Civil War* (Lexington: University Press of Kentucky, 1982); Verne Johnston, *Legions of Babel: The International Brigades in the Spanish Civil War* (University Park: Pennsylvania State University Press, 1967); Cecil Eby, *Between the Bullet and the Lie: American Volunteers in the Spanish Civil War* (New York: Holt, Rinehart and Winston, 1969); Robert Rosenstone, *Crusade on the Left: The Lincoln Battalion in the Spanish Civil War* (New York: Pegasus, 1969); Peter N. Carroll, *The Odyssey of the Abraham Lincoln Brigade: Americans in the Spanish Civil War* (Stanford, Calif.: Stanford University Press, 1994).

# Index